Praise for Armor Your Self™

"Wow! *Armor Your Self*™ is a landmark, pioneering work that belongs on every cop's bookshelf. Get this book! Study this book! Apply this book! It will save careers. It will save marriages, and it will save lives! Relatives of police officers should give this book to 'your' cop. Mental health and medical practitioners, counselors, psychologists and therapists should use this book as a part of your wellness and therapeutic plan for police officers. There is no other book like this available today. It is essential and irreplaceable. And a hearty 'Well done!' to John Marx! These are hard times in law enforcement, and in our nation, and I believe John was put here 'for just such a time as this.'"

Dave Grossman
Lt. Col., USA (Retired)
Author of *On Combat, On Killing,* and *Assassination Generation*

"The book, *Armor Your Self*™: *How To Survive A Career In Law Enforcement* gives information and skills to the law enforcement professional to not only survive their career, but also to stop transferring unresolved emotional issues into inappropriate police conduct. An important contribution to the law enforcement field."

Kevin M. Gilmartin, Ph.D.
Police Psychologist, Behavioral Sciences and Management Consultant
Author of *Emotional Survival for Law Enforcement*

"If a book is weighed on the basis of how useful it is, *Armor Your Self*™ weighs a ton! Step by practical step, it coaches you on how to build the life-saving skill of resilience, the most critical quality for surviving the physical, mental, and emotional perils of a law enforcement career. A perfect gift for new recruits, an invaluable Rx for veteran officers who already are under siege from the many threats and stresses of the Job."

Charles Remsberg
Author, the *Street Survival* **book series**

"*Armor Your Self*™: *How To Survive A Career In Law Enforcement* is an essential read for all law enforcement officers. John Marx is an experienced, veteran police officer who provides practical and comprehensive information necessary for career-long officer-wellness. It is equally significant to spouses of officers and others that have an interest in the challenges confronted by modern-day law enforcement officers."

Jack. A. Digliani, PhD, EdD
Police Psychologist
Author of *Reflections of a Police Psychologist* **and** *Contemporary Issues in Police Psychology: Police Peer Support Team Training* **and the** *Make it Safe Police Officer Initiative*

"What are you willing to do to save a life? What about your own life? This comprehensive manual tells you how to find your way through the minefield of mental, emotional and spiritual assaults you experience in police work. *Armor Your Self*™ teaches you that overwhelming stress, burnout, PTSD and despair can be prevented or managed. The exercises and tactics in this book prepare you to survive, thrive, and enjoy your work and life. It's one of the best books for personal survival you will ever read."

Allen R. Kates, MFAW, BCECR
Author of *CopShock, Second Edition: Surviving Posttraumatic Stress Disorder (PTSD)*

"*Armor Your Self*™ is one of those rare resources that is truly an encyclopedia for a successful law enforcement career. From physical fitness to tactical exercises to emotional well-being, John Marx has put together a book for every cadet, rookie, trainer, administrator and senior member of every police department in North America. It should be on the shelf of every law enforcement agency and academy library and must be shared with anyone who has a cop in the family. It's one of those books that, after reading, we looked at each other and said 'Why didn't we write this?' Thankfully, John Marx did."

Dave and Betsy Smith
Law Enforcement Trainers and Authors
www.bucksavage.com

"*Armor Your Self*™: *How To Survive A Career In Law Enforcement* should be considered the 'owner's manual' for law enforcement officers. Like a vehicle's owner's manual it provides an understanding of the systems and routine maintenance required to keep yourself operating at peak performance from your 'breaking in' as a rookie all the way through a successful retirement. It provides insight, tactics, resources and applications for the individual officer to utilize in all aspects — physically, mentally, emotionally, and spiritually — of their personal and professional lives.

It also gives guidance for agencies on how to incorporate these same concepts on a departmental level. A modern law enforcement agency understand that its most valuable assets are the lives and health of the officers that it employs — an idea that all too often is given more lip service, than application. Reading it, I was struck by the amount of information contained in the book. It also strikes me as one of the most comprehensive works on the subject on how to attain a long, healthy career in the law enforcement profession.

Like any owner's manual, success and performance will be determined by the diligence and care that the individual officer and/or department choose to apply over the length of service. This book has long been needed in this profession, and I thank John for having the insight, wisdom, desire and drive to make it a reality."

Duane Wolfe
Retired police officer, trainer,
***The Warrior's Path* PoliceOne.com columnist**

"I Love, love, love this book. John's thoughtfulness and concern for the average officer is genuine, for sure. Yet, the approach he takes to make the book understandable and applicable to all of the grunts or 'boots on the ground' shines through. This book provides useful insights and suggestions that any first-responder can take advantage of. This book provides easy steps and attainable goals in a process to make yourself safe and to learn to take the same protective steps mentally as you do physically to shield yourself from harm. A must read for officers beginning their careers to those who are at the end of it."

Sergeant Stephen A. Bishopp
Dallas Police Department
And Associate Director for Research, Caruth Police Institute

"*Armor Your Self*™: *How To Survive A Career In Law Enforcement* is the most comprehensive, effective book of its kind I've ever seen. It addresses the physical, mental, emotional, spiritual, and ethical aspects of a career in law enforcement and of the people who wear the badge. The insights and techniques it provides will save lives, careers, and marriages. Get yourself a copy right away. And that cop you know — the one who is tired, angry, and demoralized — order one for him or her, too."

Cary A. Friedman
Law Enforcement Chaplain
Author of *Spiritual Survival for Law Enforcement*

"*Armor Your Self*™: *How To Survive A Career In Law Enforcement* is a must have for anyone working in or with law enforcement! This is one of the best overall compilations of resources, guidance and techniques for those who navigate the high-stress, high-performance world of police work. Whether you're an officer, family member or professional support staff, this resource will make you better at what you do!"

CDR Eric G. Potterat, Ph.D., USN (Retired)
Clinical and Performance Psychologist
Former Head Psychologist for the US Navy SEALs

"While this book would have been valuable to read a decade ago, with the incredible and ever increasing stresses on today's law enforcement practitioners it becomes a must read. It is extremely well researched with a vast array of suggestions and options for successfully addressing current challenges. Although topically designed to assist law enforcement, many segments should also be invaluable for adoption by other high-stress occupations."

Bob Pence
Special Agent in Charge, FBI (Retired)

"*Armor Your Self*™, written by former law enforcement officer John Marx is a must read for anyone in the Law Enforcement field (including family members) in order to physically, mentally, emotionally, and spiritually survive a career in law enforcement. This book goes so much farther than any other book I have read on the subject of Law Enforcement wellness. The book contains the most up to date comprehensive resources and tools available to law enforcement and their families. Thank you John for your openness of your law enforcement career and your incredible effort to keep cops alive."

Tod E. Bassett, Lieutenant
San Diego Police Department
One of the founding members of the San Diego Police Department's Wellness Unit

"Before I finished the first paragraph, I was hooked. John had me smiling and nodding my head in agreement throughout his book. Not only does he understand the all encompassing effects of a law enforcement career, he has laid out a comprehensive fitness plan for mind, body and soul. If you want to make it through your career whole, and help the people around you do the same, read this book."

Karen Solomon
Author of *Hearts Beneath the Badge* and *The Price They Pay*
Creator of Blue HELP and 1stHelp.net

"*Armor Your Self*™ is the most comprehensive book on this subject I have ever seen. John Marx does an outstanding job at a challenging time when it is really needed."

Lee Shaykhet, owner
Shaykhet Training, LLC

"We spend time working out, practicing with our tools and wearing our protective equipment to make sure we can go home at the end of the day. This book is one more tool needed to keep ourselves safe now and throughout our career. Read it and take it to heart."

Raymond Craig
Metropolitan Police Officer II
Honolulu Police Department

"The greatest asset in public safety are your people — please take care of them. Law enforcement is a rewarding and honorable profession; unfortunately, it also destroys people that are associated with it. Following the sudden death of a friend and co-worker, John Marx has utilized his life experiences as a law enforcement officer to fulfill a personal mission to help other first responders.

Armor Your Self™: *How To Survive A Career In Law Enforcement* is a straightforward guide, written by John, which highlights and educates people about the real hazards facing law enforcement today. This book offers you numerous suggestions to address these hazards with John's P.E.M.S. system (Physical, Emotional, Mental & Spiritual) to help you change individually or assist your agency. This book offers you proven solutions to improving the health and quality of life as individuals and as a group within your agency and police academy. Law enforcement is losing more people annually to heart attacks, suicide, vehicle crashes and illnesses. Most of these are preventable. John's book provides you with information for you and your agency to improve total wellness and strengthen resiliency. Take the lead and be the change!"

Sergeant Mark St. Hilaire
30+ year Veteran Police Officer
Metrowest Boston, Massachusetts

"*Armor Your Self*™ is not the conclusion but rather, the beginning of the author's, John Marx's, work and could be the owner's manual for police work. In this book, the author addresses more issues that impact officers (and their families) than any book I have ever read. Written from the perspective of a career police officer/career trainer, this book presents an understandable, comprehensive approach on how to survive the potentially, life-threatening issues in law enforcement that officers and police academy training do not address. *Armor Your Self*™, not only offers suggestions, options, and studies, it even provides practical exercises which help the reader to better understand the subject matter. This book includes information and resources for suicide prevention, dealing with shame, survivor support, agency wellness, creating effective habits, and addresses the Police Perfection Paradox. *Armor Your Self*™ has information for young men and women who might be considering a career in law enforcement, all the way to veteran police officers and retirees. I recommend this book for any person whose life is in law enforcement or touches law enforcement from any perspective."

Sgt. Clarke A. Paris (Retired)
Las Vegas Metropolitan Police Department
Author of *My Life for Your Life* and *Daddy I Worry About You*
Creator of the documentary film *The Pain Behind The Badge*

"I have such respect for John Marx and his willingness to share so openly his experience as a veteran police officer in *Armor Your Self™: How to Survive a Career in Law Enforcement*. As a mental health professional who works with emergency responders, I know how valuable it is for officers to hear from those who have done the job and who can truly speak to the impact the job has on one's personal and professional lives. John's genuine concern for others in the blue family is evident throughout the book and his insights are incredibly valuable to new and veteran officers as well as their family members."

Dr. Sara Garrido
Nicoletti-Flater Associates
Peer Support Consultant for Multiple Peer Support Teams

"John Marx has provided a desk reference for law enforcement career survival. This text provides tangible, attainable tools to aid any and all of us to survive a most challenging and rewarding career."

Tim M. Brown, M.A., L.P.C.
Police Captain

"Law enforcement is profession of heroic men and women who have chosen to serve their communities through this honorable profession. While this is a rewarding and honorable profession it can take a toll physically, emotionally and spiritually if you are not prepared for the challenges and realities of the profession. *Armor Your Self™* is a comprehensive guide for law enforcement professionals and their families. This is not a novel to be consumed in a weekend. This is a book to be studied and referenced throughout a career. Invest the time to study the contents, do the exercises and check out the references before you feel you need it. This will allow you to Armor Your Self and thrive in this career."

Sgt. Brian Willis (Retired)
Calgary Police Service
President - Winning Mind Training Inc.

"This book will empower you as long as you are willing to read it, embrace it and then put your plan into action. During my 53 years of U.S. law enforcement experience, this particular information has never been offered as it is in this book. *Armor Your Self™* will assist you to survive your law enforcement career and emerge with your physical, mental, emotional and spiritual life intact. This is a college course, guide and map to success right here at your fingertips. If you decide to really embrace this book and take it onto yourself, you really must be willing to do the needed work to benefit from its content."

Colonel Robert "Coach" Lindsey (Retired)
Jefferson Parish Louisiana Sheriff's Office
Founding Member of ILEETA and ASLET

"John Marx's book *Armor Your Self™: How To Survive A Career In Law Enforcement* has brought awareness to the inner struggles, emotional problems and behavioral issues officers deal with throughout their career. This book offers solutions for emotional wellness and stability; therefore, Armor Your Self is a must read."

Dr. Ron Rufo
Retired Chicago Police
EAP Peer Support Team Leader
and author of *Police Suicide: Is Police Culture Killing Our Officers?*

"*Armor Your Self™* is an attempt to save officers and educate departments that their officers should not be treated as a piece of fruit where the affected or problem officer is the peel that is thrown away — as in *Death of a Salesman*."

Patrick Monaghan
Retired Milwaukee Police Officer
Peer Counselor for Concerns of Police Survivors (C.O.P.S.) from 1988 to present.

ARMOR Your Self™

How To Survive A Career In Law Enforcement

ARMOR Your Self™

How To Survive A Career In Law Enforcement

Guidance and Support for Officers and Their Families

by John Marx

Armor Your Self™: How To Survive A Career In Law Enforcement
by: John S. Marx

© Copyright: 2017

Published by:
The Law Enforcement Survival Institute
11757 W. Ken Caryl Ave., Suite F-321
Littleton, CO 80127
303-940-0411

ALL RIGHTS RESERVED. No part of this material may be used, reproduced or transmitted in any form whatsoever, mechanical or electronic, including recording, photocopying or by any informational storage or retrieval system without explicit written permission from the author and the publisher.

DISCLAIMER AND/OR LEGAL NOTICES:
The information presented in this document represents the view of the author as of the date of publication. Information is changing rapidly in the fields of law enforcement and military wellness. Data obtained following publication may alter the author's opinions.

This document is for informational purposes only. While every reasonable attempt has been made to verify the information provided in this product, The Law Enforcement Survival Institute, the author, their affiliates and/or partners do not assume any responsibility for errors, inaccuracies or omissions. Any slights of people or organizations are unintentional. If advice concerning legal or related matters is needed, the services of a fully qualified professional should be sought. This information is not intended for use as a source of legal or accounting advice. You should be aware of any laws that govern business transactions or other business practices in your country and state.

ISBN-13: 978-1544661810
ISBN-10: 1544661819
Printed in the United States of America

Cover design and text layout by A Cuppa Creative and Kim Hall Design

For information or to obtain additional copies of this manual, or for reprint rights please contact:

The Law Enforcement Survival Institute
11757 W. Ken Caryl Ave., Suite F-321
Littleton, CO 80127
303-940-0411

info@CopsAlive.com

To Kevin Gilmartin, Bryan Vila, John Violanti, Jack Digliani, Allen Kates, Dave Smith, Chuck Remsberg, Cary A. Friedman, Robert Douglas, Sean Riley, Ellen Kirschman and all of the law enforcement pioneers in the areas of health, wellness and safety that built the foundation upon which this work was created.

Also to "Brother Bob" Dale, a law enforcement friend whose suicide set me on this path of writing about law enforcement resilience.

Acknowledgements

To my parents Johann and Joyce Marx and all the other people who have contributed to the information in this book or to the development of my life I say - thank you!

To Adam Simms and Brenda Cartwright, I couldn't have finished this book without you!

There are so many people to thank and I'm so worried that I might accidentally leave someone out. Thanks to all of you, and if I did forget to add your name, it's because I made a mistake not because you did!

To: Bob "Coach" Lindsey, Cary Friedman, Daniel Aldrich, Eric Potterat, Karen Amendola, Jack Digliani, Sally Spencer-Thomas, Michael Guthrie, Barry Bratt, Patrick Monaghan, AnneMarie Rossi, Lois and Stephen James, Robyn Winters, Tod Bassett, Chuck Rylant, Stephen Bishopp, Fabrice Czarnecki, Jon Sheinberg, Dave Smith and Betsy Brantner Smith, Kevin Gilmartin, Bryan Vila, John Violanti, Allen Kates, Chuck Remsberg, Robert Douglas, Ellen Kirschman, Deborah Ortiz, Dave Grossman, Teresa Tate, Gary Noesner, John Nicoletti, Sara Garrido, Evan Axelrod, Jamie Bower, Bob Dale, Marla Friedman, Lynda O'Connell, Andy O'Hara, Dwayne Fuselier, Don Gunnarson, John Garavaglia, Richard Goerling, Debbie Gutierrez, Candice Kumai, Emily Lauck, Ed LeClair, Kelly McGonigal, Michael Mejia, Heidi Hansen, Patrick Melvin, Chris Manos, Al and Eleanor Manos, Raymond Craig, Greg Morrison, John Coppedge, Mark Bella, Janet Larson, Larry Wieda, Jim Philips, Jim Wilson, Jesse Waddle, Ginger Charles, Keith Dameron, Sue Dion, Kevin Eldridge, Dave Hayes, LuzMaria and Bill Shearer, Kevin Heaton, Donn Kraemer, Janelle Kruger, Anita Martin, Rachel Nuñez, Rhonda Kelly, Faye Warren, Donna Schulz, John Wycoff, Vera Alexander, Kelly Huddleston, Kristen Borie, Robin and Jeremy Heath, Tony and Joob Pascoe, Kimber Saunders, Harold and Sylvia Bowen, Ara Marx, J.J. Jepson, Doris and Jack Inslee, John Sutton, Hal and Dorothy Sutton, Albert Turner, Troy Bowen, Peter and Laurie Van Son, Joyce Donner, Jody Wilson, Sue Veldkamp, Tom Dearth, Laurie Taylor, Karen Van Cleve, Terri Norvell, Karyn Ruth White, Diane Sieg, Terry Anglin, Roger House, John Kepler, Brian O'Malley, Tim and Kris O'Shea, Judy Sabah, Joe Sabah, Carolyn Strauss, Bob Wendover, Sheryl Kay Watson, Michael Benidt, Bill Wilson, Louis Engelberg, Troy Cooper, Amy Ruppeck, Dan Stocking, Bob Walker, Michael Parreco, Matt Barnes, Phil West, Rich and Sharon Hamilton, Carolyn Whiting, Carolyn LaRoche, Elaine Dumler, Gina Ohanesian, Christie Ward, Ruby Newell-Legner, Gwen Crawford, Pam Gordon, Mary Ann Grenewald, Dick and Carol Ann Wronski, Stephan Wronski, Karl Mulle, Alice Ehr, Don Ayers, Chuck Hahn, Jim Olp, Clarke and Tracie Paris, Sean Riley, Mark St. Hilaire, Joe Padilla, Christian Dobratz, Lisa Wimberger, Kathleen Mitchell, Mary Kelly, Julie Zielinski, Mark Sherwood, Jeff Shannon, Bobby Smith, Gary Sommers, Danny Veith, Renise Bayne, Brian Nanavaty, Don Wick, Suzie Sawyer, Dianne Bernhard, Shelley Jones, Leland Melvin, Harvey Hedden, Brian Willis, Ron Scheidt, Duane Wolfe, Lee Shaykhet, Dale Stockton, Pat Heine, Scott Hernandez, Paul Quinnett,

James Wolfinbarger, Domingo Herraiz, Scott Hinshaw, Michael Hirsch, Janice Hoffman, John Holiday, Bill Jenkins, Karen Solomon, Mark Lamplugh, Pat Landrum, Tamara Lenherr, John Moorhouse, Scott Silverii, Jeff and Carol Jones, Vaughn Pepper, Kim Barron, Tim Tripp, Steve McDonald, Paul Newton, Brent Earhart, Rita DeFrancesco, Sandy Schwab, Donna Powell, Karen Sexton, Matt Rippy, Russ Johnson, Mike Cressman, Mike McLoughlin, Larry Robbins, Don Hauptmann, Richard Infranca, Gene Boespflug, Dean Villano, Rance Okada, Tim Carlson, Paul Newton, Dan Montgomery, Lee Birk, Jim Buckner, Dave Lester, Darrell Tygart, Mike Collier, Jim McCarthy, Phil Maimone, Pat Martinez, Kurt Wetzel, Mark Lindberg, Heather Wood, Mike Kampf, Mike Spellman, Dave Tallman, Bill Mason, Rick Kempsell, Kerry Sanchez, Doug Tiller, Bill Martin, A.J. Stutson, Bob Maxeiner, Derry Upshaw, Nich Hartney, Dan Ives, Karin Hermosillo, Paula Pedigo, Jackie June, Mary Paczosa, Ralph Turano, Barb Lamana, Luis Lopez, Rob Ross, Kim Martinez, Randy Olson, Phil Paquet, Jeff Sill, Bennie South, Mark Yamashita, Doug Hall, Neil Rosenberger, Gary Pedigo, Bill Work, Herb George, Mike Schaffer, Susan Nachtrieb, Andy Mead, Deb Larsen, Patti Wright, Rachel Harlow, Kathleen Hix, Don Enloe, Kelly Young, Sharon Gibson, Ken Bohling, Sheryl Schwartz, Keith and Shelley Hoey, Robert Cook, Jennifer Williams-Cherry, Tina Bitner, Heather Tharp, Wendy Defusco, Donnie Archuleta, Jerry Hinkle, Dave Roberts, Beth Haynes, Shane Sheridan, Tim and Mary Ann Sheridan, Chuck and Suzanne Sheridan, Gaku Homma, Michelle Ponakiski, Marilyn Robinson, Deanne and Adam Thompson, David and Lisa Torrez, Matt and Brenna Alderman, Howie and Theresa Danzik, John Bishop, Glenna Trout, Ann Massei, Rob Verhaejen, Else Massei, Johan Rens, Leen Massei, Stef Vekemans, Sharron Lyons, Sandy Bosma, Steve and Amy Milliken, Joie Worthen, Ed Usher, Phil Boswell, Bernie Morgan, Mark Eichin, Steve Kent, Bill and Melody Larson, Frank and Amy Soto, Donna DeNomme, Tina Ulatowski.

Thank you!

Foreword

My brothers and sisters of the shield,

Hello, I am "Coach" Bob Lindsey and have served 34 plus years in American law enforcement, initially with the New Orleans police department then with the Jefferson Parish Sheriff's Office. The era in which I served would eventually be remembered as some of the most turbulent years in the law enforcement profession.

After reading *Armor Your Self*, I feel qualified to highly recommend this book because I became a participant and a victim of what can and often does occur to you personally unless you are willing to "armor your self" against the toxicity, chaos, horror, stress and daily demands of law enforcement.

I feel so strongly about this book because I have personally gone through and emerged from the horror of mental, emotional, physical and spiritual breakdown and destruction — most of which was at my own hand. If I had the benefit of this text, I would not have had to experience the devastation of aloneness, isolation, ridicule and the realization that I was so far out that I could not find my way back. I had forgotten how to win and was wallowing in the damnation that I was out of control and alone. I had in fact lost my family, my god, and my own self-worth.

Please avoid what I chose to do. Instead, please consider not just reading *Armor Your Self*, but studying it. You will find herein information that can and will help you to help yourself. This book is not a quick fix; however, it will empower you as long as you are willing to read it, embrace it and then put into action your newly designed plan. If you decide to really embrace this book, you must be willing to do the needed work to benefit from it's content.

John Marx successfully presents a well researched, written text that serves as a guide to you in preparing for and surviving a law enforcement career. It also provides information and techniques to help you strengthen your mental, emotional, spiritual and physical well-being.

Armor Your Self is so well thought out and well written. Many of the concepts in Kevin Gilmartin's book *Emotional Survival for Law Enforcement* are taken to a new level in *Armor Your Self*. John Marx provides resources such as training and conditioning, videos, apps, articles, websites, homework assignments, mentoring resource lists, suggested readings, resources for survivor support and resources to promote annual death prevention training. *Armor Your Self* includes substantial facts, information and ways to accomplish goals in your law enforcement career as well as you personal life. It also inspires, motivates and sets a solid foundation for you to find your path and take action to seize control of your life as you work to remove yourself from harm's way and catapult yourself into a new way of life. It empowers you with tools and instruction for a strong mental, emotional, spiritual and physical life and to survive a career in law enforcement. It also guides you with information, tools and techniques so that you can help your fellow officers and get your supervisors and department involved in supporting you and the rank and file of your department.

There are chapters on how you can and hopefully will become "willing" to protect yourself, your family and your mental, physical, emotional and spiritual well-being. Please acknowledge that telling yourself you can do something does not necessarily motivate you to do it. Willingness promotes action, and action turns into your reality and to your success on taking control of self.

I so wish I had taken control of myself earlier, but I didn't. I didn't have the tools that you can find in the Armor Your Self book. You can take control of yourself, and you should. The chapters that can help you to find your way and walk your path are filled with "can do" information. John Marx has created a foundation upon which you can learn to change your present and future mindsets so they can now be built upon rock-solid grounds.

The light is right there for you. Please read this text and turn that light on. Shine that light into whatever darkness you are terrified of and seek to emerge from. For it is written "the light shines in the darkness, and the darkness can never extinguish it".

During my 53 years of U.S. Law enforcement experience, this particular information has never been offered as it is in this book, *Armor Your Self*. It will assist you to survive your law enforcement career and emerge with your physical, mental, emotional and spiritual life intact. This is a college-course guide and map to success right here at your fingertips.

The decision to take control of your "Self" is right where it belongs, and that is with you. The things from a law enforcement career that threaten our "Selves" are not gender things, race things, age things, or rank things. These horrible and devastating things that challenge your mental, emotional, spiritual and physical "Self" can happen to anyone. Utilize the resources found in the *Armor Your Self* book, and do not permit these things to happen to you! Stand up for what you believe in. Read this text, embrace it and take it unto yourself. "Armor your Self" with a healthy professional, personal and private life.

My thoughts and prayers are with you. God bless and keep you and your family safe always.

Non soleus (never alone)

Coach

Colonel Robert "Coach" Lindsey (ret.) Jefferson Parish Louisiana Sheriff's Office
Founding Member of ILEETA and ASLET
Member and instructor for ILEETA and for Verbal Defense and Influence

Contents

Preface 1

Introduction 3

CHAPTER 1 - **Hidden Dangers** 13

CHAPTER 2 - **A New Paradigm** 37

CHAPTER 3 - **Build A System of Systems** 57

CHAPTER 4 - **Create A Comprehensive Agency Support System** 97

CHAPTER 5 - **Change the Culture** 145

CHAPTER 6 - **The Tactical Resilience Model** 179

CHAPTER 7 - **Armor Your Self™: Physically** 201

CHAPTER 8 - **Armor Your Self™: Physically Training Exercises, Tactics & Techniques** 231

CHAPTER 9 - **Armor Your Self™: Mentally** 251

CHAPTER 10 - **Armor Your Self™: Mentally Training Exercises, Tactics & Techniques** 269

CHAPTER 11 - **Armor Your Self™: Emotionally** 299

CHAPTER 12 - **Armor Your Self™: Emotionally Training Exercises, Tactics & Techniques** 327

CHAPTER 13 - **Armor Your Self™: Spiritually** 363

CHAPTER 14 - **Armor Your Self™: Spiritually Training Exercises, Tactics & Techniques** 385

CHAPTER 15 - **Now and the Future** 411

About the Author 427

Index 429

This information is presented to you in attempt to save your life or to improve the quality of your life and your career. I make no claims to be a psychologist, medical doctor, fitness trainer nor expert in any of these areas. I am just another cop who experienced the hidden dangers of a career in law enforcement firsthand and who knew a fellow officer who took his own life.

I have researched all the tips, techniques and suggestions made in this book. Some of these I tried myself; others I know have worked successfully for other people. Try these at your own risk, but I encourage you to stretch your comfort zone and be open-minded to what could help you, your family or one of your peers.

You have my best wishes for a long, healthy and happy career and life.

Stay safe and take good care of your Self!

John Marx

May 2017

Preface

The Armor Your Self™ concept is a strengthening and conditioning program designed to build Tactical Resilience™ in individual law enforcement professionals, their agencies and their communities. The Armor Your Self™ concept can make you stronger, tougher and more tactically resilient.

This program is about what you can do to make your Self stronger and better able to endure the rigors of the job. It's about peers helping each other. It's about your agency working with you to build systems of support to enable you to do your job more effectively and safely. It's also about law enforcement professionals working within their communities to build the trust, cooperation, support and social capital needed to maintain community resilience. *Resilient communities support resilient cops; resilient cops support resilient communities.*

This program is about *surviving* and *thriving* in this career. In the Armor Your Self™ program you will learn to build Tactical Resilience™ that will help your family, your peers and your agency support you.

The Armor Your Self™ program uses techniques and methods proven effective in many other industries and professions. They are now being adapted for use in law enforcement and military wellness.

This program has already been presented to hundreds of law enforcement professionals around the United States. The Armor Your Self™ program is practical and can be learned quickly. You can then apply what you have learned immediately.

The Armor Your Self™ concept is very adaptable, providing lots of options from which to choose. This allows you to adapt the program to fit your needs, today and at any point during or following your career.

There are two kinds of people: the *Gung-ho* and the *Average Joe (or Jane)*. This program will accommodate both types.

The *Gung-ho* are those who are massively dedicated toward improving themselves and who want to master the fine art of police work. This book is for you, as it will provide you with some insights and strategies that you haven't considered before. Hopefully it will challenge you to achieve all that is humanly possible for you and increase your satisfaction with life.

The *Average Joe* is a person more like me. You want to be better and are always learning and improving yourself. Yet, you are not a super-fit street monster. You might exercise sometimes and try to keep yourself fit, but it's an uphill battle and you struggle with self-discipline. I understand you; I sympathize with you. This book is for you, too! It will give you lots of ideas — some may be just what you need to succeed.

For Gung-hos and Average Joes/Janes alike, this program is for you because *I know* your life, health, and happiness are at risk from the overt and hidden dangers of your career. Included are many strategies to strengthen your Self and build Tactical Resilience™. It is my wish that these strategies will empower you to not only endure the rigors of your career, but also enjoy a more fulfilling personal, family and community life.

John Marx

Introduction

The major challenge facing the future of our law enforcement profession is not how and why our officers are *dying* but how and why are our officers *suffering*.

A growing body of research about law enforcement professionals indicates that *our* profession is very toxic to those who enter it, as evident in higher than average rates of heart disease, diabetes and cancer, and a lower-than-expected average life expectancy. Police officer suicide, on-the-job fatigue, depression and PTSD are additional serious problems.

When you include other issues like alcohol and drug abuse, relationship problems, domestic violence, financial mismanagement and other issues that attack our personalities, then you might even begin to see the dimensions of the crisis we face: Simply *being* a law enforcement officer may be enough to make sure that you won't live a long, happy and healthy life.

Whether you are a long-time police officer or just considering starting your career in law enforcement, you should ask yourself these crucial questions:

1. Are you willing to sacrifice your life to save the life of another?
2. What are you willing to sacrifice to save your own life?
3. What are you willing to do to save the life of a fellow officer?
4. What are you willing to do to save your own life?

There are many great recommendations out there about what we can do about the problems that undermine our health and the lives of those closest to us.

The *best approach* is a *compound system of approaches*. At the Law Enforcement Survival Institute, we offer comprehensive and systematic training with three programs that can impact your overall health and wellness. These programs are:

- Armor Your Self™
- Armor Your Agency™
- True Blue Valor™

In 2007 a friend of mine who we called "Brother Bob" took his own life. Bob had worked in law enforcement at two different Sheriff's Departments for over 14 years. He left his last agency as a patrol sergeant and was admired by everyone who worked with him. He retired from law enforcement at age 35 and went to work in his family's business, which was thriving at that time. Without warning, Bob completed suicide. None of us had a clue it was coming. He did it in his own home so that his peers from the Sheriff's Office would be the ones to find him. He didn't leave a suicide note, so no one really knows for sure why he took his life. Like so many other officer suicides I've heard about, Bob was always the life of the party, and his suicide devastated his friends and family.

After Bob took his life, I searched high and low for scientifically proven methods to identify and help other cops avoid whatever he went through that ended in his suicide. After all, as law enforcement officers, we are selected to be the most physically and emotionally fit to handle the rigors of protecting our society, and to be able to withstand and tolerate all the ills that create the crime and debauchery that we face.

I found, to no one's great surprise, that when dealing with human beings there is more art than science in the literature and practices out there. We humans are very complex, and we just don't know enough about how we work physically, much less mentally, emotionally and spiritually.

When I retired from my career in law enforcement, after 23 years in a Sheriff's Office and a municipal police department, I described myself as "burned out." I knew I was becoming overwhelmed by the death, destruction, trauma and tragedy that I saw. I had never been involved in a shooting, but I had seen enough in my work as a hostage negotiator, public information officer and detective. It was affecting my health, behavior and personality. I didn't believe that I was too emotionally scarred, suffered from PTSD or needed psychiatric treatment, but I knew I needed to get out of the job. I was lucky: I had planned for my retirement, invested well, started several of my own businesses and could leave the job and survive financially.

Don't misunderstand me. Despite all my good decisions and strategies I suffered, and still suffer, many of the things affecting my brothers and sisters in law enforcement. I have had periods of heavy drinking, sometimes to intentionally drown my sorrows. I have squandered money, been promiscuous, divorced and bankrupt, and I have made some poor choices in life. To this day I still struggle with my fitness and health.

After Bob's death I made a decision to find and develop practical techniques and programs that would strengthen and condition me, my friends and other cops for better health and a better quality of life. I researched techniques that seemed to help other people because I feel that if you have taken an oath to protect and serve your community, you deserve the very best options for success that I can recommend to you. I started writing about these issues at CopsAlive.com in 2008. Since then, I've conducted research, interviewed experts, attended summits and seminars and talked to cops in over 47 countries. My aim is to present the very best information that's out there, and let you decide what works for you.

Someday, science will be able to nail down what strategies best protect a law enforcement professional throughout a long career. But until that research is available, *you* are the one that will have to decide what *you* are willing to do to save *your own* life.

Definition of Terms

The four components of the Armor Your Self™ concept are **PMES**, which are designed to shield all that makes up your Self **P**hysically, **M**entally, **E**motionally and **S**piritually from all the *threats* that might affect you. That means that this book is about protecting your *body*, your *mind*, your *emotions* and your *spirit*. I think the best way to do that is to strengthen and condition your Self mentally, emotionally and spiritually — just as you would physically.

The Individual and the Team

This book is also about laying a foundation within our police culture and our agencies so that once we protect ourselves, we will have systems in place in our agencies to support our efforts. So many officers I talk to have gone to great lengths to take care of themselves, and even asked for help, only to be rejected by their peers or their agency because of ignorance, fear, or a lack of courage. This book is designed to change those reactions as well as to help you, the individual, learn to care for yourself and your peers.

Who is this book for?

This book is for everyone in law enforcement. Though I most often use the term "law enforcement professional" here, I want you to know that this book is also meant for as wide an audience as possible. The tips, tools and techniques described here will help anyone who works in a stressful job and under extreme pressure. I was a Sheriff's deputy and a municipal police officer; and therefore much of what I write about is based on my own experience and situations I have seen in law enforcement agencies as I have traveled around the world.

At the risk of leaving someone out, I want you to know that this book is for cops and all the people who support them in law enforcement agencies: police officers, Sheriff's deputies, corrections officers, detectives, parole officers, probation officers, dispatchers, communications specialists, police supervisors, law enforcement managers, records clerks, animal control officers, criminalists, crime scene investigators, coroners, coroner's investigators, district attorneys, district attorneys investigators, wildlife officers, fish and game officers, park rangers, military police officers, Air Force security police, Navy shore patrol, NCIS investigators, military police officers from any branch of any military in the world, traffic cops, SWAT cops, vice and narcotics cops, and employees working for any law enforcement or investigative service in the world.

It's also especially for *police families* — police wives, police husbands, police mothers, police fathers, police children, police brothers, police sisters, police officer peers, police officer partners, police survivors and any other extended family.

This book is for all of you!

In these pages, I use the terms "police officer," "cop" and "law enforcement officer" interchangeably to refer to all law enforcement professionals. You know who you are — just insert your title where appropriate. The same is true when I use gender terms. I know there are many female law enforcement professionals in many different jobs. I love you for it, and think that we need more of you. But the truth is that most people in this profession are men, so it's the male pronoun that shows up most often. I in no way intend to slight anyone. This book is about helping you survive. Please don't let terminology get in the way.

Layer Upon Layer

In this book you will find lots of tips, techniques, strategies and tools to help you care for yourself and others. They're drawn from the best sources I can find and presented as a series of *layers* to help you build better tactics, habits, systems and organizational culture to support your efforts.

INTRODUCTION

Here's a quick overview

Hidden Dangers provides tools to do a realistic threat assessment of what could make your life miserable or kill you.

*A **New Paradigm*** describes the new model of strategies for how to train ourselves to survive this career intact **PMES** (**P**hysically, **M**entally, **E**motionally and **S**piritually).

A System of Systems outlines how to build layers to support your efforts with systems you can implement individually, along with systems for your organization to use to support you, and systems for all of us to implement to help change and improve our police culture so that we all embrace the need to support and protect each other.

Change the Culture encourages all of us in the law enforcement profession to walk our talk, so that if we declare "We're all one big family" or "I've got your back" or "No one gets left behind," then we mean what we say and put systems in place to make those statements reality. This builds a model for a system of **True Blue Valor**™.

Create Comprehensive Agency Support System presents the **Armor Your Agency**™ process of proven, groundbreaking strategies and best practices to build a system within your agency to support all of the individual strategies employed by the Armor Your Self™ concept.

The Tactical Resilience ™ ***Model*** challenges you to identify personal and team tactics you will use in your mission to combat "Blue Trauma Syndrome" and build Tactical Resilience™.

Armor Your Self ™ ***Physically*** lays out everything for a plan to strengthen and condition your Self physically, including a multitude of physical fitness strategies incorporating proper nutrition, proper hydration and getting enough sleep.

Armor Your Self*™ *Physically Exercises sets forth specific strategies you can incorporate *right away* to strengthen and condition your Self physically.

Armor Your Self*™ *Mentally charts all that is necessary in strengthening and conditioning your Self mentally, clarifying how mental and emotional strength and conditioning differ, and focusing on important areas of mental fitness, such as multifaceted brain training, visual and auditory conditioning, personal mind-set, mind control techniques, flash recognition training and "trained observer training."

Armor Your Self*™ *Mentally Exercises offers specific strategies you can incorporate *right now* to strengthen and condition your Self mentally.

Armor Your Self*™ *Emotionally shows you everything needed to strengthen and condition your Self emotionally with descriptions of emotional wellness and methods to protect and condition your emotional Self, including arousal control techniques, stress management strategies, tactical breath control, "quiet mind" goals, and work/home buffer time.

Armor Your Self*™ *Emotionally Exercises includes specific strategies you can incorporate *today* to strengthen and condition your Self emotionally.

Armor Your Self*™ *Spiritually profiles everything I believe necessary to strengthen and condition your Self spiritually, including discussion of your moral compass, "The Police Perfection Paradox," law enforcement oaths and ethics, spirituality's relation to law enforcement, your inner strength and where to find it, the power of faith, tactical trauma control and thoughts on tactical decision making.

Armor Your Self*™ *Spiritually Exercises advances specific strategies you can incorporate *today and in the future* to strengthen and condition your Self spiritually.

What We Can Do Now and in the Future examines additional opportunities available to us individually and collectively, now and in the future, to improve ourselves, and the quality of our lives, and the lives of those who live in our communities. You will also lay the foundation for your plan to Armor Your Self™ and build Tactical Resilience™.

INTRODUCTION

How to Use This Book

I have organized this material in a sequence that makes sense to me, based on my experiences. But that's *my* logic. It may not work for *you*. So I suggest you use the table of contents as your personal guide to the topics that you need most right now. Later, you can come back and read other parts of the book. I've also included a list of some of our Web sites at the end of this introduction that may help you find exactly what you're looking for.

You will find that the heart of this book consists of pairs of chapters: one about a central concept, followed by a chapter of practical exercises. I encourage you: *Do not skip the information about the concepts.* Becoming familiar with the concepts will enable you to understand the reasons for the exercises and the research or source behind them. Also, each of the main "PMES" chapters provide information about how to use the materials on tactics to build systems, build habits and build a better police culture in your agency or organization.

You will also find that the kinds of exercises I recommend are different: Some of them are more active, and others are more passive. This stands to reason. When doing physical or mental exercises, you might be very active physically and mentally, but emotional and spiritual exercises ask you to dig more into your mind and your soul. In fact, some exercises require you to be quiet and still, and this will drive some of you crazy! But *all* of these exercises are important because this program is designed to develop you *completely* as a person and as an effective law enforcement professional. If you are not "balanced," you will not be as effective, and you may be more vulnerable to the toxic side effects of your job.

You will find exercises and "homework" for every concept in this book. But there is also a lot of great material out there, and I just couldn't cram it all into this book. So I encourage you to check out the suggested reading lists at the end of each chapter to continue your personal research into how to survive this career.

WARNING!

I have a long history as a law enforcement trainer, so I think like a trainer and would rather be talking with you. I also believe that you have to "own" this material in order to get anything out of it. For the ideas and exercises in this book to be meaningful, it has to be about *you,* and only *you* can make it meaningful. That's why I will frequently ask you to set the book aside and write something that is more personalized to your needs as "homework." To help you with these "assignments" there is a Student Handbook and the Armor Your Self™ Toolkit workbook that go along with the live, on-site seminar so that you can personalize these materials. I urge you either to order these workbooks from The Law Enforcement Survival Institute, or to start your own notebook and keep it ready while you read this book.

My Stuff vs. Your Stuff

Try to keep your notes handy in one place. I recommend a spiral-bound notebook or a tabbed, three-ring binder to organize your notes and thoughts about this material. You may read or reread this material over several months or even years. I encourage you to make notes about how *you* would get these ideas and exercises across to yourself, your colleagues and your agency or organization. What I present here is based on my experiences and the experiences of my close friends. You are different, perhaps very different. Your career may differ from mine; your job assignment may differ from mine. That's OK, because I'm convinced that no matter who you are and whatever your role in the law enforcement profession, we all share many similarities and, most importantly, we have to look out for one another. My goal is to write about what I know in the hope that you find what I know helps you. I know from experience that it will help you most if you take the time and do the work to write out your own thoughts and beliefs about your experiences in this career.

Now, words about why I trademarked these concepts

I have very specific goals in mind for the development of The Law Enforcement Survival Institute and the materials on all of our Web sites. My primary mission is to continue researching and developing materials to help law enforcement professionals around the world survive their careers and be able to live happy, healthy, productive lives, both while working and well into retirement.

Unfortunately, there just isn't enough research out there about the members of law enforcement. I intend to change that. I want our institute and foundation to grow and develop more and better tools and techniques to help cops. Please stay in touch with what we are doing, because I will always welcome your suggestions and assistance.

To that end I plan to create a nonprofit foundation to support development of these tools and techniques. There is so much more we need to know about how toxic of a career this is on us as human beings and on how we can best survive 10, 20 or even 30 years in this line of work. To be able to do that I have created a rigorous business model that will allow our institute to grow and to fund our foundation. My hope is that if these principles are universally accepted by members of our profession then the proceeds from our publications, training programs and Web sites will further work long after I am dead and buried.

You will also notice that I've created a lot of my own terminology to describe some of the things that I am talking about. The goal is to more accurately communicate my message, because it's best that we all first get on the same page so that we can have a vigorous and spirited discussion on these topics. The trademarks also help to protect the materials from dilution by others using the same terms. Please understand that I mean no disrespect to any other law enforcement author, trainer, leader, psychologist or educator. I just feel it's important to use terms that we can define, and that we maintain control of these definitions.

How is this book different from others?

1. *Here you'll find practical exercises written by a fellow cop.* I'm not a psychologist. I'm a cop who experienced a lot of the *hidden dangers* mentioned here. I'm also not a scientist, but I am a researcher who sees many problems that are not being addressed. And I'm not a police chief, but I am a leader who sees a need for our profession to improve.

2. *This book is more comprehensive than many others* which are usually focused on only one or two of the Physical, Mental, Emotional or Spiritual topic categories.

You may find that these ideas would also probably be helpful to most ordinary people. But since you're in law enforcement, you're *not* ordinary, and neither are the negative stresses and threats you face. I hope this information, although new and very different from what you may be used to, will be helpful and perhaps even save, lengthen and improve your life.

If you bought a digital copy of this book, then please take advantage of its many Web links, which will make your additional reading and research much easier. If you're reading a printed copy of this book, please copy these Web links into your Web browser to do further research. Either way, you'll have access to as much information as possible to make your journey through this process as personal and specific as you need.

If you would like to take this course online, visit the Armor Your Self™ Web site.

http://www.ArmorYourSelf.com

Additionally, if you have read the book or taken the course already, you can join our ongoing membership program. There you will learn new techniques and new exercises every month.

http://www.ArmorYourSelf.com/members

Some of our other Web sites* that you may find useful are:

http://www.LawEnforcementSurvivalInstitute.org

http://www.CopsAlive.com

http://www.TrueBlueValor.com

http://www.PoliceWellness.com

http://www.PoliceMeditations.com

http://www.TacticalResilience.org

http://www.YouTube.com/CopsAlive

http://www.YouTube.com/SurvivalTipsForCops

http://www.ArmorYourSelf.com

http://www.ArmorYourAgency.com

http://www.BloggingForCops.com

http://www.SurviveAPoliceCareer.com

http://www.FRBB.us

http://www.AskCopsAlive.com

As of this writing, not all of these are active yet. But we have big plans, so stay tuned!

Stay safe, and take good care of your Self!

John Marx

May 2017

CHAPTER 1

Hidden Dangers

I believe that this career of ours is toxic and that each of us suffers from its effects, mostly in silence. There are *hidden dangers* to this job that no one ever warned me about, and it's time we all talked about them. New people coming into law enforcement need to know exactly what threats they will face, and those of us still on the job or retired should do some realistic "threat assessment" to ensure we are adequately protecting ourselves from all these threats.

When I started my law enforcement career more than 35 years ago, the only threats we talked about were bad guys who might hurt or kill us. We trained hard to be in the best physical shape possible, and when we talked about anything to deal with the stresses of the job we were told that working out regularly was a sure cure. Looking back I now think we may not have been fighting the right battles or on the right battlefields. Physical fitness is very important in law enforcement, and indeed I believe we must think of ourselves as professional athletes. But when I look at some of the statistics and I look back at my personal experiences I now believe we have focused on the wrong things and wrong strategies.

When you consider that we are painstakingly selected as the fittest candidates for a very demanding job, you would think our agencies would want to take better care of us as valuable assets. What I find, however, is that we don't follow-up with training or evaluation for most of the qualities we are selected for, including mental aptitude, emotional and physical fitness, and honesty and integrity. When you consider that, even by the most conservative numbers, nearly twice as many law enforcement officers in the U.S. take their own lives than are murdered in the line of duty, maybe we should reconsider how we train to maintain our strength and fitness. Physical fitness is just one kind of fitness necessary for this job, and we need to strengthen and condition ourselves mentally, emotionally and spiritually as well as physically.

One reason for writing this book is that I lost a law enforcement friend to officer suicide. When I started talking about it, I realized that other suicides had occurred in the agencies around mine, and I had never even heard about them. We, as a profession, don't talk much about officer suicide, or about any of the other issues relating to emotional and mental health. No one mentioned anything about police suicide as a threat when I was in the police academy, and I think that many of us think of it as our profession's private shame. I call it our "Blue Shame" in the True Blue Valor™ training program and when I write about it on CopsAlive. We don't talk enough about officer suicide and the other threats that steal our quality of life and slowly destroy some of us. We are tested in so many ways when we are hired into the profession, including a full psychological profile, but we never address that matter again for the remainder of our careers, unless forced to.

I don't believe I am an alarmist; nor do I think the "sky is falling." I do however believe we have a major crisis in our profession. Ours is a very dangerous job, and we all knew it when we signed up. I just want to ensure that we have our eyes wide open and that we see all the dangers, even the insidious *hidden dangers*, from which we need to protect ourselves. Then and only then do I believe we can effectively establish the appropriate strengthening and conditioning systems we need as individuals and organizations to be resilient to all of the dangers inherent in this career.

I know that when I retired after 23 years on the job, I was burned out. I thought the feelings I experienced were unique to me, and that I was just no longer tough enough to handle the stresses of the job. I was lucky that I had the financial means to retire and a plan for how I was going to continue to pay my bills and recover from the effects of this career. Many cops suffer in silence, and we need to identify what is affecting them and why. We also need to get them some help to recover so that they can survive this career and live "happily ever after."

The rest of us need to change the way we train ourselves in order to ensure we are fit in all the areas necessary to enhance our Tactical Resilience™ to survive this career.

I've written this book because I want to give something back to the profession that gave me so much, and I don't want anyone to go through what my friend "Brother Bob" went through before he took his own life. I believe that anyone who takes the oath and wears the badge, as well as all of you who are in law enforcement support roles, deserve better than to suffer during or after this career. I believe that every professional who works in law enforcement, as well as our families, suffer the toxic effects of this career, and I don't want anyone ever to have to suffer in silence again. I believe all of these dangers can be managed and minimized with the appropriate tactics, habits and systems.

This book details my beliefs about how all of us can work to protect ourselves, protect our brothers and sisters, and protect our families so that we survive this career and "live happily ever after." We should be able to enjoy a good life after a career in law enforcement. We deserve that, and the only way to make these changes and improve our profession, is if *we* do it *ourselves* by working *together* with our peers and in conjunction with our agencies' managers.

We need to take care of ourselves first, in order to be better able to perform the duties our jobs require of us. We need to take care of each other and really mean what we say when we proclaim "No one gets left behind." Finally, we need to take care of our families and build systems within our agencies that support and sustain us and our way of life so that those who follow in our footsteps will have it better than we did.

With all this in mind, let's talk about some real "Threat Assessment" and see just what we are all up against.

Let's start by considering three questions:

1. What kills most cops in both the long and short term?

2. What's most likely to kill you?

3. If you aren't killed on the job, what threats are going to make your life miserable?

I believe that most people working in law enforcement, either as commissioned officers or as civilian staff, have never really done any personal threat assessment to determine what might hurt or kill them during the course of their careers. Without such information, we are wholly unprepared to safeguard ourselves against all potential threats. As we work through this chapter, I recommend that you complete some personal assessment of all the real and potential threats you will face in your career; then we will talk later about how to prepare for those threats.

Some of the threats we face are *physical* and can injure or kill us. These are the ones of which most of us are already aware and are training to prevent. It is important to point out that not all physical threats are posed by the "bad guys" or the risky situations we face. These threats can also be created by our own actions or inactions. Among them are poor choices we make about diet, exercise, sleep and recreation. Sometimes poor choices can be more devastating to our fitness, happiness and longevity than actions taken by the criminals in our society.

Other threats we face are *emotional*, and can come at us suddenly, such as when we see a particularly grisly death or horrific tragedy. These could be the kinds of threats that later trigger a diagnosis of Post-traumatic Stress Disorder (PTSD).

All these threats can arise either suddenly or slowly over time. Too often, when we haven't appropriately processed traumatic events as they arose, at a point when they were smaller and more manageable, the cumulative effect of many such events we experience and endure over a long or full career combine to incapacitate us. These emotional threats are more mysterious to most of us than the physical threats we can see, and they are more difficult for us to define and defend against psychologically or medically.

Other threats challenge us *mentally* and affect the way we make judgments, concentrate, perceive the environment around us or solve problems. These threats tend to be associated with fatigue, and can distract us and wear us down with feelings of being overwhelmed and exhausted.

Finally, other threats challenge us *spiritually*.

Before you freak out and stop reading: I'm *not* talking about "getting religion," nor am I suggesting anything about what you should believe or should establish as your basis for faith. I do, however, consider that spirituality is an underexplored area within our profession. It is an area that is very mysterious, and most of us don't want to explore it because we don't have a clear understanding of what constitutes strength in this area and we don't know how to build that strength.

Spirituality is a difficult concept for most humans to embrace, and when we try to estimate threats in this realm, we may often overlook the danger these threats pose because we don't fully appreciate and understand the parts of ourselves that are threatened. Consider threats to your honor, integrity, values and faith. This isn't just about your choice of religion, or lack thereof. Rather it's about your moral and ethical compass — your guidance system — and the choices you make about honesty, truth, justice and compassion.

Even as I've grown older and become more spiritual, being able to think of myself as a religious believer or religious person continues to elude me. And for a long time, I thought "religion" and "spirituality" were one and the same, inseparable. So I think I was probably like many of you and I didn't want to explore such unknown areas and, in fact, some of my resistance was based on the things I saw on the job. I didn't want to consider issues about God or religion, and when I saw terrible tragedy and trauma I couldn't believe in religion or a God. Like many of my friends I would say things like "If there is a God, how could these terrible things happen to good people?" As I matured, I wasn't so threatened by these topics and I began to realize that keeping spirituality at arm's length may present both our biggest weakness as well as our biggest opportunity for safety throughout our careers.

I'm not suggesting that you adopt any particular religion. Rather I'm only asking you to do an honest threat assessment — and if some aspect of your work poses a threat to your honor, integrity, values or faith, or if the source of your protection comes from your honor, integrity, values or faith, that you at least be open to *think* about it.

Here are some important things for you to consider:

> Many notes left behind by officers who commit suicide indicate, or outright declare, that they have lost *hope* — so it might be important for us to determine exactly what *hope* is, where you get it and, more importantly, how you can lose it and what can you do to avoid that.

Ask yourself:

- Where do hope, joy, love and compassion come from?
- What would happen if this job, and its side effects, threatened your ability to hope, love or find joy?

- Is there a hidden threat out there that can cause burnout or make you more angry, bitter or resentful?

In the United States over the last 20 years, the average annual number of law enforcement line of duty deaths (LODD's)[1] is right at 154 such deaths a year. If you look at the statistics about what is really killing cops on duty, you will find that most law enforcement line of duty deaths are accidental, while less than half, about 75 a year, are murders.[2] There are other threats out there that I call the *hidden dangers* of our profession, and those dangers are where most of this book's attention will be focused.

Personal Threat Assessment

Generally, those of us in law enforcement are very strategic thinkers and used to assessing risk. So perhaps a proper threat assessment is in order to help us focus on all the tangible and imaginable threats to our lives and well-being created by our profession.

For years we have focused only on what kills cops when they're on duty. The three most common causes of line of duty death, in order of frequency in the United States, are accidents, murder and job-related illness, which includes heart attacks. Most of our training is directed toward shooting, driving and arrest control. Such training is critical to the effective functioning of all law enforcement professionals, but it doesn't really assess all the risks of the job or properly prepare our personnel and us.

If you expand your threat assessment to include things that are not as well documented, like law enforcement officer suicide, the ranking of the threats changes. The new ranking would list suicide as the highest cause of law enforcement officer death in the U.S., followed by accidents, murder and job-related illnesses. Even when we use the lowest officer suicide numbers available, an estimate taken from averaging three separate studies showed 137 officer suicides per year[3], which indicates that the number of police officer suicides in the U.S. is nearly equal to the number of officers killed in the line of duty. These are only the *lowest* of all the reported suicide statistics, and that also means that *at very least* nearly *twice* as many officers take their own lives as are murdered in the line of duty in the United States.

To phrase that differently: You could say that *police officer suicides account for at least twice the number of officers murdered* — and that's only one of the threats I call a "hidden danger!"

A Toxic Profession Filled with *Hidden Dangers*

The often under-detected and often ignored physiological side effects of this job can be toxic!

All of us who get into a career in law enforcement know that violence might endanger our lives at some point. But most newly hired employees, and even some more experienced law enforcement professionals may not recognize that there are also many *hidden dangers* which are even more likely to kill us or at least make our lives miserable.

To me, *hidden dangers* are those that might kill you, might kill you slowly, or at the very least might ruin your life or your quality of life. These are the threats I believe we all need to focus on and prepare ourselves for.

What are the threats I'm talking about? Let's divide them into two categories: those that kill you and those that make your life miserable.

First, the threats that *will* kill you: line of duty death, officer suicide, accidental death, murder, and other causes, including heart disease, diabetes and cancer.

Another medical term we all need to become aware of is *Metabolic Syndrome*, and we will discuss that later. For the moment, know that the National Heart, Lung and Blood Institute of the U.S. National Institutes of Health uses this definition: "Metabolic syndrome is the name for a group of risk factors that raises your risk for heart disease and other health problems, such as diabetes and stroke."

At the same time we also need to consider threats that *don't* kill you but just make your life miserable and may shorten your life expectancy: depression, divorce, addictions including alcohol abuse, over-eating, sex, spending, gambling and being addicted to the adrenaline rush of the job. You should also consider the negative impacts of bankruptcy, the consequences of inappropriate impulsive behavior, uncontrolled anger, PTSD, cumulative negative stress and any job-related disability.

It seems obvious to me that we need more comprehensive research in this country, as well as internationally, into what is really killing cops. There is a lot of disagreement about the U.S. police suicide numbers, but even the lowest numbers show that *twice* as many officers take their own lives than are murdered on the job. Whatever the true numbers may be, I think you need to decide for yourself if those numbers are acceptable or if we (*you*!) need to take steps to reduce them.

As I was preparing this chapter I thought about including a lot of statistics and data even though I know that the research into the effects this job has on you emotionally and physiologically is very limited and the population samples are small. The research out there is good. However, we need a whole lot more of it and we need to know what we are going to face before we start on a 20-year, 30-year or longer career in law enforcement.

Equally important for those already in a career in law enforcement is knowing what dangers we face and how best to deal with them so that we can enjoy a "positive quality of life" during our careers and afterwards.

"In one study, 76% of officers had elevated cholesterol, 26% had elevated triglycerides, and 60% had elevated body fat. Other studies have shown that only police officers who exercised regularly had a lower 10-year risk of heart disease and were absent less from work."[4]

General Mortality

"It has been argued that police officers are at increased risk for mortality as a result of their occupation. The average age of death for police officer in our 40-year study was 66 years of age."[5]

Heart Disease

Dr. John Violanti states that police officers have a higher risk for heart disease than the general population, and that police officers are four years ahead of the average citizen in the progression of heart disease.[6]

Suicide

Statistics indicate that somewhere between 2-6 times more officers kill themselves each year than are killed by the bad guys.[7]

A study of police work patterns and stress, lead by researchers at the State University at Buffalo, N.Y., has shown that "A quarter of female police officers and nearly as many male officers assigned to shift work had thought about taking their own lives."[8]

Depression

"Researchers at Columbia University's Mailman School of Public Health said occupational stress in a large sample of urban police officers was significantly associated with adverse outcomes, including depression and intimate partner abuse."[9]

A survey of quality of life and depression among police officers in Kaohsiung, Taiwan, estimates a rate of probable major depression at 21.6%. Researchers concluded that police officers might have a higher estimated rate of depression than previously thought and those with depression have a poorer quality of life.[10]

Domestic Violence

Domestic violence is 2-4 times more common among police families than American families in general, according to the National Center for Women and Policing.[11]

Fatigue

Dr. Bryan Vila, a former police officer, has learned that 53% of law enforcement officers average less than 6.5 hours of sleep daily. In addition, he determined that more than 90% of law enforcement officers report being routinely fatigued, and 85% reported driving while drowsy.[12, 13]

Findings presented at the 21st Annual Meeting of the Associated Professional Sleep Societies in 2007 show "…sleep disorders appear to be highly prevalent in the present sample of police officers," and "Sleep disorder screening and treatment programs may potentially improve police officer health, safety and productivity."[14]

A study by San Francisco Veterans Affairs Medical Center researchers found that although only 7% of officers are currently reporting significant problems with PTSD symptoms, more than 45% of police officers reported sleep disturbances typical of patients in insomnia clinics.[15]

Among a group of North American police officers, sleep disorders were common and were significantly associated with increased risk of self-reported adverse health, performance and safety outcomes. Results of the 4,957 participants, most of who had not been diagnosed previously, 40.4% screened positive for at least one sleep disorder.[16]

Post-traumatic Stress Disorder (PTSD)

"Research indicates that 12-35% of police officers in the United States suffer from Post-traumatic Stress Disorder (PTSD)."[17]

"Researchers in the UK found a prevalence rate of 13% for PTSD symptoms amongst suburban police officers."[18]

Administrative Stress

"According to CopHealth.com, officers report that approximately 90% of stress in their work is a result of a highly structured, unresponsive, uncaring administration."[4]

Burnout

Different ways in which men and women in the police force deal with stress may actually cause them more stress.

"Don Kurtz, an assistant professor of social work at Kansas State University, studied the gender differences in stress and burnout among police officers. One of the biggest differences Kurtz found was the role that family played in police officers' stress. Whereas a family life can help male officers deal better with stress from the job, women may not have the same support in their own families. 'Women settle into the role of caretaker and come home to a second shift,' Kurtz said."[19]

Alcohol Issues

In a large urban police sample from Australia, Richmond et al. reported that almost half (48%) of males and more than two-fifths (40%) of females consumed alcohol excessively including continuous hazardous or harmful consumption and binge drinking.[20]

In a large sample of urban U.S. police officers, Ballenger et al. documented that 18.1% of males and 15.9% of females reported experiencing adverse consequences from alcohol use, and 7.8 % of the sample met criteria for lifetime alcohol abuse or dependence. Female officers had patterns of alcohol use similar to male officers and substantially more than females in the general population.[21]

A Summary of the Toxic *Hidden Dangers*

No matter what you think of these statistics, I believe two things: First, we as a profession have problems we need to fix; and second, we need lots more research on cops by cops.

Some of that research is beginning to come in, and it confirms that a career in law enforcement can indeed be very toxic to your health.

The Buffalo Cardio-Metabolic Occupational Police Stress (BCOPS)[22] study released findings in 2012, which "demonstrate that police work by itself can put officers at risk for adverse health outcomes."

Conducted over five years by University at Buffalo researcher John Violanti, PhD, this study of 464 police officers, found:

- more than 25% of the officers had metabolic syndrome versus 18.7% of the general employed population

- female and male officers experiencing the highest level of self-reported stress were four- and six-times more likely to have poor sleep quality, respectively

- organizational stress and lack of support was associated with metabolic syndrome in female, but not in male, police officers

- overall, an elevated risk of Hodgkin's lymphoma was observed relative to the general population. The risk of brain cancer, although only slightly elevated relative to the general population, was significantly increased with 30 years or more of police service.

Violanti adds that while police officers do have health insurance, the culture of police work often works against the goal of improving health.

"The police culture doesn't look favorably on people who have problems," he says. "Not only are you supposed to be superhuman if you're an officer, but you fear asking for help." "Police officers who reveal that they suffer from a chronic disease or health problem may lose financial status, professional reputation or both," he explains.

The answer, Violanti says, is to change the training of officers in police academies so that they understand signs of stress and how to get them treated.

"Police recruits need to receive inoculation training against stress," says Violanti. "If I tell you that the first time you see a dead body or an abused child that it is normal to have feelings of stress, you will be better able to deal with them; exposure to this type of training inoculates you so that when it does happen, you will be better prepared. At the same time, middle and upper management in police departments need to be trained in how to accept officers who ask for help and how to make sure that officers are not afraid to ask for that help," he says.

Here is some additional information from another of Dr. Violanti's studies, "Shifts, Extended Work Hours, and Fatigue: An Assessment of Health and Personal Risks for Police Officers," published in March 2012, through the U.S. Department of Justice National

Criminal Justice Reference Service: "The physical health, psychological well-being, safety and efficiency at work are important factors for any police agency to consider. When one considers the monetary and human costs of fatigued officers, it is essential to promote scientific awareness and subsequent plausible interventions. The rate of officers dying from health related problems and accidents for example have surpassed the rate of officers dying from homicide. Fatigued or tired police officers are also a danger to themselves as well as the public they serve."[23]

The Police Executive Research Foundation (PERF) conducted a study of officer fatigue in 2000. Entitled "Evaluating the Effects of Fatigue on Police Patrol Officers,"[24] it came up with these findings:

"Police accidents, injuries, and misconduct extract heavy human and economic costs. Empirical research and practical experience indicate that fatigue associated with the pattern and length of work hours contributes to these problems. Fatigue arising from sleep loss, circadian disruption, and other factors worsens mood and may be expected to increase the probability that officers will be involved in official misconduct. At the same time, it worsens relations with their co-workers, their families, and the communities they serve. Fatigue also increases the probability that police officers will be involved in accidents that put themselves and their communities at risk due to decreased alertness and impaired performance."

"The data revealed significant levels of fatigue among officers who reported that they routinely worked more consecutive hours than would be legal in other public service industries. In fact, from the objective measures, levels of fatigue six times higher than those found among shift workers in industrial and mining jobs were discovered. Additionally, high levels of sleep pathologies were found from the self-report measures of sleep quality where only 26 percent of officers reported averaging the seven or more hours of sleep per day that research finds are minimally required for good health."

One thing is very clear: In a profession that relies heavily on statistics, we are not keeping good enough data on what's happening to us. If we can't even come up with accurate figures about our own suicide rate, we should be ashamed. The International Association of Chiefs of Police (IACP) Psychological Services Section commented on this in 2009 in an article written for the U.S. Department of Justice COPS office: "The end result of the IACP committee's research points clearly to the need for improved data gathering on a national level. Since archival data cannot adequately answer the questions, forward-focused research that controls for the problems identified earlier, must be conducted."[25]

Finally, a 2012 article in *Police Chief* magazine said: "For each and every chief, the problem of law enforcement suicide can suddenly become a personal one. Losing an officer to suicide can result in feelings of guilt or loss all the way up the chain of command. Given the amount of attention, time, and resources spent on other threats to law enforcement, the time has definitely come to address this very real threat."[26] If you are concerned about the issues of police officer suicide, please order the Preventing Law Enforcement Officer Suicide — Data CD from the IACP.[27]

It's nice to have numbers, but you still may be asking yourself, "How does this apply to me?"

One way to answer that question might be to answer a simple series of subjective personal-assessment survey questions to help you decide what actions you might need to take.

Total Wellness Risk Assessment: Are You on Target?

To help you, I have created a very subjective assessment to get you thinking about your quality of life and career and to give you a starting point from which to continue your own personal threat assessment. It's 3 pages long, and while it's too long to include in this book, you can access it for free on www.CopsAlive.com/ThreatSurvey. This document can be downloaded so that you can take it in the privacy of your own home. It focuses on eight areas of your life including: Life, Career, Health, Money, Growth, Relationships, Retirement and Recreation, and it will only take you 5 to 10 minutes to complete.

I've been asked, "If these challenges are so critical, why haven't we addressed them in our own lives or within our agencies earlier?" But a more pertinent question is, "What are the obstacles to implementing change within our profession concerning how we protect ourselves and each other?"

I believe that the first major obstacle to implementing change is our law enforcement "culture." When we are hired we have been judged to be psychologically fit to perform our duties, and thereafter no one mentions these issues because we are afraid that if we do, we'll be labeled weak and then have to worry about losing our jobs and our livelihood. No one wants to take a follow-up psychological evaluation because we are afraid of what it might tell us. We also have a law enforcement culture that thrives on creating self-sufficient, lone wolves who fear they will get cut from the pack if they show any sign of weakness. This is ridiculous because we all know that the job takes its toll on everyone — but we have never accepted the fact that emotional wounds need to be treated just as proactively as physical wounds.

We need to create a culture where we Make It Safe[28] to ask for help. We need to face the fact that everyone would benefit from early intervention on mental, emotional or spiritual wounds rather than leaving them to fester untreated and unaddressed. We need to invest in building long-term resilience for ourselves and our agencies. Common sense should tell us that it would be far more economical to sustain the personnel in which we have invested so much time, energy and money to recruit, select, hire, train and equip, rather than throwing personnel away and hiring someone new.

We also need to create a new model or paradigm of how we should be training our personnel to protect themselves. For years, maybe even centuries, we have focused all of our training time and money to guard against the person who wants to murder us. We train for self-defense, hand-to-hand combat, how to shoot or don't shoot, and the best arrest control techniques. And yet our threat assessment says that most line of duty deaths are accidental. So we train for high-speed driving and make recommendations about the importance of wearing seat belts and body armor. We are loaded with lots of equipment, including lethal and less-than-lethal means of suspect control, and yet we know that more than twice as many of us will take our own lives than will be murdered.

It's time to create a comprehensive training regime that will protect us physically, mentally, emotionally and spiritually.

It's also time we correct the language we use to describe the threats that confront us. It's easy to say that the big threat we face is job stress. We can describe post-traumatic stress and cumulative stress, but really the term "stress" is inadequate when it comes to fully describing what many of us feel is the toxic nature of this job. Some of the threats against us come suddenly, while others are more insidious and chip away at our wellness over weeks and months and years.

What does it take to properly train and condition a modern law enforcement professional (civilian as well as sworn) to endure the rigors of this career?

What threats do *you* have to defend your Self against, and how are you going to do that?

Stress as a Catchall

The word "stress" has become a generic term for all that ails cops. The truth is that we don't really know all the effects this career will have on us physically, mentally, emotionally and spiritually. In truth, stress can be a good thing for a police officer or other professional in this career. We don't know what makes some officers lose hope or others become depressed. We are not really clear about what Post-traumatic Stress Disorder (PTSD) is or how you get it, or even what to do about it. There are no clear links between law enforcement and addictive behaviors like alcohol, drug abuse, excessive gambling or overeating, yet there are symptoms. We are only now becoming aware of connections between this career and major diseases like heart disease, cancer and diabetes, and only now are the connections being studied.

Because these concepts are complicated, I have had to create some new terms to describe these issues so that we can be sure we are all talking about the same thing. In this book, I will use terms like Blue Trauma Syndrome and Tactical Resilience™, which I have created and defined so that we don't become confused with what other educators or authors are talking about. I hope that the use of these terms will generate discussion and even controversy within our profession, because we could use a whole lot more discussion about what's killing us and what to do about it.

Blue Trauma Syndrome

Through the Law Enforcement Survival Institute I have defined Blue Trauma Syndrome as "a spectrum of negative physical, mental, emotional and spiritual health-effects manifested by many career law enforcement people." Blue Trauma Syndrome most certainly has its roots in large or cumulative doses of negative occupational stress and surfaces in the form of many negative physiological, mental, emotional and spiritual symptoms.

Blue Trauma Syndrome is an interesting enemy. You can't see it, you can't touch it, and most times you can't even describe it. But it's there, and it attacks us every day. We must defend ourselves and armor ourselves against its effects; otherwise a career's worth of battle fatigue will overtake all of us. I'm speaking in generalities here, but I think even a small amount of introspection will reveal this is true for the vast majority of us.

Keep in mind that some stress within our bodies is good and may be especially important for law enforcement officers. You can also read all the research that's out there about the effects that negative stress has on law enforcement officers, but it still doesn't give us enough information about *which* stresses will get to us. Part of the problem is that the same stress will affect different officers differently, and its effect is different on different days and at different points during your career. Its dangers are also cumulative and attack you drip-by-drip, day-by-day over the life of your career. We see the signs but we dismiss them as "burnout," bad moods, anger, frustration and withdrawal. These symptoms are really representative of depression, grief, misery, hopelessness and emotional exhaustion created by cumulative stress. I believe that all of these symptoms can be collected into one general category that I call Blue Trauma Syndrome.

The Bucket Metaphor

As much as I liked the movie *The Bucket List*, directed by Rob Reiner, written by Justin Zackham, and starring Jack Nicholson and Morgan Freeman, I believe in a different kind of bucket list.

When I speak to groups of officers, I like to use the metaphor of an imaginary bucket you might carry with you throughout your career. As you move through life, and especially a law enforcement career, you fill your bucket full of stuff. Now, you can define "stuff" any way you like, but for the purposes of my story, "stuff" consists of the bad effects you absorb from seeing death, destruction, trauma and tragedy. Your bucket collects things like memories, emotions and traumas that negatively affect you. I'm sure that there are ways to minimize the effects of the stuff in your bucket, and the techniques taught in this book can help you do that. What I have noticed in my peers and myself is that if you don't manage what's in your bucket, it eventually becomes too full and starts to splash all over you and the people you care about. If you wait too long, the stuff in your bucket becomes part of the toxic effect that can be part of this career.

For example, when I examined my bucket I found a lot of memories and emotions having to do with other peoples' dead children. In my early career I was known as the "King of SIDS deaths" (Sudden Infant Death Syndrome) because I responded to five of them in my first year-and-a-half on the job. During my career I also witnessed two house fires that took the lives of seven children, and I was the first officer on the scene of an auto accident that decapitated a six-month-old infant. Because I worked as a hostage negotiator, detective and media spokesman during different times in my career, I think I responded to every murder, major accident, major crime and major disaster we had in my jurisdiction during my 20-plus-year career. When I retired my bucket was very full and I had what I described as "burnout." I was tired of the job and all the negativity that went with it.

It's in the nature of a law enforcement career that threats come at us from all sides. And they're not only physical; they're mental, emotional and spiritual, too.

The big issue is that none of this matters unless it affects you and those that you care about. So let's put all this information to one side and ask: What's real in your world?

Let's do some Self-inspection. What is it about your job that's affecting you? And more important, *how* it is affecting you?

A "What's in Your Bucket?" Exercise

Image you have an invisible bucket (or two) in which you carry around all the trauma and crap you pick up in your life and career — the psycho-motor, mental, emotional, and spiritual garbage, the memories, horrible images, smells, sounds, photos, descriptions and experiences you have had with events that most humans would find unimaginable.

So: "What's in your bucket?"

The answer is probably different for every one of us. But no matter where you are in the world, if you work in law enforcement then, there is probably some very toxic stuff in your bucket. Most human beings, and especially cops, have an ability to process these things so that they don't do us excessive or prolonged harm. However, there are times when we're not very good at doing what it takes to properly process this toxic waste, and so it continues to build up and sometimes overflows the bucket. It's up to you to deal with it or not; but it won't go away if you just ignore it. If you choose to do something to manage the toxicity of this job, then read on and I hope this book provides you with enough material so that you can effectively manage your bucket. Part of the Armor Your Self™ concept is about how you strengthen and condition your Self to avoid some of this toxicity in the first place; but it's also about how to effectively mitigate the toxicity so that it doesn't excessively harm you or your family.

Take a few minutes to put this book aside and write (yes, I said *write*) a list of what's in your bucket.

Another issue we have to deal with is the Police Perfection Paradox, which is demonstrated in situations where we foolishly expect our personnel to be superhuman and not have to cope with the excessive negative stress and emotional trauma caused by what they encounter on the job. The paradox is that we know this profession is toxic, and we really do understand that it will take a toll on the people working within our profession. When that toll and its side effects appear, we seem to forget that we knew it would happen and we talk as if no one saw this coming. What's worse is that most agencies have nothing in place to support and heal their employees when the psychological and emotional trauma happens.

As you read through this book, let your #1 goal be to start a personal training program to create a *positive quality of life* for yourself, your peers and your family.

It is my recommendation that you learn to respond to all threats against you, your co-workers and your family, and that you create a Comprehensive Threat Response Plan to fight against those threats that can kill you or ruin your life and well-being.

The Right Battlefield?

It's time to prepare for all the dangers that threaten us. We need to be fighting to survive all the battlefields on which we might suffer. I'm talking about physical, mental, emotional and spiritual threats that might wound, cripple or kill us.

We need to create a Comprehensive Threat Response Plan — a battle plan, if you will. And to do so, you need to beware that there are several battlefields upon which you will likely be called to fight.

One reason why it's important to talk about the *hidden dangers* of law enforcement is that we can then begin to see we might be fighting on the wrong battlefield. For years all of our training has been directed toward dealing with line of duty death. Perhaps we should be training and conditioning ourselves to become resilient against *all* the real and tangible threats to our lives and the quality of our lives. To that end you will find that this book tackles three different battlefields.

First, you will spend most of your time on helping strengthen and condition yourself physically, mentally, emotionally and spiritually to defend against all the threats that might endanger you and your family. It's important to build what I call Tactical Resilience™, which is defined as the intentional tactics and techniques used by a police officer (or other law enforcement or military professional) that allows them to resist and withstand the rigors and hidden emotional, physical, spiritual and physiological dangers of continuous high-threat/high-stress situations. These techniques, when used properly and conditioned regularly, will build strength and well-being, and will create whole person fitness, as exhibited through the mind, body, brain and spirit.

Second, we will spend one chapter on the concept of armoring your agency so that you can help build all the networks, systems and programs necessary to support you and your peers throughout your career. None of us stands alone, and the Armor Your Agency™ concept works to build systems to support all of you.

Finally, we will discuss our concept of True Blue Valor™, a third approach to threat assessment and prevention. Even if we are strong as individuals and agencies, we still have to tackle the norms and stigmas of our police culture. True Blue Valor™ is about changing our law enforcement culture so that it supports and sustains us as we tackle this very challenging career. One of the biggest hurdles is getting us to actually walk our talk. We say that "no one gets left behind," that "we are all one big family" and we tell each other "I've got your back." But reality shows that we lack follow-through with these promises. The True Blue Valor™ concept works with the concepts of Armor Your Self™ and Armor Your Agency™ to create a platform so that all three concepts work in cooperation and as an effective system.

You will also see that these new ideas have required me to create new language for us to use with concepts like Blue Trauma Syndrome and Tactical Resilience™.

In conclusion, I suggest that we have problems in our profession that are not being adequately addressed and which, in many cases, we are fighting on the wrong battlefield. I believe that with the Armor Your Self™ program we can create a new model or paradigm for the future to address those problems effectively.

Let's Create A New Paradigm

Let's create a new paradigm or model for both your training and for developing a Comprehensive Threat Response Plan. In the next chapter we'll start to tackle the concepts of Armor Your Self™ and what we can do individually to strengthen and protect against the *hidden dangers* of law enforcement. In that chapter I will make some recommendations about what model or paradigm we need to be using, and then use that model to build the whole Armor Your Self™ process.

Recommended Resources

If you would like to do more research on your own about all the dangers in law enforcement, here are some Web links to resource organizations and Web sites that may have more data for you to review:

- The Federal Bureau of Investigation (FBI):
  http://www.fbi.gov

- The International Association of Chiefs of Police (IACP):
  http://www.theiacp.org/

- The U.S. Centers for Disease Control (CDC):
  http://www.cdc.gov

- The U.S. National Institutes of Health (NIH): http://www.nih.gov

- The U.S. Department of Justice (DOJ): http://www.justice.gov

- Below 100 is an Initiative to Reduce Police LODD's to Fewer Than One Hundred Per Year: http://www.below100.com

- *Breaking the silence: Suicide prevention in law enforcement video and resource guide* created by the Carson J Spencer Foundation; International Association of Chiefs of Police (IACP); National Action Alliance for Suicide Prevention; American Association of Suicidology (AAS):
  Video:
  http://youtu.be/u-mDvJIU9RI
  Discussion Guide:
  http://www.carsonjspencer.org/files/4314/4225/7835/20150817_LE_Video_Guide.pdf

- Jack Digliani's "Make it Safe Police Officer Initiative:"
  http://www.jackdigliani.com/index.html

- Bryan Vila's report, "Tired Cops," from the U.S. Department of Justice National Criminal Justice Reference Service:
  https://www.ncjrs.gov/pdffiles1/jr000248d.pdf

- John Violanti's page at the University of Buffalo: http://sphhp.buffalo.edu/social-and-preventive-medicine/faculty-and-staff/affiliated-faculty-directory/violanti.html

Here are some additional resources from our family of organizations that offer information and training:

http://www.CopsAlive.com
http://www.LawEnforcementSurvivalInstitute.org
http://www.PoliceWellness.com
http://www.TrueBlueValor.com
http://www.PoliceMeditations.com
http://www.SurviveAPoliceCareer.com
http://www.BlueWarrior.us
http://www.BloggingForCops.com
http://www.AskCopsAlive.com
http://www.ConcentratedNutrition.com
http://www.YouTube.com/SurvivalTipsForCops
http://www.YouTube.com/CopsAlive
The Center for Tactical Resilience: http://www.TacticalResilience.org

Suggested Homework for Your Own Personal Development:

1. Do your own research on the numbers.

2. Decide what threats you need to worry about and when.

3. Set your plan to take some actions now to reduce those dangers and keep reading this book to learn more.

4. Continue your research and due diligence as your career develops. This is a profession that requires you to continue to hone your skills and develop your craft for the rest of your life.

Recommended Reading:

Digliani PhD, Jack. *Reflections of a Police Psychologist.* Bloomington: Xlibris Corporation, 2010 revised 2015.

Douglas, Robert. *Death With No Valor.* Pasadena, MD: Keener Marketing Inc., 1997.

Douglas Jr., Robert E. *Hope Beyond The Badge.* Pasadena, MD: Keener Marketing Inc., 1999

Gilmartin, Kevin M. *Emotional Survival For Law Enforcement.* Tucson: E-S Press, 2002.

Hackett, Dell P. and John M. Violanti, Ph.D. *Police Suicide.* Springfield, IL: Charles C. Thomas Publisher, 2003.

Kates, Allen R. *CopShock. Second Edition: Surviving Posttraumatic Stress Disorder (PTSD).* Cortador, AZ: Holbrook Street Press, 2008.

Kirschman, Ellen. *I Love A Cop: What Police Families Need To Know.* New York: Guilford Press, 2006

Sapolsky, Robert M. *Why Zebra's Don't Get Ulcers.* New York: Henry Holt and Company, 2004.

Vila, Bryan. *Tired Cops: The Importance of Managing Police Fatigue.* Washington, DC: Police Executive Research Forum, 2000.

Violanti, John M. and Douglas Paton. *Who Gets PTSD?* Springfield, IL: Charles C. Thomas Publisher, 2006.

Violanti BCOPS Research:
http://www.buffalo.edu/news/releases/2012/07/13532.html
(Accessed 12-27-12.)

Footnotes

1. Information from the U.S. Law Enforcement Officers Memorial Fund http://www.nleomf.org/ (Accessed 4-12-16.)

2. Data on the causes of law enforcement line of duty deaths (LODD) from the National Law Enforcement Offers Memorial Fund http://www.nleomf.org/facts/officer-fatalities-data/causes.html (Accessed 10-18-14.)

3. Badge of Life National Study of Police Suicides (NSOPS) **http://www.policesuicidestudy.com/id16.html** (Accessed 4-4-16.)

4. Violanti, John M., PhD. "Dying from the Job: The Mortality Risk for Police Officers" http://www.cophealth.com/articles/articles_dying_a.html, http://www.cophealth.com (Accessed 10-5-06.)

5. Ibid.

6. Violanti, John M., PhD. "Police Officers Are At Increased Risk For Heart Disease" http://www.lemha.org/id23.html http://www.lemha.org (Undated). (Accessed 12-8-11.)

7. Varying statistics collected from www.psf.org and www.badgeoflife.com

8. "Depression and suicidal thoughts among police officers differ based on gender and work shift" http://www.news-medical.net/news/2008/10/19/42041.aspx (2008). (Accessed 12-8-11.)

9. "Police Work Stress Linked to Depression" http://www.upi.com/Health_News/2009/03/13/Police-work-stress-linked-to-depression/UPI-81261236980499/#ixzz1DgebHphr (2009). (Accessed 9-22-11.)

10. "A survey of quality of life and depression for police officers in Kaohsiung, Taiwan" http://www.ncbi.nlm.nih.gov/pubmed/16721651 (2006). (Accessed 9-22-11.)

11. "Police Family Violence Fact Sheet" http://www.womenandpolicing.org/violenceFS.asp#notes National Center for Women & Policing. (Accessed 9-22-11.) HeavyBadge.com (Undated). (Accessed 12-9-10.)

12. "No Rest for the Weary" http://www.justnet.org/TechBeat%20Files/NoRestforWeary.pdf (Accessed 3-17-11.)

13. "Sleep Deprivation: What Does It Mean for Public Safety Officers?" http://www.ojp.usdoj.gov/nij/journals/262/sleep-deprivation.htm, National Institute of Justice, 2009. (Accessed 3-17-11.)

14. "Sleep Disorder Highly Prevalent Among Police Officers" http://www.medicalnewstoday.com/articles/73968.php (2007). (Accessed 9-22-11.)

15. "Police Officers Who Experience Traumatic Event Have Greatest Risk of PTSD" http://www.universityofcalifornia.edu/news/article/3968 (2002). (Accessed 9-22-11.)

16. "Sleep Disorders, Health, and Safety in Police Officers" http://jama.ama-assn.org/content/306/23/2567.short *Journal of the American Medical Association*, 2011. (Accessed 12-27-11.)

17. "The Relationship between Critical Incidents, Hostility and PTSD Symptoms in Police Officers" https://idea.library.drexel.edu/bitstream/1860/1118/1/Clair_Mary.pdf, Drexel University, 2006. (Accessed 2-11-11.)

18. "Post-traumatic stress disorder in UK police officers" www.greenmedicolegal.com/ PTSDPOLICE.pdf Green Medico Legal, 2004. (Accessed 2-11-11.)

19. "K-State Social Work Professor Finds That The Differences In How Male and Female Police Officers Manage Stress May Actually Accentuate Their Stress On The Job." http://www.k-state.edu/ media/newsreleases/feb09/policeebp22409.html, Kansas State University, 2009. (Accessed 2-11-11.)

20. Richmond RL, Wodak A, Kehoe L, Heather N. "How healthy are the police? A survey of life-style factors" *Addiction*. 1998; 93:1729–1737. [PubMed: 9926535] https://www.ncbi.nlm.nih.gov/pubmed/9926535 (Accessed 4-4-16.)

21. James F. Ballenger, Suzanne R. Best, Thomas J. Metzler, David A. Wasserman, David C. Mohr, Akiva Liberman, Kevin Delucchi, Daniel S. Weiss, Jeffrey A. Fagan, Angela E. Waldrop, Charles R. Marmar. "Patterns and Predictors of Alcohol Use in Male and Female Urban Police Officers" https://www.ncbi.nlm.nih.gov/pmc/articles/PMC3592498/pdf/nihms243246.pdf (Accessed 4-4-16.)

22. 2012 findings released by the Buffalo Cardio-Metabolic Occupational Police Stress (BCOPS). http://www.buffalo.edu/news/releases/2012/07/13532.html (Accessed 4-8-14.)

23. Violanti Study March 2012, "Shifts, Extended Work Hours, and Fatigue: An Assessment of Health and Personal Risks for Police Officers" https://www.ncjrs.gov/pdffiles1/nij/grants/237964.pdf (Accessed 4-8-14.)

24. Evaluating the Effects of Fatigue on Police Patrol Officers. Final Report. www.ncjrs.gov/pdffiles1/nij/grants/184188.pdf (Accessed 4-8-14)

25. "By Their Own Hand: Suicide Among Law Enforcement Personnel." Prepared for the U.S. Department of Justice COPS office by the International Association of Chiefs of Police Psychological Services Section (2009). http://cops.usdoj.gov/html/dispatch/April_2009/suicide.htm (Accessed 4-8-14.)

26. "Law Enforcement Suicide: Current Knowledge and Future Directions" *Police Chief* (magazine). http://www.policechiefmagazine.org/magazine/index.cfmfuseaction=display_arch&article_id=2669&issue_id=52012 (Accessed 4-8-14.)

27. Preventing Law Enforcement Officer Suicide — Data CD. http://www.theiacp.org/ViewResult?SearchID=988 (Accessed 4-8-14.)

28. Jack Digliani's "Make it Safe Police Officer Initiative" http://www.jackdigliani.com/index.html (Accessed 4-8-14.)

CHAPTER 2

A New Paradigm

I believe that we need a new paradigm, or model, for training and conditioning law enforcement professionals. I say this because I think the old model is outdated and may actually be hurting us.

We need to understand that this world is filled with tragedy, and just because we are in law enforcement we are not exempted from that misery in our personal lives. However, we have chosen a profession that thrusts us into the pain and suffering of others, and we need to be strong enough to endure what we encounter. I don't believe that we are all born with a body or personality that is resilient enough to withstand all the negative stresses and trauma this job brings. That's why we need to train and condition ourselves to build what I call Tactical Resilience™. To better cope with all that is thrown at us on the job, we need to strengthen and condition ourselves in many ways to be the best we can be at our law enforcement roles. I am also convinced such conditioning will help make our personal lives stronger and richer as well.

If you consider the profile of the ideal and most capable police officer, that person might have incredible strength physically, mentally, emotionally and spiritually. That officer might possess what we call the "Warrior Spirit." That spirit helps prepare an officer to risk or sacrifice his or her life to save another's, to have the courage to engage in life-and-death combat with some very bad people and to still have the inner strength to be able to take a life when necessary. This is the largest responsibility anyone in a civilized society, outside of a war zone, is asked to accept. We need to acknowledge the honor that is conferred upon us, and rise to the challenge to be the best and strongest we can be in order to maintain public trust. These role model officers will also probably be very understanding and empathetic, as well as possess a huge amount of compassion for others that helps them truly serve and protect their communities.

As a group, these model officers will be master communicators, and will have the skills to empathize with and respect all those in need of help or in need of arrest. It takes very strong personal character, filled with honor and integrity, to be able to serve and protect effectively while impartially enforcing the law by warning, court summons or arrest, or even by taking a life to protect others. This is a huge responsibility, and if you aspire to be that role model officer then you must make sure you are fully prepared to make a total commitment. If you aspire to greatness in our profession, make sure you train and condition yourself in every possible way to deliver both effective performance as a protector and compassionate assistance as a community servant.

You read in the previous chapter that there are *hidden dangers* to a career in law enforcement. So? We all know this job is dangerous. That's what we signed up for, right? Maybe.

Maybe it's time for our profession to acknowledge that we need to be putting systems in place —from the beginning, when someone is hired — that will support, care for, and protect us from all the dangers we will experience throughout our careers. And maybe we as individuals need to recognize and acknowledge that there are both many obvious and many *hidden dangers* in this profession, and we need to strengthen and condition ourselves to endure these challenges and maintain our resilience throughout a long and full career.

I propose that we need new threat-oriented training strategies, and suggest that we have been using outdated survival preparation and training strategies for years, and that it's now time we become more proactive. We need a new model for training and personal preparedness that addresses *all* the threats and inoculates us from *all* the dangers inherent in this career. We need a new *paradigm* to accomplish that. In this context paradigm means a new model or new pattern to follow. We need new support systems within our agencies that must also support and encourage individual initiatives that each one of us may propose to bolster these systems.

Finally, we need to change our professional culture so that it supports and endorses these new concepts, particularly the concept of asking for help right away when we need it instead of postponing a request for help until the situation has deteriorated to the point where simple help may not be enough to solve the problem.

When we hire people into law enforcement, we test them for honesty, for communications skills, for common sense. We also test them for medical and mental fitness. After that, we encourage them to stay involved in medical evaluation and physical fitness programs, but we rarely encourage, support or require them to stay mentally fit. Most agencies in the United States don't have an on-staff, on-site psychologist, and very few agencies work with a trained police psychologist. We put everyone through psychological testing when they get hired, and then it seems that we never evaluate them again until its time to fire them or put them out to pasture.

Medical Paradigm

We should adopt a *proactive* medical-style model rather than our current psychological model for dealing with mental fitness. When officers receive a minor injuries or wounds, we send them to a doctor to treat them and then put them on light-duty while they recover and are ready to go back to duty. We should do this with those who are brave enough to admit they have some kind of emotional injury or mental wound.

What we too often *don't* recognize is that *we* have created an environment in which *we* tease and punish our peers and prevent them from even admitting they need help to deal with an emotional trauma. *We* have created an environment in which we never treat any mental or emotional wound until it's at its worst and is incapacitating us.

Occasionally a doctor decides when an officer is ready to go back to work after a physical injury. But what happens when we have a psychological injury? I am familiar with the "Psychological Fitness-for-Duty Evaluation Guidelines" and the "Guidelines for Consulting Police Psychologists," published by the International Association of Chiefs of Police (IACP) Psychological Services Section. But I also know that conscientiously following these guidelines is the exception rather than the rule. I hope most agencies have adopted the IACP's recommendations about officer fitness-for-duty and the use of a consulting police psychologist, but I expect many have not. I suspect that many agencies facing an officer with an emotional crisis have not considered the possibility of engaging such psychological services prior to needing to assist an employee in distress, and I also suspect that many of the people currently administering such psychological evaluations don't have much, if any, experience working with law enforcement officers.

The IACP's "Psychological Fitness-for-Duty Evaluation Guidelines" read in part: "Referring an employee for a Fitness-for-Duty Evaluation (FFDE) is indicated whenever there is an objective and reasonable basis for believing that the employee may be unable to safely and/or effectively perform his or her duties due to a psychological condition or impairment. An objective basis is one that is not merely speculative but derives from direct observation, credible third-party report, or other reliable evidence."

The IACP's "Consulting Police Psychologist Guidelines" suggest, "Consulting police psychologists should be competent to conduct, evaluate, and/or utilize science-based research in the practice of consulting police psychology."

You can learn more about these guidelines and the IACP's Psychological Services Section by following these links:

- http://www.theiacp.org/portals/0/documents/pdfs/Psych-FitnessforDutyEvaluation.pdf
- http://www.theiacp.org/psych_services_section
- http://www.policechiefmagazine.org/magazine/index.cfm?fuseaction=display_arch&article_id=699&issue_id=92005

The real problem we face is not so much the quality of mental health care available to law enforcement. Rather, the problem is that too often we do not want or don't accept such help until it's really long overdue. We have created a culture that values sucking it up and never allowing or showing any weakness. When officers become wounded emotionally, we struggle with what to do with them. We value strength and courage, yet we do nothing to build mental and emotional strength and do nothing to support someone with the courage to ask for help! We need to work toward encouraging a culture of proactive mental, emotional and spiritual health *and* find ways to make those things acceptable to everyone so that asking for help, when you feel overwhelmed by negative stress or trauma, won't be a problem for you or your agency.

We also tend to react with an "all or nothing" mentality when someone is injured emotionally or psychologically. We either treat problems as major injuries (if we treat them at all) or we ignore or "blow off" anything that could be considered a minor injury. And there seems to be no in-between. We all, as part of a professional culture, need to change our attitudes about mental health and accept our own responsibility to care for ourselves and to support our peers. When we or someone we work with require mental health care, we need to accept early interventions that have the probability of greatly reducing long-term trauma and disability. We need to accept mental and emotional wellness as a regular part of the job, and mental health treatment as preventative care that will keep us all healthy and effective. We also need to train and condition our cognitive functioning (brain), emotional stability (mind) and internal compass (spirit) regularly, just as we train and condition our bodies physically.

When you think about it, the way we now ignore problems is foolish and more likely to create more massive trauma and make the people affected more vulnerable and less likely to back us up when we need them. This would not be the case if we just changed our attitudes about mental health treatment and early intervention.

Using our current paradigm: mental fitness is something we believe in, and hire for, yet after hiring we only train for physical threats and confrontations, and not against the mental and emotional threats we face every day.

Questions to ask yourself:

- Now that you've done a personal threat assessment, what are you going to do to protect or armor your Self from all of the threats we are analyzing?
- What is your current survival strategy? Is it appropriate? What does it need to be in order to be appropriate?
- What is your agency doing to help you survive (or even thrive) in your career or life?

For so many years we have been focused on what causes line of duty deaths. We know that the majority of these deaths are accidental and that a smaller minority of all line of duty deaths involve officers who were murdered.

We need to construct a new system that will support all of us and help us find our way through the maze of *hidden dangers* and toxic traumas. We now have in the United States the "Below 100" program, which is doing an excellent job of reducing accidental line of duty deaths. But what are we doing about the other *hidden dangers*?

We need a new paradigm that guides us to prepare ourselves to survive this profession and to support each other throughout this career. Perhaps we need to adopt a *sports model* rather than the military model for our training and conditioning programs, and to consider ourselves professional "Police Athletes." This sports model would include the concepts of having the mind-set of being a professional athlete, along with the supporting concepts of teamwork and the concept of coaching for success, rather than stressing authority and chain of command in an attempt to force conformity.

Our Old Paradigm

Paradigm is a good word. In this context paradigm means a model or pattern to follow.

The Merriam-Webster dictionary defines *paradigm* as "an example, pattern; *especially*: an outstandingly clear or typical example or archetype."
(Source: http://www.merriam-webster.com/dictionary/paradigm [Accessed 3-4-13.])

The Old Paradigm of Law Enforcement Survival Training:

The Old Paradigm = Bad guys are Enemy No. 1.

The Old Paradigm = Line of duty death is the only danger to prepare for.

The Old Paradigm = Focus on what might kill you, *not* what might ruin you for life.

The Old Paradigm = Physical fitness solves everything.

The Old Paradigm = Mental health is for victims.

The Old Paradigm = If officers develop PTSD, cut them from the herd and hire someone new.

The Old Paradigm = If you succumb to stress or trauma, don't ask for help or you will be labeled as weak and lose your job or the support of your peers.

The Old Paradigm = Doesn't even consider emotional and spiritual well-being.

A New Paradigm for Your Personal Survival Planning

This new paradigm uses the Tactical Resilience™ model of Armor Your Self™ to strengthen and condition your Self physically, mentally, emotionally and spiritually. These four areas of emphasis are abbreviated as **PMES**. This new paradigm also provides a system that starts with good tactics and then builds positive habits, supportive systems and personal character — or in the case of an agency, a positive and healthy organizational culture. These four building blocks of *t*actics, *h*abits, *s*ystems and *c*haracter/*c*ulture are abbreviated as **THSC**.

For our purposes in law enforcement or the military Tactical Resilience™ is defined as a human quality of intentional strength and fitness exhibited through the mind, body, brain and spirit of police officers or other law enforcement or military professionals that allows them to withstand the rigors and hidden emotional, physical, spiritual and physiological dangers of continuous high-threat, high-stress situations.

The New Paradigm of Law Enforcement Survival Training:

The New Paradigm = New Mind-set for Training and Conditioning the "Police Athlete."

The New Paradigm = Armor Your Self™ through Comprehensive Physical, Mental, Emotional and Spiritual (PMES) Strengthening Programs.

The New Paradigm = Build Support Systems using Tactics, Habits and Systems to build Character/Culture (THSC).

The New Paradigm = Target "Blue Trauma Syndrome" so that we can minimize its effects.

The New Paradigm = Build character by developing your own Personal Code.

The New Paradigm = Strengthen your character by developing your own Personal Credo.

The New Paradigm = Develop both Personal and Agency Comprehensive Physical, Mental, Emotional and Spiritual Training and Conditioning Systems.

The New Paradigm = Develop Agency Systems that promote and support Health and Well-being.

The New Paradigm = Develop a Positive and Healthy Agency Culture that supports those who need help rather than throwing them away.

The New Paradigm = Create an organizational culture that promotes an individual's *willingness* to ask for help when first needed and not waiting until after it's too late to salvage a career.

The New Paradigm = Create an organizational culture that "Makes It Safe" for, and supports, people who choose to ask for help when it's needed.

The New Paradigm = Train everyone to be a "Fire Spotter" looking for hot spots or co-workers who need help and then supporting them through a process of early intervention and treatment.

The New Paradigm = Create proactive organizational systems of peer, family, psychological and chaplain's support to be utilized before intervention is needed.

The New Paradigm = Create a crisis intervention plan for those who need but don't ask for help early enough.

The New Paradigm = Target career success and positive quality of life on the job and in retirement.

The New Paradigm = Create an organization that starts the wellness process at hiring and continues and tracks it well into an employee's retirement.

Let's create a new paradigm about how we train ourselves to survive this career.

This is about quality of life. I believe the best way to survive a career in law enforcement is to strengthen and condition your Self in every way possible so you can endure the threats and rigors that come with this job. You need to do this when you begin your career, and you need to continue strengthening and conditioning your Self for the rest of your life.

Let's also acknowledge that surviving a law enforcement career is a team effort. While you have to work hard individually, it also takes a lot of support to keep everyone safe and healthy. Support comes from your peers, your supervisors, your agency administrators, your spouse or significant other, your family and your team of supporters. That team of supporters could include your doctor, your accountant, your lawyer, your fitness trainer, your minister, priest, rabbi, imam or chaplain and all the other individuals you pay or engage to help make you successful.

The primary purpose of this book is to be very proactive and to propose a series of "How To" examples to deal with those *hidden dangers* that affect so many in law enforcement. Keep in mind, too that there are also "What To Do's" in this book because once you know what you need to do, you will find appropriate "How To's" that will fit perfectly into your life.

I've heard many people in the field of health and wellness use the metaphor that taking care of your Self is very much like taking care of an automobile: both need fuel, fluids, lubricants, regular maintenance and occasional repairs. The unfortunate fact is that we all take better care of our machines than we do our bodies and our minds. We are in a business whose very nature means we are assaulted in many different ways every day. We need to armor our Selves to be able to perform our duties effectively and survive a 20-plus year career.

Only a fool would suggest that a career in law enforcement has no negative effects on your mental and physical health. Why, then, is it that when those negative effects materialize, we shun those who ask for help and act surprised that they might not be able to cope with the trauma and tragedy they have endured in one particular incident or in many incidents over many years?

We expect people to be in excellent mental health when we hire them, and we test for it, but over a period of years we act like nothing will change despite being exposed to some of the most toxic human experiences imaginable.

Just protecting our Selves physically and mentally may not be enough. When we do an effective and comprehensive threat assessment, we can't help but acknowledge that the other areas of emotional health and spiritual strength need to be addressed as well.

The new paradigm I'm proposing for our law enforcement profession — and you — is a comprehensive system of training and development for individuals, organizations and our professional culture.

The Sports Paradigm

Again: Maybe we should be looking to the sports world for our paradigm. Professional athletes are focused on health, fitness, conditioning and coaching for success, and they have huge systems in place to support them. Why then, should we not consider ourselves to be *professional police athletes*?

No matter what your opinions about threats posed by a career in modern law enforcement, I hope you agree we need to do a better job preparing ourselves, and our comrades, to endure its rigors. The million-dollar question is: How do we do it? For my entire twenty-plus year career, all the training I received focused on things physical: Physical fitness, arrest control, shooting, driving, first aid, etc. The only thing I think could have counted as mental conditioning would have been our annual legal update sessions. When it came to emotional or spiritual conditioning, there was nothing. We never discussed many of the threats we all now know are real. We never talked about officer suicides, PTSD or even how to handle ordinary, everyday stresses of the job. In my entire 23-year career the only stress management class I ever received was a couple of hours as part of DEA's 80-hour Basic Narcotics Investigations course.

How about you? Are you receiving or have you received any training in the areas that would protect you mentally, emotionally or spiritually?

Most important of all, are *you* doing anything to strengthen or condition your Self physically, mentally, emotionally or spiritually on a regular, frequent basis?

Whatever your answers, don't worry — this book is designed to train you to strengthen and condition your Self physically, mentally, emotionally and spiritually. It's what I call PMES Conditioning.

Strengthening activities as those activities you do repetitively to build strength, whether it's muscular strength or "strength" in any PMES category. I think of conditioning as the process doing strengthening activities repetitively so that when you need that strength or ability, like calming your stressed-out mind, you can call up that ability and put it into effect *instantly*, based on all of your repetitive conditioning practice.

That is the real gist of this book. We *all* need to take control of our own lives and be responsible for our own fitness-conditioning program. We need to establish our own threat assessment protocols and then initiate our own training programs to combat those threats. We need to be vigilant because such threats are forever changing and always elusive.

One way to describe this new Tactical Resilience™ model is as a system of systems to promote personal and organizational strength and fitness at the same time that it supports individual and agency wellness, resilience and success.

A Quick Overview of the Major Concepts in this Book

Our overriding goal in using this book is to be the best we can be, both personally and professionally. That means we will always work to nurture and develop skills, talents and habits that will keep us alive, make us very proficient at our jobs, and help us to reach retirement relatively unscathed so that we continue to live long and happy lives. In my training programs I say this is about creating the systems necessary to get to "ollie-ollie-oxen-free" in order to live "happily ever after." For many of us this is easier said than done when following the old paradigm of survival training, and that's why you need to Armor Your Self™.

The power to *build positive habits* and *change negative habits* is at the root of many of these concepts, and so you will learn how to identify and develop positive tactics that develop and layer together into healthy habits to build a system that helps you navigate the *hidden dangers* of a career in law enforcement. You can think of this as mind-and-body control to build strength and change habits using positive Habit Coaching and a systems approach. You will also get some suggestions and strategies to change bad habits that don't support your health, wellness and long-term career survival.

Here you'll find suggestions about how to use the concept of True Blue Valor™ to develop a positive, supportive and tactically resilient professional culture that will keep you alive and support you well into a positive retirement. These are responsibilities we all have as professionals in this most honorable of all professions.

You'll also gather ideas about ways to Armor Your Agency™ so that your individual efforts will be supported with an agency system designed to promote both individual and organizational success with a positive culture. This teamwork-oriented program also includes a community-wide support network that supports you, your family and peers as it creates a cooperative team effort. When everyone works toward mutual success and happiness, everyone thrives rather than simply survives.

Finally, all of these things converge to become a system of systems that promotes Tactical Resilience™, which, again, is defined collectively as *a quality of intentional strength and fitness that can be developed and exhibited through the mind, body, brain, spirit and organization of police officers (or other law enforcement or military professionals) in ways that allow them to withstand the rigors and hidden emotional, physical, spiritual and physiological dangers of continuous high-threat, high-stress situations.*

Think of a three-legged stool: It won't stand without all three legs to support it. And just like a the three-legged stool, the formula for success in law enforcement wellness is made up of the three key concepts of Armor Your Self™, Armor Your Agency™ and True Blue Valor™, which together constitute the Tactical Resilience™ Triad.

New Terminology

To best understand this Tactical Resilience™ Triad, here are some definitions:

Armor Your Self™

The process we call Armor Your Self™ works toward achieving Tactical Resilience™ by intentionally improving our emotional toughness, cognitive elasticity, ethical clarity and physical effectiveness. The goal is to increase our ability to withstand and recover from excessive or cumulative stresses we confront in the hardships, traumas, tragedies and adversity we see every day. Armor Your Self™ is a training system we can use to strengthen and condition our Selves to combat the threats and *hidden dangers* that I have collectively labeled "Blue Trauma Syndrome."

But Armor Your Self™ is not just a process. It is also a comprehensive concept of wellness training systems, which are layered over each other so that they work together to build both healthy and effective law enforcement professionals and organizations. We'll talk more about these concepts and how to implement them in the middle chapters of this book.

Armor Your Agency™

Armor Your Agency™ is a training program and an agency profile model. The agency profile includes best practices I call "Primary Strategies," as well as additional "Secondary Strategies." I suggest that in addition to using this book, you also look outside your agency to discover what additional resources might be available from within your community or within our law enforcement community, and then establish other benchmarks from those.

The Armor Your Agency™ Model Agency Profile includes these components:

Primary Strategies

- Proactive Peer Support Program
- Chaplain's Program
- Mentoring Program
- Family Support Network
- Psychological Services Support

- Annual Resilience Training
- Critical Incident Support System
- Annual Line of Duty Death Prevention Training — Driving, Firearms, Arrest Control — Below 100
- Survivor Support System
- Medical Services
- Crisis Intervention Plan
- Officer Selection focused upon wellness beliefs and practices
- Separation From Service ongoing wellness activities support
- Wellness Program & Education — Diet, Hydration, Fatigue Management
- Departmental Fitness Program — including paid or volunteer fitness trainers
- Departmental Resource Library
- Officer Recovery Case Management
- True Blue Valor™ Training
- Suicide Prevention Training
- Community Support Systems

Secondary Strategies

- Dr. Jack Digliani's Make It Safe Initiative
- FTI Training that encourages wellness
- Ongoing Roll-Call Training that encourages wellness
- Supervisors Training in support of wellness and as wellness leaders
- Supervisors Support Systems
- Dr. Paul Quinnett's Question/Persuade/Refer (QPR) Training

We'll talk more about all of these concepts in Chapter 5.

Blue Trauma Syndrome

Blue Trauma Syndrome is our Number #1 enemy, and is defined as a spectrum of negative physical, mental, emotional, and spiritual health effects manifested during a career in law enforcement. Because I feel that many issues we are going to discuss have not been well defined, and in order to make sure the terminology I use is not confused with other terms or other research, I propose Blue Trauma Syndrome as a neutral term we can all understand.

Tactical Resilience™

I define Tactical Resilience™ as a human quality of *intentional* strength and fitness that can be developed, and which is exhibited through the minds, bodies, brains and spirits of police officers (or other law enforcement or military professionals) as a quality that allows them to withstand the rigors and hidden emotional, physical, spiritual and physiological dangers of continuous high-threat, high-stress situations.

The Seven Key Factors in Building Tactical Resilience™:

- The Physical Factor
- The Mental Factor
- The Emotional Factor
- The Spiritual Factor
- The Mind-set Factor
- The Willpower Factor
- The Social Factor

We will talk more about this concept and how to build your Tactical Resilience™ in Chapter 6.

The THSC Systems Approach

T = **T**actics to create the desired positive results

H = **H**abits to enhance and encourage successful wellness behaviors

S = **S**ystems of wellness tactics and habits that layer upon one another to forge a strong, positive, individual character or positive organizational culture

C = **C**haracter for the Individual, or **C**ulture for the Organization

We will talk more about all of these concepts and learn how to piece them together into systems for success in Chapter 3.

True Blue Valor™

The concept of True Blue Valor™ describes a situation in which one law enforcement professional has the courage to confront a peer who is slipping professionally or personally and, because of that unhealthy behavior, endangers him- or herself, peers and the public.

True Blue Valor™ is about having the courage and integrity to "do the right thing" even when it's painful, unpleasant or unpopular. True Blue Valor™ is about walking our talk when we say things like "we take care of our own" or "no one gets left behind" or "we are all one big family."

True Blue Valor™ is policing leadership at every level and involves extreme bravery directed at helping a law enforcement peer or organization do the right thing and make positive change when necessary. It takes a system, organizational commitment, and professional leadership to support and foster the concept of True Blue Valor™.

True Blue Valor™ is necessary so that officers will risk asking for help when they need it, or risk taking a chance to help a peer in trouble. One of the biggest hurdles to a true system of True Blue Valor™ is our existing culture, which says that (somehow) we all need to miraculously possess the inner strength to (somehow) magically endure all the traumas of this career while *never* needing any outside help. That approach is simply ridiculous and needs to be replaced with a belief system that says we are all human and each of us can be hurt in ways that may or may not affect others. We need to acknowledge that it's not *if* but rather *when* this job will tax us physically, mentally, emotionally or spiritually, and that we need to expect to need help with those threats in order to maintain our optimal performance. Our public needs to have the strongest and most effective law enforcement professionals serving and protecting it every day. We should also recognize that our peers will be in a better position to back us up if they are healthy and happy. I have never understood how we can watch people slip out of wellness and not say anything until it's too late, and yet at the same time we complain about their competence or commitment to us!

Our belief system needs to expect that we will all need some help sometime in our careers, and that we need to "Make It Safe" to ask for help as such occasions arise. We need to change our culture to one in which our mental, emotional and spiritual health, just like our physical health, is maintained by including preventative measures that incorporate early diagnosis, intervention and treatment without stigma or disgrace.

Police Psychologist Jack Digliani, says: We all need to "Make It Safe" for everyone to ask for help! Learn more about Jack's Make It Safe Initiative at www.JackDigliani.com

Programs we can use to change our culture, build True Blue Valor™, and "Make It Safe" to ask for help, will be discussed further in Chapter 4.

Abbreviations for these new concepts:

AYS	= Armor Your Self™
AYA	= Armor Your Agency™
TBV	= True Blue Valor™
TR	= Tactical Resilience™
The TR Triad	= AYS + AYA + TBV
BTS	= Blue Trauma Syndrome
PMES	= Physical, Mental, Emotional and Spiritual (Strength)
THSC	= Tactics, Habits, Systems, and Individual Character/Organizational Culture

Think of these new terms as building blocks for success. We will add to them and layer them to create ongoing systems for your success.

My formula for Comprehensive Law Enforcement Wellness is:
$$AYS = (PMES + AYA + TBV) \times (THSC) = TR \neq BTS$$

In other words, the Armor Your Self™ (AYS) model of PMES strength is developed by layering Tactics, Habits, and Systems that build individual Character, and which work with the Armor Your Agency™ concept to create a Culture of True Blue Valor™ — all of which promote Tactical Resilience™ and combine to prevent Blue Trauma Syndrome.

Wow! That *is* a mouthful, so let's make it a reality for you so that you don't have to think about equations!

Now that we have discovered the need for a new model of training and personal preparedness that addresses *all* the threats and *hidden dangers* inherent in this career, we need to implement personal training and conditioning systems to create PMES (strength) and to insulate us from harm. We also need to create support systems within our agencies to encourage and uphold our individual initiatives. The next chapter will discuss how to build this system of systems so that you can start today to build the habits and supportive environment you need to thrive in life and this career.

Resources

www.SafeCallNow.com —This is the Web site for the Safe Call Now crisis hotline for first responders and their families. It was created by former police officer Sean Riley and others. Their hotline assists cops, other first responders and their family members who are in crisis. Riley and his associates have done an immense amount of work to ensure your legal anonymity so that when you need help you will feel comfortable asking for it. I can't mention their Web site or their crisis hotline phone number — 1-206-459-3020 — enough in this book. You need to write down the number, put it in your phone and then go to their Web site (or CopsAlive.com — see below) and download a free poster for your workplace. If you or people you know need help, call Safe Call Now as soon as possible to find the resources (near to where you live) that can help. One way or the other they are there for you 24/7/365 if you need to talk.

www.CopsAlive.com — Most of the ideas in this book, as well as additional ideas, were previously published on the blog at CopsAlive, which I started about eight years before this book was published. Please come to visit and submit an article if you have something to contribute. CopsAlive has always been a wellness Web site *written by cops for cops*, as well as for other law enforcement professionals, to ensure that we all survive to live long and happy lives. Our motto for CopsAlive and for the Law Enforcement Survival Institute has always been: "Saving the Lives of the People Who Save Lives." Come visit and please contribute your ideas.

www.JackDigliani.com — This is the Web site for Police Psychologist Jack Digliani, who provides the best Proactive Law Enforcement Peer Support Team training program I've ever seen. It's also home for his "Make It Safe" initiative. Jack also offers a number of free downloadable resources on his Web site as well as on CopsAlive.com

www.QPRinstitute.com — Dr. Paul Quinnett's, of the QPR Institute, developed this Question/Persuade/Refer (QPR) technique into a proven system for suicide prevention. Just as people trained in CPR and the Heimlich Maneuver help save thousands of lives each year, people trained in QPR learn how to recognize warning signs of a suicide crisis and how to question, persuade, and refer someone to help. Visit their Web site to learn more.

www.Below100.org — It's the mission of the Below 100 program to permanently eliminate preventable law enforcement line of duty deaths and injuries through innovative training and awareness. They focus on five tenets: Wear Your Seatbelt, Wear Your Vest, Watch Your Speed, What's Important Now? (WIN), and Remember That Complacency Kills! Check it out!

www.PoliceWellness.com — This is our ongoing project to collect tips, ideas, suggestions and best practices from law enforcement professionals from around the world who are devoted to helping their peers survive. The Web site's material will be assembled and published free for anyone in our industry whenever we have enough material for publication or revision.

www.YouTube.com/SurvivalTipsForCops — This is our video version of the Police Wellness project, and which law enforcement professionals from anywhere around the world can submit their tips, ideas, suggestions and best practices to exchange with their peers in short video form.

www.LawEnforcementSurvivalInstute.org — This is the home of our training and consulting programs. If we can do anything for you or your agency, please contact us.

Homework

You'll find in this book that I'm big on having you write down your thoughts. Some people call this journaling, but whatever you call it I would suggest that you get a notebook or three-ring binder to keep track of your thoughts as you proceed through this book. A three-ring binder may be best because you can create tabs for the major topics and then just open the binder to add your notes in the appropriate section. You could also do this in your computer.

Before you go much further in this book, write down your thoughts on paper and start adding them to your notebook. You can review them again after you finish reading the whole book to see if your answers have changed.

Here are some questions to ask yourself now:

- What threats do you see from your job, now or in the future, that might hurt or disable you? Consider threats to your life, safety, health, happiness and family.

- What are you doing right now to protect your life, safety, health, happiness and family?

- Write down anything you are doing right now, on a regular basis, to strengthen and condition your Self physically, mentally, emotionally and spiritually. I want you to become clear about this concept because there is no need to reinvent the wheel; if you are already doing some of these things successfully, then I want you to build on those strategies and add some new ones that are mentioned in later chapters of this book.

Visit:

http://www.CopsAlive.com/suggests?pmesworksheetonca/aysbook to download the PMES 4 Quadrants Worksheet to assist you in making notes for this assignment and others yet to come in this book.

CHAPTER 3

Build A System of Systems

Systems keep things in order and help them to function more effectively. I believe we need to build systems into our personal lives as well as into our organizations if we want our wellness processes to be more efficient and more effective.

In this chapter you will learn how to develop effective systems for your Self to help you nurture positive tactics that will build successful habits and cultivate a strong personal character. You will also learn to build systems that will enhance positive agency procedures and wellness support systems. And finally, you will learn how to promote systems to help create a positive culture within our law enforcement profession so that it, too, supports and encourages wellness success and career survival.

Before we start, you might write out your answers to these questions:

- How do I make effective changes in my life?

- What tactics, habits or systems do I need to put into place to help me survive my law enforcement career?

- How can I make lasting change in my life?

I'm asked these questions all the time, and I'll attempt to give you information and resources you need to answer these questions yourself. That way you'll be able to make effective changes in your habits and your life that will help you be more resilient. At the same time you will also Armor Your Self™ against the *hidden dangers* and toxic effects of this career.

Now, write out your thoughts to these questions:

- What do I need to do to prepare myself for and strengthen myself against all of the threats and *hidden dangers* of this job?
- What do I need to do to help my agency create support systems that help me be more resilient and make our agency more effective?

This book is focused on your health, well-being and career survival, and I hope that what you learn here will help you in any facet of your life.

Why Do We Need a Systems Approach?

The world is filled with systems because systems get things accomplished effectively. Effectiveness is what we need when it comes to maintaining our health and wellness. Since this book is about law enforcement career survival, we need to know how to build effective systems to help you survive your career and live a happy and successful life.

In our law enforcement profession we operate within a number of very long-standing and effective systems most of us have been using for years.

We operate within a law enforcement and legal system built of many computer systems, report writing systems, paperwork filing systems and statistical reporting systems. We even have systems of procedures — for example, checking out equipment, responding to serious calls, and even for vehicle usage. Aside from some common age-old complaints about all of our systems being broken and not working to our satisfaction, we know these systems, and we know they will get the job done.

Now we're going to capitalize on this programmed behavior that's been part of our profession for decades so that we can build a systems approach to our personal health, wellness and survival.

Let's Define The Term "System"

Systems are simply a series of measures intended to get things done efficiently. In this instance I'm defining a system as the processes and networks that build upon the effective tactics and positive habits we are using to reach our desired goals. Your system might be as involved as a series of processes and procedures, or something as simple as a checklist, a regular series of activities, or a collection of small habits that support your success. Most of us know what the words tactics, habits, systems, character and culture mean, but let's build on that knowledge and add some substance to those words that can help keep you alive and healthy.

Let's start with the most basic definitions of a "system." The Merriam-Webster online dictionary defines "system" in many ways, but the specific definitions that seem to be the most appropriate for our use here include:

- a group of related parts that move or work together
- a body of a person or animal thought of as an entire group of parts that work together
- a regularly interacting or interdependent group of items forming a unified whole
- a form of social, economic, or political organization or practice
- an organized or established procedure

For the purposes of our discussion of "systems" in this chapter, we are going to talk about systems from the largest (the police culture) to the smallest (the individual). Then, in following chapters, I'm going to elaborate upon the concepts involved, first, by talking about the largest concepts, and then narrowing our focus down to the individual systems that are at the heart of this book and the Tactical Resilience™ and Armor Your Self™ models.

Examples of Systems

Here are examples of systems you're already familiar with:

- A library card-catalog filing system
- Your process of paying bills every month

- Our systems of measurement — weights, time, volume, etc.
- Our traffic laws
- The election process in the United States

The world is filled with systems, and you can see by the definitions noted earlier that your body is a system, your agency is a system, and the culture that we produce when we interact within social or professional groups or organizations is a system. Here we will focus on systems that we can create ourselves, and on already existing systems that we can fine-tune to help us be safe, effective and healthy.

What is a "System of Systems?"

We are also going to expand upon the basic concept of a simple system and talk about a "System of Systems." I'm going to suggest that in order for us to strengthen and condition ourselves as well as our organizations, we need tactics, habits, processes and systems that are layered over one another and that build upon each other as they work to keep you safe, healthy and happy. That's what I mean by a "system of systems."

Some examples of complex systems made up of other systems:

- The world economy
- Our democratic form of government
- Worldwide research projects directed toward eradicating cancer and HIV/AIDS
- The processes NASA used to land a human being on the moon
- Any modern automobile
- The human body

One of the first things you should do is put down this book and ask yourself: *What are my goals?* Write out some notes about:

- Your goals for long-term and lasting personal health, wellness and resilience to support my personal happiness and professional effectiveness.

- Our goals for long-term agency growth and development that build systems and programs to ensure that we provide the most effective service possible to our community.

Here are some of the challenges you can expect:

- You will need to exert personal and organizational leadership to get this done.
- You need to be patient and remember that effective change takes time.
- You will need willpower and perseverance to get things finished.
- Some people, and cops in particular, can be very resistant to change.
- You and others may encounter fear — fear of change and fear that this won't work.
- Laziness — perhaps from you, and certainly from others who haven't bought into these ideas.

Model Systems

Here are model systems we might want to observe and learn from:

- The Mayo Clinic Model of the 5 Elements for comprehensive physical fitness
- The U.S. Navy SEALs' Operational Readiness Model
- The U.S. Army Resilience Model based upon Karen Reivich's work
- Tony Robbins' "Unleash The Power Within" Model
- The AA 12-Step Model for changing behavior
- The Tactical Resilience Model of Armor Your Self™
- The Armor Your Agency™ Model
- The True Blue Valor™ Model
- The McDonald's Restaurant System Model

I've always marveled at how efficient and lucrative the McDonald's system is for producing almost identical, successful and productive restaurants around the world. This is possible only because founder Ray Kroc built an effective and reproducible system for success early in the company's history. As I was writing this book, I spent many, many afternoons at my local McDonald's because I could work there productively and have a chance to observe many of their success systems firsthand. If you ever want to benchmark a personal or business system, I encourage you to learn a little about the McDonald's model and then spend a few hours at a McDonald's restaurant watching how they get things accomplished. They've broken a lot of processes into their most basic components and all of them are carefully documented into step-by-step procedures anyone can learn.

The Armor Your Self™ System for Building Effective Systems

1. Establish your goals: Put them in writing!

2. Develop effective tactics: Use other successful people as models for your success.

3. Develop effective habits: Success comes from positive, repetitive actions. Ask for help and support from family and friends.

4. Layer effective habits into systems and then onto other effective systems. Use teamwork to support you and build momentum.

5. Keep a written record of your progress and then evaluate your effectiveness on a monthly basis.

6. Continuously benchmark new tactics from the examples of other successful people. Examine, dissect or reverse-engineer and then adapt a great tactic or process for your own use.

7. Evaluate regularly or as needed (and probably before you think it's needed).

Visit this Web address to download our free Armor Your Self™ Systems Building Checklist: http://www.CopsAlive.com/suggests?systemschecklist

In the Armor Your Self™ program we are focused on building wellness and Tactical Resilience™. You will work, while reading this book, to establish goals and then design tactics to take you closer to these goals step-by-step. You will build effective habits to reinforce these tactics and ensure that your goals are met. Finally, you will layer systems made up of tactics and habits to reach your goals and stay healthy, happy and resilient. This process is exactly the same as if you were working to make your agency or organization a healthy, happy and resilient organization that supports your wellness and survival goals.

Since positive habits are the building blocks of effective systems, for the rest of this chapter we are going to focus on habits and building your positive habits. The majority of the chapters in the middle of this book are specifically designed to help you identify useful tactics to strengthen your Self mentally, physically, emotionally and spiritually. The most important thing we can work on to make us stronger, smarter, braver and more ethical is our set of personal habits. If we can find a way to identify and instill positive and effective habits into our lives, we can then build strength and fitness in all the areas we need to improve in order to be the best we can be at our jobs and in our personal lives. If we can identify and establish in our agencies the best-standardized practices and the most positive belief and support systems in our professional culture, then we will have the support and encouragement we need to foster healthy organizations and strong people.

The THSC System for Wellness and Resilience

The THSC System approach to personal and organization improvement consists of:

    T = *Tactics* that create the desired positive results.

    H = *Habits* that enhance and encourage successful wellness behaviors.

    S = *Systems* that layer upon one another to forge positive individual character and positive organizational culture.

    C = *Character* for the individual, or *Culture* for the organization.

I encourage you to adopt the THSC System as a platform for your personal success. Use the THSC System to create lasting and effective change systems with the tactics or processes that you will build into positive habits, and then build those habits into systems. You will then merge those systems with your other effective systems and use them to build a strong personal character or a positive organizational culture. (See Figure 3.1)

How Do We Make Good Ideas Work For Us?

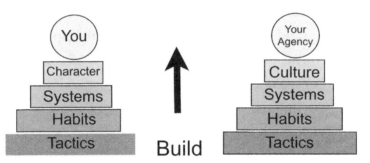

Figure 3.1

You undoubtedly already have some idea what the words strength, fitness, conditioning, tactics, habits, systems and character or culture mean. Let's build on that knowledge and add some substance to these words that can help keep you alive and healthy. Let's start with a few definitions.

THSC Process Definitions

Strength

The Merriam-Webster online dictionary defines *strength* as "the quality or state of being physically strong: the ability to resist being moved or broken by a force; the quality that allows someone to deal with problems in a determined and effective way." In our discussions of police wellness and survival techniques I will define *strength* as *a human quality of excellence in health and fortitude that may be manifested physically, mentally, emotionally or spiritually.*

Fitness

The Merriam-Webster online dictionary defines *fitness* as the "quality or state of being fit." For our purposes I will define *fitness* as *a superior quality of human well-being manifested through strength, stamina and resilience physically, mentally, emotionally and spiritually.*

Conditioning

Merriam-Webster's online dictionary defines *conditioning* as the "process of becoming stronger and healthier by following a regular exercise program and diet." For our purposes I will define *conditioning* in this context as *a repetitive wellness process used to build human strength and resilience physically, mentally, emotionally and spiritually.*

Tactic

The Merriam-Webster online dictionary defines *tactic* as "an action or method that is planned and used to achieve a particular goal." *Tactic* is additionally defined as "a device for accomplishing an end." We know all about tactics in law enforcement, but sometimes we don't use that same kind of strategic thinking in our personal lives. It's time for us all to start thinking *tactically* and *strategically* about how we train and condition ourselves to survive the job. In this book I define a *tactic* as *a technique or process used by a law enforcement or military professional to achieve a strategic advantage, specifically in health and wellness.*

Habit

Merriam-Webster's online dictionary defines a *habit* as "a usual way of behaving; something that a person does often in a regular and repeated way." Additionally, it defines a *habit* as "a behavior pattern acquired by frequent repetition or physiologic exposure that shows itself in regularity or increased facility of performance" and as "an acquired mode of behavior that has become nearly or completely involuntary." For our purpose in regard to law enforcement, I define a *habit* as *one or more tactics repeated regularly or instilled into your behavior so that they are performed without resistance — even subconsciously.*

System

Merriam-Webster's online dictionary defines a *system* as "a group of related parts that move or work together." Wikipedia defines a *system* as "a set of interacting or interdependent components forming an integrated whole." For the purposes of Armor Your Self™ I'll describe a *system* as *the coupling of tactics and habits into a process used to achieve tactical or personal success.*

In this chapter I will go beyond defining a simple system and will refer to a *System of Systems,* by which I mean *the layering of individual or organizational tactics, habits and processes to achieve a positive organizational culture or strong individual character.* I'm frequently asked how my concept of system compares to the concept of a strategy. Merriam-Webster's online dictionary defines a *strategy* as "a careful plan or method for achieving a particular goal usually over a long period of time." I think that ties in very closely with what I refer to as a *system.* If you prefer the consistency of the concepts of tactics and strategies rather than systems, that's fine with me — but let's always ensure that we are talking about the same things so as to avoid misunderstanding. This is important because I've noticed things can easily get derailed if people are not "on the same page" or not using the same definitions and language for important concepts.

Character

Character is defined by the Merriam-Webster online dictionary as "reputation," "the way someone thinks, feels, and behaves," and "the complex of mental and ethical traits marking and often individualizing a person, group, or nation." I define *character* as *personal traits and behaviors that reflect a law enforcement professional's beliefs, values and driving principles.*

Culture

Merriam-Webster's online dictionary defines *culture* as "the beliefs, customs, arts, etc., of a particular society, group, place, or time" and "a way of thinking, behaving, or working that exists in a place or organization." I go a step further and define *culture* as *the beliefs, customs and ways of thinking, behaving and working that exist in a law enforcement agency or organization.*

The THSC System for an Individual

The THSC System for an individual focuses on personal conditioning, fitness and wellness issues.

Tactics are simple things done over and over again to reach your goals. Here are some examples:

- Use one part of the five-part Mayo Clinic Workout for 15 minutes every day.
- Do some kind of brain training for 15 minutes daily.
- Drink a glass of water before every meal to ensure you stay properly hydrated.
- Eat an apple a day for quick energy and lots of necessary fiber.
- Plan 15 minutes of quiet time or an easy workout every day to achieve the relaxation response between the end of work and the beginning of your time at home.
- Strengthen your spiritual core with study and contemplation for 15 minutes every day.

Habits are activities that become a daily routine:

- Do daily workouts that include strength, balance, aerobic, core and flexibility conditioning.
- Use your breaks at work to sneak in some kind of PMES conditioning exercises.
- Set a daily goal of drinking 64 ounces of water or more.
- Pack a healthy lunch to carry with you every day.
- Plan some buffer time between work and home every day to relax, unwind and manage your stress.
- Read something every day that will test and enhance your core belief systems.

Systems are daily routines that become regular processes:

- Having a workout plan that incorporates the entire five-part Mayo Clinic physical fitness program every week. Record your progress and measure your improvements.
- Doing daily online brain training with Lumosity five or more times a week.

- Carrying a water bottle every day so you can monitor your water intake and stay hydrated every day (refilling regularly to ensure you meet your goal of drinking 64 ounces or more.)

- Having written daily goals for your body's fuel intake of fiber, protein, green vegetables, etc. Use a log to capture your progress and successes.

- Planning buffer time to disperse your stress with quiet time or an easy workout every day before going home from work.

- Building time into your week that allows reading or discussions that examine your core beliefs.

Character refers to routine systems that become part of your behaviors and personal character:

- You are physically fit.
- You are mentally fit.
- You are emotionally fit.
- You are spiritually fit.
- You are high functioning.
- You possess high levels of honor and integrity.
- You are happy.
- You are healthy.

The THCS System for an Agency or Organization

Tactics are things the organization does regularly to enhance wellness and resiliency:

- A volunteer team provides Proactive Peer Support on all shifts.
- You are connected to your police families through effective communications and support programs.

- Everyone in the agency supports success and treats new recruits like family.
- We "walk our talk" every day: We say what we mean and mean what we say.
- Agency mentors and field training instructors are assigned to each new recruit.
- Agency mentors are available to everyone at every level of the organization.

Habits are developed through team support tactics to build good organizational patterns:

- The peer support team coordinator assists team members through regular communications and reminds them to stay proactive.
- The agency promotes regular weekly or monthly family network communications through email and a telephone tree.
- Agency mentors contact new recruits weekly to discuss goals and progress.
- Agency mentors meet with or communicate with their protégées once a month.
- Everyone is considered a "fire spotter" looking for "smoke" or potential problems, and makes referrals for peer support when necessary.

Systems are the processes that support people and are built atop many strong habits:

- The peer support team has top-down leadership support and is defined by policy to ensure it stays proactive and has support for the supporters.
- The agency has a policy about, and a supervisor to support, the family network.
- The agency mentor program is defined by policy and operating procedures. The program is overseen by a supervisor and provides regular reports to the command staff.
- The peer support, mentor program and chaplains program coordinators meet regularly with psychological services to ensure support and consistency for the team members and the people they serve.

Culture that supports its members is built atop many strong systems:

- A strong, healthy culture is critical for effective law enforcement.
- The agency has a written vision, mission and values statement.
- The vision, mission and values statement is displayed, reinforced and remembered.
- The agency has a proactive peer support team system that displays individual and organizational caring for the individual.
- The agency has a strong family support network with regular training and social events to encourage family and agency interaction and assistance.
- The agency has a multilevel mentoring program to nurture successful people.
- The agency works to maintain a culture of True Blue Valor™.
- The agency works to establish as many of our Armor Your Agency™ recommended initiatives as possible.

How Do You Create Effective Systems?

The simplest definition of a system is a collection of basic steps that work together to get you to a desired goal. An effective system is one that would help you or your organization achieve all the goals you set for yourself or your organization. In this instance we are talking about wellness systems and systems that build organizational and personal resilience. In law enforcement we go one step further and build Tactical Resilience™.

In your personal life you may not often think about building systems, so let's first talk about creating effective systems for your organization. Your primary goal is first to set your vision about where you or your organization should go. Then decide what an effective system is or what an effective system looks like. You can do this by using a standard or benchmark as your baseline to help you create a solid foundation upon which to construct your useful processes. Look for other agencies doing great things and, when you find them, learn from what they are doing. If you find an agency that is doing particularly great work please, send me an email so that we can add them to our Armor Your Agency™ model agencies list.

This is a good place to talk about the concept of benchmarking. Benchmarking is a process of finding effective processes or systems from elsewhere in business or industry, or powerful tactics utilized by other individuals, and then adapting them for your own use. There is *no reason* to reinvent the wheel when it comes to finding success. We in law enforcement are very good at borrowing or adapting ideas from other professionals or agencies and making them work for us. We should not be embarrassed by this and should encourage it because it's the quickest way to compound proven and effective strategies. Our success is vital to the public good, and all of society benefits when we learn from the successes of others and capitalize upon them.

You might first use the process development loop. (See Figure 3.2, below.)

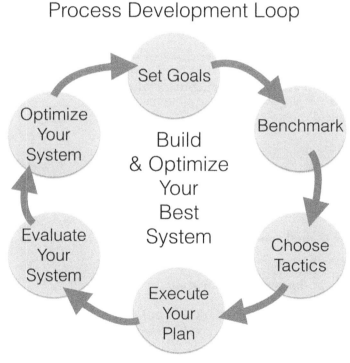

Figure 3.2

Next you set goals, establish a mission, state values, and create policies and procedures to support your organizational wellness vision.

As an organization you will want to put into place effective programs and policies to support a healthy and resilient organization with a positive and supportive culture. Our Armor Your Agency™ list of programs can assist you in this process. The most important part about creating effective systems is to evaluate and correct procedures you use in order to ensure you're not wasting your time and energy on systems that are not serving your purposes.

Just as you go about building systems for an organization, you as an individual will be layering tactics upon positive habits that become effective systems.

In order to create effective systems for your life, career or organization, you need only to establish the most basic steps needed to get you to your goal. This might take some research on your part or it might require that you find a successful role model from whom you can adapt or benchmark your own effective basic steps or processes.

Qualities of an Effective System

The qualities of an effective system include:

- Being created from an effective benchmark when possible.
- Being of simple design.
- Being efficient.
- Having built-in processes for testing, evaluation and improvement as needed.
- Being replicable based upon specific written standards.
- Producing the desired results.

What Are the Steps to Build Excellent Systems?

- Seek a suitable system to benchmark for your system or create new processes/tactics as necessary.
- Quantify all necessary processes/tactics and outcomes.
- Document every step of each process/tactic.
- Educate all potential users.
- Test each process/tactic within the system.

- Evaluate the effectiveness of each process/tactic.
- Evaluate the effectiveness of the system.
- Modify any ineffective processes/tactics.
- Reevaluate the effectiveness of the new process/tactic.
- Reevaluate the effectiveness of the new system.
- Launch and utilize the system.
- Reevaluate the effectiveness of the system on a regular basis.

I am told that in Japanese the word *kaizen* means "improvement," and it has been incorporated into American English as meaning "the philosophy or practice of continuous improvement." *Kaizen* has been used quite a bit in the total quality management initiatives utilized by the corporate world and is credited to post-World War II statistical works on quality that were promoted in Japan and worldwide by W. Edwards Deming. If you want to take your agency systems-building to an advanced level, I encourage you to read Deming's works, and review his famous fourteen key principles for management. Although Deming's work was focused primarily on manufacturing processes, the insights can nonetheless be valuable guidance for law enforcement.

I suggest that you adopt a strategy of *kaizen* to represent your constant striving for improvement, and utilize that word as a motto or slogan to motivate you for continuous improvement in the areas of your strength, health and wellness.

In his book, *The Power of Habit*, Charles Duhigg quotes winning football coach Tony Dungy: "Champions don't do extraordinary things. They do ordinary things, but they do them without thinking, too fast for the other team to react. They follow the habits they've learned."

Let's Build Your Systems

Building successful systems, whether personal or organizational, involves finding small things that work effectively to make incremental changes (tactics), and then repeating and building upon them until they become regular pattern of behaviors (positive habits). In an organization, that might mean developing effective procedures and then building them into standardized practices. A standardized practice or process for an organization is very much like a habit for an individual. It's important to notice this distinction because there will be many times over the next couple of years when you will be working to improve yourself or your organization and you'll find a really effective personal habit or organizational practice that you can dissect or reverse engineer to adapt for use elsewhere. That process is one of the concepts that you can use to layer systems that will create rapid, positive change.

First, Use Effective Tactics

We start by identifying a goal we want to accomplish and then we find tactics we can condition into our daily routines in order to reach that goal. We exercise our tactics in every one of the PMES categories — just like we do in the physical category — through repetition and continuous improvement. The Armor Your Self™ System is about balanced conditioning, and not all conditioning is action oriented. You will learn later in the book that the *physical* and *mental* components of your Self require *active* conditioning that involves exercises like strength training, aerobics, running, brain games and puzzles, etc. The *emotional* and *spiritual* sides of your Self require *inactive* conditioning exercises like quiet time, reading, study, contemplation and meditation.

Positive tactics combine to build positive habits.
Tactics and habits combine to build systems.
Excellent personal systems build excellent character.
Excellent organizational systems build an excellent culture.

Chapters 8, 10, 12, and 14 will provide effective tactics to apply to your life and career in each of the four primary Armor Your Self™ categories of physical strength, emotional strength, mental strength and spiritual strength. What you will need to do is to pick tactics that work for you and then build them into habits and systems that will create your personal success. If you already have an effective system that includes all four of the PMES categories, then use this book as motivation to maintain those systems for the rest of your life. You are a professional police athlete, and you need to always Armor Your Self™ to stave off the *hidden dangers* and toxic effects of this career. I've been retired for 14 years at the writing of this book and still see the negative effects of the job trying to intrude into my life. I believe that the practice of always working to maintain our strength and conditioning habits is a lifelong commitment.

Creating New Effective Habits

Once we have identified our goals, we start with practical and positive tactics that work together to achieve those goals. Then we repeat those positive tactics over and over again until they become part of our normal behavior and are systematized as "habits."

I only have time and space in this book to give you an elementary overview of how to build positive habits and effect positive changes in your life. More challenging is how to modify or eliminate harmful habits that, in their more complex forms, may become addictive behaviors.

Throughout this book I refer to many excellent sources about these and other important subjects. I encourage you to do your own advanced research on the subjects that interest you or which you feel merit further research on your part.

There are also other components that help us effect positive change and instill positive habits. Consider the issues of mind-set, reward and reinforcement, as well as discovery or creation of things that might cue or initiate a new, positive habit.

In the book, *The Power of Habit: Why We Do What We Do in Life and Business*, Charles Duhigg provides insight into the "the habit loop" that moves from a cue to a routine and to a reward. If you want to build new habits or modify destructive habits, his system is excellent. For the purposes of our discussions about law enforcement professionals I will change the language slightly and use terms more suited to our profession to describe our habit cycle. We will be using the terms: Trigger → Tactic → Reward. (See Figure 3.3, below.)

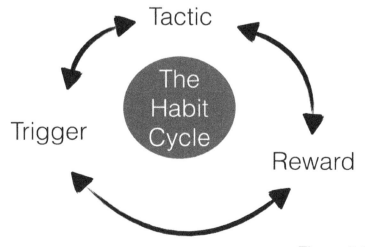

Figure 3.3

If we are talking about one of your own personal systems, then we also need to take into consideration not only the steps or procedures needed to build the system, but we must also factor in the human components that require the proper motivation, resolve or determination, which are sometimes referred to as "mind-set."

Good habits are built with three things:

- Proper mind-set
- Repetition
- Habit coaching

I use the term "habit coaching" to suggest that you seek some outside counsel to assist you with the instillation of positive and effective habits. This person could be a professional coach or a friend or a family member, but he or she should be someone who will fully understand your "habit goals" and will be available to reinforce the positive traits, tactics and processes you are implementing. Your habit coach will also provide feedback on observable negative traits or tactics.

You might make a plan and set a personal goal to find someone to provide you with positive habit coaching as you develop your personal success system.

Habit coaching is also a method for positive mind-set reinforcement, which is an important part of an effective systems approach to success.

In the case of our Armor Your Self™ program, a good habit coach will encourage you to meet your PMES conditioning goals on a daily or weekly basis. Those goals have to do with repeating your strength-building activities (tactics) until they become part of your normal daily or weekly routine. Once those tactics become part of your regular routine, they will become systematized as part of your regular positive habits and therefore part of your normal behavior.

A good habit coach will also ask you *how* you want to be supported rather than just pressure you with their processes and beliefs.

Finally, a good habit coach works with you to set up and reinforce the proper motivation, or mind-set you will need to accomplish your short-term Armor Your Self™ PMES goals and to ensure that they become life-long systems.

Mind-set and Examples of Mind-set to Help You

Mind-set is also very important in building healthy and effective habits and systems. What mind-sets are you using?

Your mind-set goals must be to visualize yourself as extraordinary, and then to find the pathway to maintain that high level of physical, mental, emotional and spiritual conditioning.

The U.S. Navy SEALs operational readiness training program includes sections on building a positive mental attitude and mind-set through focus and concentration, positive visualization and positive self-talk. We will explore that more in later chapters, and you can learn more about this concept on CopsAlive with our interview of CDR Eric G. Potterat, Ph.D., USN (Retired) Clinical and Performance Psychologist and Former Head Psychologist for the US Navy SEALs at: http://www.CopsAlive.com/train-like-a-u-s-navy-seal/

Some common law enforcement mind-sets:

- "To Serve and To Protect" (LAPD Officer Joseph S. Dorobeck)
- "Keep Fighting"
- "I Must Win"
- "I am a Sheepdog" (Lt. Col. [ret.] Dave Grossman)
- "I am a Warrior"
- "WIN or What's Important Now?" (Brian Willis, of Winning Mind Training and the Below 100 Program)
- "I am a Blue Warrior" (Law Enforcement Survival Institute ethical policing training)
- "Semper Fi" or "Semper fidelis" or "Always Faithful" (U.S. Marine Corps)
- "Semper Aequus" or "Always Just"
- "To Protect with Courage, To Serve with Compassion" (motto of the Minneapolis Police Department)
- "An Honor To Serve, A Duty To Protect" (slogan of the Colorado State Patrol)
- "Live and protect with honor! Serve with pride!"
- "The Thin Blue Line"

- "In Valor There Is Hope" (Gaius Cornelius Tacitus, Roman Senator from c. 56 AD to c. 117 AD)
- "No One Left Behind"
- "I've Got Your Back"
- *Kaizen*

Mind-set Reinforcement for Your Systems

A great example of positive mind-set reinforcement in law enforcement is how we use our mottoes, credos, codes of ethics and oaths of office. Mission statements and statements of values and goals — placed in areas where they are easily seen on a regular basis — are also ways to reinforce positive mind-sets.

The famous law enforcement motto "To Protect and To Serve," submitted in 1963 by Officer Joseph S. Dorobeck as part of a contest, was chosen as the Los Angeles Police Department (LAPD) as their motto. http://www.lapdonline.org/history_of_the_lapd/content_basic_view/1128

Dr. John C. Norcross, author of *Changeology: 5 Steps to Realizing Your Goals and Resolutions*, said in an interview with National Public Radio: "Let's think of resolutions as marathons, not a hundred-yard dash. We need to prepare for the long haul, the changed lifestyle. And we should keep in mind that even if you're not successful this year, our research shows that virtually everyone who doesn't succeed this year will try again next year. This is a life-long quest for improved behavior."

Again, consider making the concept of *kaizen*, or continuous improvement, a part of your personal philosophy and use it to set your mind-set everyday.

> To me, good health is more than just exercise and diet.
> It's really a point of view and a mental attitude you have about yourself.
> — Albert Schweitzer, *physician, philosopher and musician*

> The difference between the impossible and the possible
> lies in a person's determination.
> — Tommy Lasorda, *Major League Baseball player and coach*

Mind-set can also be used as seed for creating the spark of a new trigger or tactic in the building of new habits for success. (See Habit Seeding in Figure 3.4, below.)

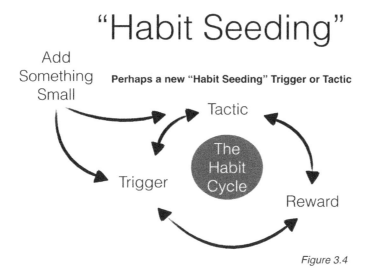

Figure 3.4

Build Your Individual Wellness Systems

Start building your individual wellness systems today!

1. Establish your individual wellness goals: *Write them out.*

2. Choose effective individual wellness tactics: *Use this book or find your own.*

3. Promote effective individual wellness habits: *Keep a journal of your activities.*

4. Layer effective wellness systems onto other effective systems — *so they work in concert, not in opposition.*

5. Build a strong positive personal character: *Write out your values, personal vision and personal credo.*

1. Establish Your Individual Wellness Goals

Spend some time thinking about how you want to live and what constitutes health and wellness. Also think about how you need to be conditioned as a professional police athlete to be strong enough to do all the things that may be required of you on the job, and what you need to do to protect your Self, including dealing with the toxic side effects of a full career in this profession. Write down all your thoughts and use them to build your plan. Later, when your plan has become a system, you can use these same notes to reevaluate your progress and perhaps reestablish new goals. Baseball great Yogi Berra was quoted as saying, "If you don't know where you are going, you might not get there."

2. Choose Effective Individual Wellness Tactics

I have defined a *tactic* as a technique or process used by a law enforcement or military professional to achieve a strategic advantage. So think about tactics you can employ in your daily life to achieve your wellness goals. Here are some examples:

- Drink a glass of water before each meal.
- Eat an apple a day.
- Pack your lunch every day with a healthy meal and snacks.
- Do 15-30 minutes of physical exercise every day.
- Set a reminder in your smartphone to drink more than 64 oz. of water daily.
- Strengthen your Self in all the individual Armor Your Self™ PMES categories.
- Post reminders (habit triggers) to yourself on the bathroom mirror, refrigerator, at your desk and/or in your car.

3. Promote Effective Individual Wellness Habits

I have defined a *habit* as one or more tactics repeated regularly or instilled into your behavior so that they are performed without resistance — even subconsciously. Now you need to choose some of the tactics you believe will work for you and build them into regular, daily habits. Consider some of these examples:

- Carry a water bottle with you to remind you to drink more than 64 oz. of water every day. Use it to drink at least 8 oz. of water before each meal.
- Do Armor Your Self™ PMES exercises repetitiously five or more times a week to condition strength in all areas and build Tactical Resilience™.
- Get 7-8 hours of sleep every night (or every 24 hours when you work night shifts) to reduce fatigue and improve your operational effectiveness.
- Strengthen your brain by using brain-training activities 5-7 times a week to condition your memory, communication skills and problem solving abilities.
- Do things that *feed* your healthy habits and to reinforce the behaviors of your success.

(See Habit Feeding Figure 3.5, below.)

Figure 3.5

Feed a Positive Habit by Watering or Reinforcing the Trigger, Tactic or Reward

4. Layer Effective Wellness Systems onto Other Effective Systems

Remember that we are defining a *system* as the coupling of tactics and habits into a process used to achieve tactical or personal success. Here are examples of personal systems you might already be using:

- The filing system you use for your bills.
- The procedures you follow to make soup (recipe is the system; the ingredients are the tactics).
- The layout of your closet.
- The Building plans for a house.
- Mowing the lawn for example, you fill the mower with gas, start in the backyard, do the trimming and edging first, mow back and forth, etc.
- Brushing your teeth (top teeth first, back to front, then the bottom teeth).
- Your workout process in the gym (Monday cardio, upper body: Tuesday cardio, lower body, etc.).

In his book, *Work The System: The Simple Mechanics of Making More and Working Less*, Sam Carpenter writes: "The pathway to control is to discover, examine, optimize, and then oversee your mechanical and biological processes." He continues, "The essence of your work, health, and relationships lies within systems, and although they are veiled behind the buzz of everyday consciousness, there is nothing magical or convoluted about them—or about their management."

Soon it will be time for you to work to create your own personal systems for building physical, mental, emotional and spiritual strength. When you are ready, you will assemble a list of all the successful wellness habits you are already using. You will identify areas that you are not covering well and set some goals for those areas. You will write out a daily, weekly and annual plan for all the successful habits that you will use on a regular basis to active your wellness goals. Finally, you will keep a log of your progress and make changes when needed or to reward successes when deserved.

5. Build a Strong Positive Personal Character

Character consists of personal traits and behaviors that reflect a law enforcement professional's beliefs, values and driving principles.

A Strong, Positive, Personal Character is composed of a collection of strong, positive, personal traits that build upon tactics and habits which strengthen you and tells the world that you are a person of courage, integrity and honesty and that you will always be trustworthy, loyal and reliable. As a warrior, you know how to use both deadly force *and* compassion. You respect and honor truth and justice, and you exemplify a code of honor by exhibiting the highest ethics, courage and strength as you prepare and meet the challenges of the world. You are a leader who is skilled, proficient and competent in your craft.

In *Mindset: The New Psychology of Success*, Carol S. Dweck quotes former UCLA head basketball coach John Wooden: "I believe ability can get you to the top, but it takes character to keep you there… It's so easy to… begin thinking you can just 'turn it on' automatically, without proper preparation. It takes real character to keep working as hard or even harder once you're there. When you read about an athlete or team that wins over and over and over, remind yourself, 'More than ability, they have character.'"

I believe that the components of a strong individual character (a system of personal character) include integrity, honor, trustworthiness, honesty, timeliness, reliability, loyalty, professionalism, courtesy, empathy, compassion, etc.

So let's break down just one of these parts of character into its components: What is your definition of *integrity* in personal terms? What are the tactics that you would use to build a system of personal integrity? Your definition of *integrity* probably contains the following components:

- You are true to your word. Your word is your bond.
- You do what you say you will do.
- You are always on time (or even early).
- You are honest to a fault. You always tell the truth.
- You don't ask for loans.
- You repay debts and favors immediately.

- You walk your talk — your actions speak louder than any of your words.
- You are not arrogant or vain.
- You are dependable and competent in your work.
- You constantly strive to improve yourself.
- You are compassionate to the needs of others.

List some real world descriptions of habits you can use to build a system of personal integrity for yourself. You can consider adapting some of these descriptions for your own use:

- You hold yourself to the highest standards and are constantly looking for opportunities to reinforce your personal commitments.
- You make sure that you always do what you say you will do — or you don't promise it.
- You set reminders and alarms that make sure you are always on time or early.
- You are very conscious of what you say and make sure that you always tell the truth.
- You are very self-reliant financially, and you don't ask for loans as a matter of principle.
- You ask for help when needed, and you repay favors immediately.
- You consider your word your bond and you don't make promises you can't keep.
- You find times to surprise people with an unexpected, positive comment or gesture.
- You look for opportunities each day to be humble and gracious in your words and deeds.
- You work hard at taking classes, attending training and improving your skills.
- You surprise people as often as possible by completing tasks early or without being asked.
- You do more than is asked, and you always look for new knowledge or skills to enhance yourself.
- You volunteer your time to perform community service and frequently place the needs of others ahead of your own.

How Do You Change Ineffective Personal Habits?

Make a list of some *ineffective* personal habits you would like to change.

In Charles Duhigg's system he calls for tinkering with the trigger, tactic or reward in order to change a negative or counterproductive habit. I will describe this in terms of Habit Feeding or Habit Weeding. I suggest that you feed, or reinforce, the habits that are serving you well and that you weed the habits that are not helping you. In the concept of Habit Weeding I believe that you make changes to your tactic by modifying or removing either the trigger or reward. (See Figure 3.6, below.)

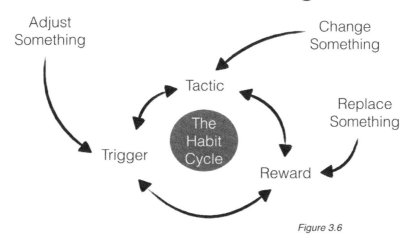

Figure 3.6

Look at the whole cycle and focus on its three components: trigger, tactic, and reward. Choose one of the three for weeding and adjust or replace it with something different.

Weed out a bad trigger and replace it with something new. For example, many smokers always light a cigarette when they drink a cup of coffee. If you are trying to stop smoking, substitute something else when you finish your coffee. (One idea is to immediately go and brush your teeth.) If you are not getting the tactic you want (for example, you are not working out every day), then weed out the reward that's not working and replace it with something else — like using a log of you workouts, and when you reach five within a week, treat yourself to your favorite healthy dessert or beverage.

Experiment with changing the trigger and rewards until you get the outcome you desire.

Build Your Agency Wellness Systems

An agency's success and reputation (or even its downfall) can be built on a foundation made up of its systems. Effective and compassionate systems build a good reputation and public trust, while a negative culture built upon inappropriate or ineffective systems for governing the people within or outside of the agency will always surely fail.

Here is the foundation for building a successful wellness system within your agency:

1. Establish your collective Agency Wellness Goals.
2. Develop Effective Agency Wellness Tactics.
3. Develop Effective Agency Wellness Habits.
4. Layer Effective Systems onto other Effective Systems so they work in concert, not in opposition.
5. Develop a Positive Agency Culture and an Effective Agency Culture of Wellness.

1. Establish Your Collective Agency Wellness Goals

These are goals for both the health of the agency and the health and well-being of its staff. Together these goals build a positive and healthy organizational culture that promotes and maintains the health and well-being of its personnel. To repeat Yogi Berra's observation: "If you don't know where you are going, you might not get there." It's important to have a plan for where you are going or you may never get there. Consider these examples:

- We are professional police athletes and we maintain the highest levels of physical fitness.
- We are emotionally tough and mentally sharp. We maintain our mental edge with regular training.
- We are compassionate and understanding of human frailty and work to protect and serve our public and each other.

- We value honor, integrity and ethical clarity and strive to maintain the highest levels of each.

- We value our public's trust and work constantly to maintain our legitimacy and transparency and eliminate bias as we promote fairness and openness in our policing processes.

- Our integrity is exemplary and we promote impartiality, fairness, respect, openness, compassion and empathy in our dealings with all people both inside and outside our agency.

2. Develop Effective Agency Wellness Tactics

Tactics are techniques or processes used by a law enforcement or military organization to create a positive organizational culture and achieve an advantage in the wellness of their personnel. You may be the leader that's needed to promote new and innovative wellness tactics within your organization. Consider implementing some of these concepts:

- We use an Agency Decision-Making Mantra to assist with decisions made in the field.

- We encourage proper nutrition and proper hydration of our personnel through educational and informational campaigns and use reward systems to promote and encourage compliance.

- We provide refillable water bottles for our people as part of their wellness program and provide a lunch area with a refrigerator and healthy snacks and beverages in the vending machines.

- We have a wellness resource library with books, video programs and online accessible resources to provide the most up to date wellness education available.

- We utilize volunteer and paid fitness trainers and nutritional educators.

- We promote fatigue management concepts and encourage our people to get proper amounts of sleep by managing overtime hours and maintain a sleep room at our stations.

- We use motivational posters and social media support to remind our people about what's important in the areas of their health and fitness.

3. Develop Effective Agency Wellness Habits

Habits are repetitions of organizational tactics employed to reach a desired goal until the goal is reached. Just as with our individual programs, we need to condition regular wellness habits into our organizational processes by using repetition and reminders. Consider some of these activities to build strong, healthy agency wellness habits:

- Our agency Decision-Making Mantra is prominently posted in all of our agency's facilities.

- We have given everyone a water bottle with measure markings to encourage them to drink between 2.2 and 3 liters of water daily.

- We offer a reminder to everyone to fill their water bottles right after roll call, and we reward those who we find regularly carrying or filling their bottles.

- We have established Armor Your Agency™ programs to promote agency and individual health and wellness, and we are continuously contacting other agencies to learn about newer and more effective processes and programs.

- We provide a workout room or gym membership and promote regular physical fitness activities in conjunction with our wellness program's reward system.

- We provide a sleeping room so that fatigued employees don't have to drive home, and supervisors are vigilant in watching for employees who seem excessively fatigued. We use the question: Good to go, or dragging to low?

- Supervisors use the agency's wellness library to retrieve books, videos and online resources about wellness for use in regular roll call training programs.

- We orchestrate regular weekly roll call wellness training. We use CopsAlive's RC10m Roll Call Discussion Guides to help us. (Visit www.CopsAlive.com and click on the "Resources" tab to find that free information.)

4. Layer Effective Systems onto other Effective Systems

Systems are the coupling of tactics and habits into a process used to achieve tactical or personal success. For our agency, we should consider processes and networks that build upon the tactics and habits used to reach the desired goals. Consider building some of these strategies into your agency's policies:

- The agency has an organized Wellness Program with a staff coordinator.
- The agency has a Wellness Library of books, audio programs and wellness videos.
- The agency has a Wellness Program that provides water bottles to personnel.
- The agency has workout facilities and personal trainers.
- The agency has a sleep room in each facility.
- The agency utilizes ongoing mentoring for personnel of all levels within the organization.
- The agency endorses positive ongoing Armor Your Agency™ concepts such as a chaplains' program, psychological services, a family support network, and a peer support team that works proactively to ensure fitness and discover those in need of help.
- The agency conducts annual, conversational "check-ins" conducted by an on-staff psychologist or an outside contracted police psychologist.
- The agency posts the "Safe Call Now" crisis hotline phone number around its buildings and encourages everyone to record the hotline phone number in their personal contact lists.
- The agency promotes stress reduction and mindfulness training.

The part can never be well unless the whole is well. — Plato

*When an organization is healthy
(when the leader at the top is doing his or her most important job),
people find a way to get things done. — Patrick Lencioni,*

*The truth is, being the leader of a healthy organization is just plain hard.
But in the end, it is undeniably worth it. — Patrick Lencioni*

(Patrick Lencioni is the founder of The Table Group organization and author of ten business and leadership books, including *The Advantage: Why Organizational Health Trumps Everything Else in Business*.)

5. Develop a Positive Agency Culture and an Effective Agency Culture of Wellness

Culture. The culture of a law enforcement agency or organization consists of the beliefs, customs, and ways of thinking, behaving, or working that exist in that agency or organization.

Positive Agency Culture. Therefore, a *positive* culture is made up of positive beliefs, customs and ways of thinking, behaving and working within a law enforcement agency or organization, and which create an effective platform for success and excellence.

Culture of Wellness. A culture of wellness is made up of positive beliefs, customs and ways of thinking, behaving and working within a law enforcement agency or organization that promote the health, happiness and well-being of its personnel.

Using the definitions above, how would you promote a culture of wellness within your organization? Consider some of these examples and see if they will help you:

- The agency leadership promotes and participates in the wellness initiatives.

- The agency utilizes wellness incentive-and-reward programs to encourage everyone's participation in wellness activities. The incentives include simple rewards like tickets to movies and sporting events.

- Agency supervisors and peer support team members bring some of the wellness library's resources to meetings and roll calls to remind people what's available.

- The agency supervisors encourage employees at roll call to drink more than 64 oz. of water throughout the shift.

- The agency encourages supervisors and peers to look out for tired employees and get them a ride home or suggest they use the sleep room.

- The agency follows the True Blue Valor™ concept of "Walking Our Talk."

- The agency has established a "no bullying" personnel policy.

- The agency has an "open door" policy utilized by all supervisors.

- The agency has adopted police psychologist Jack Digliani's "Make It Safe" initiative that makes it safe for officers to ask for psychological support.
- The agency promotes a stress reduction buffer time between work and home.
- The Decision-Making Mantra is routinely discussed and reinforced in staff meetings and at roll call.

The components of a positive organizational wellness culture include clear purpose and mission statements about health and fitness. A positive wellness culture will have value statements that encourage interpersonal respect and support for one another. A successful wellness culture promotes supervisory behaviors that show a commitment to excellence in personal integrity and wellness oriented activities. Finally, an effective wellness culture supports leadership strategies that promote mutual trust, openness, fairness and employee engagement. The organizational methods of a positive wellness culture will demonstrate strong traditional values, stability and team-oriented processes.

You should consider adding wellness-oriented wording to your mission statements, statements of vision and values, your agency motto, your agency's oath of office and appropriate policies and procedures.

How Do We Change Ineffective Systems or Negative Cultures?

I believe that there are three keys to changing ineffective systems or breaking negative organizational cultures: *leadership*, *determination* and *perseverance*.

Leadership needs to come from *everyone* in *every* level of the organization.

Determination is the fuel that drives change, and if you feel the need for change then you must combine your individual leadership with your strong sense of determination to work diligently for change for as long as it takes.

Perseverance is the differentiator between those who have leadership and determination and those who don't. If something needs to change in your organization, I don't care who you are or what your rank is, you should fight for what is right, or you should leave the organization and find a better one. Only *you* can tell how much perseverance is needed and when to give up the fight.

My Recommendations for Building Your Systems

Develop your Armor Your Self™ system by writing and discussing your thoughts on these ideas. Look back at all the notes you took (or should have taken) while reading this chapter.

Armor Your Self™ is not just a concept. It is a life-long practice whose goal is Tactical Resilience™. I know that all of this can all seem overwhelming, but I encourage you to experiment with the ideas and see if any of them work for you.

As an individual I suggest:

1. Start small.

2. Decide where you want to be, and set your goals to get there.
   (This could be about physical health, emotional stability, spiritual strength or even mental acuity. Choose to be more than just resilient; rather, focus on Tactical Resilience™.)

3. Choose your tactics.

4. Look for examples to follow.

5. Condition your tactics with repetition to build positive habits.

6. Build your systems for success by building systems made up of your positive habits.

7. Examine all of your habits — good and bad. Feed the good ones; weed out the bad ones.

8. Don't give up: persistence and determination win this race.

9. Remember to evaluate your system every few of months to see if it's working properly.

10. Correct or optimize your system until it's perfect for you.

11. Layer effective systems on top of other effective systems to achieve your personal goals.

To build systems within your organization I recommend:

1. Look back on all the notes you took on this chapter for your ideas on what improvements need to be made, and how you think they can be implemented. You are a leader and you should think like a leader.
2. Establish your vision for a healthy and resilient organization.
3. Ensure that all of your policies and procedures are in compliance with your vision. If necessary, write new ones, and get rid of ones that don't align with the vision.
4. See Chapter 5 for our Armor Your Agency™ list of recommended programs to establish your goals.
5. Find other agencies with successful programs you can use as benchmarks for your success.
6. Find policy and program tactics that reinforce the wellness tactics of your personnel.
7. Find ways to support and encourage the health and positive habits of your personnel.
8. Use all of these tools to build a system for a positive culture that supports a healthy organization.
9. Evaluate your system periodically to see if it's working as it should.
10. Correct or optimize your system to perfection.
11. Layer effective systems on top of other effective systems to achieve your vision.

Recommended Web Resources

(If you don't have the eBook version of *Armor Your Self*™: *How to Survive a Career in Law Enforcement*, type these links into your computers' browser window.)

Sam Carpenter's Work The System Web site offers a free, downloadable copy of his book. There are also some excellent resources there to help you and your organization. http://www.workthesystem.com/

Charles Duhigg's Web site especially its "About" page describe how he became interested in habits as a reporter during the war in Iraq, when he heard about an army major who had

been analyzing videotapes of riots. The major told him that the U.S. military was one of the biggest habit-formation experiments in history. "Understanding habits is the most important thing I've learned in the army." That experience helped the major make an interesting change in how they supported the Iraqi government in dealing effectively with civilian riots.
http://charlesduhigg.com/

Dr. John C. Norcross' Changeology Web site offers self-assessments and self-change exercises. He also offers several excellent articles on change.
http://www.changeologybook.com

Dr. Carol Dweck's Mindset Online Web site allows you to test your mind-set and offers four simple steps to begin to change your mind-set. There are also some excellent links to articles and interviews in which Dr. Dweck describes her research and findings about motivation and mind-set.
http://mindsetonline.com

You can download a free copy of Tony Robbins' eBook version of *Re-Awaken the Giant Within* at his Web site. He offers a large number of resources as well as personal coaching and live seminars.
http://www.tonyrobbins.com/

In 2002, *Forbes* named *The 7 Habits of Highly Effective People* one of the top-ten most influential management books ever. A survey by *Chief Executive* magazine recognized the work as one of the two most influential books of the 20th century. Visit the Stephen R. Covey Web site to learn about Dr. Covey's 7 Habits, as well as many of his other ideas about personal improvement.
https://www.stephencovey.com/7habits/7habits.php

Please also visit our Web site, where we are always adding articles and resources to help law enforcement professionals improve their wellness, Tactical Resilience™ and chances of surviving this career.
www.CopsAlive.com

Suggested Homework

Here are some homework exercises you can do on your own to further your personal development.

1. Make a list of life and career goals covering the next one, five and ten years.

2. Examine what helpful tactics you are using in your life.

3. List all of the goals for which you do not have any tactics in place.

4. Find or create tactics that will help you with those goals. Ask others what tactics they use to maintain their overall health and wellness. Look at the PMES exercise-specific chapters in this book for suggestions.

5. Set a plan to turn your positive and useful tactics into successful habits.

6. Find a way to piece together your positive and effective habits into a daily or weekly system that will support your success.

7. Look for support systems within your agency to support you, and then tie yourself into these to build upon your success.

8. If your agency does not have all the positive support programs that you need for support, see if you can volunteer to assist in implementing them. Use our Armor Your Agency™ guidelines, which can be found in Chapter 5 of this book, or online at our Web site to guide you.
www.LawEnforcementSurvivalInstitute.org

Recommended Reading

Carpenter, Sam. *Work the System: The Simple Mechanics of Making More and Working Less*. Austin, TX: Greenleaf, 2009.

Covey, Stephen R. *The 7 Habits of Highly Effective People*. New York: Simon & Schuster, 2005.

Duhigg, Charles. *The Power of Habit: Why We Do What We Do in Life and Business*. New York: Random House, 2012.

Dweck, Carol S. *Mindset: The New Psychology of Success*. New York: Random House, 2008.

Lencioni, Patrick. *The Advantage: Why Organizational Health Trumps Everything Else in Business*. San Francisco: Jossey-Bass, 2012.

Norcross, John C., Kristin Loberg and Jonathon Norcross. *Changeology: 5 Steps to Realizing Your Goals and Resolutions*. New York: Simon & Schuster, 2012.

Robbins, Anthony. *Awaken the Giant Within: How to Take Immediate Control of Your Mental, Emotional, Physical & Financial Destiny*. New York: Summit, 1991.

CHAPTER 4

Create A Comprehensive Agency Support System

Now that we are focused on your personal systems thinking, let's look at the big picture and how it affects officer survival and wellness. Nothing you do to protect yourself can be done in a vacuum. You can try very diligently to Armor Your Self™ by doing all the things I talk about in this book, but without support from a strong team and a supportive organization, all of your hard work might be in vain.

Even if you follow all of my recommendations about armoring your Self physically, mentally, emotionally and spiritually, that alone may not be enough if you can't get support, resources and encouragement from your agency.

So first, let's talk about strengthening your organization, and in the next chapter we'll talk about strengthening and conditioning your agency's culture so that it is positive and supportive and works in conjunction with your personal wellness tactics and your agency's support systems.

When I started conducting the Armor Your Self™ training program I knew that it could not stand independently without agency support. So very early on I started the Armor Your Agency™ research project to identify the best practices to support and encourage the individual wellness of an agency's personnel. What you will read in this chapter is the result of my research into best agency practices that support individual wellness. The Armor Your Agency™ project has become a training program that augments the Armor Your Self™ program, but it will always be an ongoing research project as we hear from you and others about great examples of successful and healthy law enforcement organizations.

As in previous chapters, I'll ask you to take a minute now to set aside this book and write down your thoughts about what your agency is doing *today* to support your wellness and promote your career survival. Next, write a list of successful programs that you may know about at neighboring agencies or agencies in which your friends work. Finally, make a wish list of programs or activities you wish your agency were doing to support you.

We can all work very hard to strengthen and condition ourselves individually, but if our agencies and our law enforcement culture don't have support mechanisms to sustain our efforts, then we will be doomed to always fight an uphill battle. In this chapter we'll focus on how to build agency systems to support and reinforce our individual efforts.

When I talk about Armor Your Self™, I recognize that no matter how hard you work as an individual to strengthen and condition your Self to avoid the *hidden dangers* of a career in law enforcement, you can't be effective unless you have a system to support you. That system has to have its foundation within the law enforcement agency or organization for which you work. It is critical that we, as individuals and as agency leaders, establish systems to reinforce and support the concepts of Armor Your Self™. From an organizational perspective, I call this an Armor Your Agency™ systematic strategy that will have its place in the overall strategy of building officer Tactical Resilience™.

The support mechanisms that make this possible are peer and organizational support you get from your agency. Remember also that I'm defining Tactical Resilience™ as a process of intentionally strengthening and conditioning the mind, body, brain and spirit of a police officer or other law enforcement or military professional to withstand the rigors and hidden emotional, physical, spiritual and physiological dangers of continuous high-threat, high-stress situations.

In order to accomplish this I have developed a *four-tiered system-of-systems* that builds upon individual tactics, habits and systems to enhance individual character. This system-of-systems also encompasses an organizational system that has its own agency tactics, agency habits and agency systems that work to build organizational culture. This chapter focuses on building such agency systems.

And this raises a very big question: What is our organizational responsibility? To answer that, I propose two things:

1. Get together with other willing people within your organization and have several long discussions about what you, as an organization, are willing to do to care for, encourage and support the health and well-being of your personnel. Discuss what you are offering now and what you would like to offer to your personnel. Part of this process should include examining what coverage your insurance carrier really provides. Ask your carrier what it covers for physical as well as emotional injuries.

2. Start creating the components of the system *you* think you need for *your* organization.

I've done some research into what the most progressive agencies in the world are doing to take care of their people, and I've developed some recommendations I call the Armor Your Agency™ Model Agency Profile. This profile includes "Primary Strategies" and "Secondary Strategies." I also suggest that you look outside your agency to discover what additional resources might be available to you from within your community.

Now it's time to create a comprehensive agency support system so that you can Armor Your Agency™ (AYA).

Questions to ask yourself:

- What does your agency do now to support and encourage your wellness and resilience?

- What would you like your agency to do to support your efforts toward individual wellness and resilience?

- How well and resilient is your own agency?

- What can you do *personally* to improve both your own and your agency's wellness and resilience?

The goal here is simple: Build a healthy and resilient organization that supports and encourages individual wellness and resilience using the Tactical Resilience™ Model. In order to have a healthy and resilient agency, you first must build strong, healthy individuals; they, in turn, will make up and support your healthy and resilient agency. This is a cycle: Healthy individuals build healthy agencies and, in turn, healthy agencies support and encourage strong and healthy individuals. Ultimately both of those will build and support a healthy community.

What are the obstacles to achieving an Armored Agency?

The obstacles here might all come under the heading of leadership challenges, namely: How do you create a healthy and resilient agency and then put into place measures to encourage and support individual wellness and resilience?

When I say *leadership*, I'm referring to the *concept of leadership*, not simply the people who are in roles of authority. I firmly believe that leadership is a quality that *everyone* in law enforcement possesses. Whether or not everyone chooses to exercise it is another story.

My point is that *you* — the reader of this material — have all the leadership qualities you need to move this concept forward in your agency. Whether or not you exercise that leadership is just a matter of conviction about whether you believe you can make a difference. I agree with Henry Ford, who said, "Whether you think you can, or you think you can't — you're right."

As we go about building individual strength and conditioning, we can also create a healthy and resilient agency by putting into place simple measures to Armor Your Agency™ which, in turn, support and encourage the Tactical Resilience Model.

The Armor Your Agency™ concept helps law enforcement agencies armor and strengthen their people and organizational culture in order to build and sustain Tactical Resilience™. Armor Your Agency™ also includes the concepts of Armor Your Self™ and True Blue Valor™ as protection against the stresses and traumas inherent in high-stress and high-risk careers in law enforcement and the military.

If you would like to get quick subjective reading about where your agency is right now, you can use our Armor Your Agency™ Model Organizational Support System Checklist to conduct a brief assessment of the status or your current support systems. You can downloaded the checklist for free from our CopsAlive Web site. www.CopsAlive.com/suggests?ayagencyorgrisk/aysbook

The assessment should only take you a couple of minutes, and it will give you a snapshot of where you are now, as well as some ideas about what programs and systems you need to put into place.

Do you believe that your agency scored as highly as it should have?

Based upon my research I believe we can accomplish the goal of creating comprehensive agency support systems if we add a cluster of programs, training and behaviors that collectively constitute the Armor Your Agency™ Model Agency Profile. You can use the programs in this Model Agency Profile to bolster your agency's services to your personnel. Here are the primary and secondary strategies involved in the Armor Your Agency™ Model Organizational Profile (see also Figure 4.1).

The 20 Primary Strategies of the Armor Your Agency™ Model Organization Profile

1. Wellness Program including Wellness Education
2. Proactive Peer Support
3. Psychological Services or Employee Assistance Program (EAP)
4. Chaplains' Program
5. Law Enforcement Mentoring Program (at all levels of the agency)
6. Family Support Network
7. Anonymous Crisis Hotline
8. Medical, Health and Wellness Services and Education
9. Intervention Plan for employees in crisis
10. Law Enforcement Officer Suicide Prevention Training and Suicide Tracking

11. Critical Incident Support System and Response Plan
12. Wellness Resource Library
13. Departmental Fitness Program
14. Survivor Support
15. Annual Line of Duty Death Prevention Training: Vehicle Operations, Firearms Training, Arrest Control, Below 100, etc.
16. Positive Culture of Wellness — True Blue Valor™ Training
17. Annual Resilience Training and Education
18. The "Make It Safe" Officer Initiative
19. Community Support Network
20. Internal and External System of Transparency, Fairness and Respect

The 12 Secondary Strategies of the Armor Your Agency™ Model Organization Profile

1. Community Resources for Strength and Support
2. Long-term Health and Wellness Tracking
3. Employee Recovery Case Management
4. Employment Separation Supporting Ongoing Wellness Activities
5. Employee or Officer Selection Criteria based on Wellness Beliefs and Practices
6. Disability Insurance and Disability Response Plan
7. Wellness as part of all Departmental Training
8. Wellness as part of Field Training Instructor (FTI) Training
9. Executive Leadership Training on Wellness Issues
10. Wellness as part of Supervisors' Training
11. Supervisors' Support for Wellness Initiatives
12. Designated Fitness Trainers (Paid or Volunteer)

CREATE A COMPREHENSIVE AGENCY SUPPORT SYSTEM

Figure 4.1

A PDF of the Armor Your Agency™ Model Best Practice Support System Chart shown in Figure 4.1 can be downloaded for free at the CopsAlive Web site. www.CopsAlive.com/suggests?ayagencychart/aysbook

Armor Your Agency™ Model Profile Resources and Information

If your agency doesn't have all the support systems you would like, here are some resources to assist you in creating these programs, as well as my thoughts about how to Armor Your Agency™.

1. Wellness Program and Education

Every agency that provides law enforcement services should have a wellness support and education program. This might be a program run within the law enforcement agency itself;

it might also be operated by the governing municipality, township, county, state or federal organization.

A good wellness program will involve at least one paid staff member, and it can also include a number of volunteer staff who have the expertise to assist other personnel with issues addressing diet, nutrition, health planning and wellness management.

A progressive organization will offer annual doctor visits, as well as medical screening and blood tests for a variety of health related risk factors. Consideration should be given to screening for heart disease, cancer, diabetes, obesity and the other major medical factors that contribute to the greatest percentage of deaths worldwide, and are especially prevalent within the law enforcement profession.

In 2012, the U.S. National Governors Association issued a report entitled "Strategies for Curbing Health Insurance Costs for State Employees: Benefit Design, Wellness Programs, and Data Mining." It found that

> Offering wellness programs and providing incentives for state employees to participate in them is in states' interest. State employees tend to stay in their positions longer than employees in the private sector, making it more likely that state employees' longer-term health will affect a state's cost of providing insurance coverage. Moreover, many states are more likely than private employers to retain at least partial responsibility for their employees' retiree health costs. Because states are typically among the largest employers in a state, wellness programs offer an opportunity to improve health outcomes measured for the state population as a whole by preventing chronic diseases and reducing the costs of treating them.

A 2013 Workplace Wellness Programs Study by the RAND Corporation for the U.S. Department of Labor and the U.S. Department of Health and Human Services examined the wellness programs provided by a diverse set of employers, and described characteristics of wellness programs, use of financial incentive and engagement strategies, facilitators and challenges to success, and impact of programs. Read a summary of their report at the U.S. Department of Labor Web site.
http://www.dol.gov/ebsa/pdf/workplacewellnessstudysummary.pdf

CREATE A COMPREHENSIVE AGENCY SUPPORT SYSTEM

Wellness Program Resources

- Tufts Health Plan offers an excellent two-page planning document entitled "Worksite Wellness Program Development Model." http://www.tuftshealthplan.com/employers/health/pdfs/development_model/development_model.pdf

- The U.S. National Governors Association report, "Strategies for Curbing Health Insurance Costs for State Employees: Benefit Design, Wellness Programs, and Data Mining:" http://www.nga.org/files/live/sites/NGA/files/pdf/1210StrategiesForCurbingHealthInsuranceCosts.pdf

- The Commonwealth of Massachusetts Department of Public Health's "A Model Wellness Guide Investing in Good Health" is an excellent resource. http://www.mass.gov/eohhs/docs/eohhs/wellness-tax-credit/model-wellness-guide.pdf

- The Texas Department of State Health Services' State Agency Employee Wellness Assistance and Wellness Plan Writing Guide is a downloadable booklet that provides information on the enabling legislation; a model employee assistance and wellness plan, and samples of essential materials necessary for state agencies to develop an effective wellness program.
https://www.dshs.state.tx.us/wellness/resource/sabody.pdf

- A wonderful list of activities you can do as part of your program is available from the Texas Department of State Health Services. https://www.dshs.state.tx.us/wellness/healthed.shtm

- The U.S. Centers for Disease Control and Prevention's Web site offers a concise overview of a program created for mass transit workers entitled "Development of a Logic Model for a Physical Activity—Based Employee Wellness Program for Mass Transit Workers."
http://www.cdc.gov/pcd/issues/2014/14_0124.htm
It is also available for download.
http://www.cdc.gov/pcd/issues/2014/pdf/14_0124.pdf

- The Society for Human Resource Management (SHRM) Foundation report, "Promoting Employee Well-Being: Wellness Strategies to Improve Health,

Performance and the Bottom Line," will help you assess your organization's health risk, lower your health care costs and develop a healthier workplace culture. http://www.shrm.org/about/foundation/products/documents/6-11%20 promoting%20well%20being%20epg-%20final.pdf

2. Proactive Peer Support Program

I define *proactive peer support* as more than simply having a list of employees you can contact if you are having problems. Being proactive means that the peer support team should have members on all shifts and in all areas of the department. Team members should be charged with being visible and available to employees who might need support. Team members should also touch base preemptively with employees they are concerned about before issues become crises.

In his Police and Sheriff Peer Support Team Training Manual police psychologist, Jack Digliani, Ph.D., Ed.D., has written:

> The availability of EAP [*Employee Assistance Programs*] and health plan psychological counseling for police officers represents a significant advancement in the delivery of counseling services. However for officers, EAPs and health plan counseling, although helpful, appear insufficient. They are helpful in that they are utilized by some officers who might not otherwise seek assistance. They are insufficient in that despite their availability, they do not and cannot meet the needs of many police officers. Peer support teams occupy a support niche that cannot be readily filled by either an EAP, health plan provisions, or a police staff psychologist. If an agency wants to do the best it can to support its officers, a peer support team is necessary.

Training for a proactive peer support program should include information about warning signs, intervention techniques, active listening skills, available resources and legal requirements, just to name a few. I highly recommend Jack Digliani's Law Enforcement Peer Support Team Training Program to kick-start your program. You can find a copy of Jack's Law Enforcement Peer Support Team Training Manual on the CopsAlive Web site. www.CopsAlive.com/resources

Proactive Peer Support Program Resources

- International Association of Chiefs of Police (IACP) Peer Support Guidelines: http://www.theiacp.org/portals/0/documents/pdfs/Psych-PeerSupportGuidelines.pdf

- Jack Digliani's Law Enforcement Peer Support Team Training Manual is available for free download on the CopsAlive Web site. http://www.CopsAlive.com/suggests?diglianimanual/AYSbook

- Jack Digliani has many other documents and materials available to assist peer support teams on his Web site. www.JackDigliani.com

- CopsAlive "Peer Support Infosheet:" http://www.CopsAlive.com/suggests?peersupportinfo/aysbook

3. Psychological Services

It is becoming clearer each year that the state of our law enforcement personnel's mental and emotional health is as important, if not more important, than their physical health. If we are truly to improve the professionalism, sensitivity, effectiveness and compassion of our law enforcers, then it is only logical to care for their mental and emotional health as much — and as often — as we do their medical health. But we don't.

It is a sorry state of affairs that we don't have a more prevalent and stronger network of police psychological services. Every agency with more than 100 sworn and 300 support staff should have, at the very least, a trained consulting police psychologist. Every agency with more than 500 staff ought to have an on-staff police psychologist who is a specialist in law enforcement issues and familiar with the emotional needs of our first responders and support staff. Unfortunately, the presence of such well-trained and experienced professionals is rare. Even private, consulting psychologists who have experience working with law enforcement personnel are rarely available to most law enforcement professionals in the United States.

I recommend that you read Dr. Jack Digliani's book, *Reflections of a Police Psychologist*, an account of his experiences, thoughts, and observations as a seasoned police veteran and law enforcement psychologist. Dr. Digliani discusses how stress management becomes life management within the concepts of life-by-design and life-by-default. Inside the parameters of life management, a list of "Some Things to Remember" functions as an instrument for transactional change. His discussion of issues related to traumatic stress and exposure is based on years of treating officers exposed to traumatic events. He examines the role of police peer support teams and presents models for a peer support team policy and operational guidelines, along with information related to the confidentiality of peer support interactions (a topic of current controversy).

Equally valuable is Dr. Digliani's treatment of traumatic incident debriefings and their applications in policing, as well as his presentation of phase and freeze-frame models of debriefing, and a discussion of current efficacy research pertinent to traumatic incident debriefings. He also outlines police family issues and the Foundation Building Blocks of Functional Relationships; identifies various family patterns of interaction, and provides information for families of traumatized officers, which includes a discussion of coping with death and loss (a critical matter for police officers). Toward the end of the book, he addresses retirement transitions ranging from separation from service and the return to civilian life, addressing issues that need to be considered before retirement.

Reflections of a Police Psychologist is an excellent read, and Jack has some very progressive suggestions about how we can improve the way we care for and support each other throughout this very toxic profession. He has also expanded on those discussions with his newer book, *Contemporary Issues In Police Psychology.*

I recommend that you investigate Dr. Digliani's "Make It Safe" initiative, which endorses making a cultural change in your agency to promote the understanding that mental health is as necessary to our profession as physical fitness.

Finally, I support Jack's ideas about proactive annual mental health check-ins. Laying such a foundation early in an officer's career is an important part of maintaining mental and emotional wellness throughout years of service in law enforcement. You can learn more about all of Jack's training and initiatives on his Web site. www.JackDigliani.com

All of these issues are critically important because the state of a police officer's mental and emotional health has a direct impact on professionalism, effectiveness, compassion, competence, empathy, kindness, courtesy and racial and cultural sensitivity. It is time for our profession to take a more progressive approach to supporting and maintaining the mental and emotional health of our personnel.

Psychological Services Resource List

- International Association of Chiefs of Police (IACP) Guidelines for Consulting Police Psychologists: http://www.theiacp.org/portals/0/documents/pdfs/PsychConsultingPolicePsych.pdf
- Jack Digliani's Law Enforcement Peer Support Team Training Manual: http://www.CopsAlive.com/suggests?diglianimanual/aysbook
- Jack Digliani's book *Reflections of a Police Psychologist*: http://www.CopsAlive.com/suggests?reflectionsbook/aysbook
- The book *Contemporary Issues In Police Psychology*: http://www.CopsAlive.com/suggests?contempissues/aysbook
- *IACP Employee Mental Health Services Model Policy*, available for purchase from the IACP: https://www.theiacp.org/PublicationsGuides/ModelPolicy/tabid/135/Default.aspx

4. Chaplains' Programs

Chaplains' programs are not about bringing religion into law enforcement agencies. Police chaplains' programs are a necessary part of mental health support networks, and chaplains are equal players within proactive peer support as well as with on-staff police psychological services. When you consider the part of the law enforcement psyche that protects the very core of every individual, that part of the psyche includes the concepts of honor, integrity and a moral compass, as well as a person's religious or spiritual beliefs. This spiritual side of law enforcement is different for everyone, but it is not limited by beliefs of faith or religion. This is an area of each individual that can be most vulnerable to the many tragedies, traumas and excessive negative stresses that all of us face throughout our careers. An effective police chaplain deals with these issues and provides support regardless of an employee's religion or faith (or lack thereof).

The National Sheriffs' Association Chaplains Reference Guide notes:

As long as there is crime, there will be officers and a host of persons supporting the criminal justice system. Occasionally, these men and women will need additional support to handle overwhelming emotions that are hazards of the job. Most agencies cannot afford a full time staff person to attend to such needs. The type of people and criminal actions law enforcement encounter in communities and jails can sometimes be shocking. This emotes feelings the average person is very often not equipped to process alone. As a community oriented profession, we train law enforcement not to disclose feelings at such incidents. The nature of the profession asks that feelings and normal reactions to the extraordinary be put aside. This can result in higher rates of alcoholism, drug abuse, divorce, and, sometimes, suicide. In a service profession to law enforcement, as well as to the incarcerated, and former inmates, the chaplain has a unique perspective of, and possibly is better equipped to address basic problematic events and emotions. An effective chaplaincy program should be an integral part of any sheriff's office.

Law Enforcement Chaplains' Program Resources

- National Sheriff's Association /Chaplains Resource Manual: www.sheriffs.org/sites/default/files/tb/ChaplainsResourceManual.pdf

- Cary A. Friedman's book, *Spiritual Survival for Law Enforcement.* Linden, N.J.: Compass Books, 2005: http://www.spiritualsurvivalbook.com/

- Serve & Protect is a 501(c)(3) nonprofit corporation of international scope based in Brentwood, Tennessee. It serves law enforcement, fire rescue, EMS, dispatch and corrections professionals, as well as their families, through its unique combination of crisis line, chaplain alliance and four networks of mental health professionals. Serve & Protect was founded by former mounted police and Norfolk Police Detective Robert Michaels, who also serves as Tennessee Fraternal Order of Police State Chaplain. http://serveprotect.org/

- The International Conference of Police Chaplains was founded in 1973 by Chaplain Joseph Dooley to help unite chaplains from many agencies around the United States. Today the International Conference of Police Chaplains seeks to maintain professionalism in law enforcement chaplaincy. http://www.icpc4cops.org

- The International Police & Fire Chaplain Association is a nonprofit, faith-based organization dedicated to the response and support of all federal, state and international law enforcement, fire department and homeland security agencies, as well as other emergency agencies through out the United States and overseas. http://ipfca.org/

5. Law Enforcement Mentoring Programs

Law enforcement seems far behind other professions in recognizing the value of formal mentoring programs for personnel at all levels of our agencies and organizations.

The Center for Creative Leadership, in its 1997 publication, "Formal Mentoring Programs in Organizations: An Annotated Bibliography," suggested that mentoring programs are very beneficial in helping organizations create mechanisms for feedback, counseling, coaching, skill-building, preparation for advancement, role-modeling, and reinforcement of an organization's mission and values.

In a 1988 study entitled "Formal vs. informal mentoring in law enforcement," Michael Fagan found that "Individuals who had completed the training program reported higher job satisfaction, a stronger work ethic, and less of an age/experience gap with their mentor than the control group." (*Career Planning and Adult Development Journal.* 4:2, 1988, pp. 40-48.) http://www.ccl.org/Leadership/pdf/research/FormalMentoringPrograms.pdf

What is mentoring and how does it fit into a law enforcement organization?

In the International Association of Chiefs of Police (IACP) Best Practices Guide entitled "Institutionalizing Mentoring into Police Departments," IACP defines law enforcement mentoring as "a mutually beneficial relationship in which a knowledgeable and skilled veteran officer (mentor) provides insight, guidance and developmental opportunities to a lesser skilled and experienced colleague (protégé)." The IACP suggests that the goals of law enforcement mentoring are to "1) To promote professional growth, 2) Inspire personal motivation, 3) Enhance effectiveness of police service."

I believe the importance of the mentoring concept in law enforcement extends from the bottom of the organization to its very top. You can create mentoring programs for new officers, veteran officers, sergeants, lieutenants, captains and commanders — all the way to the top with an executive mentoring program.

- Both the IACP and National Sheriff's Association in the U.S. have executive mentoring exchange programs. The IACP Training Division offers a class called "Developing a Mentoring Process."

- The National Association of Women Law Enforcement Executives (NAWLEE) also provides mentoring opportunities for women in mid-level management positions and those new to senior management positions and senior management roles. NAWLEE provides opportunities for men and women in senior management positions to better understand how to retain and mentor women in their organizations.

- Also, the FBI National Executive Institute Associates (NEIA) works to mentor law enforcement executives. NEIA is a private, nonprofit organization, with a membership of more than 1,300 chief executives of the largest law enforcement agencies throughout the U.S., Canada, Australia and Europe. Representing a broad range of key federal, state and local agencies, these top officials are all graduates of the FBI's National Executive Institute (NEI), an intensive, three-week leadership-training program held at the FBI Academy at Quantico, Virginia. Established in 1976 in response to a request by the Major Cities Chiefs' Association (MCCA) for a program designed specifically for the nation's highest-ranking law enforcement executives, NEI soon opened its classes to international students. The NEIA provides a learning environment where its members can network, mentor and share unique executive leadership experiences.

I recommend that you consider a system of mentoring programs within your agency. Ask yourself what you want to accomplish with a mentoring program and how you will ensure it will be effective. I believe that to be effective your program should start with new officers as they enter the academy. Once hired, they can be paired with a mentor to guide and encourage them, from a distance, through their academy experience. The program should then continue as new officers transition through the field training program with the mentor in a supportive, nonsupervisory role that provides encouragement but does not contradict the field training instructors. Other levels of mentoring should also provide guidance to veteran officers, sergeants, lieutenants, captains and commanders — all the way to the top with an executive mentoring program.

The list below cites a number of law enforcement agencies that have successful mentoring programs, or contact the Law Enforcement Survival Institute about information and training regarding starting or reviving your law enforcement mentoring program.

Mentoring Program Resource List:

- IACP Best Practices Guide for Institutionalizing Mentoring into Police Departments: http://www.theiacp.org/LinkClick.aspx?fileticket=33FBrH%2b8xRE%3d&tabid=392

- Fontana, California, Police Department Mentoring Program: http://www.fontana.org/index.aspx?NID=518

- Kent, Washington, Police Mentoring Program: http://www.ci.kent.wa.us/content.aspx?id=9956

- The Indianapolis Metropolitan Police Department's Mentoring program. Aaron Snyder of the Indianapolis Metropolitan Police Department discusses his department's "My Legacy" mentoring program on the PoliceOne Web site. http://www.policeone.com/chiefs-sheriffs/videos/6878208-Law-enforcement-mentoring-programs

- The Los Angeles County Sheriff's Department Performance Mentoring and PPI Initiative: http://www.parc.info/client_files/lasd/27th%20semiannual%20report.pdf

- The IACP, under the auspices of its Discover Policing recruitment initiative and the New Police Chief Mentoring Project, has launched an online mentoring center. http://mentorboard.jobtarget.com/dpo

- The National Association of Women Law Enforcement Executives (NAWLEE): http://www.CopsAlive.com/suggests?nawlee/AYSbook

6. Family Support Network

Many people in law enforcement may fear and dread this concept, and yet I believe it is one of the most important. Our first line of defense against emotional distress in law enforcement is our family support system made up of our loved ones and closest family members. If they are not connected to our law enforcement agencies in any way, then we lose valuable intelligence about how well our personnel are functioning or, more importantly, suffering. Our families are not spies — I believe, rather, that they are our frontline "first responder support network," and as such are necessary supporters of our uniformed first responders on the streets and our plainclothed personnel in the detective bureaus.

A family support network can be as simple as a communication system between our families and our agencies, or it can be as complex as a strong social and volunteer organization. Just as a volunteer program or a Citizens Academy Alumni Association can give strong support to agencies, a strong network of family support can be critical to our very well-being.

Consider asking new employees and their family members to fill out important paperwork during a departmental orientation session at which you provide a benefits overview. During that orientation you can also create a communication tree with email, telephone or social media links. You might provide monthly or quarterly training for family members that cover important information about law enforcement operations, legal issues and departmental resources. Consider creating a 12-month training calendar that covers an important topic at each monthly meeting. Conduct training sessions about financial and retirement planning, the possibility of a line of duty death, and what paperwork should be filled out and on file early in an officer's career. Anything that is important to teach community members in a citizen's police academy would be more important for our families to have.

Consider involving family members in community or department activities as volunteers. Family members can be valuable resources during a natural disaster, major community event or serious crime spree. They can answer telephone calls, conduct computer queries, provide information and any other functions for which you may already be using explorers, citizen volunteers or citizen academy alumni.

Law Enforcement Family Support Network Resources

- CopsAlive PDF document, "Suggestions for the Implementation of a Family Support System within your Organization:"
  http://www.CopsAlive.com/suggests?cafamilysupport/aysbook

- The Law Enforcement Family Support Network:
  http://www.CopsAlive.com/suggests?lefamilysupportnet/aysbook,
  www.lawenforcementfamilysupport.org

- The Law Enforcement Family Support Network administrator's guide to free and low-cost strategies for improving officer and family support:
  http://www.lawenforcementfamilysupport.org/cleo.php

- National Police Wives Association:
  http://www.CopsAlive.com/suggests?npwa/aysbook
  www.nationalpolicewivesassociation.org

- Wives Behind the Badge:
  http://www.CopsAlive.com/suggests?wivesbehindthebadge/aysbook
  www.wivesbehindthebadge.org

- 911 Dispatchers:
  http://www.CopsAlive.com/suggests?911dispatchers/aysbook
  http://911-dispatcher.com

- Concerns of Police Survivors (C.O.P.S.):
  http://www.CopsAlive.com/suggests?cops/aysbook
  www.nationalcops.org

7. Anonymous Crisis Hotline

I recommend that you have as many support programs as possible available to your personnel — from an on-staff police psychologist to an active and proactive Peer Support Team, and from a Chaplains' Program to a Family Support Network. But even if you have all of these programs in place, you still may not be reaching everyone in your organization who needs help; and in many cases those who avoid support and assistance will be the ones who don't ask for help until they are well into a crisis state.

For this reason I believe that every agency should have some form of *anonymous hotline* through which these last few individuals can reach out for a last-chance bit of assistance. You and your agency may not want to assume the expense and liability of hosting such a hotline, and even if you did your personnel still might not trust it enough to use it.

For that reason I recommend an independent anonymous crisis hotline focused specifically on law enforcement or first responder issues, whose service should also offer resources for family members who seek assistance.

It is my belief that just having a great and proactive peer support program is not enough. Some employees are so afraid of losing their jobs that they won't seek out help when they feel information might be sent back to their employer. For this reason I believe that we must provide some form of seeking help that protects anonymity while connecting a person in crisis with a treatment provider, and one that asks for no more than information about their insurance providers. We will never know how many officer suicides might have been prevented if an opportunity to place an anonymous call to a crisis hotline existed. I think that if only one life is saved, we still need to make that service available.

There are a number of crisis hotlines for first responders available in North America, including Safe Call Now, Cop2Cop, and CopLine. I have the most experience working with Safe Call Now (1–206–459–3020), and I recommend promoting it to all your personnel.

Safe Call Now provides a simple and confidential way for public safety employees, all emergency services personnel and their family members anywhere in the nation to ask for help. Staffed by officers, former law enforcement officers and public safety professionals, Safe Call Now is a secure place to turn for help from individuals who understand the demands of a law enforcement career. These trained call-takers provide assistance and referrals for any public safety personnel and their families who are experiencing an emotional crisis or need someone to listen. Legislation was passed in 2009 to maintain confidentiality for public safety professionals nationwide when they call Safe Call Now for help. Safe Call Now is also a registered 501(c)(3) non-profit organization and is not funded at the state or federal levels.

Crisis Hotline Resources

- Safe Call Now:

  http://www.CopsAlive.com/suggests?safecallnow/aysbook

  www.SafeCallNow.org

  You should also visit the Safe Call Now Web site to download a brochure about the Safe Call Now crisis hotline for first responders, suitable for passing along or posting on an agency bulletin board.

  http://www.CopsAlive.com/suggests?scnbrochure/aysbook

- Cop2Cop:

  http://www.CopsAlive.com/suggests?cop2cop/aysbook

- Copline:

  http://www.CopsAlive.com/suggests?copline/aysbook

- The U.S. National Suicide Prevention Lifeline:

  http://www.CopsAlive.com/suggests?suicidepreventionlifeline/aysbook

8. Medical, Health and Wellness Services and Education

I know this sounds so simple that it "goes without saying," but I'll say it anyway: I'm constantly surprised by horror stories I hear from cops around the United States about the poor health insurance they have or how poorly they were handled, especially when seeking treatment for emotional or mental health issues. Given the number of agencies which don't recognize Post-traumatic Stress Disorder (PTSD) as a viable side effect of a career in law enforcement, is it any wonder that so many agencies are underinsured and unprepared for the eventuality that one of their own will be negatively affected by trauma and tragedy?

I have always believed that we should be proactive in this profession, and I suggest that we should expect the same from those who provide services to us. Your agency should provide adequate medical insurance to provide proactive medical and wellness services. These include annual health screenings, education programs and regular input that will help you plan for your health and wellness needs. If you are not covered as you believe you should be, then form a committee to investigate alternatives and seek support from your agency and governmental leadership, as well as from any fraternal organizations or associations to which you belong. Even if you feel your agency provides the best possible coverage, it doesn't hurt to conduct regular reviews of services and comparisons with agencies of similar size within your region of the country. The buying power of some of our largest police associations and organizations should be leveraged to assist agencies and individuals who can't receive the kinds of coverage we deserve in law enforcement.

Resources on Medical, Health and Wellness Services & Education Programs

- "Developing a Law Enforcement Stress Program for Officers and Their Families:" http://www.ncjrs.gov/pdffiles/163175.pdf

- The Healthy Community Network and the Wellness Institute of Greater Buffalo, NY, has a great model with information. http://www.healthycommunitynetwork.com

- The Texas Department of State Health Services page on Cardiovascular Health and Wellness -Wellness Programs has a Community Wellness Index, which is a self-assessment and planning guide to help identify the strengths and weaknesses of your community's wellness and health-promotion policies and programs, as well as help you develop an action plan to implement a community wellness program or improve an existing program. http://www.dshs.state.tx.us/wellness/healthed.shtm

- Indian Health Services Wellness Program Model: http://www.ihs.gov/california/default/assets/File/GPRA/BP2012- WellnessProgramModel-Carmichael.pdf

- I was heartened to read that the Canadian Province of Ontario enacted an amendment to existing legislation to create a presumption that first responders diagnosed with PTSD have a work-related illness. http://www.CopsAlive.com/suggests?ontariofirstrespact/aysbook

9. An Intervention Plan for Employees in Crisis

As with so many other matters discussed here, a crisis intervention for a colleague is a situation we could have avoided had we done the due diligence we should have been doing long before the intervention became necessary. Many times a simple discussion with the person early in a potential problem situation can lead to a voluntary request for help. However, it is very reasonable to believe that at some point, no matter how large or small your agency, you will have to intervene with colleagues who are faltering and don't acknowledge the severity of their problems. Personal issues, financial problems, alcohol issues, and even the abuse of prescription drugs, can intrude into the law enforcement workplace and can absolutely prevent an employee from providing the services and expertise they have sworn to provide to the public. Therefore, it is critical that we have the courage to take charge and intervene before small problems blossom into major crises.

An intervention plan should include a survey of your insurance coverage and a list of available treatment facilities for various issues. You should have someone on call who can provide or oversee clinical supervision — hopefully a police psychologist, or at least a psychologist familiar with the kinds of stress and trauma issues that affect law enforcement professionals. Your plan should provide guidelines about who should be involved in an intervention team, and where and how the team might do the actual intervention. There have been instances in which law enforcement personnel handled an intervention poorly, and which led to a violent altercation or suicide.

At a minimum, you should have a mental health professional available to you on a contractual basis, preferably a psychologist, familiar with law enforcement issues. If your agency doesn't have a staff police psychologist or a consulting police psychologist, then please contact the International Association of Chiefs of Police - Psychological Services Section to get a referral for an appropriate mental health professional in your area. http://www.theiacp.org/psych_services_section

Resources to Assist You in Creating an Intervention Plan

- "Signs Of Excessive Stress & Warning Signs," excerpted from Jack Digliani's Law Enforcement Peer Support Team Training Manual:
   http://www.CopsAlive.com/suggests?warningsigns/aysbook

- Information on "How To Recover From Traumatic Stress" excerpted from Jack Digliani's Law Enforcement Peer Support Team Training Manual:
   http://www.CopsAlive.com/suggests?recoverfromtraumaticstress/aysbook

- The National Center for PTSD's Psychological First Aid Manual:
  http://www.CopsAlive.com/suggests?psychologicalfirstaid/aysbook

- A free copy of Jack Digliani's Critical Incident Handbook:
  http://www.CopsAlive.com/suggests?diglianihandbook/aysbook

- CopsAlive Employee Intervention Checklist:
  http://www.CopsAlive.com/suggests?cainterventionchecklist/aysbook

- Visit www.CopsAlive.com periodically to check for our latest Officer Intervention Guidelines document. You can find it by searching the site for "Officer Intervention Guidelines."

10. Law Enforcement Officer Suicide Prevention Training and Tracking

As I have made abundantly clear in this book, I believe we have a severe problem in our industry with law enforcement suicides. There is a lot of discussion, and even some argument, within our industry about the numbers; but all that tells me is that we need to be keeping better track of the numbers. Even when you consider the lowest numbers out there, and I believe they're inaccurately low; we are still losing twice as many officers to suicide than murder in the line of duty. Yes, that's correct: We are killing ourselves at twice the rate that the bad guys are killing us! This is a major problem within our profession and *we* need to deal with it. You don't deal with an issue by ignoring it and failing to respond to its symptoms.

What should we do? First, someone needs to be tracking the numbers and all agencies need to be reporting them. Lest we ever forget, each agency should keep track of all suicides of its officers, supervisors, civilian personnel and retirees. We do no one a service by hiding the numbers or dismissing the problem. It seems logical that the Department of Justice should be the keeper of these records and should collect them along with all the other NIBRS statistics it gathers through the Federal Bureau of Investigation (FBI). We also need to talk about this problem openly in our roll calls and staff meetings. You can download a free roll call discussion guide from our CopsAlive Web site. http://www.CopsAlive.com/suggests?officersuicideprev/aysbook

Finally, we need to conduct regular and ongoing training to address this problem until it isn't an issue any longer. I've heard arguments that police suicides aren't any higher than those in the general population, and my response is that *we aren't the general population*. We have recruited, selected, tested and trained like no other profession. If we have people committing suicide, it's a problem — end of story. The only real question is: *What are we going to do about it?*

I truly believe the Tactical Resilience™ concepts contained in the Armor Your Self™ program will work effectively to diminish police suicides. There are also plenty of other great programs out there focused specifically on police suicide issues.

In 2014, the International Association of Chiefs of Police (IACP) released a new resource for law enforcement on police officer suicide, with information and resources about prevention and responses to the problem. The resources on their Web site are from their symposium entitled "Breaking the Silence: A National Symposium on Law Enforcement Officer Suicide and Mental Health," and their Web site is loaded with lots of downloadable and reproducible materials.

According to the IACP Web site: "To address the mental health stigma within law enforcement as well as the critical issue of law enforcement suicide, the International Association of Chiefs of Police, in partnership with the Office of Community Oriented Policing Services, U.S. Department of Justice (COPS) hosted Breaking the Silence: A National Symposium on Law Enforcement Officer Suicide and Mental Health in July 2013. The participants at the symposium, which included the National Action Alliance for Suicide Prevention, law enforcement and mental health professionals, worked together to develop a national strategy to address officer mental health wellness and suicide prevention."

There is also a video entitled *Breaking the Silence: Suicide Prevention in Law Enforcement* and discussion guide you can use to create your own in-house suicide prevention program. CopsAlive also offers a roll call discussion guide.

The excellent 18-minute video was produced by the Carson J Spencer Foundation, in partnership with the International Association of Chiefs of Police, National Action Alliance for Suicide Prevention, and the American Association of Suicidology. It's a clear call to action to police chiefs around the world to make suicide prevention a health and safety priority.

The video was produced by the Carson J Spencer Foundation, a Denver-based nonprofit leading innovation in suicide prevention, and was supported financially by the Kenosha Police Department. Additional support was also provided by the Denver Police Department and police psychologists from Nicoletti-Flater Associates.

Resources for Suicide Prevention Training

By using our CopsAlive Roll Call Discussion Guide RC10m "Law Enforcement Suicide Prevention — Take Charge," along with the video produced by the International Association of Chiefs of Police (IACP) and the Carson J Spencer Foundation, you can create your own quick-and-easy and effective suicide prevention training program. http://www.CopsAlive.com/suicideprevention

Also visit these sites for more ideas and approaches:

- The International Association of Chiefs of Police (IACP) Center for Officer Safety and Wellness — Preventing Law Enforcement Officer Suicide Program:
  http://www.theiacp.org/preventing-law-enforcement-officer-suicide

- National Police Suicide Foundation:
  http://www.CopsAlive.com/suggests?psf/aysbook
  Ask about their NPSF Police Suicide Awareness (PSA) Model with Tempe PD.

- Pain Behind The Badge:
  http://www.CopsAlive.com/suggests?painbehindthebadge/aysbook

- In Harm's Way:
  http://www.CopsAlive.com/suggests?inharmsway/aysbook
  http://policesuicide.spcollege.edu/

- Paul Quinnett's excellent work with the QPR concept at the QPR Institute and the QPR Institute's Suicide Triage Training for Law Enforcement Personnel:
  http://www.CopsAlive.com/suggests?qprletrng/AYSbook
  https://www.qprinstitute.com/le.html

- Badge of Life:
  http://www.CopsAlive.com/suggests?badgeoflife/aysbook

- The Blue Wall Institute:
  www.CopsAlive.com/suggests?bluewallofsilence/aysbook

- Rescue Team Wellness:
  http://www.CopsAlive.com/suggests?rescueteamwellness/aysbook

- Safe Call Now:
  http://www.CopsAlive.com/suggests?safecallnow/aysbook

- Leading Resilience:
  www.CopsAlive.com/suggests?leadingresilience/aysbook

11. Critical Incident Support System and Critical Incident Response Plan

Many people confuse the concepts of critical incident support and peer support. I define *critical incident support* as specific measures put in place prior to a critical event and the support measures activated immediately following a major traumatic incident. These measures are different than *proactive, day-to-day, exemplary peer support*. Having a proactive peer support program that touches base with employees on a regular basis (even if there haven't been critical incidents) will certainly enhance your response to a severe incident when it occurs. There are a number of organizations that train for and coordinate critical incident response measures, and I encourage you to do your homework to find a system that works for your agency.

Critical Incident Stress Debriefing (CISD) is a specific, seven-phase, small-group, supportive crisis intervention process. It is just one of the many crisis intervention techniques which are included under the umbrella of a Critical Incident Stress Management (CISM) program.

The concept of having a written critical incident response plan is as necessary as having any other written policies or procedures. In your written critical incident response plan you should designate who should take on specific tasks during, and immediately after a critical incident, along what actions need to take place. You may want to create your own blank template or checklist to keep everyone accountable.

Critical Incident Support System Resources

- The mission of the International Critical Incident Stress Foundation (ICISF) is to provide leadership, education, training, consultation and support services to the emergency response professions, other organizations and communities worldwide regarding comprehensive crisis intervention and disaster behavioral health services. http://www.icisf.org/

- Jack Digliani's "Critical Incident Handbook:"
  http://www.CopsAlive.com/suggests?diglianihandbook/aysbook

- "Signs of Excessive Stress & Warning Signs" excerpted from Jack Digliani's Law Enforcement Peer Support Team Training Manual:
  http://www.CopsAlive.com/suggests?warningsigns/aysbook

- "How To Recover From Traumatic Stress" excerpted from Jack Digliani's Law Enforcement Peer Support Team Training Manual:
  http://www.CopsAlive.com/suggests?recoverfromtraumaticstress/aysbook

- "IACP Post-Shooting Personnel Support Model Policy 1/12," available for purchase from the IACP: https://www.theiacp.org/PublicationsGuides/ModelPolicy/tabid/135/Default.aspx

- "IACP Line of Duty Deaths and Serious Injury Model Policy 3/11," available for purchase from the IACP: http://www.iacp.org/model-policy

I also recommend that you read the following articles:

- "A Primer on Critical Incident Stress Management (CISM)," by George S. Everly, Jr., Ph.D., C.T.S., and Jeffrey T. Mitchell, Ph.D., C.T.S. (May 20, 2011), available from The International Critical Incident Stress Foundation: http://www.icisf.org/a-primer-on-critical-incident-stress-management-cism/

- "Crisis Intervention: A Review," from the International Critical Incident Stress Foundation (ICISF), originally published in the *International Journal of Emergency Mental Health*, Spring, 2000: http://cism.cap.gov/files/articles/Crisis%20Intervention%20%20A%20Review.pdf

12. *Wellness Resource Library*

I believe every organization ought to have materials available to assist its personnel to improve their personal and family wellness and well-being. The costs are minimal and the long-term effects by far outlast the short-term expenses.

The entire concept of Armor Your Agency™ is to provide mechanisms to support your law enforcement personnel in all the ways that they might need to be and want to be supported.

Just as peer support, chaplains' programs and psychological services might be different ways to get mental and emotional support to our personnel, a resource library is a simple and cost-effective way to get good information about a lot of subjects into the hands of people who choose the library system of learning. More importantly, it also shows that the organization cares enough to have all of these programs and materials available so that employees can learn at their own pace. Resources can include books, videos, audio programs, professional journals, special reports, and even a computer workstation where personnel can access the Internet or take online courses that the organization has a license to distribute. A well-stocked resource library with materials about all the areas covered in this book is an inexpensive, cost-effective way to provide employees with necessary knowledge and information they can digest at their leisure. Topics should include physical fitness, diet, nutrition, promoting resilience, mental toughness, mindfulness, fatigue issues in law enforcement, PTSD, police suicide, stress management, managing fear, spirituality, brain training, grief issues and all forms of mental and emotional health care.

Resource Library Suggestions

- I offer a complete list of all the books and materials that I recommend on our CopsAlive Web site.
  http://www.CopsAlive.com/library-list

13. Departmental Fitness Program (Including Paid or Volunteer Fitness Trainers)

Earlier in this book, I suggested that we need to think of ourselves as professional police athletes, and that as such we need to condition and maintain ourselves physically in order to be able to endure the physical challenges and hardships this career brings. To be professional police athletes we need to have our own individualized physical fitness plans that we maintain weekly for the rest of our lives.

It seems only logical that we would have someone to provide not only workout design but also coaching and support to assist us in this endeavor. Unfortunately, most agencies don't have anyone who fits this bill, despite the fact that most agencies I've visited have one or more people with the training, education and certifications to provide these services. Even if you can't afford to hire someone for this role, volunteers can provide these necessary services.

There are many programs out there, and of them all I have always had great faith in the Cooper Institute's Law Enforcement fitness standards and training programs. The institute has programs both to help you personally and to train people to bring back information to your agency. Do your research and find a program that suits your organization — and please don't reinvent the wheel, because there are many great programs out there to adapt.

The Cooper Institute says: "There is broad consensus that a lack of physical fitness is a strong predictor of disability, early retirement, and premature death. Because of this, many professional groups such as IACP and various state peace officer standards and training councils have proposed policy changes to counteract the adverse effects of low physical fitness in the law enforcement population." In fact, the IACP has stated that "the functions of a law enforcement agency require a level of physical fitness not demanded by many other occupations, and fitness requirements should be specified."

The Cooper Center Longitudinal Study (CCLS) has shown repeatedly that having a moderate-to-high level of cardiorespiratory fitness significantly decreases the risk of developing coronary artery disease, Type 2 diabetes, hypertension, certain cancers and metabolic syndrome.

All branches of the military around the globe have excellent fitness programs. There is no need to create your own program when you can adapt one. Here in the United States all of the materials about military fitness programs is available free online. (Based on my own personal research and working relationships, I have a preference for the programs of the U.S. Navy.)

The U.S. Navy SEALs physical fitness program is a balanced, albeit extreme, fitness program and builds on its systems of mental toughness training. Create a system that works for you or your agency, and put it into your weekly routine. You should also ensure that your physical training and conditioning is the best it can be for you.

Fitness Program Resources

- The Law Enforcement fitness standards on the Cooper Institute's Web site:
  http://www.CopsAlive.com/suggests?cooperinstitute/aysbook
  http://www.cooperinstitute.org/law-fire-military

- Consider sending an officer through the four-and-a-half day Law Enforcement Fitness Specialist course conducted by The Cooper Institute. This course will prepare

the officer to be a fitness coordinator who can set up a testing and training program in the department.
http://www.CopsAlive.com/suggests?cooperinstitute/aysbook

- The Cooper Institute's three-and-a-half day Military and First Responder Exercise Leader Training:
http://www.CopsAlive.com/suggests?cooperinstitute/aysbook

- The Law Enforcement page of the Cooper Institute:
http://www.CopsAlive.com/suggests?cooperinstitute/aysbook
http://www.cooperinstitute.org/law-fire-military

- The U.S. Navy SEALs training preparation workout:
http://www.CopsAlive.com/suggests?sealtrngworkout/aysbook
http://www.navy.com/inside/fitness/physical-training.html

- The U.S. Navy's Web site has lots of resources that can be downloaded. These U.S. Navy SEALs BUD/S preparation materials include:
Naval Special Warfare Physical Training Guide (BUD/S NSW PT Guide);

- Naval Special Warfare Injury Prevention Guide (BUD/S NSW IP Guide); and Special Operations Nutrition Guide (NAVSPECWARCOM Nutrition Guide).
http://www.CopsAlive.com/suggests?sealtrngguides/aysbook https://www.sealswcc.com/navy-seals-buds-prep-docs.aspx#.UYmRtIJ5-54

14. Survivor Support

Survivor support is where the rubber meets the road in law enforcement. We always say "I've got your back" and "If anything happens to you, I'll take care of your family" — but often we don't follow through. I believe every agency needs a formal survivor support program in place, even if it has never had a line of duty death. If you add families of police suicide victims into the mix, we are much more likely to need to assist and support those extended family members. I am an active supporter of Concerns of Police Survivors (C.O.P.S.) and currently serve on my state chapter's board of directors (www.nationalcops.org). Another suicide survivors organization, S.O.L.E.S. — the Survivors Of Law Enforcement Suicide — has a Web site at: http://www.tearsofacop.com/police/SOLES.html

We can talk all day about supporting survivors, but if we don't have a plan in place before we need it we are just barking at the wind. The first step in this process is to decide as an agency just what you are willing to commit to. Are you willing to mentor children of fallen officers? Will you go to their soccer games, dance recitals, graduations and weddings? Are you or someone else willing to mow that lawn every week or shovel snow? If you are not willing to do these things, then don't make empty promises.

I will tell you from personal experience that the most important thing you can do as an individual or an agency is to show that you care by expressing continuing interest and staying in touch. I've heard so many stories that can be summed up in the statement "Once the bagpipes stop playing, everyone disappears." It's hard for all of us (and co-workers are survivors, too), but when it comes to the family — the parents, siblings, in-laws, spouses and children — our promises are more important and our absence is much more noticeable.

If you have survivors connected to your agency now, ask them what they want from you. You might be surprised by their answers, and they might be surprised you asked. Take steps today to form a committee of people who take charge of drafting a written policy, and plan for how you will support and assist your agency's survivors. Make a decision right now about whether or not you will support the survivors of a law enforcement suicide. Will the family receive a funeral with full honors? We have always said "We recognize our heroes not by how they died but how they lived." Do we mean it?

Resources for Survivor Support

- Concerns of Police Survivors:
  http://www.CopsAlive.com/suggests?cops/aysbook http://www.nationalcops.org/serv08.htm

- National Concerns of Police Survivors (C.O.P.S.) resource page:
  http://www.nationalcops.org/agenciesforms.htm

- List of Local Concerns of Police Survivors (C.O.P.S.) chapters:
  http://www.nationalcops.org/chap.htm

15. Annual Line of Duty Death Prevention Training

When you really look at the statistics for line of duty deaths, you will recognize that most of them are accidental deaths, not homicides. Nonetheless, these accidental deaths may be preventable and every agency should have in place annual training that targets the most vulnerable of law enforcement's liability concerns: vehicle operations, firearms training and arrest control training. As former police officer, attorney and law enforcement consultant Gordon Graham frequently says, "What is measurable is preventable."
http://www.gordongraham.com

Resources to Promote Annual Line of Duty Death Prevention Training

- *Vehicle Operations*
  "International Association of Chiefs of Police (IACP) Vehicular Pursuit Model Policy," July 22, 2004:
  https://www.theiacp.org/LinkClick.aspx?fileticket=pnMib083hyU%3d&tabid=392

- *Firearms Training*
  "International Association of Chiefs of Police (IACP) Use of Force Model Policy 2/06," available for purchase from the IACP:
  https://www.theiacp.org/PublicationsGuides/ModelPolicy/tabid/135/Default.aspx

- *Arrest Control*
  "International Association of Chiefs of Police (IACP) Reporting Use of Force Model Policy 2/97," available for purchase from the IACP:
  https://www.theiacp.org/PublicationsGuides/ModelPolicy/tabid/135/Default.aspx

- *Below 100*
  The "Below 100" program sponsored by LawOfficer.com and Law Officer Magazine:
  www.CopsAlive.com/suggests?below100/aysbook

16. Create a Positive Culture with True Blue Valor™ Training

I have a selfish interest in mentioning the True Blue Valor™ concept: It's my brainchild, and it is the only program I know of that addresses the issue of our negative law enforcement culture.

We talk about being "True Blue" and supporting the "Thin Blue Line," and yet in most cases we don't really walk our talk, and in some cases we subvert the honorable intentions of these concepts with something negative like a Blue Code of Silence that enables negative, dishonorable and unspeakable behaviors. True Blue Valor™ is a code of conduct and a mentality that says those of us who take the oath and put on the badge of law enforcement should be the best and most noble of community servants, and that we should support one another, and expect the best from each other and our agencies.

True Blue Valor™ means having the strength of character and integrity to guide, support, encourage and mentor our peers for success. Encouraging their strength might just save our lives. It also means having the courage and strength to intervene when appropriate by starting a "courageous conversation" with someone who is struggling. Minding our own business is not a luxury we can enjoy when our "business" is law enforcement. If we are willing to risk our lives protecting and serving of our citizens, then we should be willing to have the strength and courage to protect and support our peers. This also means we should have the strength and courage to accept help when our peers think we need it.

I strongly encourage you as a leader (no matter what your rank) to promote these discussions within your agency. If we at the Law Enforcement Survival Institute can help you, please contact us.

Consider using our written Code of True Blue Valor™ and our True Blue Valor™ challenge coin to reinforce you personal code of conduct or to start a program at your agency in order to make a larger difference.

We will talk further about this concept in the next chapter, which deals with changing our culture. You can also visit the True Blue Valor™ Web site for additional information. www.TrueBlueValor.com

Resources to Create a Positive Culture and for True Blue Valor™ Training

- True Blue Valor:
  http://www.TrueBlueValor.com

- The Law Enforcement Survival Institute:
  http://www.LawEnforcementSurvivalInstitute.org

- Jack Digliani's Make it Safe Police Officer Initiative and implementation guide: http://www.CopsAlive.com/suggests?jdmispackage/aysbook

Below are some of my favorite books on building a strong, positive organizational culture:

- Buckingham, Marcus, and Curt Coffman, *First Break all the Rules: What the World's Greatest Managers Do Differently.* New York: Simon & Schuster, 1999.

- Buckingham, Marcus, and Donald O. Clifton, Ph.D., *Now Discover Your Strengths.* New York: The Free Press, 2001.

- Collins, James C., *Good to Great: Why Some Companies Make the Leap — and Others Don't.* New York: HarperBusiness, 2001.

- Collins, James C., and Morten T. Hansen, *Great by Choice: Uncertainty, Chaos, and Luck — Why Some Thrive Despite Them All.* New York: HarperCollins, 2011.

- Gladwell, Malcolm, *The Tipping Point: How Little Things Can Make a Big Difference.* Boston: Little Brown & Co., 2002.

- Kouzes, James M., and Barry Z. Posner, *The Leadership Challenge.* San Francisco: Jossey-Bass Publishers, 1997.

- Lencioni, Patrick. *The Advantage: Why Organizational Health Trumps Everything Else in Business.* San Francisco: Jossey-Bass, 2012.

- Peters, Tom, *Thriving on Chaos: Handbook for a Management Revolution.* New York: Perennial Library/Harper & Row, 1988.

- Peters, Tom, and Nancy Austin, *A Passion for Excellence: The Leadership Difference.* New York: Warner Books, 1986.

- Stubblefield, Al. *The Baptist Health Care Journey to Excellence.* New Jersey: John Wiley & Sons Inc., 2005.

17. Annual Resilience Training and Education

Resilience training like Armor Your Self™ or our Tactical Resilience™ training isn't magic and it doesn't take effect without continued or daily practice and regular or at least annual reinforcement. This profession is a tough one and the negative side effects don't always make themselves known unless you are really paying attention. If you believe, as I do, that this career requires a professional athlete's mentality, then you know that these are concepts you need to embrace early in your career and build them into lifelong habits.

When it comes to building Tactical Resilience™, one size does not fit all. You have to search to find an exercise regime that works for you. You have to find and build a repertoire of tactics, techniques and exercises that you can build into habits that work for you and that you enjoy. You must be dedicated, and you need to do your daily practice in as many of the four PMES areas as you can. Take it from me, as someone who is probably a little further down this career path, it's so much easier to build these systems and habits when you are young than when you are older.

If you are designing a program for your agency, you need to do your research and be sure to use as broad a spectrum of materials as possible. And remember: it is important to strengthen and condition the whole person, not just the physical parts, to build a truly resilient human being.

Resources for Promoting Annual Resilience Training and Education

- NIJ Developing a Law Enforcement Stress Program for Officers and Their Families: www.ncjrs.gov/pdffiles/163175.pdf

- The Law Enforcement Survival Institute has three main programs include Armor Your Self™, Armor Your Agency™, and True Blue Valor™. We have other training programs available as well.
  http://www.lawenforcementsurvivalinstitute.org/training.html

- The Centers for Tactical Resilience™ and Ethical Policing, affiliated with The Law Enforcement Survival Institute, promote further research and training in the areas of building human strength and fitness of the mind, body, brain and spirit in police officers and other law enforcement or military professionals, which allows them to withstand the rigors and hidden dangers of continuous high-threat, high-stress situations.

www.TacticalResilience.org

- International Association of Chiefs of Police (IACP) Center for Officer Safety and Wellness: http://www.CopsAlive.com/suggests?iacpsafetywellnessctr/aysbook
http://www.theiacp.org/CenterforOfficerSafetyandWellness

- U.S. Department of Justice, Bureau of Justice Assistance VALOR: Preventing Violence Against Law Enforcement Officers and Ensuring Officer Resilience and Survivability Program:
http://www.valorforblue.org

- "Stress shield: a model of police resiliency" in *International Journal of Emergency Mental Health*. Spring, 2008 10(2):95-107.

18. The "Make It Safe" Initiative

I've mentioned the "Make It Safe" police officer initiative several times in this book because I think it is such an important idea and deserves its own section here as part of your overall Armor Your Agency ™ strategy. The initiative was conceived by police psychologist Jack Digliani, Ph.D., Ed.D., and is about creating an organizational climate where it is safe to ask for help when you need it. It's also about taking away the stigma that mental/emotional health is anything different than physical health,

Make It Safe Resources

- Jack Digliani's Make It Safe Initiative and implementation guide:
http://www.CopsAlive.com/suggests?jdmispackage/aysbook

- Jack Digliani's Web site:
http://www.CopsAlive.com/suggests?jdcom/aysbook

19. Community Support Network

Every agency will thrive if it has the support of its community. This seems so simple, but what is simple is not always easy. First, we must make it a priority. Nothing will degrade community support and enthusiasm faster than neglect. When we lose sight of *why* we do this job we then lose touch with the people we serve and protect. During my career I was a community policing project administrator, and I believe in the power of strong police/community interactions. I also believe that resilient individuals build resilient agencies which, in turn, build resilient communities. The reverse is also true: if you want to enhance your personal or agency resilience, begin by building strong bonds with your community.

Resources for Building Community Support

- Community Policing Defined materials from the U.S. DOJ COPS Office:
  http://www.cops.usdoj.gov/pdf/vets-to-cops/e030917193-CP-Defined.pdf

- The Implementation Guide for the President's Task Force On 21st Century Policing:
  http://www.cops.usdoj.gov/pdf/taskforce/Implementation_Guide.pdf

- Co-Producing Public Safety Communities, Law Enforcement, and Public Health Researchers Work to Prevent Crime Together:
  http://ric-zai-inc.com/Publications/cops-w0800-pub.pdf

- Police Perspectives: Building Trust in a Diverse Nation – No. 1. How to Increase Cultural Understanding:
  http://ric-zai-inc.com/Publications/cops-p344-pub.pdf

- Police Perspectives: Building Trust in a Diverse Nation – No. 2. How to Serve Diverse Communities:
  http://ric-zai-inc.com/Publications/cops-p345-pub.pdf

- Police Perspectives: Building Trust in a Diverse Nation – No. 3. How to Support Trust Building in Your Agency:
  http://ric-zai-inc.com/Publications/cops-p346-pub.pdf

- Resource Guide For Enhancing Community Relationships And Protecting Privacy And Constitutional Rights:
  https://www.bja.gov/Publications/CommRelGuide.pdf

20. An Internal and External System Of Transparency, Fairness and Respect

A lot of attention has been given to the concepts of fairness, transparency, legitimacy and open communications in law enforcement. To me these are just facets of the concept of Community Policing I always practiced; however, I suspect to some they are new, and perhaps frightening. What is most critical to understand is that these are principles of human interaction that when practiced effectively will enhance policing services in any community — but they are also principles that will also enhance organizational management practices within any law enforcement organization. Because of the value of this two-edged advantage, I believe that every agency ought to learn and incorporate these concepts.

Resources for Transparency, Fairness, Respect, Legitimacy and Open Communications in Law Enforcement

- The Fair & Impartial Policing Project of Dr. Lorie Fridell:
  http://www.fairimpartialpolicing.com

- The National Initiative for Building Community and Justice:
  www.nnscommunities.org

- Rand Corporation Report: "Respect and Legitimacy—A Two-Way Street

- Strengthening Trust Between Police and the Public in an Era of Increasing Transparency:"
  http://www.rand.org/pubs/perspectives/PE154.html

- COPS Office resource page on procedural justice:
  http://cops.igpa.uillinois.edu/procedural-justice-resources

- COPS Office publication on Procedural Justice:
  http://www.cops.usdoj.gov/pdf/conference/2011/ProceduralJustice-Kunard.pdf

- BJA publication on Procedural Justice and Police Legitimacy:
  https://www.bja.gov/bwc/pdfs/Procedural-Justice-and-Police-Legitimacy-Paper-CPSC-Feb-2015.pdf

- COPS Office publication on Racial Reconciliation, Truth-Telling, and Police Legitimacy:
  http://ric-zai-inc.com/Publications/cops-p241-pub.pdf
- Strengthening the Relationship between Law Enforcement and Communities of Color:
  http://ric-zai-inc.com/Publications/cops-p307-pub.pdf
- Strategic Communication Practices: A Toolkit for Police Executives:
  http://ric-zai-inc.com/Publications/cops-p222-pub.pdf

Other Important Programs and Concepts

Community Resources for Strength and Support

Law enforcement should never operate in a vacuum, and building a strong and supportive network within your community is as important to your agency's wellness as it is to the health and wellness of your personnel. When major conflicts arise in police and community interactions, the agencies that come through smoothly are also the ones that have taken the time to build strong bonds to their community well in advance of any incident that might cause conflict.

Some call this Community Policing. When I was the administrator of our agency's program, we expanded that to call it Community Oriented Governance because we involved all departments within our city government in teams to build strong ties to our community organizations in those areas within our city. We invited school, business, religious, cultural, nonprofit and other leaders to be involved with us. We held regular meetings of city leaders and community representatives, and we operated in a spirit of mutual problem solving and innovation. Whatever you call your program, I highly encourage you to invest the time and commitment into building strong bonds within your community now — before you need them in a crisis.

Both the U.S. Department of Justice and The International Association of Chiefs of Police (IACP) are creating resources for building sustainable community trust. The IACP recently held a *National Policy Summit on Community-Police Relations: Creating a Culture of Cohesion/Collaboration.* This summit was held partly in response to recent events that have shined a spotlight on law enforcement agencies and officers and, the tactics and equipment employed to protect our communities. Resources are already available to help you, and more will be added as time goes by. Whichever ideas you chose to promote, find a model that works for you and set your program into motion before you need it.

Resources for Building Community Strength and Support

- The U.S. Department of Justice initiated a national effort called Building Community Trust and Justice to build trust between law enforcement and the communities they serve. Funded with a $4.75 million grant in 2014, the initiative will create a substantial investment in training, evidence-based strategies, policy development and research to combat distrust and hostility between law enforcement and the communities they serve. The three-year grant has been awarded to a consortium of national law enforcement experts led by John Jay College of Criminal Justice. Yale Law School, the Center for Policing Equity at UCLA, and the Urban Institute make up the rest of the consortium. You can learn more and watch for updates online.
  http://www.justice.gov/opa/pr/justice-department-announces-national-effort-build-trust-between-law-enforcement-and

- The U.S. Department of Justice Community Oriented Policing Services (COPS) office is dedicated to community policing. Learn more about COPS and what services they offer.
  http://www.cops.usdoj.gov/

- The U.S. Department of Justice Community Oriented Policing Services (COPS) office offers a document entitled "Community Policing Defined."
  http://www.cops.usdoj.gov/Publications/e030917193-CP-Defined.pdf

- The U.S. Department of Justice NCJRS has published a report entitled "Community Building Measures: How Police and Neighborhood Groups Can Measure Their Collaboration."
  https://www.ncjrs.gov/pdffiles1/nij/grants/213134.pdf

- The U.S. Department of Justice's Bureau of Justice Assistance (BJA) offers a document entitled "Understanding Community Policing — A Framework for Action" to assist you.
  https://www.ncjrs.gov/pdffiles/commp.pdf
- The COPS Office of the U.S. Department of Justice, in cooperation with the International Association of Chiefs of Police (IACP), have created a document entitled "Building Trust Between the Police and the Citizens They Serve: An Internal Affairs Promising Practices Guide for Local Law Enforcement." www.nccpsafety.org/assets/files/library/Building_Trust_Between_Police__Citizens.pdf
- International Association of Chiefs of Police (IACP) article entitled *Resources for Building Sustainable Community Trust*:
  http://www.iacp.org/CommuityPoliceRelations

Long-term Health and Wellness Tracking

Wellness tracking should start with new hires and then continue through their careers, from the academy and into retirement. I'm not talking only about commissioned law enforcement officers; I'm talking about *all* of our personnel. The statistics are pretty thin for officers, and they are practically nonexistent for our civilian support staff. I can't imagine that their stress is very much less than ours, and if we are really serious about wellness we should be serious about the health and well-being of all our personnel.

The Optum® Resource Center for Health & Well-being has been monitoring ongoing trends in workplace health management programs for the last several years. In its Fifth Annual Wellness in the Workplace Study, Optum® found: "Nearly half of employers have either a formal, written, long-term strategic wellness plan or an annual health management plan, a slight increase from last year. Not surprisingly, large employers are much more likely to have any kind of plan (73%) than mid-sized companies (44%) and small firms (43%)."

When Optum® analyzed the measurements of success it found: "For the first time among employers of all sizes, health risk reduction is the top factor in determining program success. Last year, claims reduction was the biggest factor for large and mid-sized companies, while health risk reduction was most important for small firms." Optum® also reported: "The fact that health risk reduction has become the leading success metric is important since health risks are linked to lost productivity and increased medical costs. But there is still opportunity for employers to build a more complete business case for health management which includes quality-of-life indicators and operational performance metrics."

One of the important issues here is that *no* national or international standards exist for what we should be tracking in law enforcement or any other profession. In that case, we should be setting the standards ourselves. We ought to look at job performance metrics, quality-of-life indicators and long-term career survivability measures. John Violanti, PhD, a former New York State Trooper and professor of social and preventive medicine in the University of Buffalo School of Public Health and Health Professions, is doing the most thorough research in our profession. He is the principal investigator on a major scientific study of the Buffalo Police Department called Buffalo Cardio-Metabolic Occupational Police Stress (BCOPS). The study has been conducted over several years at the University at Buffalo and is funded by the National Institute for Occupational Safety and Health. I think we can look to Dr. Violanti's research as a window into the future for finding the metrics we need to understand thoroughly the toxicity and survivability measures of our profession.

Resources on Long-term Health and Wellness Tracking

- The Optum® Fifth Annual Wellness in the Workplace Study: https://www.optum.com/content/dam/optum/resources/whitePapers/042313-ORC-wellness-in-the-workplace-WP.pdf

- Information about Dr. Violanti's research: https://sphhp.buffalo.edu/epidemiology-and-environmental-health/faculty-and-staff/affiliated-faculty-directory/violanti.third.html

- Dr. Violanti's work on the BCOPS study: https://sphhp.buffalo.edu/home/news-events/aspph-friday-letter/2015-archive.host.html/content/shared/sphhp/home/aspph-friday-letter/2015-articles-archive/2015-08-28-john-violanti.detail.html

Officer Recovery Case Management

The concept of medical case management is relatively new, and there are lots of conflicting opinions about its use and usefulness. Based upon personal and professional experiences, I believe that when dealing with the complexities of mental and emotional health issues faced by law enforcement personnel, a recovery case management system is very appropriate, if not just plain necessary. These are issues you need to address with your medical and mental health providers, but keep in mind that they may not be supportive of your efforts.

A recovery case management system utilizes a clinically trained medical professional who acts as a liaison and patient/organizational ombudsman between the care provider and the patient. Usually case management is appropriate when it involves complex or long-term care. Consider a simple case of sending an officer to an alcohol treatment facility. Many treatment plans call for a 30-day inpatient plan that is probably covered by insurance and may be sufficient for many people.

But I'm sorry to say that police officers and other law enforcement professionals are not like "other people." Many times the issues that lead to alcohol abuse are multi-layered and complex; may involve many years of poor coping skills, and may be layered with event-specific trauma, as well as with the cumulative effects of other emotional, relationship and work related issues. Law enforcement professionals have to see and deal with so much more than is required of many other professions within our society, and because of this their issues may be many times more multifaceted and compounded with other difficulties.

In my CopsAlive interview with John Southworth, an intervention specialist, he suggested that a treatment program might need to last up to 12 weeks in order to be successful, not just the 30 days that insurance companies want you to believe it should take; and that we should utilize a case management system for up to five years to keep track of people who are trying to make major life changes — because it might take that long — with the support of a case management system, to hold them accountable and give them the support they need. You may not agree with all of John's suggestions, but my job here is to raise the proper questions. I believe that the proper question here is: What do we have to do to get a useful employee back to full and effective fitness for duty after having suffered with a trauma or addiction and who wants to successfully receive treatment and fully recover?

I encourage you or someone within your organization to do some research to find successful treatment and case management programs for law enforcement.

Treatment and Case Management Resources

- The Case Management Society of America published a helpful document entitled "Standards of Practice for Case Management:" http://www.cmsa.org/portals/0/pdf/memberonly/standardsofpractice.pdf

- The North Carolina Department of Health and Human Services has created a document about case management and care management that will give you a quick overview of the processes. http://www.ncdhhs.gov/dma/provider/budgetinitiative/CaseCareMgmtComponents.pdf

- A BeyeNETWORK white paper prepared for ASG by Scott Wanless entitled

- "The 7 Key Components For An Effective Case Management Methodology:" http://www.emrremedies.com/images/whitepaper-7key.pdf

- John Southworth and Southworth & Associates: http://CopsAlive.com/suggests?southworthassociates/aysbook http://www.southworthassociates.net/

- Safe Call Now: http://www.CopsAlive.com/suggests?safecallnow/aysbook http://www.safecallnow.org

Employment Separation Supporting Ongoing Wellness Activities

Most agencies don't think about what to do with their retirees. Retirees can be a valuable resource of knowledge, experience and manpower, if managed properly. They also have health and wellness issues that probably affect your group health insurance rates, and so it really does "pay" to keep them healthy and contributing. You might consider offering pre-retirement planning and, as part of your discussion about financial planning, health insurance coverage, etc., include discussion about keeping in touch with your retirees and offering them ongoing access to the wellness programs, services and treatments that you make available to your employees.

The State of New Jersey is very progressive in its services to retirees and includes a Retiree Wellness Program. Its State Health Benefits Program (SHBP) says: "It is the hope of the SHBP that active program participants will enjoy a longer, active, and healthier life." Upon retirement, employees start their enrollment by signing a "Pledge for Healthier Living."

The University of Minnesota, and Rutgers University understand the value of retiree wellness. Rutgers sees two main benefits of enrolling retired employees in its retiree wellness program: Participation in the program results in waiving of the employee's required retiree health insurance contribution in the program, and participation encourages a healthy lifestyle and promotes wellness as well as preventing future disease.

Harris County, Texas, supports its retirees with a wellness program, and states: "At this point in your life it is time to enjoy those hard-earned years of retirement. Staying healthy by being socially and physically active, eating well and managing disease is key to having an enjoyable retirement. As part of the employee wellness program, Harris County has extended its programs, activities and initiatives to encompass covered retirees and their covered dependents by providing the retiree wellness program. Retirees are still a part of Harris County and because of this, we want you to be informed about your health, stay active and celebrate those successes in life. We work to bring retiree health information, wellness seminars, team challenges and other programs to all retirees."

Resources for Employment Separation Supporting Ongoing Wellness Activities

- The State of New Jersey State Health Benefits Program (SHBP) Retiree Wellness Program:
  http://www.state.nj.us/treasury/pensions/epbam/exhibits/pdf/hr0817.pdf

- The Rutgers University Retiree Wellness Program:
  http://uhr.rutgers.edu/policies-resources/faqs-2/faq-retiree-wellness-program

- The Harris County Texas Retiree Wellness Program: https://www.wellathctx.com/cms/retirees-of-harris-county/about-retiree-wellness/

- The University of Minnesota Retiree Wellness Program:
  http://www1.umn.edu/ohr/benefits/retirees/wellness/index.html

Thoughts for Your Continued Research

I have listed the 20 primary best-practice programs and strategies of the Armor Your Self™ model agency profile of best practices, plus a couple of extra secondary strategies. Now you might consider adding some others to augment the primary 20. Here are some thoughts for possible additional secondary strategies:

- Employee or officer selection criteria based upon wellness beliefs and practices
- Disability Insurance and Disability Response Plan
- Wellness as part of all departmental training
- Wellness as part of Field Training Instructor (FTI) Training
- Executive Leadership Training on Wellness Issues
- Wellness as part of Supervisors' Training
- Supervisors' Support for Wellness Initiatives

In order for these ideas and suggestions to have any effect, it is critical that we as individuals and agency leaders establish systems to reinforce and support these concepts. These systems must be consistent and permanent in order for these concepts to take hold and matter. This book provides several different personal and organizational models to help you build the foundations for your continued success.

If your agency is too small or doesn't possess the resources to provide all the services I've suggested, I encourage you to reach out to neighboring or larger agencies with which to partner with to create regional resources to serve several agencies. Consider creating regional networks to provide these resources, perhaps through a regional intergovernmental agreement or mutual aid pact. Every law enforcement professional and agency deserves to have these services. Your challenge is how to make that happen.

This completes our discussion about agency responsibility. It's time now to go further and consider the importance of the culture within our organizations so that it supports our individual and agency efforts. If you organizational culture is not healthy, your organization and your people won't be healthy either. The next chapter considers how to change the culture of our profession so that it supports individual and agency wellness.

CHAPTER 5

Change the Culture

Now that we are focused on thinking about systems, let's look at the big picture and see how systems like your agency's culture can affect both your personal wellness and your agency's overall effectiveness. If your organizational culture doesn't encourage wellness and supportive behaviors, then all the best individual strategies and agency programs in the world won't help combat the detrimental effects of a negative organizational culture.

One would think that in a profession as tough as law enforcement the culture would be very supportive and team oriented; but I think that in many agencies it is not. You might expect that as professionals we would recognize the negative stresses we're all under and that each individual would be more supportive and encouraging of the others — we are, after all, all going through the same things, only at different times. In reality that's not how our culture functions. Our law enforcement culture can be as toxic as the profession is, and that is one additional risk factor when we consider what hurts us. I think our culture could use an overhaul.

Don't get me wrong. Most people in law enforcement talk a good game. We talk about being a family. We talk about taking care of our own. We say things like "I've got your back" and "I've got your six." But I don't think we really mean those things. Sure — it's easy to have someone's six during a high-risk warrant service, and it's not hard to have someone's back when they're involved in a justifiable shooting. But the real, telling circumstance is when someone makes a mistake, or shows weakness or indecision. The situations are when someone has done something that raises questions in their own mind, or when their peers in the agency seem to separate those officers from the pack. We tend to shun them rather than listen to and support them. Right or wrong, they are still our brothers and sisters, and with only a slight change of circumstance or timing it could have been you or me in that same situation. Our job is not to judge; our job is to support and be empathetic. That doesn't mean that you should support colleagues who abuse their power or are malicious or biased in their actions. This is about not allowing simple differences in style or behavior become the reason we exclude someone from the team.

To me, "having someone's back" means that you're there to support him or her through thick and thin and for the long haul — not just when it's easy or fashionable, but especially when it's difficult and takes some work. That especially means the times when you see someone slipping or messing up, like abusing alcohol or prescription drugs. You need to have the courage to say something about it rather than looking the other way.

I've always found it frustrating that even though we have the roughest job in the world — where at any minute someone might try to kill you, or you might be thrust into some horrible tragedy — most of us report that the highest amount of negative stress we experience comes from inside the walls of our law enforcement agencies. Many people want to blame that on "management" or the "bosses." But in reality a lot of it comes from our pears, in the form of teasing, hazing, negativity and other crap, which builds up and makes us much less tolerant of other challenges to our patience. In our line of work, that's just dangerous. When hazing happens, it's like being part of a dysfunctional family: We feel it's okay to be mean to the people who we are closest to, and frequently we take that attitude home with us. Also when we see such hazing (or worse, harassment) happen to others, we realize it could easily be happening to us, so we try to separate ourselves emotionally from the bad circumstances rather than standing up for someone who is being beaten down.

We attribute a lot of this bad behavior to the notion that we are making people "tougher" and "building character." In reality we are just venting our own anger and frustrations on the people who might have to save our lives on the next shift. I don't know of any sports or

Olympic coaches who would encourage athletes on their teams to browbeat each other the way we do. But, then again, we don't have any pressure to win, maintain excellence or even show up. *Or do we?*

Finding the Best Model for Our Law Enforcement Processes

Maybe we need to use a sports model instead of the current military model for our management and leadership principles.

> The Sports Model: The Police Officer as Professional Athlete
> Concept: Team, Teamwork, Coaching, Leadership, Open Structure
>
> The Military Model: Rigorous Chain of Command, Police Officer as Warrior
> Concept: Lone Wolf, Strict Supervision, Rigid Structure

I see some value to a military model in areas of discipline and order, but with some maturity and a little coaching the sports model will accomplish the same goals. I like the Warrior mind-set because I think we need to get back to the original meaning of warrior: those who hold themselves to the very highest standards of excellence in both "personal" character and professional mastery; but note that these qualities are also valid in a sports model.

While military methods of building tough individuals are very appropriate for those who are going into combat — which sometimes happens in law enforcement — such methods may not always be appropriate for individuals who have to spend the next 20 or 30 years dealing with people as a servant-leader. We are Peace Officers, which means we Protect *and* Serve. We deal with good people *and* bad people, and we have to treat them the same. We deal with traumas and tragedies, and we have to maintain our professional demeanor when we deal with the poor or the wealthy — and no matter who the people or what the circumstances, we have to be friendly, calm, courteous, capable and proficient.

We have to be friendly and courteous to everyone, and we have to withstand angry people who spit on us, insult us, and try to fight with us. We are held to the highest standards of human behavior and are expected always to perform with ease, composure and compassion. That's a big challenge. You'd think that given these tasks, ours would be the most cohesive and supportive of cultures. But it's not. You'd think we'd understand the challenges we each face and we'd be there to support and encourage one another; yet we don't always. You'd think we'd stand by each other through the worst of things; yet we frequently fall short, especially when it has to do with each other's mental health. We scatter like a flock of startled pigeons at the first sign of "scandal," and we cut the weak from the pack like a bunch of rabid wolves. We can be extraordinarily cruel, like bullies, to our peers. So when will we start to protect and serve each other?

It's not always our actions that are the problem. It's as much our *inaction* that can cause pain for our peers. When we don't know what to say, we say nothing, even when some supportive words are needed. Instead of supporting someone when we should, we turn away; and when someone's recovery takes too long, we abandon him or her; and worst of all, sometimes we top off abandonment with ridicule. We tell each others' families that if something happens to their loved ones, we'll take care of them — but we don't. We can be hypocrites.

From a management perspective I think we frequently take the cowardly route. We have an obligation to take care of our people. We have an obligation to our public to ensure that the human resources of our agencies function at optimal capacity and perform with the highest levels of skill and precision. We usually have solutions when individuals fail to perform their jobs physically; it's when they have trouble mentally, emotionally or spiritually that we struggle.

Sadly, many agencies have nothing in place to deal with these circumstances. Many agencies are small, understaffed and underfunded. Unfortunately, that's not going to be an effective legal excuse when we are taken to court after one of our personnel, due to anger, fear, fluster or fatigue, causes someone's death. We should devote time and energy to preventing and overcoming these challenges, yet many agencies fail to address these challenges until it's too late and a catastrophe has already occurred.

Our Agency Mind-set

There's another issue we need to address beyond capability, preparation and performance, and that's *mind-set*. I think that many of us still believe that mental health services are for victims. If one of us needs mental, emotional or spiritual guidance, we think they are weak or broken. I call this "Our Blue Shame:" ignoring, avoiding or outright refusing to accept our responsibilities to each other. Just as police officer suicides are the "dirty little secret" of our profession, Our Blue Shame is our failure in not addressing the problems that need addressing early, before they are irreversible.

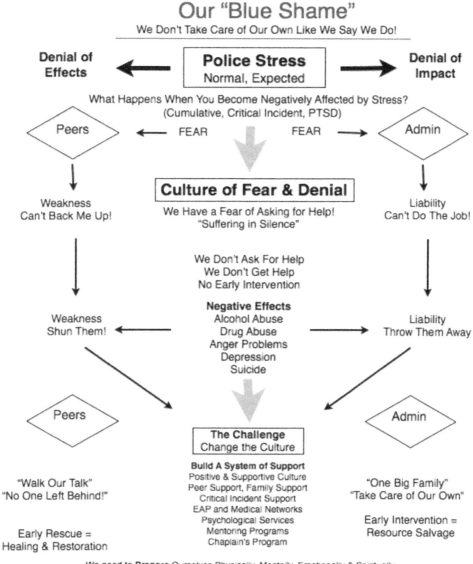

Figure 5.1

As we have already discussed, modern law enforcement professionals face challenges caused by all kinds of trauma and tragedy that they see every day. If these traumas and tragedies are severe enough, or if enough of them build up and the negative stresses that results are not attended to, the police officer may experience fatigue, depression, PTSD and, in the worst scenario, may contemplate suicide. Other aftereffects like — alcohol and prescription drug abuse, relationship problems, domestic violence and financial mismanagement (among others) — are all manifestations of a personal crisis for any officer. We should know that something like this might occur, but we frequently reject it as "unexpected" when, in reality, we all get very heavy doses of cumulative negative stress that can develop into problems like physical ailments, depression or Blue Trauma Syndrome.

In law enforcement and criminal justice we focus a lot of attention and keep statistics on crime rates, numbers of arrests and even police line of duty deaths. But we don't keep *any* statistics on the numbers of officer suicides or of officers forced to retire after being disabled. It has been proposed that the very occupation of law enforcement may be a negative health risk factor of its own — but we know all of this! We know it from the time we're hired. But sometimes we don't see the effects it has until we are well into our careers.

Issues that we might start to see "On the Job" include:

Mental Fatigue
Depression
Cumulative Stress
Post-traumatic Stress Disorder (PTSD)
Burnout
The Police Perfection Paradox
(Expecting humans to be superhuman)
Anger and Frustration

Issues that we might start to see "Off the Job" include:

Marital Problems
Relationship Problems
Domestic Violence
Gambling
Drinking
Drug Dependence
Financial Problems
Problems with Our Kids

The greatest challenge facing the future of our law enforcement profession is not how our officers are dying, but rather *how our officers are suffering.* Which raises another hidden danger of this job that we never really talk about: the Police Perfection Paradox.

The Police Perfection Paradox

I define the Police Perfection Paradox as the conundrum created by trying to reconcile law enforcement officers' personal expectations with those of their agencies' and the public's. The agency and/or the public may expect you always to be perfect in your decision making, yet reality frequently proves that human beings don't always meet this standard. When you do make a mistake, your agency, the media, the public and your peers will judge you. Frequently their expectations about how an ideal police officer is supposed to behave don't match the responses of a human being while under stress. So a massive conflict ensues. Sadly, sometimes, despite the best of intentions, we make a fatal decision under stressful circumstances and split-second timing pressures and even when everyone around you says that they understand, you might not ever be able to reconcile your own split-second decision emotionally.

The Police Perfection Paradox is created by the requirement to make split-second, life-and-death decisions without allowance for mistakes; but well after your split-second decision, your actions and the outcomes will be second-guessed by people who weren't even there. The public, the media, the courts, your supervisors and even your peers will scrutinize your actions for years.

The Police Perfection Paradox is fueled by our macho image of law enforcement super-heroes, an image that won't let us be weak or acknowledge that we have feelings emotions or even any personal problems. We all fear that management won't promote us if we show any sign of "weakness." It is a damned-if-you-do/damned-if-you-don't paradox.

Examples of the Police Perfection Paradox

Public Expectations	*vs.*	*The Reality of Life*
Be super-human		We are not perfect
Make perfect decisions		We make split-second decisions
Shoot the gun out of his hand		Reality is not like TV
Run fast, shoot straight, be strong		We are only human
Never be rude or cranky		We get frustrated too
Never suffer from trauma and stress		We suffer, and sometimes it shows!

Symptoms of the Police Perfection Paradox:

    Macho self-image vs. vulnerability to mistakes

    Fear of making a mistake

    Anger caused by unachievable expectations

    Very negative views and opinions

Problems with the Police Perfection Paradox:

    May lead to indecisiveness

    May cause inaction or laziness based on fear

    The officer becomes angry and burned out

    The officer begins to blame problems on outside forces —

    (police administration, family or "them")

The old-school, macho style of policing isn't working. We have groomed many generations of police officers who are "strong and silent" types, who believe that we just have to be strong enough to emotionally suppress all of our traumas and tragedies, including the fears, stresses, anger and other emotions that we can't even label, and then hope that these feelings will never come back out again. This simply does not work. We need to learn that and find a better system to deal with our pain.

We have created a "pressure cooker" environment in which our personnel bottle up all of their feelings, emotions and natural responses to negative stress and then never release them, until they practically explode from the build up of these internalized pressures.

It certainly is all right — even appropriate — to suppress our reactions to the things we see and experience while on the streets at work. Compartmentalization is an effective method of dealing with immediate emotional distress when you are in the middle of a serious or life-threatening event. What causes problems is that we never release those bottled-up emotional reactions, nor do we *ever* effectively process them with the appropriate professional help or peer support. Instead we let the pressure cooker boil until the next event, and the next, and we keep adding pressure to this already over pressurized caldron filled with all of our traumas and pain. We have created a culture that's about being tough without providing appropriate first aid for the wounds that this career can inflict, and if left unattended those wounds will fester, and all that was put into the pressure cookers will explode. We have to learn to deal with emotional wounds early, when they are easily treatable, just as we would with a physical injury.

Natural and logical responses to negative stress and trauma will not go away just because we internalize our reactions. We need to realize that this ineffective emotional management system is what is killing us, causes so many problems within our careers, and even intrudes into our personal lives.

Ideally, we should be tough and stoic while in the middle of a crisis and then, when in a safe place afterwards, be able to talk and express our feelings to someone who understands. If the emotional aftereffects of responding to a crisis are more serious, then professional mental health support is an appropriate and necessary first-aid measure to ensure any law enforcement professional's long-term effectiveness. Continuing to deny the importance of mental health and emotional and spiritual care is foolhardy.

We can correct this problem ourselves by recognizing the reality of the job and making sure the public does too, through good individual and organizational leadership and appropriate public and media education.

No one is exactly sure what effect negative stress has on the human body, especially what effect it has with the high doses of stress police officers take in. It's time for us to start anticipating these negative effects created by the job and to start preparing ourselves to deal with them through education, prevention, treatment and intervention. We need to acknowledge that negative physical, mental, emotional and spiritual forces will challenge us all. We need to learn how to manage these negative effects and to armor our selves.

Each of us will handle the negative effects of trauma and tragedy differently. Some of us will handle negative trauma better than others, and each of us might handle those negative effects well one day and not well another day. Whether the cause is a buildup of strong negative cumulative stress or something else has yet to be discovered. But what is known is that the phenomena I call Blue Trauma Syndrome has a profound and negative impact on many officers, and I believe we can prevent much of that by preparing ourselves in advance. Even if you start late in your career you should be able to reverse some of these negative effects, especially if you have support from your peers and your agencies.

It's time to pay greater attention to prevention and intervention. We know about crime prevention and injury prevention, and are trained in time management and suspect management. But what about PTSD prevention and trauma management? We can dress a colleague's gunshot wound in the field, but we can't seem to care for emotional wounds. Maybe this is a matter of obliviousness, or perhaps we're just afraid to ask for guidance. If that's the case, then our task is to educate ourselves so that we are better equipped to care for ourselves and to help our peers. As the airline safety briefings tell us: "Put your own oxygen mask on first, before you try to help someone else."

Large Cumulative Doses of Negative Stress (and even PTSD) Are Treatable

It's important that our personnel know there are effective treatments for excessive stress and PTSD, and these afflictions need not be fatal to one's career. Our personnel also need to know that the earlier they begin treatment the better chances they have for a full recovery. So it's to your benefit to ask for help, and to ask for it early. The U.S. Department of Veteran's Affairs runs an excellent Web site through the National Center for PTSD, which states that there are many new and effective treatments for PTSD:

> Today, there are good treatments available for PTSD. When you have PTSD, dealing with the past can be hard. Instead of telling others how you feel, you may keep your feelings bottled up. But talking with a therapist can help you get better.
>
> Cognitive behavioral therapy (CBT) is one type of counseling. Research shows it is the most effective type of counseling for PTSD. The VA is providing two forms of cognitive behavioral therapy to Veterans with PTSD: Cognitive Processing Therapy (CPT) and Prolonged Exposure (PE) therapy. To learn more about these types of therapy, see the V.A.'s fact sheets listed on their Web site's "Treatment" page.
>
> There is another kind of therapy called Eye Movement Desensitization and Reprocessing (EMDR) that is used for PTSD with very positive effects. Also, medications have been shown to be an effective treatment for PTSD. According to the V.A. "a type of drug known as a selective serotonin reuptake inhibitor (SSRI), which is also used for depression, is effective for treating PTSD."

To learn more visit the V.A.'s Web site.
http://www.ptsd.va.gov/public/treatment/therapy-med/treatment-ptsd.asp

In the United States, officers who seek help for emotional or mental health-related traumas may be provided some protection through the Americans with Disabilities Act. I'm not a legal expert. You should do your own research on the issue of legal protections for yourself, your peers or your agency. One way or another you're always better off asking for help than trying to tough it out and then being ordered into treatment or, worse, waiting so long that you get fired for performance issues before you can get help. We all need to believe that it's critical for us to seek help early when things are bothering us.

I realize there are some gaps between art and science here — but are we even trying? We've prepared ourselves to fight and shoot — but have we prepared ourselves to counsel and care? We can do an intervention on a drunken subject or a suicidal party, but do we use those same skills with peers when we need to?

Where are the classes on "Mental First Aid," "Emotional Survival Techniques" and "Spiritual Damage Assessment?" Where is the training on how to help a peer who's suffering on the inside? Where is the training for finding the courage to tell colleagues they are screwing up?

It's Time We Rebuilt Our Police Culture from the Inside Out

We need to correct all of these problems, and we need to create an environment in which we all understand and support each other. We need to make it safe to ask for help. Stresses, both positive and negative, are part of our job. We need to face it as fact. We need to learn to work within parameters that make dealing with negative stress a part of the process of keeping ourselves and our peers strong and sharp enough to do the job.

Why do we tease and pick on our peers? Isn't it tough enough for them on the streets? We think we're "helping" them get stronger and that the weak should get out of this profession. Perhaps that's true — but that is their decision, not yours!

Bullying in Law Enforcement

You would think that in a job filled with so much danger and trauma we'd work hard to take care of each other rather than make each other feel worse. You'd think that if your life depended upon someone else's capacity to handle tough situations, you'd work hard to make sure they were always mission-ready. But that's not really the case, is it? You'd think all that talk about the "Thin Blue Line" would really mean we looked after each other rather than dividing into cliques and ignoring peers we don't like or understand.

It's time to change, and I'm going to recommend several things for all of us to initiate. In addition to implementing the Armor Your Self™ strategies for yourself individually, and the Armor Your Agency™ best practices for your organization, let's talk about what I call True Blue Valor™.

True Blue Valor™ Definition

True Blue Valor™ is about cops having the courage to confront their buddies who slip professionally and personally, and endanger themselves, their peers and the public. I think the hardest thing we might ever have to do in this profession is to intervene when a peer is slipping. I think most of us would rather confront someone holding a gun than confront those of our own who aren't taking care of themselves as they should or who aren't upholding our code of honor.

True Blue Valor™ is also about taking care of yourself, supporting your peers and working hard to make sure everyone on your team is strong and capable. It takes a system of organizational support and professional leadership to support and foster the concept of True Blue Valor™.

True Blue Valor™ means having strength of character and integrity to guide, support, encourage and mentor our peers for success. Encouraging their strength might just save our own lives. It also means having courage and strength to intervene, when appropriate, by starting a "courageous conversation" with someone who is struggling. Minding our own business is not a luxury we can afford when our business is law enforcement. If we are willing to risk our lives to protect and serve of our citizens, then we should have the strength and courage to protect and support our peers. Providing protection and support is not about endlessly bullying peers to "make them stronger." That's not helpful, and we need to stop it. We all face enough trauma, tragedy and danger on the streets and in our jobs; we don't need more piled on from our peers.

Ask yourself:

- Are you willing to sacrifice your life to save the life of another?
- What are you willing to sacrifice to save your own life?
- What are you willing to do to save the life of a fellow officer?
- What does the phrase "I've got your back" mean to you?
- What are you really willing to do to support your friends? What about the rest of your peers?

Let's do a quick culture check. Rate your answers to each of these ten questions with a 1-10 score with 10 being the highest, most positive, answer:

1) Is the law enforcement culture around you positive and helpful?
2) Does it provide support in times of need?
3) Does it encourage excellence?
4) Does it have an early warning system to detect emotional injuries?
5) Does it take care of your survivors?
6) Does it support and encourage wellness?
7) Does it support and encourage looking after your partner?
8) Does it provide for early intervention in the case of trauma?
9) Does it care for those who have fallen in battle but not died?
10) Does it enforce a strict code of honor?

Add up the total and give your culture a grade-school assessment of effectiveness. Would you score an "A (90-100%)?" How did you do? An 80? A 60? Whatever your score — *was it acceptable?*

Here are some strategic goals we might all adopt to build a positive and healthy culture within our agencies *and* all agencies in law enforcement:

1. Create a positive wellness culture that embraces and accepts the four areas of physical, mental, emotional and spiritual health.

2. Create a positive culture that truly walks it's talk and takes care of its own.

3. Create a leadership environment that fosters the concepts above, and encourages all to be leaders in their own right to support one another.

4. Create a leadership model that encourages executives and supervisors to recognize the value of maintaining the Tactical Resilience™ and well-being of their personnel.

5. Create a positive environment that encourages everyone to support everyone else rather than a culture that breaks down and provides little or no support.

6. Create an environment that *makes it safe* for anyone to ask for help.

7. Adopt a positive wellness culture that supports those who need help in any of the four areas of physical, mental, emotional or spiritual health.

8. Implement a two-pronged Top-Down/Bottom-Up approach to create a positive, wellness-oriented awareness within your agency.

Let's Talk Specifics

What's your action plan to adopt and implement a system of True Blue Valor™, personally and within your organization?

Develop a process for your personnel to initiate "Courageous Conversations." A courageous conversation is one that tactfully cuts to the critical issue and paves the way toward a successful resolution. Courageous conversations are neither easy nor painless. Nonetheless they are a critical part of any organization's health and development and a critical component of True Blue Valor™.

Converge International, an Australian Employee Assistance Program consulting and training firm, has on its Web site an excellent article entitled "Anatomy of a Courageous Conversation," adapted from Susan Scott's 2002 book, *Fierce Conversations*.
http://www.convergeinternational.com.au/news/article-library/anatomy-of-a-courageous-conversation

The article suggest's that you structure your conversation like this:

- Name the issue succinctly.
- Select a specific example that illustrates the behavior or situation you want to change.
- Describe the impact on you.
- Clarify what is at stake.
- Identify your contribution to this problem.
- Indicate your wish to resolve the issue.
- Invite the other person to respond.
- Listen, don't interrupt.

Susan Scott's book, *Fierce Conversations* is an excellent resource, and she offers extensive training on a broad array of "fierce conversations" through her firm, Fierce Inc., a global leadership development and training company that drives results by improving workplace communication. http://www.fierceinc.com/conversations-training

The Make It Safe Police Officer Initiative

Police Psychologist Jack Digliani, Ph.D., Ed.D., has created an initiative that he calls "Make It Safe," which was created to support and encourage officers to ask for psychological support when they need it. Jack has created 12 elements and an implementation guide to help you start the initiative at your agency. We have both together on our CopsAlive Web site. www.CopsAlive.com/suggests?jdmispackage/aysbook

Jack makes it safe *and* easy to ask for help since he also recommends a proactive, annual check-in with a mental health professional. This is a simple check-in, not a check-up, and can be done with a staff psychologist, a member of the Peer Support Team, a department Chaplain, private counselor, or other support resource. You can find more information on both of these programs at his Web site.
www.JackDigliani.com

I suggest that you do both personal and agency action planning about how you will work to change your organization's culture for the positive. Follow the link below to download my True Blue Valor™ Agency Cultural Change Action Planning Worksheet and True Blue Valor™ Personal Action Planning For Cultural Change Worksheet. Please use the sheets along with the ideas in this chapter to initiate actions in both your personal life and within your agency. http://www.CopsAlive.com/truebluevaloractionplanning/

Suggested Individual Actions:

- "Up" your integrity.
- Be responsible.
- Be compassionate.
- Don't play games or fall into unhealthy groups.
- Don't hang out with toxic people.
- Take care of your peers.
- Be honest.
- Be trust "worthy."
- Don't tease people about traumatic events.
- Find a better way to express "dark" humor.
- Don't kid yourself about how tough you are.
- Admit weakness.
- Ask for help.
- Make it safe for others to ask for help.
- Protect and serve your peers and your Self.
- No bullying.
- Have the courage to support colleagues who are supportive and to challenge people who are not.

Suggested Agency Actions:

- Have a comprehensive oath of office.

  The Clark County Sheriff's Office in Ohio has a comprehensive Oath Of Office that includes phrases like:

  "I will, keep my private life unsoiled as an example to all; maintain courageous calm in the face of danger, scorn, or ridicule; develop self restraint; and be constantly mindful of the welfare of others," and "I will never act officiously or permit personal feelings, prejudices, animosities, or friendship to influence my decisions."

- Have a comprehensive mission statement. Google "police mission statement examples" and you'll find examples adopted by some of the biggest agencies in the U.S. Thanks to Colonel Scott Hernandez, chief of the Colorado State Patrol, you can read his patrol's 2014-2018 Strategic Plan online. It's one of the best such documents I have ever read.

  https://www.colorado.gov/pacific/sites/default/files/2014-2018%20Colorado%20State%20Patrol%20Strategic%20Plan%20Final.pdf

- Have your current personnel write or update a statement of your organization's values and vision.

- Establish an agency motto or credo. I like the one from the Colorado State Patrol. It reads: "An Honor To Serve — A Duty To Protect."

- Establish an agency code of ethics. You can find samples at the PoliceCodes Web site. http://www.policecodes.org/police-code-of-ethics

- Make the oath, mission statement and values statement part of your agency's training so that each of them means something. All new hires should receive an orientation that includes the traditions, mission, values and goals of the agency.
    - Reinforce them.
    - Discuss them.
    - Update them.
    - Live them.
    - Walk your talk.

- Hold yourself and everyone else in the agency accountable.
- Promote leadership at every level of the organization — from everyone.
- Promote servant leadership.
- Get rid of the people who don't get it.

Jim Collins, author of *Built to Last*, *Good to Great* and *Great By Choice*, created one of the best business metaphors of all time in *Good to Great*, he suggests that a great leader is like a bus driver: where, in his "First Who — Then What" strategy,

You are a bus driver. The bus, your (agency), is at a standstill, and it's your job to get it going. You have to decide where you're going, how you're going to get there, and who's going with you.

Most people assume that great bus drivers (read: business leaders) immediately start the journey by announcing to the people on the bus where they're going — by setting a new direction or by articulating a fresh corporate vision.

In fact, leaders of companies that go from good to great start not with "where" but with "who." They start by getting the right people on the bus, the wrong people off the bus, and the right people in the right seats.

Maybe in law enforcement we should use a "police cruiser" or "paddy wagon" as our metaphor instead of a bus — but you get the idea.

Do you need to get your bus going in the right direction? I hope that you, as a law enforcement leader, will consider getting the right people onto your bus, getting the right people into the right seats, and getting the wrong people off your bus. You can learn more at Jim Collins' excellent Web site.

http://www.jimcollins.com/article_topics/articles/good-to-great.html

And here are additional resources from Jim Collins' Web site:

- Good to Great® Diagnostic Tool developed by Jim Collins
  http://www.jimcollins.com/tools/diagnostic-tool.pdf

- Jim's 12 Questions
  http://www.jimcollins.com/tools/12Questions.pdf

Forces That Change Culture:

Someone once told me you can't change a culture — you can only change people. That same person suggested that to do so you have to provide incentives for people to change their behaviors. Once their behaviors change you can start to mold a new and better organizational culture. *You* decide what will work in your agency.

Create Culture Change from the Top Down

- Write meaningful statements of your Mission, Values and Goals.
- Practice true visionary leadership.
- Establish a wellness program.
- Build a gym and add some personal trainers (either as paid staff, or volunteers from within the organization).
- Hire someone who knows about proper nutrition, and let that person stock the vending machines.
- Ensure that your personnel have access to knowledgeable psychological support, preferably from a staff police psychologist or at least a competent contract psychologist who knows about law enforcement people and programs.
- Create a proactive Peer Support program.
- Start a Mentoring Program for all levels of your agency.
- Establish a Family Support program.
- Take care of your survivors with a support program.
- Create a Chaplain's program.
- Implement True Blue Valor™ training.
- Write an agency Officer Intervention Plan.
- Establish a Critical Incident Response Plan that utilizes your peer support team and police psychologist.

- Review your disability insurance coverage and create a Disabled Employee Response Plan.
- Host annual Tactical Resilience™ training.
- Ensure that you provide training covering the primary areas of LODD (Line of Duty Death) Prevention — including arrest control, shooting, driving and the use of body armor and seat belts.
- Create a Wellness Resource Library.
- Build a sleep room.
- Create a quiet place for people to relax.
- Promote positive police community interactions.
- Practice true community policing.
- Institute role modeling regarding fair and impartial policing.
- Protect and serve inside the agency and out.
- Discuss what should be included in a Courageous Conversation.

Culture Change from the Bottom Up

- Be a person of integrity.
- Write your own personal motto or credo.
- Practice positive encouragement.
- Be a leader in all that you do.
- Be a servant leader.
- Support your peers and your administration.
- No bullying.
- Honor others both in your agency and in your community.
- Practice compassion.

- Express your gratitude daily.
- Protect and serve your Self, your family, your peers and your public.
- Offer help when it's needed.
- Ask for help when you need it.

Let me remind you that I believe law enforcement is the most noble profession on the planet, and that I have utmost faith in our ability within our profession to police ourselves as we grow and improve both ourselves and our culture.

- We are brave and honorable when it comes to the easy stuff.
- We honor our dead, and we say nice things at the funeral.
- We drive fast, and we carry guns.
- We catch bad guys, and we crack heads (when necessary).

But do we have courage and integrity when it comes to doing the really hard stuff:

- Taking care of those who are suffering from the work.
- Dealing with weakness and corruption.
- Recognizing that we are all human and can make mistakes.
- Telling colleagues that they are drinking too much or abusing their power.
- Looking after the families of those who have given the ultimate sacrifice.
- Showing compassion to the people we serve — *all* of them!

If we could start over and go into a factory to build a law enforcement culture, you would think we'd pay a lot of attention to making sure that the people backing us up:

- Have respect for race and diversity
- Understands that the more diverse our team — with men and women, all races, all religions, all orientations, different strengths, different mentalities — the better
- Are service oriented

- Are compassionate
- Are supportive of the whole team
- Have a team-first attitude
- Don't give up
- Are happy
- Are friendly
- Are well adjusted mentally and emotionally
- Are strong physically, mentally, emotionally and spiritually
- Are true professionals
- Have good communication skills
- Are curious
- Are intelligent
- Are honest and filled with integrity
- Are personally responsible
- Are community and customer focused
- Accept responsibility
- Are effective at problem solving
- Work to maintain organizational resilience and promote personal resilience
- Are positive team players
  You should aim to be this person!

As opposed to:
- Burned out
- Grouchy
- Prejudiced
- Biased

- Lazy
- Out of shape physically
- Always tired
- Always stressed
- Always angry
- Unethical
- Corrupt
- Spiteful

Don't be this person!

The FBI Law Enforcement Bulletin has an excellent article on this subject: "Characteristics of an Ideal Police Officer," by Larry E. Capps, M.S., the retired assistant chief of the Missouri City, Texas, Police Department. http://leb.fbi.gov/2014/december/perspective-characteristics-of-an-ideal-police-officer

I also highly recommend the book *The Advantage: Why Organizational Health Trumps Everything Else in* Busines,s by Patrick Lencioni.

So How Do We Build and Maintain a Healthy Culture?

We do this by building systems into the structure of our organizations with the use of displays, museums and educational programs that promote the traditions of our agencies. We state and support the mission, values and goals of our organization with posters and training throughout the year and throughout the agency, highlighting with rituals and symbolism, its mottoes, credos, pledges and codes of honor.

Consider the LAPD Motto: "*To Protect and to Serve.*"

Do you know the history of the Los Angeles Police Department's motto? In February 1955, the Los Angeles Police Department, through the pages of its internally produced *BEAT* magazine, conducted a contest for a police academy motto. The contest stated, "The motto should be one that in a few words would express some or all the ideals to which the Los Angeles police service is dedicated. It is possible that the winning motto might someday be adopted as the official motto of the Department."

Officer Joseph S. Dorobeck submitted the winning entry: "*To Protect and to Serve.*" It became the official motto of the Police Academy, and it was kept constantly before the officers in training as the aim and purpose of their profession. With the passing of time, the motto received wider exposure and acceptance throughout the department and has been adopted by law enforcement agencies around the world.

On November 4, 1963, the Los Angeles City Council passed an ordinance, and the credo has now been placed alongside the City Seal on the Department's patrol cars.

Reprinted from BEAT magazine, December 1963: http://www.lapdonline.org/history_of_the_lapd/content_basic_view/1128

What's Your Personal Motto or Credo?

Just as your agency should have a motto to promote professionalism and positive actions, so too should *you* have a personal motto or personal credo. Ask yourself these questions:

What's *your* personal motto or credo?

What's the motto or credo of *your* agency?

What's *your* pledge or code of conduct?

Write them yourself, do it as a team project, or even adopt the motto of LAPD: "To Protect and to Serve;" or the Colorado State Patrol's: "An Honor To Serve — A Duty To Protect."

Write them and then live by them! It's a matter of attitude.

Read our CopsAlive article about The Credo Project, which is a special educational initiative of the Police Chaplain Project dedicated to unlocking the power of CREDO in daily life.
http://www.CopsAlive.com/whats-your-credo

The Credo Project also offers Personal Credo development ideas.
http://www.chaplainusa.org/#our-story-1

There's even a downloadable suggestion sheet to help you write your own credo.
http://www.chaplainusa.org/s/writing-Your-CREDO.pdf

The Credo Project also offers a Credo Leadership Guide that provides strategies for putting Credo to work in your department.
http://www.chaplainusa.org/new-index-1/#credoleadershipguide

What About Our Attitudes And The Language We Use?

Just as positive "self-talk" is important to your personal resilience, you will find that positive attitudes and positive agency talk will build a positively resilient agency culture. What are people in your agency saying?

Phrases that promote an unhealthy agency culture:

- "Suicide is for psychos"
- "Mental health is for victims!"
- "He's a coward"
- "Don't let the door hit you in the ass on the way out"
- "If you don't like it here, we can hire ten more just like you to replace you tomorrow"
- "Toughen up and don't act like a wussy"
- "If I want your opinion I'll beat it out of you"
- "Your opinion doesn't count for shit around here"
- "Nobody cares about your problems"
- "Get tough or get out"

Using negative language can become habit — and when that occurs those negative thoughts and words become our beliefs. I choose to err on the side of being positive. As the Bible tells us: "As a man thinketh in his heart, so is he."

Consider how this applies to the concept of the Police Perfection Paradox:

Our own Expectations	The Reality of Cumulative Stress
I'm tough! I can handle anything!	Wrong! It will catch up with you!
If I keep quiet, problems go away	Untreated problems get worse
I'm as good as I was at age 21	Wrong! You're human, and you age
If my family only knew what I do…	Talking is good for everyone
It's too horrific to share	Wrong. They need to know to help — and they want to know

| If I need help I will lose my job | Ask early — when problems are small and treatable |
| Mental health is for victims! | Preventative care is all good — and good for all! |

Remember: The Armor Your Self™ concept is about building strength through physical, mental, emotional and spiritual repetition and conditioning *before* you need that strength so that you will have it when you or someone else needs it.

What else can we do? We can speak positively — and mean it!

Phrases that promote a healthy agency culture:

- When I say I've got your back, I mean it.
- When we say we are all one big family, we mean it — and we take care of our own.
- We protect and serve because we care.
- Law enforcement is a dangerous profession, but you are safe here at headquarters.
- You can feel safe asking me for help.
- We are all role models and mentors; we are masters at our craft.

Codes, Coins, Credos and Calls

As in many professions, we in law enforcement use many techniques to teach and remember important concepts — things like codes of honor, challenge coins, mottoes and credos, as well as what are called call/response phrases.

Honor Codes and Codes of Conduct

The IACP Oath of Honor reads:

> On my honor,
> I will never betray my badge,
> my integrity, my character,
> or the public trust.
> I will always have
> the courage to hold myself

and others accountable for our actions.
I will always uphold the Constitution,
my community and the agency I serve.

I have written a Code of True Blue Valor™ as a statement-of-integrity based upon the most cherished of law enforcement and human beliefs and ethical principles. It is a standard upon which we can base our ethical and compassionate decisions and about how to work with and support our peers. Being "True Blue" means supporting and developing the profession of law enforcement and its members by all means honorable, ethical and professional. In other words, it means being "True to the Blue."

The Code of True Blue Valor™ is a law enforcement honor code that says we will protect our brothers and sisters behind the badge from all the dangers, hidden and otherwise, that threaten life, health, family and happiness. If this code works for your agency, please use it. If you use it, please send us an email to let us know so we can brag on you.

The Code of True Blue Valor™

To maintain a code of honor and integrity to protect and to serve my community and to protect and support my peers.

True Blue Valor™ means having the courage to do what is right and to do the right things.

To Armor my Self physically, mentally, emotionally and spiritually so that I am better able to protect and to serve.

To Armor my Agency so that it is best able to protect and serve its people and its community.

To have the courage to walk my talk and look after my peers. If I say "We are all one family" and "I've got your back," then I will mean it.

As a matter of honor I pledge that on my watch, "No one gets left behind."

Challenge Coins

As I understand it, the modern challenge coin may have its roots all the way back to Roman times. But there is a common story of a well-to-do fighter pilot during World War I who had medallions struck for everyone in his flying squadron. Each member wore one in a small pouch around his neck, and in one instance that coin was the only way a pilot downed behind enemy lines was able to prove his identity to the resistance forces that found him.

Since then, many elite military and law enforcement units have used challenge coins to validate a person's membership in the unit. One form the challenge takes is that members found not to have their coins within arm's reach when challenged need to buy a round of drinks for the unit. Another way it's used is that if someone is noticed to be bragging in a bar about once being part of an elite military unit, someone else from that unit can issue a challenge by rapping their coin on the bar. If the braggart doesn't have a coin, the choice is either to buy drinks or take a pounding.

I think it's time we put the "challenge" back into Challenge Coins, and I think taking care of our own and True Blue Valor™ lends itself to this perfectly. That's why we have created a True Blue Valor™ Challenge Coin, which includes a pledge to protect and serve your brothers and sisters behind the badge and to take care of each other. As of this writing, the coin comes with a copy of the Code of True Blue Valor™, the True Blue Valor™ Challenge and a call/response phrase — all of which are used to instill these concepts into the psyche of your department. If you are interested, you can learn more about our True Blue Valor™ challenge coin our Web site.

www.TrueBlueValor.com

    The True Blue Valor™ Challenge Coin reads:

        On My Honor I Pledge

        We Take Care Of Our Own

        No One Gets Left Behind.

When we issue the True Blue Valor™ Challenge Coin we recite this challenge:

        I will offer help when it is needed

        I will accept help when it is offered

        I will ask for help long before it's too late

What are you willing to do?

Create your own Pledge

Here is an example pledge:

>When I say, "I've got your back," I mean it.
>
>When I say, "No one gets left behind," I mean it.
>
>My word is my bond.
>
>Partner to partner, I will support, protect and defend you.
>
>Peace Officer to Community, I will honor, protect and serve you.

Sean Connery, as King Arthur, issues a pledge in the movie *First Knight*:

>*May God grant us the wisdom to discover right, the will to choose it,*
>*and the strength to make it endure.*
>
>— *From the 1995 Columbia Pictures film about King Arthur called* First Knight, *directed by Jerry Zucker and starring Sean Connery, Richard Gere and Julia Ormond.*

The True Blue Valor™ Pledge:

>On My Honor I Pledge:
>
>>To Uphold The Code of True Blue Valor™
>>
>>First I Will Do No Harm
>>
>>I Am A Protector, Not a Bully
>>
>>I Will Treat My Co-workers with Respect and Dignity
>>
>>Because We Are All One Family
>>
>>I Will Not Look The Other Way When a Peer Is in Crisis
>>
>>I Will Offer Support and Encouragement When Needed
>>
>>I Will Take Charge and Intervene When Necessary
>>
>>I Will Protect and Serve My Country, Community, Family and Peers
>>
>>I Will Support and Encourage My Brothers and Sisters in Law Enforcement
>>
>>I Do All of This Because:
>>
>>>I "Walk My Talk"
>>>
>>>And I say:
>>>
>>>"We Take Care of Our Own"
>>>
>>>And On My Watch
>>>
>>>"No One Gets Left Behind."

Credos

In the 1976 Paramount Pictures film *The Shootist*, directed by Don Siegel, and starring John Wayne, Lauren Bacall, Ron Howard, Harry Morgan and James Stewart, John Wayne's character, the Shootist, has a personal credo: "I won't be wronged. I won't be insulted. I won't be laid a hand on. I don't do these things to other people, and I require the same from them."

Visit the Credo Project Web site and investigate its Personal Credo development ideas and its Credo Leadership Guide.

http://www.chaplainusa.org/#our-story-1

Call/Response Phrases

Call/Response phrases have been around for centuries and are used by law enforcement, the military, Hollywood films, comedians, musicians and teachers. For example:

Call: Who you gonna call?   *Response*: Ghostbusters!

In the 1995 Jerry Zucker film *First Knight*, here is the call/response used by the Knights of the Round Table, in which the call and the response were the same phrase:

"Brother to brother, yours in life and death."

The U.S. Army sometimes refers to these as "Jody Calls," and they are used to set cadence during long training runs. The best-known call is probably "Sound Off:"

Sound off! 1 — 2!

Sound off! 3 — 4!

(Cadence count) *1 - 2 - 3 - 4; 1 - 2 — 3 - 4!*

Known as the "Duckworth Chant," named after Private Willie Duckworth, this cadence still exists with variations in the different branches of the U.S. military. Duckworth's simple chant was tweaked and embellished by Army drill sergeants and their trainees, and the practice of creating elaborate marching chants spread to the Air Force, Marine Corps and Navy.

U.S. Navy pilots are said to use the following call/response cadence while running:

I don't know, but it's been said

Air Force wings are made of lead

I don't know, but I've been told

Navy wings are made of gold

A law enforcement call/response cadence for running is:

> *A six gun, a tin star, a horse named Blue*
> *In 1890 a cop held these true*
> *In 1930 the Tommy gun*
> *It made police work a lot more fun*

The Fire Service uses a variation of this call/response cadence while running:

> *When my grandmamma was 91*
> *She did PT just for fun*
> *When my grandmamma was 92*
> *She did PT better than you*
> *When my grandmamma was 93*
> *She did PT better than me*

Our True Blue Valor™ call/responses read:

> Call: *I protect you*   Response: *You protect me*
> Call: *I ask for help*   Response: *I help*
> Call: *You ask for help*   Response: *You help*
> Call: *Why?*   Response: *Because nobody gets left behind*
> Both: *Partner to Partner, Yours In Times of Crisis and Success*

A Second True Blue Valor™ call/response goes:

> Call: *I will help you if you ask*   Response: *I will help you if you ask*
> Call: *I will offer to help you, even if you don't ask*   Response: *I will offer to help you, even if you don't ask*
> Both: *Partner to Partner, Yours In Times of Crisis and Success*

Perhaps you can use a similar, powerful tool to instill the values and ethics you want to instill in your troops. Check out the IACP's Ethics Toolkit. It offers an excellent resource page with lots of great resources on these topics.
http://www.theiacp.org/Ethics-Toolkit

What Can You Do?

Focus on Prevention!

- Start a family support program.

- Acknowledge the importance of mental health.

- Change the stigma with the words: We have to take care of our own mental health and watch out for that of our peers.

- Implement police psychologist Jack Digliani's Make It Safe Initiative, and investigate his recommendation for an Annual Check-In.
http://www.CopsAlive.com/suggests?jdcom/aysbook
www.JackDigliani.com

- If you don't have a Proactive Peer Support Program at your agency, start one.

- Implement our True Blue Valor™ "Fire Spotters & Smoke Jumpers" Concept. The Fire Spotters & Smoke Jumpers Concept is meant to be somewhat less formal than a Proactive Peer Support Program and should not be used as a replacement for effective peer support. In a nod to the Fire Service's quick response to forest fires, "fire spotters" are employees to whom you provide training to look for problems and summon assistance for a person in trouble. A "smoke jumper" is someone with more specialized training who can do an immediate check-in with an employee about whom someone has a concern and who can make appropriate referrals to mental health professionals if needed. This program must be tied into your existing psychological support process.

- Start a Mentoring Program at your agency. Mentoring is a great way to create and maintain a positive culture of excellence and success. Mentoring can be used to reinforce positive traditions and organizational best practices so that every member of the agency has a chance to receive support and guidance from a more experienced mentor.

- Start a Law Enforcement Suicide prevention discussion within your agency.

The first thing to do, no matter where you are on this continuum, is to start a discussion. This is no easy, black-and-white subject. There are lots of gray areas here and, because we are dealing with human beings, there are lots of variables. You have to create something that works for your people and your organization. You can find free resources to help you on our CopsAlive Web site.
www.CopsAlive.com/SuicidePrevention

We all know that most people who need help don't want help. We see it every day in our jobs and it's only worse when the person who needs help is one of our own.

Final thoughts about True Blue Valor™

The best way to protect the "thin blue line" is not through a "code of silence" but with a code of honor and excellence.

When you have the kind of expectations placed upon us because we're in law enforcement, then what we do off duty is just as important as what we do on duty. The bottom line is that it's about a *sense of duty*.

Earlier in the chapter I asked whether we have prepared ourselves to counsel and care.

We can do an intervention on a drunken subject or a suicidal party — but do we use these same skills on our peers when we need to?

Where are the classes on "Mental First Aid," "Emotional Survival Techniques" and "Spiritual Damage Assessment?" Where is the training for how to help a peer who is suffering on the inside, or how to find the courage to tell colleagues they are screwing up?

While this chapter is about changing the culture, this book is about giving you ideas and actionable tactics to effect change right after you put this book down. Even if I don't get around to answering all the above questions within these pages, know that I and everyone on the faculty of the Law Enforcement Survival Institute is dedicated to answering these questions and creating those training programs if they don't already exist. If they do exist, we are determined to help spread the word. You don't have to reinvent the wheel. There is a lot of work still to be done in this area, and we are doing our best to pioneer new tools and techniques while supporting all the good men and women who are trying to help those of us in law enforcement.

Resources to Help You

The resources section for this chapter alone was lengthy, so we turned that into a PDF document and put it up on our CopsAlive Web site for you to download at your leisure, and for free.

http://www.CopsAlive.com/suggests?ch5resources/aysbook

CHAPTER 6

The Tactical Resilience™ Model

What Is Resiliency?

Thus far I've discussed the Armor Your Self™ model and building support systems within your agency and organizational culture. I've also talked about the hidden dangers of a law enforcement career and changing your strategies for coping with those dangers. These strategies must be comprehensive, as you'll use them to condition your Self to build strength physically, mentally and emotionally, as well as spiritually. It's critically important to build systems, which include tactics and techniques that grow into positive wellness habits and will make up the building blocks for your personal systems that strengthen your character as a human being. It's also important for you to consider the tactics and behaviors that serve as your contribution to building organizational systems that will build a positive wellness culture within your agency.

I am aware that what I've just written is a tad abstract, and I ask you to bear with me. It's necessary to look at the big picture before we dive into the next chapters, which are devoted to giving you concrete examples of techniques and tactics that will help you survive — and even thrive — as a law enforcement officer.

The key to the Armor Your Self™ model is that it's a system for building *Tactical Resilience*™. So let's look at what Tactical Resilience™ is so that we have a clear idea of what we are trying to accomplish.

Here are a couple of questions to ask yourself:

- What is *resiliency*?
- Why do I need it?
- What do I want to accomplish in life?
- What do I want to accomplish in my career?
- How can I do these things safely and effectively?
- What's the best I can be as a person?
- How can I get to be that person?
- And how can I make sure I remain that person?

These are important questions, because your truthful, candid answers will set you on the road of living with the highest possible quality of life; to building a safe and rewarding career; and to achieving all that you can possibly hope to achieve.

When we think about *resilience*, we're basically talking about the ability to be flexible, adaptable and tough enough to withstand extreme psychological distress *and* still bounce back to your normal state — or something stronger.

The American Psychological Association defines resilience as "the process of adapting well in the face of adversity, trauma, tragedy, threats or significant sources of stress — such as family and relationship problems, serious health problems or workplace and financial stressors. It means 'bouncing back' from difficult experiences."

Studies also show that one primary factor in resilience is having caring and supportive relationships within and outside the family — relationships that create love and trust, provide role models and offer encouragement and reassurance, which help to bolster a person's resilience.

Additional factors associated with resilience include:

- A capacity to make realistic plans and take steps to carry them out.
- A positive view of yourself and confidence in your strengths and abilities.
- Skills in communication and problem solving.
- A capacity to manage strong feelings and impulses.

All of these are factors that people can develop in themselves.

Source: http://www.apa.org/helpcenter/road-resilience.aspx

Tactical Resilience™ goes beyond these APA definitions and descriptions because law enforcement is an occupation that challenges its employees with the prospect of confronting extreme traumas and tragedy almost daily. I define Tactical Resilience™ as a quality of *intentional* human strength and fitness that can be developed and, once developed, exhibited through the mind, body, brain and spirit of a police officer or other law enforcement or military professional. Such resilience allows officers to withstand the rigors and hidden emotional, physical, spiritual and physiological dangers of continuous high-threat, high-stress situations.

Everyone has the ability to be resilient, and some people are naturally more resilient that others. Different people, in the same situation, demonstrate different levels of resilience, and everyone demonstrates different levels of resilience on different days or in different circumstances. Your goal should be to build a system that allows you to leverage and develop your natural resilience so that you can reach a more powerful state of tactical or intentional resilience.

Along with the four factors of conditioned *physical, mental, emotional* and *spiritual strength* of the Armor Your Self™ concept, *three other factors* bind with these elements to create an effective system of Tactical Resilience™. These three other factors act as the glue to hold this Tactical Resilience™ system together and they are:

- A positive mind-set,
- Self-mastery — perhaps called willpower, self-control or self-discipline, and
- Positive social support.

Building Tactical Resilience™ is not easy and can't be done overnight. It's not a magic potion or a quick fix. It takes time and effort to develop and even more energy and effort to maintain it. What's more: Resilience is *not* a substitute for professional mental health support or services, and you have to build resilience *before* you need it.

Tactical Resilience™ is what we have to strive for in order to survive our careers in law enforcement with a sound mind, body and spirit. It is what we need to be able to muster in order to function well during our careers so that we thrive and can enjoy many more happy and productive years after we retire. What's important to grasp is that making your Self resilient is a very challenging process, and the steps needed may be different for you than the steps others must take to achieve their resilience.

A key part of building Tactical Resilience™ is getting to know yourself and discovering what works for you — and what doesn't. Be open-minded, experiment, and do your own research. Try things out and keep records of how they affect you. Talk to your peers and ask what works for them. Talk to people in other departments and learn what they think is important. The most important thing is that you must do the work required to build healthy habits.

Steven Pressfield, author of *The War of Art*, which I highly recommend, wrote: "Socrates demonstrated long ago that the truly free individual is free only to the extent of his own self-mastery." The worst thing you can do is what so many of us have been doing for years, and that is to live in denial about how this job negatively affects you and to do nothing to minimize those negative effects.

Do Your Own Threat Assessment

I've described "Blue Trauma Syndrome" as a spectrum of negative physical, mental, emotional and spiritual side effects that manifest themselves as a result of a career in law enforcement. Simply saying, "all that ails law enforcement are large doses of negative stress" is too simplistic. Rather, I choose to use a larger, more encompassing term that leads us to further discussion, research and self-discovery. Our goal in building Tactical Resilience™ needs to be more than merely surviving; we need to thrive. To do that, we need to build a plan and a system that intentionally develops resilience not only to withstand these hidden dangers, but also to avoid those hidden dangers so that we can flourish in our personal lives and our careers.

The process I call Armor Your Self™ is the foundation of Tactical Resilience™. Armor Your Self™ is designed to improve our emotional toughness, physiological elasticity and psychological effectiveness so that we can increase our ability to withstand and recover from excessive or cumulative stresses, which lead to Blue Trauma Syndrome. As we build our Tactical Resilience™, we strengthen our physical and spiritual fitness, and make ourselves more able to endure the hardships, traumas, tragedies and adversity we see every day.

Ask yourself: Are you thriving? What are the threats to your physical, mental, emotional and spiritual health? What drains your resolve and depresses your attitude? What ruins your day and causes you anger and frustration?

These questions are about the threats you might be taking for granted as "just the way things are." Well, I suggest that "just the way things are" is not acceptable. These threats and influences can be removed or minimized with a good dose of resiliency. Think about this as Blue Trauma Management. The goal of Blue Trauma Management is more comprehensive than stress management alone. Whereas stress management is about managing physiological effects that occur within the body, Blue Trauma Management is about managing all of the physiological, mental, emotional and spiritual influences that have a negative impact on the body of a law enforcement professional. Consider adopting the Tactical Resilience™ Model and building a system that will work in your life.

The Tactical Resilience™ Model

The Tactical Resilience™ Model embodies seven key factors that work together cumulatively to produce a strong, healthy, ethical and well-grounded individual. It's a process made up of techniques and tactics that you *consciously*, *intentionally* and *regularly* use to build positive daily habits.

The Seven Key Factors in Building Tactical Resilience™:

- The Physical Factor
- The Mental Factor
- The Emotional Factor
- The Spiritual Factor
- The Mind-set Factor

- The Self-mastery Factor
- The Social Factor

Ideally, all these factors are also coupled with the concepts of building a healthy and resilient agency with Armor Your Agency™ strategies, as well as with a strong and healthy police culture fortified with the concept of True Blue Valor™. Additionally, the Social Factor is a two-way street and can be amplified through a strong network of community policing and leadership, which supports both law enforcement professionals and the community members they serve and protect.

The Tactical Resilience™ Model involves building the three pillars of individual, agency and community resilience, and each pillar works synergistically to buttress the other two.

Since most of the rest of this book is about the first four key factors in building Tactical Resilience™, I'll spend most of this chapter discussing the last three factors.

The Mind-set Factor

The Merriam-Webster dictionary describes mind-set as "a mental attitude or inclination, a fixed state of mind." For our purposes "mind-set" is *the physical, mental, emotional and spiritual programming that sets our mind onto a positive task*. The task can be a simple daily activity, or the process of overcoming an immediate crisis or an impending challenge. The positive or negative focus of our mind-set can either help or hinder the outcomes of those daily tasks or those major crises and challenges — hence its relationship to attitude.

Let's focus our attention on creating positive mind-sets for success and operate with the assumption that we can intentionally, proactively and consciously manifest positive mind-sets to accomplish our desired goals no matter how challenging the situation confronting us. Having a positive mind-set is all about having the proper commitment and determination. I'm convinced you have nothing to lose and everything to gain by adopting a positive, success-oriented mind-set, and I'm absolutely sure that you can be damaged if you accept a fear-based, losing mind-set. This is as simple as changing your "mind" and can be done in an instant. Simple does not mean easy, and I think you can condition strength in this area with regular, daily practice and conditioning.

The argument could be made that for *The Book of Five Rings* that Miyamoto Musashi wrote after spending his life studying both Buddhism and swordsmanship in order to teach about not only the art of fighting but also the art of living, and in which he used his knowledge to create a philosophy that includes both the concepts of willpower/self-control and mind-set. If you examine his final *Book of Emptiness*, you will find some of his musings in which he suggests that if you can rid your Self of "stopping mind" you can achieve a state of *Satori* or enlightenment. I don't know enough about enlightenment to advise you, but I believe that if you can learn to master your Self in both the areas of self-control and mind-set, you can achieve Tactical Resilience™.

Think of mind-set as your way of programming your internal *mental computer processor* for success or failure. On a practical level, let's think of mind-set as a definitive statement you make to yourself about what you resolve to do. You will then support and encourage a positive mind-set with positive self-talk and vivid, positive success focused visualization in your mind's eye.

You activate your mind-sets by repeating a phrase in your head that motivates you to take the right actions or make the right decisions, and you support that motivation with a mental image of your success. By repeating these positive affirmations, you support the successes you intend to achieve.

This is very much like strengthening your mind by the regular, daily conditioning of strong positive thoughts. Don't sidetrack your success by thinking of this as some kind of self-help mumbo jumbo (negative mind-set), rather, think of it as a proven technique (positive mind-set) used by many high performers and world-class athletes. It is also important to note that many of us don't even notice the negative mind-sets we slip into and which derail our positive intentions. Negative mind-sets are corrected by first noticing them, and then by reprogramming them with positive self-talk.

Here are some examples of positive mind-sets to help you in your life:

Winning Mind-sets

1. "Warrior Mind-set"

    Lots of officers have indoctrinated themselves with a *Warrior Mind-set* for surviving life-and-death situations. Based on the warrior codes of many ancient and current cultures, the Warrior Mind-set is designed to generate an unstoppable will to survive and take a life only when absolutely necessary. This mind-set is also coupled with a code of ethics and integrity about how warriors conduct themselves in a peaceful society. Components of this code of conduct include: Service, Compassion, Honesty, Justice, Honor, Strength, Courage, Leadership, Peace, and Integrity.

What's your code of conduct?

Activate this mind-set with the phrase:
"*I Am an Honorable Warrior*" or "*I Am a Noble Warrior.*"

2. "Guardian Mind-set"
    The Guardian Mind-set offers a different perspective on protecting and serving our citizens by thinking of ourselves as protectors, not as soldiers. Currently there is a lot of talk in our profession (as well as among politicians and the public) about replacing law enforcement's Warrior Mind-set with that of a *Guardian*. While I fully understand the principles of this argument, and while I believe that in some cases it may be appropriate, I believe that most people overlook the fact that the concept of a warrior is deeply rooted in the history of many cultures, and contains guiding principles of ethics and integrity about warrior conduct in a peaceful society. I believe that the Guardian Mind-set is a more passive approach and overlooks the issue that we may have to proactively act to take a life or sacrifice our own life to protect the lives of others. I still prefer the Warrior Mind-set because it not only prepares officers to be willing to risk their lives, but also prepares them for the possibility of having to take another person's life, and these are not passive actions. If you think the Guardian Mind-set does those two things, then that mind-set would be fine; but I do not believe that it does.

    If, however, you decide to adopt this mind-set, activate it with the phrase:
    "*I Am a Guardian*" or "*I Am Society's Guardian.*"

3. "Discomfort Mind-set"

    Many people in many parts of the world cherish being uncomfortable or even miserable. Only in the West have we become so complacent and focused upon our comfort that we don't remember what life was like when times were hard. Consequently, we only encounter the *Discomfort Mind-set* when we need to bear down and get tough. Many extreme athletes and high performers understand this mind-set. They focus on drawing strength from their discomfort and pushing through the pain.

    Activate this mind-set with any of these phrases, or create your own, to help yourself toughen up and go the extra mile:

    "*A little cold, a little hungry and a little miserable.*"
    "*When we're expecting the worst, the best always seems easy.*"
    "*The only easy day was yesterday.*"
    "*When the going gets tough, the tough get going.*"
    "*No pain, no gain.*"
    "*No one said that life was going to be easy.*"
    "*Hara hachi bu.*"*

    * "Hara hachi bu" also known as the "80% Rule" has it's origins in Okinawa, where people remind themselves to stop eating when their stomachs are 80% full.

4. "Community Leader Mind-set"

    A leader is someone who sees a problem and takes action to solve it. That's what law enforcement professionals do every day, and by taking on the mind-set of a *Community Leader*, you don't need to solve problems all by yourself. Rather, you assemble information, resources and the necessary people to solve them within your neighborhood, community or patrol beat. We need to spend more time being *proactive* rather than reactive.

    The Community Leader mind-set for law enforcement takes ownership and responsibility to its ultimate outcome. This does not mean that we solve every problem by ourselves, but rather we are masters at assembling teams from within the community that can solve these problems cooperatively. By the very nature of our business we are the people who others call when they have a problem, and it's our job to try to help them. Many a modern officer has lost sight of this in the belief that the job is to simply make arrests. We may not be able to solve every problem, but we usually have a good idea about who can and about additional resources are available to our community's members. Our job as law enforcement community leaders is to bring all of those components together for success. This is just good, old-fashioned police work that's sometimes called Community Policing today.

Activate this mind-set with the phrase:
"I Am a Community Leader."

5. "Protect & Serve Mind-set"

    The motto of "To Protect and to Serve," so common in law enforcement today, was created by Los Angeles Police Department Officer Joseph S. Dorobek in 1955 as a motto for L.A.'s police academy. According to the LAPD Web site, "'To Protect and to Serve' became the official motto of the Police Academy, and it was kept constantly before the officers in training as the aim and purpose of their profession. With the passing of time, the motto received wider exposure and acceptance throughout the department, and on November 4, 1963, the Los Angeles City Council passed the necessary ordinance and the credo [was] placed alongside the City Seal on the Department's patrol cars."

What are your beliefs about the words "Protect" and "Serve?" Can you use "To Protect and to Serve" as an activator to create a positive mind-set of positive policing service in your life?

Activate this mind-set with the phrases:
"To Protect and to Serve" or *"My Job Is to Protect and to Serve."*

6. "Talk It Out Mind-set"

    We have been unconsciously programming such unproductive and unhealthy mind-sets as "Don't Be A Pussy" and "Suck It Up" for years in law enforcement. They are not serving us, and these and other mind-sets like them have to go. They keep us from asking for help when we really need it, and they keep us from talking about what's bothering us. The problem with these old and outdated notions is that they cause people to bottle up emotions for years, and instead of the negative emotions going away, they percolate and act as toxins in our bodies and minds. By not treating traumas and emotional problems when small and easily managed, we instead suppress them and allow them to fester and grow.

    We need to *get real* and really serious about our mental and emotional health. We wouldn't leave a physical wound untreated, so why do we think that suppressing emotional wounds makes them go away? Certainly, in combat you have to pack these issues away until after the battle when you can deal with them; but in law enforcement the battle should be over at the end of our shift. We need to make it safe to ask for help so that we can get help when we need it.

    One simple way to treat basic emotional and psychological trauma is to talk to someone about how you're feeling. Talk to a friend, chaplain or loved one; talk to a peer support team member, or talk to someone from EAP or Psychological Services — but talk to someone. You should also be willing to listen when someone else asks you for help. Remember: we also need to build support *before* we need it, and talking to others about small issues is one way to build the foundation for the support we might need when something becomes a crisis for us. Finally, I'm not just talking about telling tough-guy war stories and "yucking it up" at the end of a shift. This is about trusting each other enough to express what's *really* on your mind and what's bothering you. In order to do that, though, you need to be self-aware enough to recognize things that are, or should be, troubling you emotionally.

    Activate this mind-set with the phrases:
    "*Talk It Out*" or "*It's Important To Talk.*"

7. "Ask For Help Mind-set"
   One of the hardest things to do in life is to ask for help — but in law enforcement it's critical to our success, health and well-being. Even though we act independently in our jobs, we are always dependent upon a team that's there to support us with answers, assistance, back-up and peer support. We need to be brave enough to ask for all these things when we need help. That help can be anything from a simple question on a case or assistance in dealing with the emotional aftermath of a particularly disturbing call.

   The "Tough It Out" mentality we've had for years isn't working and it's not healthy. "Tough It Out" can be a positive mind-set in the heat of battle or during challenging moments, but it works against you as a negative mind-set if you rely upon it all the time. You have to know when to trust others enough to let down your guard. We need to take on a sports mentality here and fall back on our team for support. We need to be able to ask for support as well as to offer it when someone needs it. We need to change our culture so that it's acceptable, expected and safe to ask for help and, where it's appropriate, to be a team player in providing it.

   Activate this mind-set with the phrases:
   "*It's Okay to Ask for Help*" or "*Ask for Help.*"

8. "No Regrets Mind-set"
   I love Lee Ann Womack's song, "I Hope You Dance." The lyrics present a list of opportunities in life that we all confront, and suggest that when you have to make a choice between two conflicting opportunities, you choose the one where you can "dance." What she suggests, I think, is that none of us wants to get to the end of our lives, look back and see all the opportunities we didn't take and regret that we missed them. Rather, we should dance and take risks and then enjoy life when we can because such opportunities may never come again. This is about creating an attitude about living life to its fullest so that we don't later regret opportunities we let pass.

Activate this mind-set with the phrase:

"*No Regrets*" or "*Dance*."

Losing Mind-sets

I don't want to give losing mind-sets anything more than a passing glance; I just want to help you identify and remove them from your mentality. Here are a few destructive mind-sets you ought to reject: the *Suck It Up Mind-set* (which focuses on the negative instead of the positive and is used to punish rather than encourage); the *Don't Be A Wussy Mind-set*; the *You're A Loser Mind-set*; the *Power Rules Mind-set*; the *Arrogance Mind-set*; the *I'm Invincible Mind-set*; the *I'm Superman Mind-set*; and, as we talked about earlier, the *Get Tough Mind-set* taken to the extreme so that you don't know or notice when you need help. Be on constant lookout for losing mind-sets and program them right out of your head with positive self-talk and success-oriented visualizations. Use your mind-set to program your brain and immediately replace losing mind-sets with positive ones.

The Self-mastery Factor

At this point you can probably see there is still a missing piece, one that's more about strength than about motivation. The missing piece is the *inner strength* that is part mental, part emotional, part physical and part spiritual — the inner strength that we draw from some hidden wellspring and which encourages and sustains us when we need it most. That missing piece is sometimes called *willpower, mental toughness, self-discipline* or *self-control*. I use the term self-mastery because I believe it's all-encompassing and overarching, and incorporates all of the other terms I just mentioned. I also like the term self-mastery because by it's very essence is something you have to work hard at to obtain in order to build inner strength and character.

The Merriam-Webster dictionary defines self-mastery as "the power to control one's actions, impulses, or emotions," and I believe that encapsulates this missing piece because it involves the intentional segment of Tactical Resilience in developing mastery over your responses to external and internal stimuli. Self-mastery is about the Do's and Don'ts in your life: Doing the things you should do and not doing the things that you shouldn't do. As easy as that sounds, it confounds most human beings in the areas of diet, health, hard work, drinking, exercise, spending, dating, and a host of other critical life activities.

Willpower is our human capability to muster the energy to make change, handle tough decisions or complete difficult challenges, etc. And willpower has lots of other names: self-discipline, grit, determination, perseverance, resolve, drive, strength of mind, strength of will, iron will, resolution, restraint, decisiveness, doggedness, steadfastness, indomitable spirit, and on and on. In the end it's all about mastering your Self.

Building Willpower and Self-control

Willpower is actually three powers — "I will, I won't and I want" — according to Kelly McGonigal, Ph.D., in her book, *The Willpower Instinct: How Self-control Works, Why It Matters, and What You Can Do to Get More of It.* (New York: Avery, 2012.)

We all must master not only our willpower, but we must also build and enhance it continuously. The very act of doing your daily strengthening and conditioning routines will build self-discipline to do things you need to do when you need to do them. You will also learn that, as you get stronger physically, mentally, emotionally and spiritually, you're building your own inner strength.

Think of your will as a muscle that needs to be strengthened and conditioned regularly. Willpower can become flabby and weak if you neglect it. But every time you fulfill a commitment or avoid a bad habit, you're strengthening your will and gaining mastery of your Self. You can consciously, and intentionally test your Self regularly by making promises and commitments that you must meet. When you do, your will becomes stronger. Also, when you intentionally don't do things that you know are wrong or bad for your health, you're also building that same strength of will.

I encourage you to do more research to find out as much as you can about strengthening and maintaining your self-discipline. You'll learn that your willpower can be weakened if you are fatigued or not properly fueled and nourished.

Willpower isn't just a skill. It's a muscle, like the muscles in your arms or legs, and it gets tired as it works harder, so there's less power left over for other things.

If you want to do something that requires willpower — like going for a run after work — you have to conserve your willpower muscle during the day,
— Charles Duhigg, The Power of Habit: Why We Do What We Do In Life And Business.
https://www.goodreads.com/work/quotes/17624817-the-power-of-habit

Willpower Training

Willpower is the ability to control your Self, either to do something positive, or to avoid doing something negative, or to find the balance between what you want and what's good for you. Think of willpower in terms of impulse control to deal with dieting, exercise or abstinence from things like drugs, smoking, gambling or the like. Willpower is also the inner power or strength to get things done, such as working out, cleaning out the garage, writing a book, etc.

You can use willpower to make things happen — resist doing unhealthy things — and you develop it the same way you build strength and precision in your life: by repeated practice.

Try These Simple Willpower Exercises:

Resist snoozing (sleeping in) for 30 days

Resist dessert for 30 days

Resist drinking any alcohol for 30 days

Resist chocolate for 30 days

Resist sex for 30 days

Resist watching TV for 30 days

Do a daily workout for 30 days

Do your four 15-minute AYS workouts every day for 30 days

Wear your seat belt every day — forever!

Floss your teeth every day for 30 days

Remember the concepts of Habit Seeding, Feeding and Weeding. How does that apply to your willpower development? What habits can you add to, or delete from your life to strengthen it?

Try willpower development as a team exercise that uses positive peer pressure and positive Habit Coaching.

Habit Coaching is having a professional or peer assist and encourage you as you build positive and healthy habits. Your coach works with you to identify the right tactics and techniques to help you seed and nurture positive habits. Your coach also helps you weed out any distracting or negative habits by helping you identify the bad triggers or working to get those triggers to spark positive tactics instead of negative ones. Finally, your coach works with you to identify proper rewards for your positive habits and to adjust the reward system for negative habits so that they are not as appealing as they once were. Your Habit Coach could be a full-time coach helping you strengthen yourself, or it could be a partner with whom you are trading support so that each of you works on what you each need by trading encouragement and coaching.

Who can you get to be your Habit Coach?

The Social Factor

Despite what you may have heard from your drill instructor in the military or police academy, all human beings need love, encouragement and emotional support. The fact that we see such high numbers of police officer suicides, as well as a host of other negative side effects from this career tells me that *support* is one factor of resilience that many have neglected.

The *Social Factor of Tactical Resilience*™ is the support system you build for your Self. It can include family, peers, professionals, your support team, or any of a host of mechanisms that you surround yourself with to nurture, love, encourage and support you. You have an obligation here, too, and that's that you have to invest *trust* in your support system and share the honest truth about what's going on in your mind and spirit with the people who are part of it. I know our law enforcement culture hasn't been very good at encouraging this in the past, and our suicide statistics make the case for why this isn't working. We all need a support network — and it doesn't just appear automatically. You have to build it, and you have to build it *before* you need it. You build it by sharing little bits of your Self over time and by investing your time in helping others so that they trust you and so they might reciprocate when you need their help. Remember, too, that the community that you serve and protect can, and should, be a part of your support system.

The Social Factor in Building Officer, Agency and Community Resilience

Creating a positive law enforcement culture is only one part of building a strong law enforcement profession. We also have to build trust and support within the communities we serve. Strong bonds between the people and the police support serve our officers, just as strong officers can better support our community. No one can thrive in law enforcement for very long if everyone you meet in your community hates you. Community support and trust will also encourage and sustain us as a critical part of our Social Tactical Resilience™ Factor. I don't think this happens easily. It takes individual leadership and initiative, and I encourage you to be the person to initiate that interaction. I believe that one of the core responsibilities of effective law enforcement is to develop strong police-community ties that stem from strong law enforcement officers as community leaders.

> *Be the change that you wish to see in the world.*
> — Mahatma Gandhi

The Law Enforcement Officer Community Action Leadership (LoCAL) Project

The Law Enforcement Officer Community Action Leadership (LoCAL) Project is an offshoot of the Law Enforcement Survival Institute's belief that resilient communities support resilient officers, and unhealthy communities promote unhealthy officers. To that end we at the Institute have created a project to encourage beat cops to develop their personal leadership skills by promoting old-fashioned community policing strategies in cooperation with neighborhood leaders. LoCAL's cooperative teams work to promote healthy police/community relationships and build social capital in neighborhoods.

We believe that the Four Pillars of Procedural Justice (Fairness, Voice, Transparency and Impartiality) are also the mainstays of Community Policing and promote good practice for internal agency activities, as well as mainstays that build and maintain community trust. The concepts of Fairness, Voice, Transparency and Impartiality work hand-in-hand with individual, agency and community resilience. The Law Enforcement Survival Institute (LESI) will continue to develop programs and projects that build upon these principles and concepts.

Examples of the Tactical Resilience™ Model in Action

I've proposed in this chapter some general strategies important for your most efficient daily functioning. Some simple *tactics* you can use to build your *physical* strength include: getting regular exercise, eating a nutritious diet, drinking at least 64 ounces of clean and pure water daily and getting 7 to 8 hours of sleep every 24 hours.

Other simple tactics you can use to build your *mental* resilience include brain training, or simple exercises that boost your strength in areas such as situational awareness, memory, mental flexibility, problem solving, decision making, reaction times and attention of mental focus.

As for *emotional* and *spiritual* strength, some simple tactics you can try are to include scheduling into your daily activities quiet time, reading, study, contemplation, discussion and meditation.

To promote a positive *mind-set* I've suggested that you can work daily to program your attitude with positive internal Self-talk and mental visualization of success and accomplishment. You have control of the outcomes of your attitude, and weeding out negative mind-sets is one way to reprogram your Self for success.

Self-mastery is the constant and ongoing process to build your inner strength by doing the things you should do and not doing the things you shouldn't. It also involves having the self-discipline to balance your needs with your wants.

Strong *Social Support* comes from our loved ones, our family, our peers, supervisors, and even the people we serve and protect. They all serve as our emotional "first line of defense." We all need social connections to make us stronger, and we build them by investing trust in others and being someone whom others can trust. Talk and openness are the currency of social support and even the most old-fashioned and conservative of law enforcement professionals should invest in them.

Our individual resilience is supported by *agency resilience*, which is built upon the programs and policies the agency uses to support its resilient people. Critical among these programs and policies are psychological services, peer support, family support, chaplain's services, and health and wellness education and resources.

Also, anything within our profession that works to develop a *positive law enforcement culture* of support and wellness also promotes the Tactical Resilience™ model. Programs such as True Blue Valor™ or Jack A. Digliani's Make It Safe Police Officer Initiative work toward accomplishing the goal of developing Tactical Resilience™.

Finally, the Tactical Resilience™ model becomes a healthy cycle as it works to support individual, agency and community resilience by building social bonds between law enforcement professionals and the people they serve through active community police interaction. I've mentioned our LoCAL project, but there are many others serving as models around the United States and elsewhere.

Programs such as the Mount Kisco, New York, Police Department's "Police and Community Together" (PACT) program accomplish this very well. PACT worked to build a relationship between police and their city's immigrant Latino population by organizing community meetings at local houses of worship; providing cultural competency training for police officers, and recruiting volunteer community liaisons who assisted the police by connecting them with their communities.

Another example is the Teen/Police Dialogue Workshops created by the Hawthorne, California, Police Department. This initiative provided a positive and tangible engagement opportunity between African-American teens and police officers.

These two examples are described the U.S. Department of Justice COPS Office's publication, "Police Perspectives: Building Trust in a Diverse Nation #2. How to Serve Diverse Communities." (You can find a link to download a copy in the resources section at the end of this chapter.)

In sum, the Tactical Resilience™ model is a good foundation for law enforcement because it focuses on comprehensive strategies like whole-person wellness and whole-organization wellness and combines them with whole-community wellness processes. Resilience is about being flexible and bouncing back from challenges that apply to us as individuals, organizations and entire communities. Because law enforcement is such an integral part of every community, it makes sense that we should lead initiatives that build social capital and foster community resilience. When we do this, we all become stronger.

The Tactical Resilience™ System

The Tactical Resilience™ System takes everything I've described about the Tactical Resilience™ model and shapes its components into processes that make the theories come to life. Remember that a system is a set of connected parts, which form a complex whole — in particular, a set of principles or procedures that build an organized scheme or method. So in order to turn our model into a system, we need to create processes and procedures. We also need to do some action planning that begins with individual, agency and community threat assessments. The results of those assessments form the basis for developing our strategies, which in turn we use to build our system.

In this book, I talk about doing just that by taking the Armor Your Self™ strategies of strengthening your Self physically, mentally, emotionally and spiritually, and then using these tactics and techniques to develop strong, positive habits. These habits are then assembled into personal systems to develop individual character and, in a law enforcement agency, to build organizational culture.

Our system of Tactical Resilience™ also includes the components of individual mind-set, Self-mastery for willpower and social connection, and these are all coupled with agency and community support programs to create a comprehensive system of health and wellness.

Resources to Help You

- "Police Perspectives: Building Trust in a Diverse Nation #2: How to Serve Diverse Communities." Edited by Caitlin Gokey and Susan Shah:
  http://ric-zai-inc.com/Publications/cops-p345-pub.pdf

- If you want to do some quick reading about willpower, read Steven Pinker's review of the book *Willpower: Rediscovering the Greatest Human Strength* by Roy F. Baumeister and John Tierney: Steven Pinker, "The Sugary Secret of Self-Control," *New York Times*, September 2, 2011 at:
  http://www.nytimes.com/2011/09/04/books/review/willpower-by-roy-f-baumeister-and-john-tierney-book-review.html?pagewanted=all&_r=0

- Maia Szalavitz, "Improving Willpower: How to Keep Self-Control from Flagging," Times Magazine, September 19, 2012 (Accessed 1-6-15.)
  http://healthland.time.com/2012/09/19/improving-willpower-how-to-keep-self-control-from-flagging/

- Equally informative is Ian Newby-Clark's article, "Three Effective Ways to Enhance Your Willpower," (Accessed 1-6-15.)
  http://zenhabits.net/three-effective-ways-to-enhance-your-willpower/

Suggested Reading

Asken, Michael J., Dave Grossman and Loren W. Christensen. *Warrior Mind-set.* Millstadt, IL: Warrior Science Group, 2010.

Baumeister, Roy F., and John Tierney. *Willpower: Rediscovering the Greatest Human Strength.* New York: Penguin, 2011. Print.

Benson, Herbert, and Miriam Z. Klipper. *The Relaxation Response*. New York: HarperCollins, 2000.

Benson, Herbert and Marg Stark. *Timeless Healing — The Power and Biology of Belief (Integration of Body, Mind and Soul.)* New York: Fireside, 1996.

Berns, Gregory. *Satisfaction: The Science of Finding True Fulfillment*. New York: Henry Holt & Co., 2005.

Kabat-Zinn, Jon. *Full Catastrophe Living: Using the Wisdom of Your Body and Mind to Face Stress, Pain, and Illness*. New York: Bantam Dell, 1990.

McGonigal, Kelly. *The Willpower Instinct: How Self-control Works, Why It Matters, and What You Can Do to Get More of It*. New York: Avery, 2012. Print.

McGonigal, Kelly. *The Upside of Stress: Why Stress Is Good for You, and How to Get Good at It*. New York: Avery, 2015. Print.

Pressfield, Steven. *The War of Art: Break Through the Blocks and Win Your Inner Creative Battles*. New York: Black Irish Entertainment, 2012. Print.

Reivich, Karen, and Andrew Shatte. *The Resilience Factor: 7 Keys to Finding Your Inner Strength and Overcoming Life's Hurdles*: New York. Broadway Books. 2003.

Sieg, Diane. *Stop Living Life Like An Emergency*. Washington D.C.: Lifeline Press, 2002.

Seligman, Martin E. P. *Flourish*. New York, NY: Atria Paperback, 2013. Print.

Southwick, Steven M., and Dennis S. Charney. *Resilience: The Science of Mastering Life's Greatest Challenges*. New York, Cambridge University Press. 2012.

CHAPTER 7

Armor Your Self™: Physically

The concept of armoring your Self physically is much more complex than simply running three times a week or lifting weights. In order to be truly physically conditioned and fit, the Mayo Clinic suggests you consider a five-part physical fitness program which includes: aerobic fitness, the development of muscular strength and stamina, flexibility achieved through a regular stretching routine, core body stability, and a well-developed sense of physical balance. You also need to fuel your body with a proper diet filled with fresh, high quality, nutritious ingredients and lots of clean pure water. Finally, in order to be fully physically fit and conditioned for a job in law enforcement, you need to get enough quality sleep each and every day.

Let's examine all the things that you need to do to maintain, strengthen and protect yourself physically in order to be effective in your job, and to allow you to lead a happy and healthy life. These things include your physical fitness, proper nutrition and hydration, as well as your ability to get enough daily sleep and/or recover from fatigue.

My bottom line is: *It helps to think of yourself as a professional police athlete!*

The Professional Police Athlete Concept

Your goal must be to train yourself to survive both short-term combat and the long-term rigors of a law enforcement career. You must also include the qualities of resilience that at the same time allow you to enjoy a happy and healthy personal life.

- To survive a short-term combat situation, you may want to train like a wrestler for short-term strength and endurance. This will give you stamina and aerobic capacity to sustain a number of short, powerful bursts of strength to win a struggle with someone twice your size and half your age.

- To survive the toxic effects and hidden dangers of a long-term career in law enforcement, you may want to train like a marathon runner, who works constantly over years to improve overall fitness and nutritional habits. This will help you to cultivate a body that can handle the long and continuous pounding that challenges your strength over long periods of time.

Other resilience qualities you need to develop to enjoy happy and healthy life are covered in the other three chapters on mental, emotional and spiritual health. Overall, you should think about physical recreational activities that bring you joy, physical challenge, companionship and social connections as you exercise. This chapter is about building the physical resilience factor of what I call Tactical Resilience™ for both long-term survival in a police career and the ability to thrive in your personal life.

You could also think about your body as one of the most important pieces of your job-related equipment. I've heard a lot of people suggest that we take better care of our handguns and vehicles than we do of our bodies. Your body is the one piece of equipment no one else is going to maintain for you — and it needs maintenance to perform at peak ability every day and be able to last a long lifetime.

The ideas and techniques described in this chapter are probably the easiest ones to incorporate into your daily routine, since you're probably more in touch with your physical Self than all the rest of your being. But let's not make assumptions, and so we'll start from the beginning.

Your body is what most physically represents your Self, since everyone else can see it. Your body is also a profound component of your being, since all of its physical functions and issues are directly and intimately linked to your mental, emotional and spiritual Self.

Here are some important questions to ask yourself:

- What physical job-related tasks do I need to be able to perform well and to maintain consistently over a full career?
- How do I prepare myself physically for this job?
- How will I determine whether I am functioning effectively physically?
- What am I doing to be able to enjoy the physical side of my life?
- What else do I need to do that I'm not doing now?

Conditioning Physical Strength

I am by no means a fitness trainer; neither am I a finely tuned, "meat-eating" physical specimen of a patrol monster that you might be. I served on a SWAT team as a hostage negotiator for 19 years, and had to maintain the same levels of physical fitness as the rest of the team. We used the Cooper Institute's standards, and while (thankfully) I was not held to the same additional physical fitness standards as our Entry Team Operators, I still had to work hard for 19 years to meet those Cooper standards.

In addition to the Copper Institute, there are two other sources of fitness and conditioning whose expertise I trust: the Mayo Clinic, and the U.S. Navy SEALs.

The Cooper Institute's Recommendations

The Cooper Center Longitudinal Study (CCLS) has repeatedly shown that a moderate-to-high level of cardio respiratory fitness significantly decreases risks of developing coronary artery disease, type 2 diabetes, hypertension, certain cancers and metabolic syndrome. All of those ailments are things that challenge us as a profession.

According to the Cooper Institute, "studies have shown that on average, officers die relatively early due to an increased prevalence of suicide, cancer, and cardiovascular disease. It is estimated that 80% of law enforcement professionals reach full retirement age, 14% take early retirement or go on disability, and 6% die during employment. Most agencies report that cardiovascular disease, orthopedic problems such as back injuries, and stress disorders (anxiety, depression) are the major reasons for disability and early retirement."

The Cooper Institute also reports "there is broad consensus that a lack of physical fitness is a strong predictor of disability, early retirement, and premature death. Because of this, many professional groups such as IACP and various state peace officer standards and training councils have proposed policy changes to counteract the adverse effects of low physical fitness in the law enforcement population. In fact, the International Association of Chiefs of Police (IACP) has stated that 'the functions of a law enforcement agency require a level of physical fitness not demanded by many other occupations, and fitness requirements should be specified.'"

One of the reasons I like the Cooper Institute is because it has been doing research and setting standards in law enforcement fitness for years. There are some who disagree with their recommendations, but I can attest that they served me well during my career. You should consult with your personal or departmental fitness trainer and make your own decisions.

Among the Cooper Institute's recommendations is a physical fitness assessment to measure specific underlying fitness capabilities for law enforcement personnel:

Aerobic Capacity (Cardio respiratory)	1.5 Mile Run ***
Anaerobic Power (Sprinting Ability)	300 Meter Run ***
Anaerobic Power (Explosive Leg Strength)	Vertical Jump***
Muscular Strength (Upper Body)	One-Rep Max Bench Press ***
Muscular Endurance (Upper Body)	1 Minute Push-Ups **
Muscular Endurance (Core Body)	1 Minute Sit-Ups **
Muscular Strength (Lower Body)	One-Rep Max Leg Press*
Flexibility (Lower Back and Hamstrings)	Sit-and-Reach*
Body Composition (Percent Body Fat)	% Fat (caliper/underwater weighing/impedance)*

*** Highly predictive of performing job tasks in all cases
** Predictive of performing job tasks in most cases
* Not predictive or predictive in only a few cases

Accompanying these categories of capabilities, the Cooper Institute recommends the following standards:

Test	Range
1.5 Mile Run	14:40 –15:54 minutes
300 Meter Run	64.3 – 66.0 seconds
Vertical Jump	15.5 – 16 inches
1RM free weight bench press raw score	151 – 165 lbs
1RM free weight bench press ratio	.78 – .84 of body weight
Push-Ups	25 – 34 reps
Sit-Ups	30 – 38 reps

Learn more on the Internet by going to:
https://www.cooperinstitute.org/vault/2440/web/files/684.pdf

Cooper Institute also provides individual and agency support training that you might want to investigate. At the time of this writing they were updating their programing but these were the offerings they had for law enforcement. Even if they change the design of their courses, these outlines might give you some insight in planning your own development.

- A 4.5-day Law Enforcement Fitness Specialist course prepares officers to be fitness coordinators who can set up a testing and training program in their departments. Course topics include:
    - Fitness and Wellness
    - Coronary Risk Factors
    - Medical Screening
    - Exercise and Safety
    - Anatomy and Kinesiology
    - Body Composition (Skinfold method)
    - Fitness Assessment for Law Enforcement/Public Safety
    - Exercise Physiology
    - Goal Setting
    - Exercise Safety
    - Strength Training and Prescription

Flexibility Training and Prescription

Cardiovascular Training and Prescription

Nutrition

Motivation and Adherence

Physical Fitness Testing in Law Enforcement/Public Safety

Physical Fitness Standards in Law Enforcement/Public Safety

https://www.cooperinstitute.org/law-enforcement-fitness-specialist

http://www.cooperinstitute.org/pub/class_list.cfm?course_id=257

- You might consider their 3.5-day Military and First Responder Exercise Leader Training course. Topics include:

    Leadership and Motivational Skills

    Fundamentals of Circuit Training

    Basic Anatomy and Developmental Circuit Exercises

    Class Design and Group Planning

    Exercise Guidelines and Safety Programming

    Exercise Modification and Amplification Guidelines

    Resistance and Cardiovascular Training Guidelines

    Body Mechanics and Controversial Exercises

    Static Stretching, Dynamic Stretching and Athletic Warm-up

    Sports Nutrition and Application as a Fitness Leader

    Interval Training and Running Drills

    Partner Strengthening Exercises

    Exercise Prototypes and Sample workouts

    https://www.cooperinstitute.org/military-first-responder

    https://www.cooperinstitute.org/pub/class_list.cfm?course_id=246

The Cooper Institute suggests that "the key issue and the one necessitating considerable planning, thought, research and effort is what level of physical fitness is required to do the job? In other words, which fitness cut points or standards will be chosen and implemented. The standards your agency selects for applicants, recruits and incumbents have legal, scientific and practical issues. The recommendations put forth by The Cooper Institute reflect [their] judgment as to the legal and scientific validity requirements for tests, standards and programs. However, your department's legal and HR specialists should be included when fitness testing, fitness standards, and policies are being made."

I'm neither paid by, nor do I receive any compensation from, the Cooper Institute. I encourage you to learn more about them at these links so that you can make up your own mind:

http://www.CopsAlive.com/suggests?cooperinstitute/aysbook

http://www.cooperinstitute.org/law-fire-military

www.cooperinstitute.org

Mayo Clinic Recommendations

The Mayo Clinic recommends a five-part physical conditioning program, which includes focus on these distinct areas of physical conditioning: aerobic fitness, muscular strength, regular stretching, developing core stability and regular balance training. I really like the Mayo Clinic as a resource for cops because they are a well-respected medical center and health care system, and they also have an excellent and very accessible Web site that has a wealth of information. When I have medical questions, the first thing I do is to go to its Web site.

https://www.mayoclinic.com/health-information/

I recommend that you incorporate this five-part model into your weekly fitness routine. Your physical strengthening and conditioning program should include the elements recommended above.

Additionally, I recommend doing two kinds of physical workouts: one to build strength and endurance (using the Mayo Clinic model), and another to act as a physical stress-reduction buffer between your time at work and when you go home. I also suggest that you add a separate "quiet mind" session of pure stress management every day. We'll talk about that in the chapter, Armor Your Self™ Emotionally.

U.S. Navy SEALs Fitness

The U.S. Navy SEALs offer a wealth of excellent, reputable information about physical fitness. If you want to look beyond the Cooper Institute's training standards and really challenge yourself with more demanding workouts, investigate the U.S. Navy's general information (listed below), or the Navy Challenge Programs.

All of this is public information available on the Internet from the U.S. Navy. Also, feel free to research your favorite branch of the U.S. military for its standards and specialty programs.

According the U.S. Navy's Web site, the Physical Readiness Test (PRT) is a standard Navy fitness test consisting of push-ups, curl-ups (sit-ups) and a 1.5-mile run.

Navy Physical Screening Test (PST)

While fitness is important for all Navy sailors, it is imperative for those who make up communities like Special Warfare/Special Operations, which includes SEALs, Special Warfare Combatant-Craft Crewman (SWCC), Explosive Ordnance Disposal (EOD) Technician, Navy Diver, and Aviation Rescue Swimmer (AIRR) professionals. Qualification standards and training programs for these specialties — referred to as Navy Challenge Programs — are far more demanding.

The chart below highlights the current *minimum* Navy Physical Screening Test (PST) requirements of Navy Challenge Programs for aspiring service members who are in the Delayed Entry Program (DEP), in boot camp, or who already serve in the Navy. For the physical fitness standards of the SEALs training preparation workout refer to the CopsAlive Web site.

http://www.CopsAlive.com/suggests?sealtrngworkout/aysbook

Minimum Physical Screening Test

	SEALs	SWCC	EOD	Diver	AIRR
Swim 500 yards (450 M) — breast or sidestroke (in number of minutes)	12.5	13	14	14	12
REST: 10 MINUTES					
Push-ups (in 2 minutes)	42	42	42	42	42
REST: 2 MINUTES					
Sit-ups (in 2 minutes)	50	50	50	50	50
REST: 2 MINUTES					

Pull-ups (in 2 minutes)	6	6	6	6	4
REST: 10 MINUTES					
Run 1.5 miles (in number of minutes)	11	12.5	12.75	12.75	12

*AIRR may use sidestroke or breaststroke and utilize American crawl/freestyle or a combination of all.

Use the CopsAlive link or visit the Navy's site to download their training guides:
Naval Special Warfare Physical Training Guide (BUD/S NSW PT Guide),
Naval Special Warfare Injury Prevention Guide (BUD/S NSW IP Guide), and
Special Operations Nutrition Guide (NAVSPECWARCOM Nutrition Guide).
http://www.CopsAlive.com/suggests?sealtrngguides/aysbook

Prescription for Professional Wellness Called "Rx3x"

The prescription "Rx = 3x Daily" is a combination of physical and emotional workouts for you to do three times a day for your overall wellness. I recommend this prescription of physical exercise and stress reduction for every workday.

The *first physical workout* is exercise to strengthen and condition your body. For this, you should plan and coordinate with your personal or department fitness trainer, and it should include the Mayo Clinic's five-part recommendations.

The *second physical workout* is one I call a "Buffer Workout for Stress Reduction," which specifically targets the physiological "Relaxation Response" and is used as a buffer between your time at work and your time at home. In other words, I suggest that you create a buffer time period before going home from work and spend 15-30 minutes trying to achieve the physiological "Relaxation Response," suggested by Dr. Herbert Benson that couples some kind of rhythmical exercise with a repeated word in an attempt to lower your blood pressure, heart rate, respiration rate and slow your metabolic rate. The purpose of this session is strictly for relaxation and anxiety release, not exercise. I don't care whether you are going home to someone (or not) — you need this for your well-being as much as theirs!

Then the *third and final workout* in the Rx3x concept is not a physical workout. Rather, it's a relaxation session of some sort, and I will give you ideas about that in the Armor Your Self™ Emotionally chapter and the chapter on Emotional Tactics and Exercises.

Find out more about the Rx3x concept by downloading our CopsAlive "10 Minute Roll Call Discussion Key 'Rx3x' 3x Prescription for Stress Management in LE" at the Cops Alive Web site.

http://www.CopsAlive.com/suggests?rx3xrc10m/aysbook

Target The Relaxation Response

Every day your target should be to achieve the "Relaxation Response" in both of your stress reduction workouts — 1) a physical stress-reduction buffer workout between your time at work and when you go home and 2) a separate "quiet mind" session of pure stress management.

Herbert Benson, M.D., Associate Professor of Medicine at Harvard Medical School, and author of the book *The Relaxation Response*, characterizes the relaxation response as a "physical state of deep rest that changes the physical and emotional responses to stress and the opposite of the fight-or-flight response."

Described simply, the Relaxation Response triggers a decrease in heart, breathing, blood pressure and metabolic rates which, with dedicated practice, can be called upon on demand to relax the body and mind and counteract the harmful effects of negative stress.

The Relaxation Response is a physiological reaction stimulated within your body through a combination of rhythmical physical activity and a meditative exercise that triggers a decrease in your internal physiology. Dr. Benson predicts, with regular practice, the Relaxation Response can counteract the harmful effects of negative stress.

Benson's original research indicated that you could accomplish this with four components: A quiet environment, a mental mnemonic device (like repeating a word or phrase), a passive attitude (putting aside distracting thoughts and always focusing on your breathing), and a comfortable position. Further research found that only the *passive attitude* and *mental mnemonic device* are really needed, and these two practices can be performed with exercise as long as your physical activity is repetitious and your intent is always to clear your mind of distractions and return your focus to your repeated word in sync with your breathing rate.

You can think of this as "meditative exercising" if you prefer but there are many ways to accomplish it. Some of the words you might use as your mental mnemonic device might be "calm," "relax," "slow," or "one." Repeating in your mind a word while you focus on your breathing works to activate this response.

You can learn more about Dr. Benson's work and the steps necessary to achieve the Relaxation Response at his Web site.
http://www.relaxationresponse.org/steps/

More About the Professional Police Athlete Concept

I again encourage you to think of yourself as a *professional athlete*. There is a lot of support for this "sports model" concept, since we are paid, as part of our jobs, to be in top physical condition and our lives literally depend upon our ability to stay in that condition for the rest of our lives.

Another benefit of switching your mind-set to that of being a professional athlete is adopting all the other language that goes with that concept. Concepts like "teamwork," "team spirit," "coaching," and "playing to win" are very relevant to our profession. What would happen if you started to think of yourself as a professional athlete and your supervisors started thinking of themselves as coaches? What if we didn't operate as "lone wolves" but rather started to adopt a teamwork-and-team-spirit mentality? I think it not only fits — I think it's essential. You'll see in later chapters that social support and organizational culture play a massive role in our wellness and success. And you can imagine, these factors also play gigantic roles in our "*unwellness*." This isn't about blame. As a professional you need to be in charge of your life and career. This book is about *you taking charge and changing all the things around you to sustain your wellness and success.*

So, the only change for you in this sports model is to shift your mind-set to that of a professional person whose level of physical fitness is directly proportional to your success and career survival.

*As a Police Athlete, You Should Try
to Work Out Physically Every Day*

Create a Workout Plan

Work with your personal or department fitness trainer to create a *written plan* that will promote creation of good, daily physical fitness habits.

- Write a plan for a short 10-20 minute workout if you only have a little time
- Try to blend all 5 parts of the Mayo Clinic program into your weekly routine.
- Set some physical fitness goals for your Self.
    Consider:
    - Sit-ups, push-ups, flexibility, mile-and-a-half run, chin-ups
    - Biceps curls, triceps curls, military press, bench press, dead lift, leg press
    - Resting heart rate, blood pressure, cholesterol level, triglyceride level
    - Core body strength, balance, flexibility and stretching
    - Targeting the Relaxation Response

Build routines that continually challenge you mentally and physically, and incorporate all of the physical conditioning components needed by a police athlete. If you want to challenge yourself further, work to incorporate all of the standards set forth by the Cooper Institute or the U.S. Navy SEALs.

Check Under the Hood

Just as you check and maintain your police vehicle, you should regularly check "under the hood" on your body. Remember: you need to adopt the mind-set of a professional police athlete, and in so doing you have to take care of your body just as any professional athlete does. This means having an entire team of people to help you: a physician, fitness trainer, massage therapist, dietician and whoever else you think you need.

You should get an annual physical examination with a doctor in order to track and maintain proper health. Remember: You are a professional athlete, and you should act as such. As law enforcement professionals, we may be more at risk of developing or experiencing an early onset of long-term diseases, such as heart disease, diabetes and cancer. Also, today there are all kinds of apps and products to help you record and track your heath and fitness activities.

Metabolic Syndrome

Another physical threat being tracked in research about police officers and their health is *metabolic syndrome*. Work regularly with your physician's office to monitor your HDL cholesterol, triglyceride and fasting sugar levels. This information can be used to track your susceptibility to metabolic syndrome.

What Is Metabolic Syndrome?

The term *metabolic* refers to the biochemical processes involved in your body's normal functioning. According to the U.S. National Institutes of Health metabolic syndrome is a group of risk factors, which include traits, conditions, or habits that raise your risk for developing heart disease and other health problems, such as diabetes and stroke.

Metabolic Risk Factors

The five conditions described below are metabolic risk factors. Although you can have any one of these risk factors by itself, they tend to occur together. It takes at least three metabolic risk factors to be diagnosed with metabolic syndrome.

- *A Large Waistline* (also called abdominal obesity or "having an apple shape")
  Excess fat in the stomach area is a greater risk factor for heart disease than excess fat in other parts of the body, such as on the hips.

- *A High Triglyceride Level* (or you're on medicine to treat high triglycerides)
  Triglycerides are a type of fat found in the blood.

- *A Low HDL Cholesterol Level* (or you're on medicine to treat low HDL cholesterol)
  HDL is sometimes called "good" cholesterol because it helps remove other cholesterol from your arteries. A *low* HDL cholesterol level raises your risk for heart disease.

- *High Blood Pressure* (or you're on medicine to treat high blood pressure)
  Blood pressure is the force of blood pushing against the walls of your arteries as your

heart pumps blood. If this pressure rises and stays high over time, it can damage your heart and lead to plaque buildup, which narrows your arteries.

- *High Fasting Blood Sugar* (or you're on medicine to treat high blood sugar) Mildly high blood sugar may be an early sign of diabetes.

http://www.nhlbi.nih.gov/health/health-topics/topics/ms/

Buffalo Cardio-Metabolic Occupational Police Stress (BCOPS) Research

Recent findings reported from research underway by the Buffalo Cardio-Metabolic Occupational Police Stress (BCOPS) project at the University of Buffalo in New York state that "The daily psychological stresses that police officers experience in their work put them at significantly higher risk than the general population for a host of long-term physical and mental health effects." John Violanti, the lead researcher on this project at the University at Buffalo, and a former New York State trooper, has said, "We wanted to know, in addition to stress, what are other contributing factors that lead to cardiovascular disease in police."

Current findings, from a cross-sectional study of 464 police officers found that "more than 25 percent of the officers had metabolic syndrome versus 18.7 percent of the general employed population… Having metabolic syndrome increases the risk for developing cardiovascular disease and type 2 diabetes." The same study also found that "overall, an elevated risk of Hodgkin's lymphoma was observed relative to the general population. The risk of brain cancer, although only slightly elevated relative to the general population, was significantly increased with 30 years or more of police service."

"In an earlier pilot study of 100 police officer," says Dr. John Violanti, "shift work is a contributing factor to an increase in metabolic syndrome. Nearly half (46.9%) of officers in the BCOPS study worked a non-day shift compared to just 9% of U.S. workers… We found that as a group, officers who work nights have a higher risk of metabolic syndrome than those who work day shifts."

The BCOPS study's findings demonstrate that police work *by itself* can put officers at risk for adverse health outcomes.

"Usually, health disparities are defined by socioeconomic and ethnic factors," says Violanti, "but here you have a health disparity caused by an occupation, highlighting the need to expand the definition of health disparity to include occupaion as well."
http://www.CopsAlive.com/suggests?bcopsstudy/aysbook

In addition to tracking your waist's circumference, you can also keep track of your body mass index (BMI) to judge the effectiveness of your physical workouts and resistance to metabolic syndrome.

According to the U.S. Centers for Disease Control, "Body Mass Index (BMI) is a number calculated from a person's weight and height. BMI is a fairly reliable indicator of body fatness for most people. BMI does not measure body fat directly, but research has shown that BMI correlates to direct measures of body fat, such as underwater weighing and dual energy X-ray absorptiometry (DXA)." You can learn more from the CopsAlive or C.D.C. Web sites.
http://www.CopsAlive.com/how-is-your-body-mass-index-or-bmi/
http://www.cdc.gov/healthyweight/assessing/bmi/adult_bmi/index.html

>U.S. Department of Health and Human Services (USHHS) offers this general guideline:
>
>>If your BMI is less than 18.5, you're *underweight*.
>>
>>If your BMI is between 18.5 and 24.9, your weight is *normal*.
>>
>>If your BMI is between 25 and 29.9, you're *overweight*.
>>
>>If your BMI is more than 30, you're *obese*.
>
>Find out your BMI by using USHHS's quick online calculator.
>http://www.CopsAlive.com/suggests?bmicalculator/aysbook

Obesity Alert

A study published in the *Journal: Public Library of Science (PLOS) Medicine* found that "Extreme obesity shortens your life more than smoking."

Researchers at the National Cancer Institute compared normal-weight smokers to extremely obese nonsmokers. They found that, on average, the smokers lived longer. Healthy-weight smokers lost about nine years of their lives; nonsmoking adults who were extremely obese — defined as having a BMI of 55 to 55.9 — lost nearly 14 years on average.
http://www.cnn.com/2014/07/11/health/five-studies-missed/index.html
http://www.plosmedicine.org/article/info%3Adoi%2F10.1371%2Fjournal.pmed.1001673

Other Important Physical Fitness Considerations

The Importance of Quality Sleep and the Avoidance of Fatigue

More and more research shows that law enforcement professionals require proper sleep daily in order to avoid fatigue and drops in reaction times, judgment and performance.

Getting proper amounts of quality sleep is just one of many things you need to ensure that you are physically fit. Sleep is vitally important to all human beings, but with the rigors of a career in law enforcement, it becomes so much more important. Without proper sleep, you're up against the problem of fatigue — and fatigue can literally be a killer in our business.

Did you know that (according to Lumosity.com) "Peak performance requires plenty of rest. Sleep deprivation can cause memory impairment, induce attention deficits, and create other brain health concerns."

Also, according to the National Sleep Foundation, "being awake for 18 hours is equal to a blood alcohol concentration (BAC) of 0.08%."

Bryan Vila, a University of Washington researcher and a former cop, notes: "More than half of police officers fail to get adequate rest, and they have 44 percent higher levels of obstructive sleep apnea than the general public. More than 90 percent report being routinely fatigued, and 85 percent report driving while drowsy." I highly recommend that you read Bryan's article as it makes specific recommendations for (1) things managers can do, and (2) things officers can do.

Source: Bryan Vila, Ph.D., "Sleep Deprivation: What Does It Mean for Public Safety Officers?" http://www.nij.gov/journals/262/pages/sleep-deprivation.aspx

Drew Dawson and Kathryn Reid reported in the July 17, 1997 issue of *Nature*: "Sleep deprivation is dangerous. Researchers have shown that being awake for 19 hours produces impairments that are comparable to having a blood alcohol concentration (BAC) of .05 percent. Being awake for 24 hours is comparable to having a BAC of roughly .10 percent. This means that in just five hours — the difference between going without sleep for 19 hours versus 24 hours — the impact essentially doubles. (It should be noted that, in all 50 states and the District of Columbia, it is a crime to drive with a BAC of .08 percent or above.)"

Source: Dawson, D., and K. Reid. "Fatigue, Alcohol and Performance Impairment," *Nature* 388 [July 17, 1997]: 235.

Sleep is also important if you want to lose weight or simply stay in shape. According to the book, *New American Diet*, from the American Association of Retired Persons, "Sleep gives you energy to burn more calories during the day. People who sleep fewer than six hours a night are 27 percent more likely to become obese. Drop that number down to four hours a night, and you're 67 percent more likely to put on pounds at an unhealthy rate."

Source: http://www.aarp.org/food/healthy-eating/info-11-2012/lose-weight-quickly-photos.html#slide1

Tips for a Good Night's Sleep

- First and foremost: Protect your need and right to sleep!
- Ensure adequate time in bed, free from interruptions and demands. (Most adults require 7.5-8 hours. Teens and kids need even more.)
- Keep regular sleep habits!
- Avoid vigorous exercise shortly before retiring.
- Avoid napping to protect your main sleep time.
- The bed should be used for sleep and sex — not for reading, TV, or computer work.
- Avoid large meals and excessive fluid intake before your scheduled sleep.
- Avoid caffeine and smoking prior to retiring.
- Make sure that your sleeping area is conducive to good sleep: cool, quiet (use earplugs if necessary), and dark (use a mask or room darkening shades on windows).
- Avoid medications that can interfere with either sleep or alertness.

Source: www.CopsAlive.com, www.thewakeupsquad.com

Proper Nutrition

Tips for Good Nutrition

- Eat more plant foods, including fruits, vegetables and whole grains.
- Choose lean protein from a variety of sources.
- Limit sweets and salt.

- Control portion sizes.
- Being physically active promotes good digestion and a healthy metabolism.
- Drink plenty of water.
- Try *Hara hachi bu* which means: "Eat until 80% full."

As of the early 21st century, Okinawans, in Japan, through practicing *hara hachi bu*, are the only human population to have a self-imposed habit of calorie restriction. Almost 29% of Okinawans live to be 100, about four times the average in Western countries. They consume about 1,800 to 1,900 calories per day. Their typical body mass index (BMI) is about 18 to 22, compared to a typical BMI of 26 or 27 for adults over 60 in the United States.
Source: http://en.wikipedia.org/wiki/Hara_hachi_bu

Become a "Food Label & Menu Detective"

Try to eat whole, fresh foods. But when you need to eat food that comes in a package, you should always read the nutrition labels on the packages so that you know what you're eating.

- Check the serving size and then look for the amounts of:
    - Calories
    - Proteins
    - Carbohydrates
    - Fats
    - Cholesterol
    - Sugars
    - Sodium
- Look for hidden salt, sugars and for an excess of chemicals like colorings or preservatives (which are usually words you don't recognize or can't pronounce).
- Try to find labels that read:
    - 100% Natural
    - USDA Organic
    - Low Fat or Low Carbs

- Real Fruit
- Whole Grains
- Gluten Free

Also remember that when the manufacturer makes a packaged food that says it's "low fat," they may have substituted something else to boost the flavor — and frequently that ingredient is sugar or a sugar substitute.

The Bottom Line: **Know What You Are Eating**

There are now a number of smartphone apps to help you keep track of your wellness and fitness goals. I use and like the *Calorie Counter and Diet Tracker*, by MyFitnessPal HD, for my iPhone. A student of mine also recommended the *Lose It Diet* app. Both apps help you track your daily intake of everything you should be tracking, and both have a huge database of packaged foods, fast food and chain-restaurant menu items to help you easily understand what you're putting in your mouth.

Eat an Apple a Day

Consider the "Tactical Apple" — perhaps the perfect portable food. Just grab an apple before your shift, bring along a napkin and plastic bag to dispose of the core, and you're all set. Apples are typically rich in fiber, vitamins C, A and E, as well as beta carotene, and they act as a natural toothbrush.

- Apples have been linked to:
- Bone protection
- Asthma reduction
- Alzheimer's prevention
- Lower cholesterol
- Lung cancer prevention
- Breast cancer prevention
- Liver cancer prevention

- Diabetes management
- Weight loss

Resources:

http://www.healthdiaries.com/eatthis/10-health-benefits-of-apples.html

http://tlc.howstuffworks.com/family/an-apple-a-day.htm

Is Sugar Toxic?

I found an interesting *60 Minutes* story entitled, "Is Sugar Toxic?" that you might be interested in (first broadcast on April 1, 2012). It may encourage you to conduct your own research into the effects on your body of sugar and other things in your food. Do your own Google investigation. Here's a link to the 60 Minutes story:

http://www.cbsnews.com/news/is-sugar-toxic-01-04-2012/

Mindful Eating

- Be focused — not distracted — while eating
- Eat small portions more often during the day
- Never allow yourself to feel "starved"
- Only eat until you are 80% full — *Hara hachi bu*

Source: http://eatingmindfully.com/mindful-eating-tools/

Total Physical Wellness Planning: What You Need to Do!

As you start your own personal wellness planning, start by asking yourself these questions about how you will prepare yourself as a professional police athlete:

- What am I training for and what skills do I want to develop?
- How will those skills help me in a fight?
- How will those skills help me at home?
- How do I summon the strength I need?
- How do I turn off my body's *on-duty physiology* when I'm at home?
- How do I need to care for my body to perform at my peak level?

Here are some of my general suggestions:

- Train, exercise, sleep, hydrate, eat well, talk out challenges
- Be a team player
- Manage your life, money, relationships and stress!
- Learn, grow, share, talk some more, have some fun
- Set a plan
    - Make a habit of success
    - Get a "success or physical wellness buddy"
    - Make physical wellness *fun*
    - The three "R's" of wellness — Rest, Recreation, Relationships
    - Don't forget these:
        - Rx = 3x daily
        - Workout for exercise
        - Buffer workout for stress reduction
        - Stress management session
- You should be doing three kinds of workouts:
    - One for strength and endurance
    - One for stress reduction
    - *Plus*: Plan a session of stress management every day and practice your Relaxation Response
- Strengthen your body/mind/spirit support system and plan for Blue Trauma Management

*Life is not about finding yourself —
life is about creating yourself!*
(Unknown)

Read more about nutritional strategies

Nutrition

- Susan Albers, Psy.D., *Eating Mindfully: How to End Mindless Eating and Enjoy a Balanced Relationship with Food.*
- Former model-turned-chef Candice Kumai has written several books I love. Start with this one: *Cook Yourself Sexy: Easy Delicious Recipes for the Hottest, Most Confident You.*

  Kumai has written several books and offers great recipes on her Web site. http://www.candicekumai.com/

Caffeine

Most of us have an addiction of some sort, and for cops the most popular one might be our love of coffee and other caffeinated beverages. It's part of our culture and part of our social routines. Just as with alcohol, consumption of too much caffeine may be causing you more problems than it's worth.

In a book published by the Institute of Medicine (US) Committee on Military Nutrition Research entitled *Caffeine for the Sustainment of Mental Task Performance: Formulations for Military Operations*, the authors reported that "In a study of adult men, a dose of 4 mg/kg (280 mg/70 kg human, or about 2 to 3 cups of coffee) had a caffeine half-life of 2.5 to 4.5 hours, and was not affected by age." What that means to you is that you still have half the dose of caffeine from your coffee 2.5 to 4.5 hours later, and 2.5 to 4.5 hours after that you still have a quarter dose. This might easily disturb your sleep that night, and it will become cumulative if you drink more caffeine later in the day, or even the next day.

Also, in an article published in *Forbes* magazine in August 2012, entitled "Caffeine: The Silent Killer of Success," author Travis Bradberry writes: "Caffeine has a six-hour half-life, which means it takes a full twenty-four hours to work its way out of your system. Have a cup of joe at eight a.m., and you'll still have 25% of the caffeine in your body at eight p.m. Anything you drink after noon will still be at 50% strength at bedtime. Any caffeine in your bloodstream — with the negative effects increasing with the dose — makes it harder to fall asleep. When you do finally fall asleep, the worst is yet to come. Caffeine disrupts the quality of your sleep by reducing rapid eye movement (REM) sleep, the deep sleep when your body recuperates and processes emotions. When caffeine disrupts your sleep, you wake up the next day with an emotional handicap. You're naturally going to be inclined to grab a cup of coffee or an energy drink to try to make yourself feel better. The caffeine produces surges of adrenaline, which further your emotional handicap. Caffeine and lack of sleep leave you feeling tired in the afternoon, so you drink more caffeine, which leaves even more of it in your bloodstream at bedtime. Caffeine very quickly creates a vicious cycle."

I'm not a killjoy, and I would never tell you how to *run* your life; but my job in this book is to give you some suggestions about how to *manage* your life and career more effectively, and one suggestion I have is to learn the valuable lesson of moderation.
Source: http://www.forbes.com/sites/travisbradberry/2012/08/21/caffeine-the-silent-killer-of-emotional-intelligence/#368ddc0467c9

Alcohol

Alcohol consumption has almost become a rite in law enforcement. It surrounds our social interactions, and it's used to self-medicate and numb ourselves from the things that bother us. Stress is a critical challenge in law enforcement and despite what is commonly believed, alcohol is *not* an effective stress reliever. In fact its consumption may even exacerbate your stress problems, physiologically as well as emotionally and, like caffeine, can disrupt your ability to sleep effectively.

In research published by the National Institute on Alcohol Abuse and Alcoholism entitled *Sleep, Sleepiness, and Alcohol Use*, the authors state, "studies found that in non-alcoholics who occasionally use alcohol, both high and low doses of alcohol initially improve sleep, although high alcohol doses can result in sleep disturbances during the second half of the nocturnal sleep period. Furthermore, people can rapidly develop tolerance to the sedative effects of alcohol. Researchers have investigated the interactive effects of alcohol with other determinants of daytime sleepiness. Such studies indicate that alcohol interacts with sleep deprivation and sleep restriction to exacerbate daytime sleepiness and alcohol-induced performance impairments." None of this is good for the effective maintenance of your physical fitness.
Source: http://pubs.niaaa.nih.gov/publications/arh25-2/101-109.htm

Nutritional Supplements

I know that lots of cops take nutritional supplements, and my only suggestion is for you to do the research to make an informed decision about what you may be taking. Most of the doctors I've talked to believe that, for the most part, nutritional supplements are a waste of money. Personally, I have always taken some kind of supplement because I've always struggled with my diet. I have tried a variety of supplements but chose to take Nutrilite® products because I feel that they are the best, and most well established, vitamins and supplements to help round out my otherwise poor eating choices. I feel better taking vitamins and supplements and do not plan to stop. If you want to learn more, you can visit my distribution site at: www.ConcentratedNutrition.com. Yes, I do make a sales commission on anything you buy; however, the commission goes to supporting the Armor Your Self™ program and is part of our First Responder Business Builders initiative.

Proper Hydration

The Mayo Clinic tells us that "The Institute of Medicine determined that an adequate intake (AI) for men is roughly about 13 cups (3 liters) of total beverages a day. The AI for women is about 9 cups (2.2 liters) of total beverages a day. What about the advice to drink 8 glasses a day?

Everyone has heard the advice, "Drink eight 8-ounce glasses of water a day." That's about 1.9 liters, which isn't that different from the Institute of Medicine recommendations. Although the "8 by 8" rule isn't supported by hard evidence, it remains popular because it's easy to remember. Just keep in mind that the rule should be reframed as: "Drink eight 8-ounce glasses of fluid a day," because all fluids count toward the daily total."

Source: http://www.mayoclinic.com/health/water/NU00283

Try these suggestions to help you drink enough water every day:

- Stay hydrated: Carry a water bottle with you everywhere you go (especially on duty).

- You should drink 3 liters or a little over 101 oz. of fluids, preferably clean water, every day — that's almost thirteen 8oz. glasses a day.

- *Hint*: If you drink one glass of clean water before each meal, that's already three glasses, and it will also help to curb your appetite so that you may avoid overeating.

Building Positive Physical Wellness Habits

One way to build positive habits is to keep track of what you're doing. As mentioned earlier in this book: *Observe your physical wellness activity cues, tactics and rewards to keep your habits positive and help eliminate negative habits.*

Part of our Armor Your Self™ Program recommends that you "Count Everything," because we believe that "What gets measured gets managed," a maxim often attributed to business guru Peter Drucker, who coined the term "management by objectives."

I suggest that you keep track of:

- Push-ups
- Sit-ups
- Weight-lifting reps
- Time spent working out daily
- Miles run
- Water or fluids consumed
- Calories consumed
- Sugar consumption
- Fat consumption
- Blood pressure
- Resting heart rate
- Workout heart rate
- Your body weight
- Your body mass index (BMI)

As well as:

- Time spent
- Money spent
- Arrests made
- Deaths investigated
- Traffic stops
- Friends supported
- Miles traveled
- Time on the beach

And anything else in your life that's important to you.

To help you, we've prepared a sample spreadsheet with lots of suggestions and plenty of room to add your own ideas. It is available on the CopsAlive Web site. http://www.CopsAlive.com/ suggests?counteverything/aysbook

Small Changes: Big Results

1. Exercise daily and drink lots of clean, pure water
2. Meditate each morning
3. Eat well and ditch the processed junk food
4. Be more mindful of others
5. Cook daily and pack your own meals for work
6. Opt for natural sweeteners — there's nothing wrong with sugar, in moderation.
7. Moderate your alcohol consumption to 1-2 glasses of wine/beers a week
8. Walk more. Walk on your lunch break. Park far away and walk.
9. Eat until you are only 80% full. Stop overeating.
10. Bonus: *Let go of all things that are not serving you well. I promise you, this one works!*

Impulse Control and Action Initiation

I've talked in other chapters about impulse control and action initiation, and both have a particular use in proper nutrition and physical fitness.

Impulse control is your ability to resist a spontaneous impulse to do something that is bad for you. For example, eating something that's not healthy, or eating too much of anything.

Action initiation is your ability to take action and initiate activities that are good for you but which you might not want to do, such as daily fitness workouts or starting a diet to lose weight.

You could think of this as mind control, but it's not really mind control as much as *Self control!*

You talk to your mind to establish your mind-set

Your mind-set controls your brain

Your brain controls your body

You control your impulses and initiate actions and then:

Your body manages the stress

I will make some recommendation in the next chapter about AYS Physically Exercises, listing tactics you can develop to test and enhance your impulse control and action initiation.

The Importance of Tactical Breathing

Your breathing can be used to impact many of the physiological activities in the body, and by monitoring and controlling your breathing you can steer changes within your body, such as lowering your heart rate, blood pressure and initiating the Relaxation Response. These changes take time to materialize: however, over time you can condition the responses to happen more quickly and more dramatically.

The first priority in breath control (or *tactical breathing*) is simply becoming conscious of your breathing. The next step is gaining control over you breathing rate. It's really easy when you aren't under any stress; but when you are agitated, it's harder to do. That's why practicing breath control every day becomes so important. You can program good breathing habits for the stressful times when you need them. By programming your mind and body *now* with good breathing exercises that slow your body's physiology, you will be better able to slow and control that physiology (breathing rate, heart rate and metabolism) when you're under stress.

Typical breathing exercises focus on the length of your inhale, the amount of time you hold your breath, and the length of time you exhale. You can measure these by counting the different rates.

These strings of numbers show the length of time, in time counts, of the inhale, the hold after inhale, the exhale and the hold after the exhale.

   12-6-12-6

   8-4-8-4

These long counts are usually used in stress management and meditation sessions. Many experts who promote tactical breathing to gain control of your emotions or steady your hands in a shooting situation, propose a straight inhale then exhale with no holds in between. These are usually done to a simple 4/4 count, with a count of four on the inhale and then an immediate count of four on the exhale. The process is then repeated over and over again until the desired physiological state is achieved. The only variation on this technique is how long each count is, i.e., a very long and slow four count or a more rapid four count.

Another breath control training technique is to practice holding your breath. See how long you can hold your breath, and over time you will develop the ability to do so for longer and longer periods. As I write, a worldwide competition is being held to see who can hold their breath the longest. Famed American magician, illusionist and endurance artist David Blaine is one of those who has held and lost the record over the last several years. You can see David's TED Talk about how he held his breath for 17 minutes at:

http://www.ted.com/talks/david_blaine_how_i_held_my_breath_for_17_min?language=en

The current record (as of this publication) — over 22 minutes — is held by Stig Avall Severinsen, a three-time world free diving champion, who has written a book on the art of conscious breathing called *Breatheology*.

Both of these record holders made their attempts under strict supervision and in controlled environments, so don't try this without guidance from your personal physician.

If you want some support in your breath control training, I recommend the Tactical Breather App from the National Center for Telehealth and Technology, which is available in iPhone and Android versions. Learn more at The National Center for Telehealth and Technology Web site where it also has a number of other great apps to check out.
http://t2health.dcoe.mil/

If you look in the next chapter on physical exercises, you will find several techniques to improve your breath control. These are categorized as Tactical Breathing, Breath Control, The Heavy Sign, Out of Breath Recovery, and The Purging Breath.

Physical Wellness Resources For You

Books:

Albers Psy.D., Susan. *Eating Mindfully: How to End Mindless Eating and Enjoy a Balanced Relationship with Food.* Oakland, CA: New Harbinger Publications, 2012.

Benson, Herbert and Miriam Z. Klipper. *The Relaxation Response.* New York: HarperCollins, 2000.

Kumai, Candice. *Cook Yourself Sexy.* New York: Rodale, 2012.

Severinsen, Stig Avall. *Breatheology: The Art of Conscious Breathing.* Naples, Italy: Idelson-Gnocchi, 2010.

Sherwood, Mark. *The Quest For Wellness: A Practical & Personal Wellness Plan For Optimum Health In Your Body, Mind, Emotions & Spirit.* Riviera Beach, FL: Emerge Publishing, 2015.

Vila, Bryan. *Tired Cops: The Importance of Managing Police Fatigue.* Police Executive Research Forum, 2000. You can find it on the PERF Bookstore Web site. http://www.policeforum.org/perf-bookstore#t1

Weil, Andrew. *Eating Well for Optimum Health: The Essential Guide to Bringing Health and Pleasure Back to Eating.* New York: Quill, 2001.

Eat an apple a day:
http://www.healthdiaries.com/eatthis/10-health-benefits-of-apples.html
http://tlc.howstuffworks.com/family/an-apple-a-day.htm

Author/Chef Candice Kumai's Web site:http://www.candicekumai.com/

CopsAlive article on BMI:
http://www.CopsAlive.com/how-is-your-body-mass-index-or-bmi/

General Nutritional Resources Links:
www.MayoClinic.com/health/health-diet
www.ChooseMyPlate.gov

CHAPTER 8

Armor Your Self™: Physically Training Exercises, Tactics & Techniques

NOTE: I'm neither a doctor nor a certified physical fitness trainer. I don't pretend to be an authority on any of this. What I am is another cop on this same path, perhaps just a few years ahead of you. I've tried all the things I recommend here. Some of them I do, and some of them my friends think work great — and so you get to choose the ones that work for you.

You should consult with your doctor or a certified physical fitness trainer before you undertake a new or more challenging physical exercise program. I know you're an adult, and you know that I cannot accept any liability for injuries you might incur trying these recommendations. But having said that, my intention here is not to give you a series of exercise routines, which you probably already have or can get from your personal trainer. Rather, what I offer are some new tactics or techniques that will help add fun or something different to your daily physical exercise routine.

It is important, before any and all physical exercise that you properly stretch the muscles you are about to exert — even if you are only doing a quick or short exercise.

One *key* concept for you to understand is that what you really need to do is to *build good habits* that will carry you throughout the rest of your life. These aren't just some temporary measures to get you in shape so you can then coast through your career and life. This is about adopting the right tactics as early as possible so that you can maintain them throughout the rest of your life.

REMEMBER: As part of the Armor Your Self™ concept we want to find good tactics that we can "seed" into good habits. If we layer those habits into our daily lives, we will create a system for success. Ultimately we are building character by developing positive daily habits that will carry you through a happy, healthy and successful life. That said, here are some suggested tactics for you to try out to see if any of them fit your style, schedule and personality. Use all that suit you — or throw them all away and find others that work for you. *The bottom line:* Please find something that keeps you physically active and healthy on a weekly basis, and something that you can maintain for the rest of your long and healthy life.

REMEMBER: Positive tactics build positive habits, and these positive habits become part of your personal positive systems. The reverse is also true, so make sure you are always focused on the positives! Remember the concepts of *Habit Seeding, Habit Feeding* and *Habit Weeding*. You want to find simple goals to accomplish to *Seed* the development of a new, effective habit. You also want to *Feed* or reward effective habits so that they stay a part of your weekly activities. At the same time, you want to identify small cues or triggers for your bad habits and *Weed* those out by replacing them with triggers for positive habits. You can also substitute another positive activity to replace your bad habit.

The following tactics are arranged around the Mayo Clinic's recommended five-part physical fitness training program of aerobic training, muscular strength training, balance training, flexibility training, and training to strengthen your core stability. I've also added tactics to help you with nutrition, fatigue, sleep, and proper hydration, as well as tactical breath control.

Always have goals when you are developing your physical fitness and physical health. When you set up your physical training regime, plan the tactics you want to try for a week at a time, and create a way of recording your progress in a log or a journal.

Good luck!

Tactics To Build Aerobic Fitness

Short Hits and Wind Sprints

Short hit tactics are designed to add quick, simple aerobic conditioning tactics to your arsenal of ideas to improve your aerobic fitness. Many feel that the best way to expand your aerobic capacity and extend your stamina is to run quick, fast and short "wind sprints."

Don't have time for a long extended run? Why not run around the block twice, doing short, quick and fast wind sprints of 50-to-100 yards at a time. You can do this before work or during your meal break. You don't have to do too many, but it really helps to push yourself and do them every day or several times a week. Time yourself and try to get faster over time.

It's nice to be able to change into running shoes for this, but it might sometimes help you to run in your work shoes or boots and with all of your duty equipment, whether you work in uniform or plainclothes. If you have the opportunity to add other physical fitness tactics to this — like running a fitness or obstacle course that includes features like a pull-up bar, balance beam, incline sit-up bench or other challenges — all the better. This is a great way to enhance your overall level of physical fitness quickly, without using too much time on any one day or adding an overwhelming fitness workout routine.

"Really Get Winded" Sprints

Choose to sprint if you are in very good shape, or try fast walking if you are just getting started with your physical fitness program. *REMEMBER: The most important thing is to do something regularly.* That's always more important than how hard you push yourself. If you want to really push yourself, that's fine. But I know that most of you are not workout fanatics, and so it's important to do something regularly rather than skipping workouts.

Run or walk for 15 minutes, 3 times a week, and incorporate sprint and rest phases:

Sprint (or walk very fast) for 1 minute, then walk quickly for 1 minute; *then*
Sprint (or walk very fast) for 2 minutes, then walk quickly for 1 minute; *then*
Sprint (or walk very fast) for 1 minute, then walk quickly for 1 minute; *then*
Sprint (or walk very fast) for 2 minutes, then walk quickly for 1 minute, *then*
Sprint (or walk very fast) for 2 minutes, then walk quickly for 1 minute; *then*
Sprint (or walk very fast) for 1 minute, then walk quickly for 1 minute.

Tactics to Build Muscular Fitness

"10 PP" (Ten Perfect Push-ups)

Maintaining physical fitness is about doing many things in small steps or sets. Push-ups are great because you can do them anywhere, anytime.

If you are fit and can do 10 perfect push-ups, then do several sets at one time, or do your sets several times throughout the day.

If you struggle to do 10 perfect push-ups, focus on *quality*, not quantity, and try to challenge yourself several times a day to do 10 perfect push-ups.

You can do them in the morning, at lunch, on a break or even while you are watching TV. If this seems daunting, *remember* that you can do a set of 10 perfect push-ups in less than half a minute. You have 30 seconds to build a lifetime of health and fitness, don't you?

Try the "10 PP" Challenge

The "10 Perfect Push-ups," challenge is designed to help you focus more on doing push-ups well and doing them more often, instead of just hating push-ups and never doing them.

Try this: Every time you think about wanting to be in better shape, or about not having enough time to exercise, just drop and do 10 perfect push-ups. Focus on your form and try to make each push-up perfect. This shouldn't take you very much time and maybe you'll get a chance to do this 4-5 times a day. If you're not doing any push-ups now, then this will be 40 or 50 more a day that you can just sneaking in by doing them spontaneously. Make it a game or challenge at work. Try to define the perfect push-up. Compare styles and vote on what counts and what doesn't.

Even if you can do 10 perfect push-ups right now, this exercise challenge might just surprise you at how quickly you can get those arms into better shape.

Lee Shaykhet's 10-Minute Workout

There are a lot of simple 10-minute workouts available and you can even create your own by setting a timer for one minute, 10 times during the day, and then doing 10 different one-minute exercises.

If you are looking for great ideas for quick and easy physical fitness workouts, I recommend *Lee Shaykhet's 10-Minute Workout.* Lee is an excellent law enforcement trainer with expertise in a variety of topics, including defensive tactics, self-defense and fitness. Lee's experience ranges from training former Soviet Army officers and soldiers to providing instruction for law enforcement and military organizations in the United States and Canada. He has also offered training for security and consulting companies, and has trained bodyguards for several high-profile events.

Lee believes in teaching simple, practical fitness applications, and in his 10-minute program you are your own gym. No equipment is required and the techniques can be done anywhere. Learn more at his Web site.
http://www.shaykhettraining.com/

Tactics to Condition Physical Balance

Balance is a term that applies to all areas of your life and comes up in all four quadrants of our Armor Your Self™ recommendations. Proper balance is necessary for good health and physical, mental, emotional and spiritual wellness. You will find the concept in many chapters of this book and in many facets of your life. By focusing on physical balance you will also begin to condition yourself to recognize and initiate balance practices in the other areas of your being.

The Tactical Shoe-tie

Adding balance to your life is so important in many ways. Adding balance to your physical fitness practices is very important and can work as a nice "Seeding" exercise to get you to do other types of physical fitness activities.

The *Tactical Shoe-tie* is a simple way to add a balance activity to your everyday schedule: From now on — whether you're a sock-sock-shoe-shoe person, or a sock-shoe-sock-shoe person — try putting on your shoes and socks while standing up. Try pulling your socks and shoes on while standing on one leg, *without* leaning against something. (Some of you may think this too easy, but many may not be able to do it.) And finish by tying your shoes while standing up unassisted. *Throw away those Velcro things and go back to shoes that actually require you to tie them!*

Balancing Your Dental Hygiene

Another quick and easy way to seed balance exercises into your daily routines is to *brush your teeth while standing on one leg at a time.* Follow your dentist's instructions for good brushing techniques, but spend at least 30 seconds on each leg. Perhaps you'll brush your upper teeth for 30 seconds while balancing on your left leg, and then spend 30 seconds balancing on your right leg while brushing your lower teeth.

Your teeth, gums, and center of gravity will all be happier and healthier if you do this every day or three times a day!

Have a Ball at Your Desk

If you really want to start seeding good balance habits into your life, consider purchasing a large *fitness ball* and use it in place of your desk chair.

I use mine without a frame, but I've seen others use theirs with a frame that fits underneath the ball to stabilize it. There are also frames that have wheels on the bottom to allow you to roll your ball-chair around as you would any other desk chair.

If this works for you, also consider using a fitness ball as a chair when you watch TV or play video games.

Reverse Hand Exercise

For a different kind of "balance" exercise, try using your *less dominant hand* to do everything for an hour or even for a day. Write with your "off" hand, brush your teeth with that other hand, and try to do everything that you would otherwise normally do with your primary hand. (This one is one of those exercises that's both physical and mental, but I think it is primarily a physical activity.) It's probably better to do this on your day off and not try to add this challenge into your work day.

Walk a Tight Rope for Balance

Consider the balance exercise called *Slacklining*. Wikipedia defines slacklining as "the act of walking or balancing along a suspended length of flat webbing that is tensioned between two anchors. Slacklining is similar to slack rope walking and tightrope walking." I see a lot of people doing this near where I live. They attach the slackline webbing between two trees, a foot or so off the ground, and walk from end to end while trying to keep their balance. I've tried it and it's not easy. Google it, and see if it appeals to you!

Other Balance Exercises

The Mayo Clinic has and excellent slideshow with some suggestions about simple balance exercises you can try.

https://www.mayoclinic.com/health/balance-exercises/SM00049

Tactics To Promote Stretching & Flexibility

The Mayo Clinic promotes the value and benefits of stretching. You can learn more on the Mayo Clinic Web site.

https://www.mayoclinic.com/health/stretching/HQ01447

15-Minute TV Stretching

Feel guilty about watching TV? Well, it's not nearly as bad for you if you squeeze in a little physical fitness while you watch. You can ride a stationary bike, do sit-ups, or even spend your time getting in a really good stretch.

You can very easily add simple stretches to your daily routine. Set a timer for 15 minutes and work your way through several simple stretches designed to increase your flexibility and decrease your risk of fitness-related injuries. Consider doing a series of stretches for your lower back, calves, hips, hamstrings, shoulders, neck and quadriceps.

The Mayo Clinic offers an excellent slideshow to demonstrate these and other stretches for you on its Web site.

http://www.mayoclinic.org/healthy-lifestyle/fitness/multimedia/stretching/sls-20076840

They also have a number of other slideshows and videos about a variety of stretching exercises. Adding stretching to your daily routine is a great way to "seed" other positive physical fitness habits!

Martial Arts, Qigong, Tai Chi or Yoga

You might also consider adding a martial arts or yoga class to your schedule in order to build overall fitness, as well as to add crucial balance training and conditioning.

All martial arts will help you build strength and better balance. *Gung Fu* and *Aikido* are excellent for balance training, and *Qigong* and *Tai Chi* offer a more calming and meditative experience that can also help you learn emotional and spiritual calming. *Yoga*, although it's a four-letter word to most cops, is an excellent way to stay flexible and can help with lower back problems encountered by many in law enforcement due to the heavy equipment belts worn in patrol.

Diane Sieg, a former ER nurse and yoga coach, has a great CD program of empowering activities, which include deep breathing, yoga stretching, balance poses, meditation, and journaling, all in an audio-guided, 30-minute program. You can learn more about the "30 Days to Grace" on her Web site.

http://dianesieg.com/30-days-to-grace/

Tactics to Build Core Stability and Strength

Fast and Easy TV Core Exercises

There are all kinds of core-strengthening exercises you can do while watching television. Sit-ups, planks, crunches and crawling are exercises that provide an excellent foundation for a core-strengthening program. See if you can seed into your daily activities several sets of sit-ups, crunches, planks or crawls to maintain a strong and healthy core. There are a lot of muscles involved in keeping the core of your body upright and your spine in a neutral position. You can use simple tactics and exercises to work on building strength in your core, as well as enhancing the core stabilization of your spine. If some of these exercises become too easy, you can progress to a medicine ball or kettlebell strengthening routine, but you should seek advice from your fitness trainer for specific instructions.

The Mayo Clinic offers some excellent suggestions for simple core strengthening routines on its Web site.

- https://www.mayoclinic.com/health/core-exercises/SM00071
- https://www.mayoclinic.com/health/core-strength/SM00046
- http://www.mayoclinic.org/healthy-lifestyle/fitness/multimedia/core-strength/sls-20076575

Quick Physical Activities and Workouts

Get Up and Go

People who do lots of sitting are getting attention lately because a growing body of research shows links between a sedentary lifestyle and health risks, such as obesity and metabolic syndrome. And according to the Mayo Clinic, "Too much sitting also seems to increase the risk of death from cardiovascular disease and cancer."

Those of us in law enforcement run these risks if we spend too much time sitting in our patrol cars or behind a desk. The Mayo Clinic notes: "Any extended sitting — such as behind a desk at work or behind the wheel — can be harmful. What's more, spending a few hours a week at the gym or otherwise engaged in moderate or vigorous activity doesn't seem to significantly offset the risk."

The only solution is less sitting and adding more movement into your life. You might consider a standing desk, or doing more work on your feet. If you work patrol, you might spend more time walking your beat or getting out of the car more often. As a professional police athlete, you must find a way to become as active as possible in order to maintain your health and fitness. You can learn more about the problem and some solutions at the Mayo Clinic Web site.

http://www.mayoclinic.org/healthy-lifestyle/adult-health/expert-answers/sitting/faq-20058005

Tactics to Promote Proper Nutrition

Try Four Meals a Day

Many fitness experts tell us to eat smaller meals more often in order to stay fueled for the day, and to avoid large drops in blood sugar levels that can make you drowsy and lethargic. There is some debate about whether you should eat four smaller meals each day, or only three meals and a snack. But most agree that you not eat more often than that.

I recommend that you try eating four meals a day or one small-to-medium-sized meal every four hours. Meals that you eat early in the day should be larger than meals at the end of the day. The key here is to eat well-balanced, nutritious meals and to avoid empty calories.

You're much better off planning and packing your own meals than eating out. *At all costs:* Avoid fast food.

Good fuel should consist of lots of vegetables, especially leafy green ones, with some source of good, lean protein and high-fiber carbohydrates. Keep fruits and sweets to a minimum.

Talk to your fitness trainer or wellness coordinator to get some ideas about what best to eat, and then build a weeklong meal plan. If you still need ideas, I like the anti-inflammatory diet recommended by Dr. Andrew Weil on his Web site.

http://www.drweil.com/drw/u/PAG00361/anti-inflammatory-food-pyramid.html

Make Love to Your Chocolate

Most of us have a food item that is our special thing. Many times it is chocolate, but it can be any food item that you eat way too much of even when you know that's not good for you.

Often, our normal routine is to eat huge portions of our favorite food without really tasting or enjoying it. Many times we eat while we're distracted while we're watching TV or talking, so that we're not focused on the act of eating and enjoying our food.

Here is an exercise in *mindful eating*, in which I suggest you learn to eat slowly and savor the flavor of one bite — almost as if you were making love to it. *Focus all your attention on the food in your mouth, and sense the rich taste as it flows over your tongue.* You'll discover the rich experience of eating slowly *and* enjoying the full flavor of your "chocolate," rather than mindlessly eating mouthful after mouthful without ever noticing what you're chowing down.

It's not always the types of foods we eat that create risks, but rather the quantity. In this case, allow yourself to indulge occasionally; but when you do, really *savor and enjoy it.*

An Apple a Day

Apples have been called the "miracle food," and I have come to believe that *apples are the perfect portable food for cops.* They are very low in calories, saturated fat, cholesterol and sodium, *and* at the same time they are an excellent source of dietary fiber and vitamin C.

Apples and their skins also contain an ingredient that functions well as an antioxidant, which research suggests can help to prevent everything from stroke and atherosclerosis to cancer and heart disease. Always wash apples before eating them, and eat the peel as well as the meat of the apple in order to get maximum nutritional benefits. *But also note*: Because a large part of the calories in apples come from sugars, you can gain weight if you eat too many.

Consider grabbing an apple everyday. And if you take one to work with you, throw it into a plastic bag with a napkin or paper towel for clean up. You'll be ready to have a quick snack anytime you need it.

Be a Food Detective

There's so much junk in the foods we eat these days that if you're not eating fresh foods you really need to read the packaging on the foods you are consuming. Start paying attention to the percentages of protein, carbohydrates, fat, sugars, calories, salt — and the chemicals whose names you can't pronounce. Many experts agree that the things to avoid are high-fructose corn syrup, white flour, white sugar and hydrogenated fats.

The 2015 Dietary Guidelines Advisory Committee recommendations to the Secretaries of the U.S. Department of Health and Human Services (HHS) and the U.S. Department of Agriculture (USDA) encouraged dietary patterns which are low in saturated fat, added sugars and sodium. Their recommended goals for the general population are:

- Less than 2,300 milligrams of dietary sodium per day.
- Less than 10% of total calories from saturated fat per day.
- A maximum of 10% of total calories from added sugars per day.

You can learn more about the 2015 Dietary Guidelines Advisory Committee recommendations on the CNN Web site.
http://www.cnn.com/2015/02/19/health/dietary-guidelines/index.html

The current U.S. Government nutritional recommendations (which replaced the old "food pyramid") are available from the U.S. Department of Agriculture on the Choose My Plate Web site.
http://www.choosemyplate.gov/

You can also find some great reproducible handouts for use at your agency on the USDA's Web site.
http://www.choosemyplate.gov/healthy-eating-tips/ten-tips.html

Tactics to Fight Fatigue

Lots of factors contribute to fatigue during your waking hours, and most of them have to do with *not* doing all the things I recommend: getting 7-8 hours of quality sleep, eating well without overeating, staying hydrated and having the right amount of physical activity in your day. Other suggestions include getting some sunlight in your life, every day if possible, and not taking in too much caffeine. With all of that in mind here are some thoughts on how to fight fatigue.

Take a Nap

I am not a fan of napping because naps seem to make *me* more tired. However, I have talked to so many people who swear by napping that I can't ignore their recommendations.

People who recommend naps usually have specific rules. Most recommend napping for no longer than 30 minutes, and many say less than 20 minutes. You'll have to test what works for you.

The U.S. National Sleep Foundation says: "Most people feel refreshed after a nap that lasts approximately 20 minutes. Longer naps can leave you feeling groggy, because they require waking up from a deeper sleep. It's also important not to nap late in the day because this can make it hard to fall asleep at night."

Many law enforcement agencies are adding sleeping rooms to their buildings because fighting fatigue and giving overworked people a place to rest is very important. WebMD offers "9 Tips To Combat Fatigue And Get Your Energy Back."
http://www.webmd.com/balance/guide/get-energy-back

The National Health Service in the United Kingdom offers "Self-help Tips To Fight Fatigue."
http://www.nhs.uk/Livewell/tiredness-and-fatigue/Pages/self-help-energy-tips.aspx

The U.S. National Sleep Foundation offers many useful tips on its Web site.
http://sleepfoundation.org/
http://sleepfoundation.org/insomnia/content/should-you-nap

Tactics to Build Better Sleep Habits

Guard Your Sleep the Way You Guard Your Life

Your amount of *quality* sleep is a critical factor in your ability to do your job. You should enforce some strict rules about the importance of your sleep, just as you would enforce any other critical rules in your life.

Planning for quality sleep is an important factor in whether or not you get it. Set *a daily plan* for bedtime, and allow *at least eight hours of uninterrupted sleep time*. Set up *a room* that is *cool, dark and quiet*. *Don't allow* anyone to interrupt your sleep. *Turn off* phones and other things that could disturb you. *Don't* watch TV, work out or do anything stressful within one hour of going to bed. *Avoid* large meals, excessive fluid intake, caffeine, too much alcohol or smoking right before your scheduled sleep.

Be careful with caffeine: it has a half-life of about five hours, so what you drink in the morning can affect your sleep at night. See the report entitled *Caffeine for the Sustainment of Mental Task Performance* listed at the end of this chapter for more information.

It's critical that you protect your sleeping routine, just as you guard the time set aside for sleep. We all know that the rest of the world doesn't understand shift work and is not very considerate about your time. *You* have to enforce the rules.

"Sleep Now"

If you have trouble quieting your mind and getting to sleep (or getting back to sleep), try repeating the phrase *"Sleep Now"* to yourself while you slowly focus on your breathing. Inhale while you say the word *"Sleep,"* and exhale while you say the word *"Now."* Don't say the words out loud; rather, say them to yourself quietly in your mind. This accomplishes two things: first, you distract your mind with the two tasks of slow breathing and repeating the words; second, you activate actions that we use in several sections of this book to calm your mind and body.

If you practice these breathing exercises tactics frequently, you will condition your mind and body to respond automatically to purge stress and calm yourself. If you practice it often enough, the act of deep rhythmical breathing alone can become your pathway to stress release and relaxation.

Set an Alarm to Go to Bed

Most of us have to set an alarm to wake up from sleep. But have you ever considered setting an alarm to tell you when to go to bed?

Studies show many law enforcement officers get less than the recommended 7-9 hours of sleep every 24 hours, so it might be a good idea to set a bedtime for ourselves and enforce it with an alarm to remind us to go to bed.

Most experts suggest you get a minimum of eight hours of sleep every sleep cycle — otherwise fatigue can affect your performance and decision-making abilities.

Getting eight hours should be a firm commitment. Plan for it and try using reminders, like an alarm on your phone, to make sure it happens.

Create the Right Environment for Sleep

Having the right environment for proper sleep can be as important as having the correct amount of time for sleeping. Many of us work odd shifts, and so our sleep cycles may be different from the rest of the world — or even our families' worlds. Many experts on sleep recommend a cool, dark and quiet environment for sleeping.

If you work the night shift, it's very important to set up a room that is darkened and kept cool so that you can sleep. You should also silence phones and other distractions that will disturb your rest. Wear earplugs if you need to shut out unwanted noise. If you have ongoing problems sleeping or you feel tired all the time, talk to your doctor and consider a sleep test. Some people use white noise machines to create a background curtain of nonspecific noise that helps them *tune out* other familiar backgrounds noises.

None of these recommendations are impossible to follow if you recognize the value of getting proper amounts rest.

Tactics to Promote Proper Hydration

Water, Water — Everywhere

Do you carry a water bottle everywhere you go?

I think you should. I also think you should track the amount of water you drink daily to ensure you're drinking enough.

The Institute of Medicine determined that "an adequate intake (AI) for men is roughly 3 liters (about 13 cups) of total beverages a day. The AI for women is 2.2 liters (about 9 cups) of total beverages a day." That's an AI of 101 ounces for men and 74 ounces for women. I'll bet that's more than you are drinking now, but you will never know until you start tracking your fluid intake.

By carrying a water bottle with you and refilling it several times a day, you will know you're drinking enough. This will also ensure that you have water with you in case you get stuck on a long and involved call or case. Water is important, and you need to *consciously* stay hydrated.

The flip side of this is that you don't want to get stuck on a call somewhere and have to go pee. So think preemptively: Become more intentional about stopping for anticipatory bathroom breaks more often, which will also keep you healthier. A wise old-timer once told me to get in the habit of never passing on an opportunity to use the restroom, and that habit alone kept me better prepared to do my job.

Drink a Glass of Water Before Every Meal

We know from the Institute of Medicine that men should be drinking about 13 cups (101 ounces) of water a day, and women 9 cups (74 ounces) a day. There is also an old adage about drinking eight 8-ounce glasses of water a day, which is a little shy of the Institute's goals, but it's easy to remember. Yet many people still don't drink enough water.

One simple way to seed your habits is to drink a full glass of water *before* every meal, and then another glass of water *with* your meal. This simple tactic, along with carrying a water bottle with you everywhere, should help you ensure that you are always fully hydrated.

Tactics to Help You With Tactical Breath Control

Your breathing cycle can exercise some control over physiological responses in your body, and *tactical breathing* can either energize or relax your physiology. By monitoring and training your breathing, you can steer changes in your body to your desired level, like the Relaxation Response for relaxation, or by energizing yourself for action.

Most of the time these techniques are used to relax. With effective and regular physical conditioning, and practice in advance, tactical breathing can be used to help combat your body's natural fight/flight/freeze response and allow you to recover your normal breathing and heart rate more quickly. This is really useful to control your negative stress response during a high-stress situation or to facilitate your body's recovery when the situation is over.

Different sources recommend several ways to accomplish this, and I discuss the full range of breath control exercises in Chapter 12 on Armor Your Self™ Emotionally Tactics & Exercises.

4x4x4 Combat Breathing

Lt. Col. Dave Grossman (ret.) teaches a 4x4x4 Combat Breathing technique that follows this count routine to calm your body and mind during or after a high-stress situation:

- Breathe in through your nose for a slow 4-count.
- Hold your breath for a slow 4-count.
- Breathe out through your mouth for a slow 4-count.
- Hold your breath for a slow 4-count.
- Repeat this cycle four times.

Using Your Count for Tactical Breathing

Typical breathing exercises focus on the length of inhale, the amount of time you hold your breath, the length of time you exhale, and the pause time before repeating. You can adjust these to your own preferences by counting at different rates. You can perform a rhythmical cycle, such as a 4-4-4-4 or 6-6-6-6 count; or you can create a count that has shorter times for the hold at the top and bottom of your breathing cycle.

These longer strings show the length of time, in time counts, of the inhale, the hold after inhale, the exhale, and the hold after the exhale. You might find a 12-6-12-6 or an 8-4-8-4 cycle suits your body better.

4x4 Tactical Breathing

The 4x4 Tactical breathing cycle focuses on inhaling to a 4-count and then immediately exhaling to a 4-count without the hold at the top or bottom of the breathing cycle. This is repeated over and over again for several minutes until your body reaches your desired level of arousal or relaxation.

Using Breath to Prepare for Action

By quickly inhaling and exhaling several full breath cycles, you can energize yourself for action. Breathe in and out several times a second very rapidly, either just through your nose or through your mouth. Try to keep the duration of your inhale equal to the duration of your exhale. This is sometimes called "*bellows breathing*" because you're using your diaphragm like a bellows to draw in and expel air from your lungs very rapidly to quickly oxygenate your bloodstream. (Don't do too many cycles of this at first — practice no more than 10 to 15 seconds worth.)

Once you've gotten used to this technique, you can use it to energize yourself both physically and mentally for a tough challenge. *Note, however*, that bellows breathing can be very noisy and may not be appropriate in an immediate tactical situation.

Take a Breath Before You Speak

That old adage is really true: You should take a deep breath to trigger relaxation *before* you open your mouth and say something that you may possibly regret later. It's best, if you have the time, to go through several cycles of relaxing breaths before you express yourself. But if you have properly conditioned yourself to use a breathing technique to relax, it will be much easier to call up when you need it under duress. After much practice and conditioning, this technique will, when needed, only require one deep breath to trigger a calming response.

Once you become an expert at learning to use breath control to exercise some mastery over your body's autonomic responses, you will be able to call up your body's desired physiological response much more easily on demand. This is not something you can activate instantly without practice. It only comes after long-term practice and conditioning.

Physical Tactics to Promote Impulse Control — "Not Doing Something You Shouldn't"

Impulse control is your ability to resist a spontaneous urge to do something that is bad for you. Examples include eating something that's not healthy, or eating too much of anything, or spending more than you can afford. Impulse control could positively impact lots of human behaviors because most of us have something in our lives that's bad for us, or that we do to excess when we shouldn't.

Brush Your Teeth Right After Eating to Avoid Snacking

For many people the act of brushing their teeth is a psychological signal that mealtime is over and it's time to start the day (or go to bed). Many people say that they don't like to eat anything after brushing their teeth because the flavors of the food clash with the flavor of their toothpaste. If you fit into either of these categories, then you can use this to your advantage to help you avoid snacking between meals. I suggest that you carry a toothbrush and toothpaste with you wherever you go, and make it a point to brush right after meals to avoid over eating. You might also experiment with brushing your teeth when you have an urge to snack unnecessarily. Most toothpaste has sweetener in it so you will get a little sugar rush, and that fresh mouth taste may inhibit you from eating something you shouldn't.

Physical Tactics to Enhance Action Initiation — "Doing Something You Should"

Action initiation is your ability to take actions that are good for you — but ones that you might not want to do, like daily fitness workouts or starting a diet. You could think of this as "mind control," but it's also really *self-control* or *self-discipline*.

Think of this process:

You Talk to Your Mind to Establish Your Mind-set

Your Mind-set Controls Your Brain

Your Brain Controls Your Body

You Control Your Impulses and Initiate Actions — and then:

Your Body Manages the Effects of Negative Stress

Set Your Mind to Do Something

Try a little *habit seeding* and pick some small tactic you know will improve your health or wellness. Then, set your mind to adding it to your daily routine for at least the next three weeks.

Perhaps you want to brush your teeth after every meal but don't always remember. Start by habit seeding: Carry a travel toothbrush and toothpaste with you in your briefcase or car, and use them as reminders to add this simple habit to your daily routine. Or maybe you want to eat an apple a day or do 10 Perfect Pushups ten times a day. Choose a simple action and see if you can actually work that tactic into your other daily habits. I recommend that you keep a log of your actions and use notes or other reminders to trigger your positive actions each day.

One way to build initiative and get things done is by setting your mind to "Just Do It!" or "Git Er Done!"

CHAPTER 9

Armor Your Self™: Mentally

I differentiate between the concepts of mental and emotional strength and conditioning. When I write about the concept of Armor Your Self™ Mentally, I'm not talking about improving your mental health. To me, strengthening and conditioning your Self *mentally*, is about strengthening and improving your brain's *cognitive* abilities in terms of memory, reaction times, problem solving, communication skills, etc.

Just as you strengthen your body physically by doing strength-building exercises through regular conditioning and repetition, you can do the same with mental or cognitive strength — *and* improve your cognitive functions as they apply to law enforcement. What's more, you can negatively affect you mental functions when you neglect them through fatigue, poor nutrition, poor hydration, negative health habits, and lack of use.

Here are some interesting questions for you to contemplate as you go through this material:

- What's the difference between your *mind* and your *body*?
- What's the difference between your *brain* and your *mind*?
- What's the difference between your *mind* and your *emotions*?

- What's the difference between your *brain* and your *emotions*?
- What's the difference between your *mind* and your *spirit*?

There are no easy answers to these difficult questions, but I think you ought to consider them in your quest for mental strength and sharpness. Such questions will give you something to consider as you gather your thoughts and conduct your own internal examination when you engage in practical spiritual training for your work.

For now, we are going to talk about building strength in your brain and mind, along with some discussion about mind-set. Some of these materials may overlap with those of professionals and trainers who offer advice about mental health and mental strength and toughness. But as a law enforcement trainer (and not as a mental health professional), I think the distinction between emotional strength and cognitive strength is important enough to your survival to have this discussion.

In the various sections of this book that deal with improving your mind-set, I suggest that:

- You Talk to Your Mind
- Your Mind Controls Your Brain
- Your Brain Controls Your Body
- Your Body Manages the Stress Response
- You Get the Job Done Right!

Mental or cognitive mind-set is crucial in managing physiological stresses because a strong, properly oriented mind-set will allow your brain to function at peak levels so that your mind can perform with maximum effectiveness. Think of mind-set as the software used to program your brain, just as a computer programmer uses code to program a computer's operating system. Let's think of *mind-set* as *the operating system of your brain*.

Mind-sets for Your Mental Conditioning:

Master and use these mental mind-sets to train and condition your mind to be sharper, as well as to strengthen and condition all your brain's cogitative functions. You can have many mind-sets and you can nurture them everyday. Mind-sets don't have to work in opposition — they are completely and freely available to you right this instant so that you can grow and develop your own life-saving practices. The choice is always yours.

The "Builder of Community Trust" Mind-set

Like the Community Leader Mind-set (mentioned in Chapter 6), this mind-set envisions peace officers as grassroots leaders within their communities. You're there, in the neighborhoods, as a representative of government and society. Even if you don't feel like a *Community Leader and Builder of Trust*, you have earned that role by the very nature of your oath of office and position within the community. *So take on the leadership role you deserve*. As a leader, your job is to get to know your constituents and work with them to create a safe and secure community within which they can build a healthier society with better lives for themselves, their families, and even you.

You probably have more power than you realize and more of a network of resources than most people. Leverage your power and your network to build trust among the people you serve — and they, in turn, will support you when you need them.

The "Happy Home" Mind-set

The *Happy Home Mind-set* simply creates a happy home environment that's separate from your work. This is a state of mind that's important both mentally and emotionally, because it helps to compartmentalize your work and your home life. The goal is self-preservation and a better quality of life for you and your family.

This doesn't mean that you avoid talking about work at home. On the contrary, it means finding the right balance of what it is about your work that you talk about with your family. Just as I have talked about creating an emotional buffer time between home and work through quiet time and physical exercise, Happy Home Mind-set leaves stressful thoughts of work *at work*, and leaves thoughts and issues from home *at home*. Bringing stressful thoughts of home into your working environment can be dangerous in our line of work, just as bringing stressful thoughts about work into your home can be harmful to your state of mind and to the quality of your home life. This is about being present in the moment and keeping your head in the game (which is why I'm discussing it here under mental conditioning).

The "Never Quit" Mind-set

The *Never Quit Mind-set* is the last I will talk about in this chapter. Like all the others, it has a place within your mental Self because it provides useful physical, emotional and spiritual perspectives. The Never Quit Mind-set focuses on developing mental toughness, building inner strength and courage, and establishing an iron will to get things done.

Mentally, this mind-set is about perseverance and determination — stubbornness on a project or persistence on a case. The Never Quit Mind-set will carry you through tough times and help you strengthen your resolve in the face of overwhelming odds. These qualities are hallmarks of a true law enforcement professional, and cornerstones of great character and unwavering integrity. Nurture this mind-set regularly in preparation for the day when you will really need it most.

Mental Threat Assessment

Mental threat assessment is about examining all the things that can hurt you or impair you mentally. Mental threats that can impair your cognitive functions in law enforcement include *lack of sleep, alcohol, drugs, fatigue, medications, depression, anxiety, heavy doses of negative stress, caffeine, energy drinks and smoking* — to name just a few. And your cognitive functions will also decline with age.

Now, think about the effects these threats (to name just a few) might have on your life and career if you allow them to go unchecked:

- Being outsmarted by a crook
- Missing clues
- Decision fatigue
- Not solving cases
- Slower reaction times
- Not detecting an immediate threat

- Implicit or unconscious bias
- Poor shooting decisions
- Poor arrest decisions
- Sloppy search-and-seizure decisions
- Inadequate report-writing skills
- Inability to navigate to a emergency call effectively
- Weakened interview and interrogation skills.
- Your picture on the evening news for all the wrong reasons!

Let's examine areas of a law enforcement job where mental strength and strong cognitive functioning are critical to success. Consider the importance of cognitive strength in these situations:

- Crime scene investigation
- Traffic accident reconstruction
- Questioning suspects and witnesses
- Examining fresh and perishable evidence
- Negotiating with angry citizens
- Managing informants
- High-speed driving
- Shoot/don't shoot situations
- Low-light arrest and control situations
- Verbally controlling intoxicated subjects
- Counseling wayward teens
- Corralling unwanted wildlife
- Remembering names and other critical information given at roll call days earlier
- Recognizing dangerous people and situations

- Accurately describing a suspect after only a minimal glimpse
- Conducting a quick triage at a mass-casualty disaster scene
- Making a quick evacuation assessment at a potential hazardous materials spill

Having cognitive functions that perform at peak levels will help you to do your job better. They can also keep you alive!

- Because it's important for you in your job to have:
- Problem-solving skills to reconstruct the sequence of a complex crime scene.
- Advanced reasoning skills to conduct a complex financial crimes investigation.
- Verbal proficiency to obtain critical information from a traumatized victim.
- Language skills to interview several multilingual witnesses.
- Mental flexibility to handle multiple high-stress calls back-to-back in one day.
- Anticipation skills to recognize when a subject may be reaching for a weapon.
- Memory capacity to retrieve the names of suspects, victims and witnesses from prior cases.
- Decision-making skills to decipher a complicated shoot/don't shoot situation successfully.
- Verbal fluency to speak with people from all walks of life.
- Appropriate reaction skills to navigate a high-speed chase in heavy traffic.
- Ability to prioritize and set the sequence for critical tactics during an active-shooter call.
- Mental focus to shut out all distractions as you engage an armed subject.
- Cognitive processing speed to respond to and deal with multiple situations both on the radio and in front of you.
- Desire to be constantly learning new tactics and techniques to improve your job performance and officer survival skills.

- Self-control to stay focused and in the moment during all routine and critical decisions and activities.

In order to perform any and all of these acts at peak performance, I suggest you create *a mental strengthening and conditioning regime*, just as you would to improve your physical fitness.

- In law enforcement improving mental strength can involve:
- Brain Training
- Visual and Auditory Conditioning
- Establishing a Blue Warrior Mind-set
- Officer Survival Conditioning
- Internal Mind Control Techniques
- Memory Improvement and Flash Recognition Training
- Trained Observer Training
- Situational Awareness Expansion
- Focused Attention Training

Depending upon the branches of cognitive science you explore, you'll find different lists or descriptions of the primary human cognitive functions or domains. For the sake of our discussions, I have gathered a law enforcement specific set of the descriptions available to give you some things to consider when planning your own cognitive development.

The Big List of Different Terms Used to Define Brain and Cognitive Functions

Learning	Attention	Reaction Time
Intelligence	Memory	Executive Functions
Perception	Language	Flexibility

Processing Speed	Anticipation	Inhibition
Verbal Fluency	Problem-Solving	Concentration
Reasoning	Decision-Making	Focus
Motor Skills Processing	Insight into Human Behavior (EQ)	Visual and Spatial Processing
Emotional Self-Regulation	Prioritization or Sequencing	Distraction Avoidance
Situational Awareness	Working Memory	

Mental Conditioning

13 Primary Topics for Law Enforcement Mental Conditioning

Let's focus on 13 of these topics of mental conditioning that can be very useful in law enforcement. (You can, of course, choose your own goals for building mental or cognitive strength.)

- Situational Awareness
- Memory
- Language
- Mental Flexibility
- Anticipation
- Problem-solving
- Decision-making
- Verbal Fluency
- Reasoning
- Processing Speed
- Reaction Time
- Attention/Concentration/Focus/Distraction Avoidance
- Prioritization or Sequencing

OK — there's a major superstition about the number "13." But the reason I've chosen 13 topics not to tempt fate, but because when Ben Franklin reportedly committed himself to daily self-improvement, he established 13 core values or virtues, and then chose one to focus on each week and to write about in his journal. Ben was very clever, because the number 13 goes into 52 four times. So with 13 topics he was able review and write about each topic four times during a 52-week year.

Using this same system, you can conduct your daily mental training regime by focusing on one of these topics for a week at a time, and do that four times during the course of a year. I can't help but believe that this will help to massively improve your cognitive functioning. (And even if you can't find specific science to support each and every piece of that notion, I sure can't imagine you'll do yourself any harm.)

How Do You Prepare Yourself Mentally Now?

We in law enforcement have for decades been conditioning ourselves mentally with a number of techniques that are very valid in promoting good mental processing and better decision making:

The OODA Loop

Created by Colonel John (Richard) Boyd, a United States Air Force fighter pilot, the *OODA Loop* decision-making tool is used by fighter pilots (and now cops) to make better decisions.

OODA is an acronym for *Observe*, *Orient*, *Decide* and *Act*. When used properly in law enforcement training, OODA helps students to cognitively manage the normally split-second process of observing a situation, deciding if it presents a threat to the officer or the public, and then making a cognitive choice about what action needs to be taken.

Using the OODA Loop for Split-Second Decision Making

- ***Observation***: Collect data from all of your senses
- ***Orientation***: Analyze and synthesize data to form your current mental perspective
- ***Decision***: Determinate a course of action based on your current mental perspective
- ***Action***: Play out decisions physically

The Cooper Color-Code System

Another mental conditioning systems many law enforcement agencies use in training is the *Cooper Color Code System*, created by John Dean "Jeff" Cooper, a Marine lieutenant colonel who served in World War II and the Korean War. In 1976, Cooper founded the American Pistol Institute (API), in Paulden, Arizona, which later became the Gunsite Training Center. Cooper used the Color Code System to help students maintain a state of mental and physical readiness about their surroundings and potential threats. This system, which was probably the basis for the Transportation Safety Administration's alert system, helps to set a standard for alertness and maintaining a state of readiness as it progresses from *white* (a low level of awareness and readiness) all the way up to *red*, representing a mental and physical state needed in a fight.

Creating an Action Mind-set using the Cooper Color Code System:

- *Condition White*: Unaware
- *Condition Yellow*: Relaxed Alert
- *Condition Orange*: Specific Alert
- *Condition Red*: Fight

(Some add *Condition Black*: Actively Engaged in Combat. However, Col. Cooper did not believe in using this category, and his original system only went as high as red.)

Street Survival Seminars and In-Service Training

The world-class *Calibre Press Street Survival Seminar* has been the ultimate police training experience for decades, motivating, inspiring, and teaching officers to not only survive but to *win* critical life-and-death confrontations. Pioneered by Chuck Remsberg and Denny Anderson, this program is the gold-standard training for officer safety and street survival in law enforcement.

How Do You Train Your Mind to Survive This Career?

To answer this question, we must first recognize that there are two different functions of the word *survive* when it comes to mental preparedness.

The most obvious function is having the cognitive effectiveness and positive mental mind-set to handle any critical or threatening situation when it arises.

The second function of the word *survive* deals with having the mental capacity to endure the aftermath of both critical situations *and* the cognitive strain of staying alert to those threats throughout each day and for every day throughout a career.

Earlier I identified 13 primary areas of cognitive brain functioning that I suggest you should work to strengthen in order to build the Tactical Resilience™ necessary to maintain your mental edge and to be able to cope effectively with the negative stresses of this career. Since building strength is a task of repetitive conditioning, I suggest you find ways to regularly challenge yourself mentally in these 13 areas. There's a growing body of research about how we can (or can't) strengthen our cognitive functioning, and I suggest you do your own research and conduct your own personal experiments to test what works and what doesn't work for you.

Situational Awareness

A finely tuned sense of your surroundings and alertness for danger or distress is the cornerstone of an effective and safe law enforcement professional. Tuning your senses to your surroundings takes practice and constant mental focus. Most human beings long ago lost the priority of watching for danger, and frequently, much to our frustration in law enforcement, most people do not watch for danger at all. We do not have that luxury in our profession. The external dangers we face are real and frequent. We must make it a part of our regular, daily practice to constantly hone and perfect this skill. In the next chapter we will talk about some ways you can do this easily and effectively as part of your normal daily activity.

Memory

We all depend on memory every day, and law enforcement professionals need to have sharp, clear memories in order to remember the names of suspects, victims and witnesses, as well as remembering names and other critical information given at roll call or written in a previous report. Clear, sharp memory is also important for recognizing dangerous people and threatening situations, as well as helping to describe accurately a suspect, vehicle or location.

Language

Communications skills are critical in law enforcement when (among other situations) we talk with people, question suspects, write reports, and testify in court. Consider the skills you might use on a daily basis in police work: mediating among angry citizens, talking to addicts, calming mentally ill persons, managing the fears of informants, controlling intoxicated subjects, counseling wayward teens, or talking with multilingual victims and witnesses. Maintaining superior communication skills is paramount in this job.

Mental Flexibility

Whether you are working a crime or accident scene, or trying to solve a community problem, your ability to keep your thinking processes fluid and flexible is critical in your ability to create successful outcomes. Also, your ability to maintain mental flexibility is a very important element in your capacity to stay resilient, as well as to your ability to manage and cope with multiple high-stress cases and situations every day throughout your career.

Anticipation

Your ability to maintain the keenness of your senses, heightened awareness of your surroundings, and a well-tuned mindfulness about your Self plays a major role in how well you are able to perform your duties as a law enforcement professional *and* your ability to protect yourself from danger. Finely-tuned cognitive anticipation can mean the difference between life and death in your ability to sense danger from a suspect or unusual situation. Anticipation must also be tempered by impartiality, good judgment and restraint so that your senses don't deceive you and lead you down an erroneous path. Bias and prejudice can be the enemies of anticipation, so be sure to maintain calm detachment and a levelheaded sense of professionalism.

Problem-solving

Problem solving is the cornerstone of modern law enforcement, and centers around our ability to solve puzzles, analyze data and provide solutions to the most complex of human problems. Whether we conduct a complicated crime scene investigation, reconstruct a fatal accident, question a suspect, or just talk with a crime victim, our problem-solving skills need to be topnotch.

When you add in the split-second and convoluted decisions required in life-and-death shooting or driving situations, the need to process information quickly and efficiently is paramount in reaching a positive outcome. We need our ability to utilize logic, draw inferences, make deductions, employ reason, utilize divergent and convergent thinking, as well as be creative, while doing all of this in only a split second.

In order to be able to do this on demand and under extreme pressure, we must regularly enhance our abilities while also conditioning our skills' usefulness with constant learning and practice.

Decision-making

Ability to make split-second and correct decisions is at the root of all activities within a law enforcement career. It involves gathering information, sorting, analyzing and prioritizing data with the ultimate goal of rendering determination of facts and drawing conclusions. Make no mistake: Your effectiveness in making correct decisions is a skill that should be a regular part of your mental strengthening and conditioning process.

Verbal Fluency

Excellent communication skills are a fundamental competence in the field of public service and law enforcement. Your degree of aptitude is completely dependent upon your desire to excel in this arena.

Whether it's a broad vocabulary needed to converse with a septuagenarian minister, or streetwise banter used with gang members and pimps, or sympathetic tones taken with a juvenile victim, or provocative rants used by an inebriated agitator, you must constantly hone and develop your skills. Whether carefully nurturing a homicide confession from a sociopathic deviant, or artfully crafting a negotiation with a suicidal jumper, you must have the appropriate vocabulary, grammar, volume and tone ready on the tip of your tongue as you nurture the necessary self-awareness to communicate effectively with the vast diversity of our modern multilingual, multicultural, and multigenerational society.

Reasoning

The main characteristics of our profession is ability to bring order to chaos, to make sense of vast quantities of information by utilizing logic and other critical thinking processes in order to reach some conclusion, and to make judgments about both critical *and* mundane societal issues. Whether it is a matter of assessing body language, analyzing patterns of speech, or appraising truthfulness, keen reasoning is critical when you have to evaluate human behavior or gauge the merits of information as evidence.

The early Greeks and Romans taught reasoning skills as part of a well-rounded education, but we no longer seem to value these skills in our modern society. Reasoning, however, is a critical skill you must develop and one that you must practice so that you don't loose your edge.

Processing Speed

A finely-tuned, properly fueled brain functions quickly and effectively — and in our profession, that can mean the difference between life and death. Your split-second ability to sense danger from a person is critical to your well-being — but it can also be the difference between a successful career and one ruined by a bad judgment call that gets you fired or sends you to prison. Conditioning your Self for quick and clear cognitive functioning is an important challenge for anyone who wants to become more effective as a police or other law enforcement professional.

Reaction Time

Your reaction times are a direct offshoot of your brain's processing speed, coupled with your skills at anticipation and situational awareness. While most of these 13 mental training priorities are individual skills you can practice, your reaction speed must be cultivated by blending several of these other skills into regular practice so that the end result enhances your reaction times. Concentrating on your shooting or martial arts skills will surely improve your reaction times in these areas. But you must be careful that you are not just conditioning a fast response to the same stimuli, rather than actually enhancing your overall abilities to make the appropriate rapid responses to multiple external stimuli.

Attention/Concentration/Focus/Distraction Avoidance

Your ability to focus and maintain attention on the tasks at hand, as well as your ability to avoid distractions, is a prerequisite for anyone in law enforcement. Yet these skills are not taught in most training courses and law enforcement academies. So it's up to *you* to practice and develop your abilities with a focused effort. That's why even daily practice to sharpen your focus is useful in learning to avoid distractions, manage bias and maintain your attention on whatever task you set your mind to conquer.

Prioritization or Sequencing

Being able to address challenges in proper order and correct sequence can be a life-and-death process in certain circumstances. Even when the tasks are mundane, your ability to prioritize tasks effectively and place them or other issues in proper sequence is a vastly important skill. Because this is a skill like the other 12 cognitive functions we are discussing, you can practice and learn to get better. One way (but not the only way) to practice every day is by prioritizing calls and placing to-do tasks into their most effective sequence.

There are a number of daily brain training apps and software programs available. I've used *Lumosity* for a number of years and I also use Rosetta Stone Fit Brains. Utilizing these two will cover many of the areas I talked about in this chapter collectively — *but you should do your own research and make your own comparisons.*

Now set your goals for the 13 primary mental strength categories I have listed above, and in the next chapter I'll give you tactics you can use to condition your Self in each category.

Consider Constant, Ongoing Learning!

I am a big believer of a concept the Japanese call *Kaizen*, which translates roughly into the concept of "continuous improvement." The need for constant education, training and professional development has never been more critical to our profession as it is now during the development of the best in 21st-century law enforcement.

As a modern, law enforcement professional, your requirement to develop yourself personally has never been more critical. With so much media attention focused on law enforcement officers who make critical errors in judgment, who fail to stay objective and professional, and who exhibit bias and bigotry in the extreme, all of us are challenged to reach levels of expertise, competence and personal deportment that have never before been required. Learning and education are common, life-long processes — but ones that have never been as necessary as they are today in our profession.

When our brains are *not* strong and well-conditioned, we lose sight of our objectives, forget what's important, make bad decisions, and are unable to solve problems. In short, our minds are neither focused nor effective.

A well-conditioned brain stays sharply focused, processes information quickly, and makes the best possible judgments. A strong mind solves problems quickly and efficiently and is able to effectively communicate its intentions and objectives easily. It is imperative that we keep our brains and minds strong and well-conditioned with daily conditioning techniques.

Think of your mind or brain as one of your most important pieces of professional equipment. How you take care of it is something you should think about early in your career. Even if you didn't do so when you started out, it's not too late now, and you should add these kinds of preventative maintenance techniques into your daily conditioning routine as soon as possible. Just as we condition our bodies, we need to build new healthy habits and condition our brains!

Ask Yourself These Questions:

- How can best I prepare myself mentally for this job?
- What else do I need to be doing that I am not doing now?
- How can I begin today to train and strengthen myself mentally?
- What do I need to add to my Blue Trauma Management plan on this subject?

We do all of these things in order to armor our Selves against mental fatigue and stress, as well as to strengthen our resolve and ability to deal with all the mental and emotional challenges that come our way.

In the next chapter I will offer a number of ways to develop your cognitive abilities to make you safer and more effective in your job and your life. The challenge now is *yours*: to find the ways and time and motivation to make this part of your daily life. *Remember*: It's important — because your life and your quality of life depend upon it.

Resources for Further Research

Scientific American article: "Brain Training Doesn't Make You Smarter."
http://www.scientificamerican.com/article/brain-training-doesn-t-make-you-smarter/

Lumosity: www.lumosity.com

"Fit Brains," by Rosetta Stone: http://www.fitbrains.com/

NeuroNation: http://www.neuronation.com/

Brain Metrix: http://www.brainmetrix.com/

CHAPTER 10

Armor Your Self™: Mentally Training Exercises, Tactics & Techniques

This chapter is about tactics and techniques to help you Armor Your Self™ mentally by developing your cognitive abilities. In the last chapter I suggested that you tailor your training regimen around 13 core areas of cognitive functioning that are important in law enforcement. Now I'll give you suggestions for training techniques or tactics in each of these areas. You can then pick the ones that work best for you, or you can design your own workout plan based upon what you need to improve or maintain your cognitive functioning.

NOTE: I'm neither a psychologist nor a certified counselor, and I don't pretend to be an expert. What I am, though, is another cop like you on this same path — perhaps just a few years ahead of you. I've tried all the things I recommend. Some of them I do regularly, and some of them my friends think work great — so you get to choose the ones that work for you.

Your Armor Your Self™ Mentally Training Plan Should Include:

1. Techniques and Tactics to Heighten Your Situational Awareness Skills
2. Techniques and Tactics to Increase Your Memory
3. Techniques and Tactics to Expand Your Language Skills
4. Techniques and Tactics to Advance Your Mental Flexibility
5. Techniques and Tactics to Develop Your Anticipation Skills
6. Techniques and Tactics to Enhance Your Problem-solving Abilities
7. Techniques and Tactics to Further Your Decision-making Skills
8. Techniques and Tactics to Boost Your Verbal Fluency
9. Techniques and Tactics to Raise Your Reasoning Abilities
10. Techniques and Tactics to Amplify Your Cognitive Processing Speed
11. Techniques and Tactics to Improve Your Reaction Times
12. Techniques and Tactics to Build Your Attention, Concentration and Focus/Distraction Avoidance Skills
13. Techniques and Tactics to Better Your Prioritizing or Sequencing Skills

1. Techniques and Tactics to Heighten Your Situational Awareness Skills

Sense Your Environment

I learned this technique as a young man while hiking in the mountains of my home state of Colorado. A good friend and Outward Bound instructor asked me to sit for a few moments on a rock and to close my eyes. He then asked me to use all of my other senses to perceive my surroundings. He went through a list of my senses and asked, "What do you hear? What do you smell? What do you feel on your skin or body?" Finally, he asked me to pick up a rock, some dirt and a bunch of pine needles, and then asked me how they tasted.

I have always found this to be a useful exercise that taught me to utilize all of my senses to acclimatize myself to new environments. With practice, you learn to quickly employ all of your senses to test your surroundings, and I would recommend that you experiment with it as a way to learn to reengage all of your senses.

Mindful Driving

Here's an exercise to engage your cognitive/perceptive functions fully while driving. I suspect most of us have been driving for many years — probably practically full-time if you are pushing around a patrol car. Use this exercise to hone your perceptive skills and maintain your situational awareness all the time.

For many people, driving can become very mindless. Especially when they drive over the same routes every day. They become detached from the actual mechanics of driving, their minds wander, and they almost drive on autopilot. Perhaps you've experienced this.

In our profession we always need to be situationally aware, and we are supposed to be model drivers. This exercise of Mindful Driving asks you to be very in tune with all the mechanics of driving and what all of your senses are telling you about what's happening. Think of this as being very "in the moment," and allow your mind to observe and acknowledge everything you see, hear, smell, feel and react to. Let your mind expand; then take in everything that is happening as if your mind is supervising it all — which it really is. When you've practiced this, try the Driving Situational Awareness Exercise below.

Driving Situational Awareness Exercise

While driving, quiz yourself about what you see around you. What's the physical description of the person in the car next to you? What are the license plate numbers of the cars in front, in back, and on each side of you? What are the make, model and description of the vehicle behind you?

You can do this exercise alone and check your answers yourself, or you can do it with a partner riding in the car with you. If you are working with a partner, take turns choosing what question you'll ask next. You might ask about things around you; or, for a more difficult challenge, you might ask about things you have just passed.

Enhanced Situational Awareness Exercise

We use this exercise in our "Trained Observer Training" program to enhance and develop your awareness, find tune your senses, and enhance your powers of observation and cognition.

When you're not otherwise occupied, take a moment to look around you and observe your surroundings. Look quickly, and then take out a notepad and write down all that you observed. Make a mental description of the people you saw and mentally calculate their height, weight and age. What were they wearing and what were they doing? Estimate distances to objects, and list the color of everything you saw. What else did you notice? Did you hear anything or smell anything? (This is a good exercise to do in a busy park or restaurant.)

Then, once you've made your mental notes, look back to examine further all that you described. How did you do? What did you miss? The more you practice, the better you'll be at describing things.

If you're working with someone, make it a challenge: Sit facing each other. Person A asks Person B questions about what they can see behind Person B — like what is the woman at the cash register wearing? Or how old is the man in the blue jacket? With human subjects, it's sometimes hard to verify age or weight, but if you are brave enough you can tell them that you are sharpening your powers of observation and ask for the correct answers.

If doing this in public is too intimidating, your can do it at parties or in class or other places where the people know who you are and won't be too intimidated by answering your questions.

2. Techniques and Tactics to Increase Your Memory

Kim's Game

This exercise to improve your memory is done with a partner. It's called *Kim's Game*, and comes from Rudyard Kipling's novel *Kim*, about an Irish orphan who grows up in India. As a young man, Kim is trained for government intelligence work, and the training involves showing Kim a tray of stones and gems for one minute. After covering the tray, his trainers ask Kim how many and what kind of stones he saw. Kim's Game is now used in scouting and in the military to test people's memories and abilities to describe things.

For our exercise, place about 20 or 30 small articles on a table or floor and cover them with a cloth or handkerchief. Use things like pencils, corks, poker chips, coins, candy, nuts, stones, playing cards, toys, knives, string, photos — anything you can find around the house or office, and cover them with a cloth. Sit your partner in front of the objects and uncover them for one minute; then cover them again. Ask your partner to write down all of the articles he or she can remember, and then compare the list to the cluster of objects.

Most people can remember about half of the articles the first few times they play Kim's Game. But the more you practice, the better you become.

For a more advanced version, ask your partner to describe fully each object he or she remembers — such as: What color was the pencil? How long was it? What did it say on the side? Was the coin heads up? What date was it minted? Where is it from? You can also make the game harder by giving your partner less and less time to observe the objects. Another advanced variation involves removing one object, rearranging all the others and asking: — What's missing?

John's Listening Game

When training hostage negotiators I used an *auditory* version of Kim's Game. Instead of an assortment of 20 objects, create a list of 20 things and read them aloud to the other player or players. When you finish reading your list, ask them to write down all the things they heard. You can use a list of famous people, familiar addresses, movie titles or anything else you wish.

With regular practice, your skills should improve. This game is great for improving ability to monitor the radio, and it's an excellent training device for dispatchers and anyone who is on your radio system.

List Memorization

How many names, places or state capitals can you remember from a written or spoken list? Pretend you're in school again, and see how many things you can memorize. Make flash cards, or have someone quiz you. Take John's Listening Game (above) and have someone read a list aloud to you rather than reading the items yourself.

Try this exercise for a week, and at the end of the week see how many things you can remember and compare that number to the first day you tried this exercise. When you have finished with one subject, go on to another. These memorization lists don't have to be work-related — they can be lists of something just for fun.

Remember the Room

Practice your observation skills, but this time with items. Glance around a busy room or area. Set a time limit of five seconds for observation, and then make some detailed notes. How many people were there? What objects did you see? When you finish your notes, look around again and compare what you remember with what's actually there.

Regular practice will improve your general observation skills as well as your eye for detail. Also try our Flash Recognition technique (later in this chapter) to improve your ability to take in a whole scene in one glance.

The Line of Introductions

When meeting people at an event or party, how many names can you remember before you lose track? There are many books and YouTube videos that teach methods of memorizing long lists of things like names. Some suggest you mentally link an object or picture to a name; other techniques suggest that you mentally say the name repeatedly to yourself. Your first task is to investigate these various techniques to find one you think will work for you.

Then, the next time you are at a party or training class with a group of strangers, test yourself to see how many names you can remember. People are very flattered when you remember their names. Over time you should become the life of the party as you show you can remember the names of more and more people.

Number Memorization

How many items or numbers can you memorize in sequence? Depending on how your brain works, this can be more challenging than remembering names.

Your assignment here is the same as in the previous exercise. First, research techniques for remembering long strings of numbers, and find one that works best for you. Then, have someone read a long list of digits to you, and see how long it takes to remember 15 or 20 or 30 numbers in a row. Or try memorizing a list of phone numbers or the winning lottery numbers for the past six months.

3. Techniques and Tactics to Expand Your Language Skills

The ABC Game

Pick any topic or subject. Then find an example of a word on that topic that starts with A. Then find a word about that subject that starts with B, C, D, etc.

For example, if your subject is U.S. state capitals, then A could be Atlanta, and B could be Boston, and so on. This exercise only takes a couple of minutes, and you can practice alone or with others.

Cop Scrabble

This is very much like the ABC Game, only you use law enforcement topics and try to find a word that's an area of law enforcement and begins with each letter of the alphabet.

For a more advanced game, try finding a law or item from the criminal code that covers every letter of the alphabet. For example: A could be Arson, B could be Burglary, etc.

Learn a Language

Learning a new language is very good exercise for your brain — and with all our modern technology, there's no reason why we can't learn something new easily and simply.

There are many resources available online or free at your local library. Or join a club or social organization in your community that has a goal of acquainting you with other cultures, and you can learn to speak a language there with locals from that country.

DuoLingo (http://duolingo.com/) is a fascinating online project that will not only help you learn a new language for free, but behind the scenes it's also working (with your help) to translate the entire Internet into every language. (You'll have to do some investigating to discover what I mean by that last comment!)

4. Techniques and Tactics to Advance Your Mental Flexibility

Off-Handed Day

Try for one week to brush your teeth or try to brush your hair or eat your meals using your "off" hand — *the hand you don't normally use.* If you are feeling particularly adventurous, try learning to write with your hand that is less dominant.

This exercise really challenges your brain and builds mental muscle — but it can be very frustrating. You should also ask your agency's range master if you could have some time to practice off-handed shooting and reloading practice.

Disability for a Day

Once you've mastered working with your "off" hand, try dealing with the *challenges of the disabled.*

Go an hour, half a day or a full day without one of your senses or your mobility. Pick a disability to experiment with. Try being blind for a day, or being in a wheelchair for a day, or giving up your sense of hearing. Try not speaking for a day (and to make it even harder, try learning to communicate with American Sign Language).

Weed a Bad Habit

Earlier in this book I wrote about *Habit Weeding*, the technique I recommend for breaking bad habits. I noted that the typical cycle for a habit is: Trigger, Behavior, Reward. I then suggested that in order to break bad habits you need to figure out what the trigger is for the problem habit and replace the unhealthy behavior with a healthy one. Or you need to find a healthy substitute tactic to insert in place of the bad behavior.

For this exercise I want you to pick some *small* bad habit you have and try to weed it out over the next week. Remember that once you have "weeded" out a bad habit, that accomplishment can become the "seed" for a new and healthier replacement habit. Your success can serve to reinforce your belief in your ability to control all of your actions and behaviors.

Study Abstinence

For this exercise I want you to pick some challenge or weakness you have that might be causing trouble in your life and then try to do without it for just a day or for a week. Can you go a week without sugar, caffeine, gambling, shopping, liquor, or sex? Is there something that you would like to do without in your life? Sometimes the best way to build strength is to resist temptation. You will also find that when you are able to resist that temptation you'll feel a strong sense of satisfaction that will carry over into many other parts of your life and make all of your endeavors at strength conditioning much more effective.

5. Techniques and Tactics to Develop Your Anticipation Skills

Challenge Your Head with Improv

Most techniques to improve your reaction speed or abilities at anticipation require some physical activity as well. Some are fun; others are much more serious. The challenge in improving your anticipation skills is that not only do you have to be able to predict and anticipate what's coming, but you also have to be able to do it correctly — because if you're great at anticipation but your response is incorrect in the circumstances, the result could be fatal or could ruin your career. Some exercises to improve your anticipation abilities are very serious, but let's start with something that's fun.

Improv is a comedy technique to challenge your listening and response skills. It tests your anticipation skills and your ability to think quickly on your feet. You could go to a local comedy club or community college and take a class, but one simple exercise you can do with a partner is to tell a *fictional story*. Each person must add information, but only in small bits, usually four or five words at a time. You start the story with four or five words, and then your partner needs to add four or five more words. One key to success in Improv is never to contradict the other person's statements; rather transition with the phrase "*yes, and...*" so that you are always adding to the story rather than detracting from it. No matter how you start off, the stories never come out the same way. If you're willing to have some fun and take some emotional risks, you'll find this exercise very rewarding.

Krav Maga 360 Defense Technique

Many of the martial arts offer training techniques to build your sense of anticipation. I encourage you to investigate the *Krav Maga 360 Defense* training technique, used with a partner to build your reaction time and sense of anticipation. The essence of this training regime is that your partner throws punches and kicks at you while you block them with one of seven blocking positions. As you train together, you build speed, and your session becomes more of a sparring dance as your partner throws more and more attacks while you continue to block. This is not meant to be combat sparring; rather, it's a training exercise to build speed and heighten your awareness. By doing this regularly you quicken both your reaction times and abilities to sense an opponent's attack.

To learn more, check out John Whitman's training videos on YouTube channel. https://www.youtube.com/user/johnwhitman1967

Or you can visit the Krav Maga Alliance Culver City Web site. http://allianceculvercity.com/instructors/

Symphonic Stimulation

A 2007 study by researchers at Stanford University's School of Medicine, and reported in the journal *Neuron*, indicates that listening to short symphonic music might enhance your brain's ability to anticipate events and stay focused. Researchers found that music stimulates areas of the brain involved with paying attention, making predictions and accessing memories.

Even if you don't like classical music, try it for 15 minutes a day, and see if it has an effect on your brain. You can learn more at these sites:

https://med.stanford.edu/news/all-news/2007/07/music-moves-brain-to-pay-attention-stanford-study-finds.html

http://www.wsj.com/articles/SB122912678274103169

6. Techniques and Tactics to Enhance Your Problem-solving Abilities

The "What If...?" Game

Most of us have been trained to use the *"What If...?"* game to anticipate danger and plan responses. For example, as you approach the door of a suspect's home, you ask yourself: *"What if* he opens the door and has a gun in his hand? *How* will I respond?" Or you imagine: "*What if* gunshots come through the door? *Where* will I seek cover? *What* will I do next?"

This game is designed to keep your metal acuity heightened and your attention focused on areas of potential danger. Use it as an ongoing problem-solving process. *Anticipate* risks and then mentally *plan* your responses to decide how you would handle various problem situations.

You should always be planning a number of contingencies so that you don't have only one solution but several — in case your first scenario doesn't resolve the problem. *One word of caution:* Don't just condition yourself to negative situations requiring a deadly force response. I think this is how many cops are getting themselves into trouble these days. You might also consider what you would do if the subject comes to the door with a tray of chocolate chip cookies. Well, that might not really happen, but be careful about planning only for a deadly force response. What are the other possibilities?

"What If…" doesn't only have to be about life-threatening situations. For example, you might be backup on a call and do some mental calculations about how you would handle the situation or resolve the problem; and then you might think about sharing your thoughts and possible courses of action with the primary officer or detective on the case or call.

In the next chapter we'll go over how to turn off this kind of thinking so you can give your mind a rest.

What Would Sherlock Do?

I loved Sherlock Holmes stories and movies when I was a kid, and even though Sherlock is fictional, his techniques are not. You have an opportunity to build your repertoire of skills just as Sherlock Holmes did, one step at a time.

At the end of this chapter I've listed a couple of books that will help you build your own personalized training program. But for this exercise I want you simply to ask yourself: *What would Sherlock do in this situation?* Now, don't go around acting like a crazy person, wearing a deerstalker cap and talking out loud to yourself. Rather, just change your frame of mind when it comes to problem solving and get out of your old habits.

Sherlock Holmes had three key traits you can learn from:

- He was very *knowledgeable* — so work on learning as much as you can about the craft of law enforcement.

- He was very *observant* — so the next time you have a problem or case to solve, try to be a detached observer rather than jump to conclusions; and

- He was a master of *logical thinking* and *deductive reasoning*.

All of these skills are mentioned elsewhere in this chapter, so practice *all of them* as well. Next week, when you are faced with a tough problem, get out your notepad, begin to think of the problem as Sherlock would, and make notes about things you have objectively observed and you need to learn, but don't now know regarding how to deal with the situation. Then, use those notes to make some logical deductions about what to do next.

Focus on Using Logic

Logic problems can be very stimulating, and many are very much like working a complex criminal case. In fact, regularly solving fun logic problems can make you better at your job. To get you started, here are a variety of links to various puzzle and problem-solving Web sites:

For *logic puzzles*, visit Logic Puzzles by Puzzle Baron:
http://www.logic-puzzles.org/

For *math puzzles* (like Sudoku and KenKen), visit:
http://www.brainbashers.com/logicpuzzles.asp

For more *math problems*, visit: www.MathIsFun.com

For *riddles*, visit: http://riddles.com/

Take a look at this article about Stinkers for Thinkers: http://www.mirror.co.uk/news/technology-science/science/stinkers-big-thinkers-12-fiendish-5521443

And, finally, for *the world's hardest logic problems*, see list of links at the end of this chapter.

7. Techniques and Tactics to Further Your Decision-making Skills

The Decision Hunter

Decision Hunter gives you a better perspective about the many decisions you make in a day and how you go about making them. We all make many, many more decisions than we realize. For the next couple of days, carry a notepad and pen with you and simply count the number of decisions, large and small, you make in a day. If you want to be more thorough, you can keep a log of all of them.

After the first day, log *how* you make your decisions. What's the process you use to make your decisions? Are you slow and deliberate? Do you like to "sleep on it" when you have to make a tough decision? Or are you a swift, perhaps impulsive decision-maker?

We usually need three things to make a decision: First, we need *information*. Then we need to *weigh* the merits and detriments of a possible course of action. Finally, we need to do a *gut check* — examine our feelings and instincts about the decision.

How do *you* make your decisions? The purpose of this exercise is simply to encourage you to observe and learn about your decision-making processes, rather than to make any immediate adjustments.

Split-Second Decision Maker

As I noted in the Decision Hunter exercise above, there are many ways to make decisions. Many can be made easily and quickly, while others require more deliberation and consideration (as opposed to impulsively jumping to a conclusion). The most challenging decisions we make in law enforcement are those we are called upon to make in a split second.

I mentioned in the previous exercise three things needed to make a decision: *information*, a *cost-benefit analysis*, and a *check of your instincts*. In making a split-second decision, especially in police work, we probably rely on a fourth factor: *confidence*. If you're ambivalent about a decision, you're more likely to make a mistake, and in a critical or life-and-death situation, that can be fatal.

Now is the time for you to build confidence in your decision-making abilities. As you log your daily decisions, note how you make them, and then grade them with a *confidence score*.

Note how often you are supremely confident about your decisions and how often you are uncertain. Practice is the most important way to build confidence, so I suggest you embark on a quest to find opportunities to take risks and make challenging decisions.

One of the best arenas in which to do this is in your interpersonal relationships. We are most afraid of saying and doing things that will hurt or upset the important people in our lives. Whether you are dating or in a committed relationship, you know what I mean. Try your newly-honed, decision-making skills in situations that involve some social or familial risk.

The last part of this exercise is to work with your agency to provide more split-second, decision-making opportunities. This can be done with "shoot/don't shoot" computer simulations; in live training exercises using simunitions or paint balls, or in role-playing exercises.

Remember: *Practice* is what hones your skills best. Training is the best place to make a mistake if you're going to make one, so practice until you're proficient.

The Decision Tree

A decision tree is a matrix, mantra or other mnemonic device you use to help make better decisions. One I learned early in my career went like this: "Ask yourself: Is it *legal*? Is it *ethical*? Is it the *right* thing to do? If yes, go ahead and do it."

Other people tell me they just ask themselves: "Would my grandmother approve of this?" And if the answer is yes, they go ahead with their decision.

What saying or mnemonic device do you use to remember your decision-making priorities? If you don't have one, I think you should write one. If your agency doesn't have one, I think you should start the discussion today.

8. Techniques and Tactics to Boost Your Verbal Fluency

A Word A Day

This exercise helps to enhance your vocabulary, one word at a time, a new word every day. A simple way to do this is to have a large, printed dictionary sitting in front of you on a table; then, every day, just open it to a random page and pick a word. Learn how to spell it and what it means, and then try to fit it into your everyday conversation. At first your friends will become suspicious, then they may start to tease you about it. But you'll find that after awhile they'll start to learn with you, and some may even start to compete with you by finding their own words. And that'll only help you because then you'll be learning *two* words a day — one of your own and one from a friend.

There are even daily calendars you can buy that offer you a new word from a dictionary each day.

The Sergeant's Exam

Learning more about the criminal code and becoming more fluent in discussing it is the object of *The Sergeant's Exam*. Think of it as a preparation program for taking the sergeant's test or any other promotional exam. Pick one statute from your local criminal code and memorize its wording. Make sure you understand all the elements needed to meet the burden of proof, including the parameters of intent, possession, culpability, causation and active involvement. Then discuss it with someone else and include in your discussions consideration of its origins, its ramifications for modern society and where it might need to be improved or changed.

The purpose of this exercise is to utilize and expand your verbal skills in an area you're already familiar with while challenging you to stretch your ideas and beliefs. You can also think of it as preparing for a big, complex court case as you justify all the decisions made and how you would present them before a judge and a jury.

This exercise is best practiced out loud with someone else. When you finish one statute, move on to another. Try this with one statute a week, and think about applying it to discussions in a staff meeting or at roll call.

Not-So-Presidential Debate

Debating is a skill that challenges your cognitive flexibility, verbal skills and problem-solving capacity. Do some of your own research and learn about the art of debate. You'll find instruction about how to collect your thoughts effectively before you speak; how to frame a proposition; and how to build a logic argument involving a premise, an inference and a conclusion.

Sharpening your debate skills is *not* about arguing. Rather, it's about how to assemble and present your thoughts in a logical and structured way. Spend the next two weeks learning about the art form of debate and then take your new found skills to work. Don't be overbearing — but remember: Cops love to argue their opinions, so find colleagues with an opposite point of view and see if you can sway their opinions with your logic and debating skills. After much practice this can also help enhance your skills at courtroom testimony.

Learn more with this Web site:
http://www.virtualschool.edu/mon/SocialConstruction/Logic.html

Practice Public Speaking

Take opportunities to use your verbal skills more often by volunteering to give public presentations. Every law enforcement agency receives requests to have someone make a presentation to a corporate or community group, but very few officers and staff want to give them.

Whether it's talking to elementary school kids or to a civic group, there are opportunities available. You might also consider joining a local Toastmasters club. Check out its Web site at https://www.toastmasters.org/, where you'll find great, free information about public speaking and communication skills. Look for the page labeled "Public Speaking Tips."

9. Techniques and Tactics to Raise Your Reasoning Abilities

Think Like Sherlock Holmes

Ah-ha! Sherlock Holmes again! Learning to use deductive reasoning is a very valuable asset to a law enforcement professional. Becoming familiar and comfortable with this skill is not a simple path, but it's one you might find satisfying as part of your ongoing personal and professional development. Here is a simple problem to get you started:

> Suppose you question twin brothers, John and Bill, as suspects in a crime. You've been told that one brother is completely honest and always tells the truth, and one brother is a desperate criminal who always lies. They both look alike — so what *one* question can you ask both suspects to figure out which one is lying?

Consider some simple characteristics the fictional character, Sherlock Holmes, exhibits which might help you both in your work and in exploring deductive reasoning. First, you should always be working to build your base of knowledge. When confronted with a problem, remain open-minded and utilize your skills of observation and examination. *Don't* jump to conclusions; rather, be objective and withhold judgment until you've assembled all available facts. If you don't immediately come up with a simple solution, consider breaking things down in order to examine smaller sets of information and then work on the smaller sets of data. Finally, at the end, evaluate your solution one more time to confirm your conclusions and validate your reasoning process.

- Here is a list of Web sites to help you with logic and deductive reasoning:
- Here's an excellent Web site, with some sample problems from West Texas A&M University, to get you started:
  http://www.wtamu.edu/academic/anns/mps/math/mathlab/beg_algebra/beg_alg_tut35_reason.htm
- Here's another site with excellent examples of different kinds of logic problems:
  http://www.expandyourmind.com/logicproblems/
- Here is a great site to help you learn more about deductive reasoning:
  http://www.highiqpro.com/deductive-reasoning

And if you still haven't solved the problem about the twin brothers I posed above, you might find the solution by investigating these resources that I've listed for you. Good luck!

Puzzle, Puzzle, Puzzle

Puzzles help build reasoning power. There are many different kinds of puzzles, and I recommend trying a different kind every day, spending 10 to 15 minutes each day to build your reasoning skills. There are number- and math-oriented puzzles, like Sudoku and KenKen, as well as word puzzles, such as crossword puzzles or logic problems.

- Visit this site for Japanese-type logic puzzles (like Sudoku and KenKen):
  http://www.brainbashers.com/logicpuzzles.asp
- For KenKen puzzles, visit *The New York Times* site at:
  http://www.nytimes.com/ref/crosswords/kenken.html?_r=0
- For free daily crossword puzzles, visit:
  http://freedailycrosswords.com/daily-puzzles/

- Do the free daily mini-crossword puzzle from *The New York Times* at:
  http://www.nytimes.com/crosswords/game/mini
- Or subscribe for the full daily *New York Times* Puzzle at:
  http://www.nytimes.com/subscriptions/games/lp897H9.html?campaignId=4QHQ6
- For logic puzzles, visit Logic Puzzles by Puzzle Baron at:
  http://www.logic-puzzles.org/
- To challenge your brain with riddles, visit: http://riddles.com

And try the *Zebra Puzzle*, also known as Einstein's Logic problem. The Zebra Puzzle has been attributed to both Albert Einstein and Lewis Carroll, but neither connection has ever been verified. It's a complex logic problem, which Albert Einstein (supposedly) said 98% of the world's population could not solve. Everyone loves a good challenge, so try it out. It's not easy, so give yourself plenty of time. You can find variations and information at these Web sites:

- Wikipedia: https://en.wikipedia.org/wiki/Zebra_Puzzle
- Duke University:
  https://www.cs.duke.edu/courses/spring06/cps102/notes/zebra.pdf
- Florida Institute of Technology:
  http://lib.fit.edu/documents/library-displays/200306/puzzle2.pdf

10. Techniques and Tactics to Amplify Your Cognitive Processing Speed

Flash Recognition Training

Flash recognition training was pioneered for law enforcement in the 1950s by Rolland L. Soule, an associate director of the Southern Police Institute at the University of Louisville, in Kentucky. Law enforcement officers are seated in a darkened room and shown a projected image for only 1/100 of a second. Then they're asked to describe what they saw. The image can be words, numbers or pictures, and when applied to law enforcement, the images can be people, license plates, vehicles or crime scenes. The goal is to develop the skills of perceiving images in larger *whole* units rather than focusing on the small details.

Soule said, "Observation (perception) is visual association via the brain's memory faculty. The basic task of flash recognition training is to lower the threshold between visual perception and identification of what has been observed, to the lowest possible threshold level."

Using PowerPoint as a training tool, law enforcement officers can now use this training in short sessions at staff meetings and roll call briefings. Training needs to be done in pairs, with each partner choosing which images to project, and showing them for only a fraction of a second to a partner/observer. With practice you can increase your ability to identify, in just a single glance, license plates, facial features and images of a whole scene. Read more in Rolland L. Soule, "Flash Recognition Training in Law Enforcement Work — Next Exposure Ready Now," 49 *J. Crim. L. Criminology & Police Sci.* 590 (1958-1959), which you can access online from Northwestern University School of Law Scholarly Commons at: http://scholarlycommons.law.northwestern.edu/cgi/viewcontent.cgi?article=4784&context=jclc

Trigger, No Speed Limit and Bop It!

Trigger, *No Speed Limit* and *Bop It!* are party games that enhance your brain's cognitive processing speed. They are fun and fast-paced, and can be played with friends.

Look for those games at your local toy store or online retailer, or check out these Web sites to get more ideas:

- http://media.learningrx.com/7-toys-for-the-smart-moms-toy-box/
- http://brainbuzz.learningrx.com/october-2013/smart-moms-toy-box-october-2013/

Online Brain Training

Lumosity, *Fit Brains* and many other online brain-training sites offer fun and entertaining ways to not only improve cognitive processing speed but also to improve memory and computational abilities, as well as to condition many more of your cognitive abilities. You can learn more at these sites or the others listed at the end of this chapter.

Find *Lumosity* Brain Training at:

- http://www.lumosity.com/app/v5/personalization/account/new
- http://www.lumosity.com/personal-training-plan

Find *Fit Brains* (by Rosetta Stone) at:

- http://www.fitbrains.com/
- http://www.fitbrains.com/blog/new-app-fit-brains-logic-trainer/

11. Techniques and Tactics to Improve Your Reaction Times

Follow The Ball

Any activity that has you react to on-coming objects will work to build your cognitive muscle and improve your reaction speed. Games like tennis, baseball and soccer (better known as *futbol* anywhere outside the U.S.) are all great for improving your eye-hand or eye-foot coordination. Each of these sports also has activities in which you can use an automated mechanism to propel the ball towards you to make you react. Another idea is to find a wall and use a racquetball or tennis racket to hit the ball back and forth to yourself.

You might also check out this very interesting article with seven suggestions to improve your reflexes and an interesting video about making your own elastic head-ball punching trainer at: http://www.mightyfighter.com/top-7-exercises-on-how-to-improve-reflexes/

Running in the Woods

A football training tire-run or agility drill will improve both your aerobic performance and build reaction speeds. Any obstacle course that requires you to think and react to the unexpected is even better.

Many people like *trail running* because it constantly gives an uneven surface that requires both brain and body to react to the changes and contours. Please be careful doing this — one wrong step can have serious consequences.

You can find a great article on Bodybuilding.com about exercises to improve your reflexes and reaction times at:
http://www.bodybuilding.com/fun/bioplyo2.htm

Be the Mirror

Be the Mirror uses a partner to conduct your training. You stand facing each other and one person takes the lead in moving while the other tries to mirror the movements being made. It's as though you're trying to be a mirror and reflecting back all the movements you see your partner make, which, in fact, are the opposite of what you are doing.

I've noted this activity under the heading of mental training because, in order to improve your cognitive function in the area of reaction times, you may have to do things that are physical in order to enhance your reaction times. That's OK, since many of the techniques mentioned in this book overlap more than one of the four quadrants.

Here are some articles that might give you more ideas:

- http://www.stack.com/reaction-time/
- http://www.stack.com/2013/08/22/reactive-shuffle/
- http://www.brianmac.co.uk/reaction.htm

12. Techniques and Tactics to Build Your Attention, Concentration and Focus/Distraction Avoidance Skills

Concentrate Like the Master

Sherlock Holmes was remarkable for being able to keep a keen focus while shutting out all distractions, which allowed him to concentrate all of his deductive powers on a particular problem. Even though Holmes is a fictional character, many of the traits Sir Arthur Conan Doyle gave him were traits modeled from real people, and we in law enforcement can learn a lot from him as a role model for his ability to focus. Whether or not you read the Holmes stories, see if you can utilize regular practice to add some of his better abilities to your repertoire of skills.

First, hone your ability to focus by sitting comfortably in a quiet room and choosing an object across the room. Set a timer and study it for 30 minutes without moving. Use your cognitive skills to measure it, weigh it, describe it, and in all ways quantify it in your mind. Do this exercise several times over several weeks, and then turn your newly-honed skills to concentrating on one of the logic problems listed in the "Strengthening Your Reasoning Skills" section of this chapter. See if your new skills help you solve those problems.

Finally, use these skills to solve a real-life problem at work or home.

Trained Observer Training

At the Law Enforcement Survival Institute we teach a *Trained Observer Training* class to help improve observation skills. We've found that one way to improve your concentration and mental focus, as well as the kind of meticulous memory needed for a job in law enforcement, is to take 1 to 2 minutes and watch a person or an object while trying to remember every detail. When your time is up, look away and write down every detail you can remember. When you're finished with your written notes, look back and check your description against the real person or object.

This differs from *Kim's Game* in that the person you observe might be moving — one of the many distraction factors you find when observing the realworld. Over time *Trained Observer Training* can improve your focus and descriptive abilities.

You might start by working with people you know so that you'll be able to ask how old they are and how much they weigh. Just as in traffic enforcement class, where you used a radar or laser to validate your visual estimates of speed, this can help you improve your visual estimates of age and weight.

Once you get very good in your estimations, you can practice with strangers in real-life settings. In these situations, practice looking at them quickly and then writing down your description, then looking back and studying them for a few minutes to validate your first impressions. You can also do this in field interview situations where you're going to be asking people about their height, weight and age for your report or contact info. Just size them up before you ask and then compare your estimates to their answers.

Sketching

Sketching takes your *Trained Observer Training* to another level. Even if you're not an artist, you can learn a lot and improve your focus and concentration by trying to sketch an object that's near you. Many people find sketching difficult because they haven't trained their eyes to see the lines, shadows and contours that artists see easily. This is not all about natural talent but about training your eyes and brain to work in unison.

Take a moment to pick out an object in the room and then sketch a picture of it. Try for accurate detail. Spend 5 or 10 minutes and get your drawing to be as realistic and accurate as possible. When you finish, examine the object more closely and compare the real thing to your drawing. Make notes about how you might improve your drawing.

Repeat this exercise with the same object, or something new, and try to practice this every day for 30 days. Describe in your three-ring notebook how much your skills improved in 30 days. Make some notes about what skills you think have improved and why.

13. Techniques and Tactics to Better Your Prioritization or Sequencing Skills

The Inbox Exercise

Many modern law enforcement testing processes for the ranks of sergeant and above often include an *Inbox Exercise*, challenging you to prioritize and place in proper sequence a group of tasks and obligations. Every one of us struggles with this ability, which is very important in both law enforcement and our daily lives.

Most people procrastinate about the things that are most important because those things seem too big or too loaded with emotion. But notice that when you're planning to leave on vacation, you're probably very productive a day or two before you leave on that "big trip." We need to learn to bottle this ability and make it work for us *today and every day*. The big issue here is that most of us don't want to do the hard work first.

Start today by setting a goal to make a "to-do" list with only 3-to-5 items on it for the day. If you finish them all, you can add more later. (That said, I've found that unless they're really small tasks, you'll only finish 3 to 5 of them and you *do* want to have a sense of accomplishment when you finish your list.)

Do the most challenging task first. You'll know which one by how much you've been resisting doing it. It might not otherwise even make its way onto your list *because* you dread doing it. *Do that task first!*

After a few weeks of tackling the tough tasks first, you'll have a great sense of pride and accomplishment and it'll be easier for you to do the hard work first. I think you'll find you'll feel a great sense of confidence and a stronger sense of satisfaction based upon all your accomplishments.

First Step, Next Step

When it comes to prioritizing tasks and putting things into proper sequence, most people become overwhelmed by the data and begin to procrastinate because the overall task seems too large and daunting. This is one of those times when we need a system to guide us. That system can be remembered with the phrase "*First Step, Next Step.*" Like the old joke about "How do you eat an elephant?" (The answer, of course, is, "One bite at a time!"), the most important task is always to choose the first task to begin the process. Once we've chosen the *First Step*, we can proceed with a series of *Next Steps*.

Your challenge is to learn to implement this system for everyday challenges so that when you confront a really large or dangerous challenge, you have exercised your mental muscles to the point where you're in good shape and ready for the challenge.

Over the next two weeks, make a concerted effort to look for daunting challenges you're trying to avoid — like that project around the house or that follow-up to a case. Identify the *First Step* and go to work, one step at a time until you have worked your mental muscle so that you feel confident about your progress. Then find another daunting project. Going one step at a time, you'll get stronger and stronger.

By the way, "*First Step, Next Step*" is also the mind-set and mantra you set for yourself to get things done!

Adopt a Pet Project or Case

I love my dog and believe that everyone ought to have a pet. But what I mean here is a little different. Most of the time in law enforcement we run from one call to another, or move from one case to another. Sometimes we lose sight of why we really wanted to become cops in the first place. My suggestion is that you find a report or case that really strikes your fancy and try to follow it through to completion. Make it your *pet project*.

Whether you work patrol or the detective bureau, you get barraged with too much work and sometimes feel like you're just processing paper. This will be an opportunity to practice your prioritization skills while you make time for something you might find more satisfying than simply responding to calls or working cases that don't interest you as much.

My suggestion is to find a case that appeals to you and work on it whenever you can and do whatever you can to solve it. Follow up on more leads, talk to more witnesses, re-interview everyone, extend your canvass of the area, look for new sources of video, try using Crime Stoppers, talk to the suspects again.

I don't suggest that you waste time on a dead-end case; but I *do* suggest you remember what you love about police work, and that you really practice your craft and spend some of your free time at work on a case that really matters. When you finish with it, you'll not only feel a tremendous sense of satisfaction doing what you love — you'll also be free to find a *new* pet project!

Continue Your Training With Exercises and Tactics to Build and Strengthen Your Learning Abilities

TED Talks

One of the best and easiest *non*-reading ways I've found to expand my knowledge base is to visit the TED Web site (www.TED.com) and watch one of their thousands of videos on topics ranging from "The new bionics that let us run, climb and dance" to "The power of vulnerability"; from "The history of our world in 18 minutes" to "How great leaders inspire action"; from "How to spot a liar" to "How I held my breath for 17 minutes." Most TED talks are less than 18 minutes long. Check it out. You're sure to find something interesting — if not astonishing.

Investigate Learning

Take an afternoon to visit your local library. Look around and see all it has to offer. Talk with the staff and ask for recommendations about how to expand your horizons. Pick a topic and see what resources are available.

Beyond books, your library probably has Internet access with memberships to other sites that you might otherwise have to pay for. It also has videos and audio recordings, as well as newspapers, magazines and other publications. Library staff is trained to help you to learn and investigate the things you want to learn about — and best of all, *it's free*.

Do Some Exploring

Consider spending a day at your local zoo, aquarium, museum or botanical garden. Most offer free days, so it won't cost you anything. If you've never been to the place, you'll find a lot to learn. The experience will probably help you reduce the negative stresses of your job, and if you take time to read the signs and posters the staff has put up for you, you'll learn something you didn't know.

Learning is easy when it's something you *want* to learn about, and one of the reasons many people hate school is because they *have* to learn things they don't want to learn about. As an adult you can challenge your brain by expanding your horizons and learning something completely new to you, and which, even though it might not be relevant to your daily life, might grow your knowledge base and expand your belief systems.

It's important to keep challenging your brain and to be fluid in your training and conditioning. Don't get stuck in a rut with the same exercises. Each week seek out a new exercise for your brain and add it to your repertoire of tactics and exercises. You'll find your favorites, and that's okay because they'll keep you coming back for the enjoyment. But always add new things to keep your brain functioning at peak levels.

Now Use These Positive Tactics to Build Positive Habits and Positive Systems in Your Life

- All of these exercises are examples of positive mental development tactics and techniques.
- Choose to practice these tactics to strengthen and condition your Self mentally.
- Build those tactics and techniques into positive habits at home and at work.
- Build those positive habits into systems that will contribute to your overall character development and health.

Resources for Online Brain Training

- Lumosity Brain Training:
  http://www.lumosity.com/app/v5/personalization/account/new
  http://www.lumosity.com/personal-training-plan

- Fit Brains by Rosetta Stone:
  http://www.fitbrains.com/
  http://www.fitbrains.com/blog/new-app-fit-brains-logic-trainer/

- NeuroNation: http://www.neuronation.com/

- Brain Metrix: http://www.brainmetrix.com/

- Intelligym: https://www.intelligym.com

- Brain Gym's Interactive In-Person Brain Training courses at:
  http://www.braingym.org/ or look at their books at:
  http://www.braingym.com/store-edubooks1.html

Memory Resources

- Mnemonic techniques:
  http://web-us.com/memory/mnemonic_techniques.htm

- Human memory: http://web-us.com/memory/human_memory.htm

- How memory works (Attention > Encoding > Storage > Retrieval):
  http://web-us.com/memory/theories_and_processes.htm

- Twenty Memory Tricks from *Readers Digest*:
  http://www.rd.com/health/20-memory-tricks-youll-never-forget/

- Excellent memory tricks:
  http://www.thelearningweb.net/memory-tricks.html
  http://www.dumblittleman.com/2007/10/5-quick-and-easy-memory-tricks.html

Mind Tools

- The Major System for memorizing long numbers at:
  http://www.mindtools.com/pages/article/newTIM_07.htm

- Darren Bridger's two videos on YouTube on memory improvement at:
  Part #1
  http://www.youtube.com/user/DarrenBridger?feature=watch#p/u/3/nlCz9oh8-eQ
  Part #2
  http://www.youtube.com/watch?v=y3GE2bsjLbg

- Improve your Visual Information Process Skills (Perception, Tracking, Focusing, and Eye Teaming) at:
  http://www.eyecanlearn.com/

Problem Solving Resources

- The 10 Hardest Logic Puzzles Ever Created by Patrick Min, Calcudoku.org at:
  http://www.conceptispuzzles.com/index.aspx?uri=info/article/424
  http://gizmodo.com/can-you-solve-the-10-hardest-logic-puzzles-ever-created-1064112665

- 10 Logic Puzzles You Won't Be Able To Solve at:
  http://www.buzzfeed.com/kjh2110/10-logic-puzzles-you-wont-be-able-to-solve#.gfajB45vQ

- The Lady, or the Tiger at:
  https://en.wikipedia.org/wiki/The_Lady,_or_the_Tiger%3F

- Mazes, logic puzzles and other conundrums at:
  http://amazeingart.com/fun-stuff.html

- Logic Puzzles by Puzzle Baron:
  http://www.logic-puzzles.org/

Books To Improve Your Thinking

Kahneman, D. *Thinking, Fast, and Slow*. New York: Farrar, Straus and Giroux, 2011.

Konnikova, Maria. *Mastermind: How to Think like Sherlock Holmes*. New York: Penquin, 2013. Print.

Smith, Daniel. *How to Think like Sherlock: Improve Your Powers of Observation, Memory and Deduction*. London: Michael O'Mara Books Limited, 2012. Print.

Other Mental Homework

Set up your mental training regime. Plan what you want to do for a week at a time, and then create a method to record your progress.

I've discussed Trained Observer Training several times on the CopsAlive Web site, and we offer an on-site training course in this subject through The Law Enforcement Survival Institute.

www.CopsAlive.com
www.LawEnforcementSurvivalInstitute.org

CHAPTER 11

Armor Your Self™: Emotionally

Now let's examine *how* to strengthen and condition your Self emotionally. In this chapter I'll give you some things to think about regarding your emotional Self. I'll also suggest things you can do to improve your management of negative emotions, as well as some thoughts about how to promote positive emotions.

Your Emotional Self

I distinguish between the *emotional* and *mental* of you because I believe they are totally different and very separate things. This may be why there's some confusion within our profession about how to deal with its hidden dangers, since they aren't like the usual threats we train to deal with. Consider what toxic hidden dangers to your life and career lie within the emotional side or our law enforcement career. These dangers manifest themselves in the guises of anger, frustration, compassion fatigue, rage, crippling fear, depression and PTSD. They can also create problems such as excessive sick time, being late for work, getting fired for excessive force, as well as losing your spouse and family, burnout, frustration, surliness, and sometimes even suicide.

I believe our *mental* Self deals primarily with our cognitive functions, such as memory, logic, problem solving, language, mathematics, etc. On the other hand, our *emotional* Self deals with things like anger, fear, joy, frustration, happiness, love and courage. I also believe that, for law enforcement professionals, our emotional Self is one we really need to get in touch with if we want to endure the rigors of this career successfully.

How do you prepare your Self *emotionally* for this job?

What do you need to be doing that you're *not*?

What Are Emotions?

Let's begin by looking briefly at what emotions are. In psychological literature, emotion is frequently defined as "a complex state of feeling that results in physical and psychological changes that influence thought and behavior."

Here's a "word cloud" drawn from a list of more than 250 possible emotions, complied by members of Sonoma State University's Philosophy Department:

There is disagreement within the scientific community about the number of emotions; some contend that hundreds exist, while others posit we have just a few core emotions. Among those who believe we have only a core group of primary emotions, some scientists think there are eight polar-opposite primary emotions, including joy, sadness, anger, fear, trust, disgust, surprise and anticipation. Still other researchers have proposed new theories that there are only four core emotions: anger, fear, happiness, and sadness.

The most important thing for us to acknowledge is that there are driving forces within your Self that can sustain you — or ruin you if you don't acknowledge, examine, manage and develop them.

What does this have to do with law enforcement?

As true law enforcement professionals, we need to delve into this realm of emotions and their management in order to better understand ourselves — and to be better able to protect and to serve our public. Therefore, the central goal of Armor Your Self™ Emotionally is learning to identify the emotional state you're trying to achieve, and then strengthening and conditioning your Self to be able to achieve that state. A closely related goal is identifying emotional states you want to manage or avoid, and then strengthening and conditioning your Self to manage or avoid those states successfully.

I recognize this is a daunting task. Scientists, doctors and psychologists have been studying this challenge for many, many years. Nonetheless I believe that we, as professionals, can extract from this research some practical pointers and techniques that can be put into practice *now*.

As law enforcement professionals, we need to focus upon three sets of opposite emotional states that are the most important to manage. These are: *Anger vs. Calm*, *Fear vs. Courage*, and *Despair vs. Hope*. (As we go through a consideration of dealing with these primary emotions, I'll also take a look at *joy* and *happiness* — related to *calm* — and *grief* — related to *despair* and *hope* — and which plays such a large role in many of the calls and cases we investigate in policing.)

Our goals should be to maintain emotional control and balance in the most difficult of human conditions without losing our compassion, professionalism, joy, happiness and ability to care for and about other human beings. We have always been asked to do this in our policing, but I doubt many of us have been taught in our professional setting how to manage our emotions. I hope this book will be a catalyst for you to begin a discussion (even if only with yourself) that will spark an examination and motivate an exploration of the impact emotion has in the lives and careers of law enforcement professionals.

My favorite joke about police training is that people expect us to be trained observers, and even though we say we are, most cops I've met have never had any training to become expert observers. In the same way, we are expected to control our emotions, and yet no one has ever trained us *how* to do it. We can change that now, as you begin to train your Self to control and manage your emotional responses.

Call it "mind control" or "emotional control" or whatever you like. The simple objective is for us to be able to maintain a state of *calm* and to be able to regain a state of *happiness* and *joy* when we're *not* in the middle of a crisis. And, looking at the big picture of a career in law enforcement, you ultimately need to find a way to flourish and thrive in your life and career despite all the negative things you have to see and endure.

In this chapter and the next I'm going to outline some practical ways to go about doing this.

Balanced Conditioning

As you recall, I suggested earlier that the process of Armor Your Self™ is about *balanced conditioning*. The concepts of Armor Your Self™ Physically and Mentally are achieved through *active* conditioning, while the processes of Armor Your Self™ in the emotional and spiritual realms are achieved by *inactive* conditioning.

In the *physical* realm you achieve strength through physical activity like building muscular fitness, running, and aerobic training. In the *mental* realm you achieve strength through intellectual activity such as brain games, working on puzzles, and solving logic problems.

In the areas of the *emotional* and *spiritual*, strength is achieved through more inactive and passive means like "quiet time:" reading, study, contemplation, discussion, and meditation. Don't fret. While this may seem more daunting to you than running five miles, the challenge lies in *expanding your fitness horizons to include these more comprehensive activities*. Even though being inactive might seem boring or a waste of time, I believe these kinds of strengthening and conditioning activities are as important, if not more important, when compared with your current physical fitness activities.

What's in Your Bucket? — Negative Stresses vs. Blue Trauma

Before we talk about building emotional strength, let's look at what we're up against.

There's no doubt that large doses of cumulative negative stress contribute to the hidden dangers and toxicity I discussed in Chapter One. However, I don't believe that negative stress is the sole cause of all the problems we face as modern law enforcement officers. That's why it's misleading to suggest that physical fitness or stress management alone can deal with all the troubling issues and negative health effects I lump into the concept of Blue Trauma Syndrome.

I mentioned earlier that when I teach seminars, I use the metaphor of an imaginary invisible bucket that fills up with all the "stuff" (feel free to substitute your favorite four-letter word) that we collect in our law enforcement careers. It's that kind of negative stuff which, if not managed, manifests as Blue Trauma Syndrome.

Every day, our "bucket" fills with all the negative stuff (negative emotions, trauma, tragedy and worse) that we see and encounter in police work. If we don't manage our bucket's contents, it overflows. Sometimes what overflows splashes all over our loved ones and us. When we don't manage the stuff in our bucket, it can become toxic to us and to those around us, including the citizens we serve.

I believe that there are things you can do (consider the seven key factors of Tactical Resilience™) that can mitigate and remove some of the negative stuff in your bucket. Call it "Bucket Management" or call it Blue Trauma Management — it's all the same.

I've defined Blue Trauma Syndrome as a spectrum of negative physical, mental, emotional, and spiritual health effects which can manifest during and after a career in law enforcement. To be sure, our body's responses to prolonged negative physical stress account for many of the problems we see within our ranks. But it doesn't account for all of them.

When we consider the human mind and the toxic effects a career in police work can have on a human mind, then we can more clearly see the need for a conditioning routine that will strengthen our minds and emotions to be resilient to these negative effects. The key point to understand about Blue Trauma Syndrome is not so much its exact definition, but rather our need to find ways to prevent its cumulative effects and the negative outcomes those effects produce.

Emotional Threats

Law enforcement professionals are expected to maintain control of their own emotions. We are expected to be cool and calm in the face of danger, to be strong and composed when surrounded by trauma and tragedy, to be empathetic and compassionate when we offer assistance, and respectful as we make an arrest.

But these expectations can be difficult to meet when the person inside the uniform has been collecting buckets of trauma and tragedy day in and day out. As our emotional strength erodes, we tend to become more irritable and less friendly. We start to suffer from what's called "compassion fatigue," and we start to lose our concern for other people. We can become "burned out" and stop working as hard as we should — or worse, begin to compromise our integrity. If we succumb to anger and rage, we may become violent and abusive and exceed our authority. And, in the worst cases, we may lose our own humanity and become callous, self-serving and hollow inside.

Emotional Management Planning

Let's create a daily emotional conditioning plan that both minimizes some of the negative effects of your career and promotes the positive parts of your life. This plan will be just one of the seven key elements in your system for building Tactical Resilience™.

Your target is *Blue Trauma Management*. The goal of Blue Trauma Management is more comprehensive than stress management alone. Whereas stress management is about managing *physiological* effects that occur within the body, Blue Trauma Management is about managing *all* of the physiological, mental, emotional and spiritual influences that have a negative impact on the body of a law enforcement professional. When you get to the end of this book, you'll have a plan that encompasses all seven of the key factors in building Tactical Resilience™.

Building a comprehensive emotional management program includes: plans to create calm and joy in our lives, and a method to manage and reduce anger as it builds courage and minimizes the effects of fear. Our plan also helps us understand and manage grief, both in ourselves and in others. Finally, it includes ways to build a strong social support network of friends, family and colleagues. Ultimately, it promotes activities that allow us to thrive and flourish.

This chapter and the next provide ideas, tactics and techniques to accomplish these goals. The rest is then up to you.

But before we get to the nitty-gritty of these ideas, tactics and techniques, let's talk about the goals of your emotional management plan.

Focus on Calm, Happiness and Finding Joy

I love the second principle in Stephen Covey's great book, *The 7 Habits of Highly Effective People*, when he suggests: "Begin with the end in mind."

Here is how I translate this in terms of living a life in law enforcement: Day in and day out, we strive at all times to be cool, calm and collected. What's more, we frequently have to draw heavily from our reservoirs of courage and willpower. But as we draw from our reservoir, we have to consider how we're going to refill it. Often times we're negligent and lose sight of the importance of maintaining happiness and joy in our personal lives in order to combat the negative emotions, like anger and fear, that we have to endure in our jobs.

So in order to keep our eyes on our target of controlling and minimizing negative emotions, we are going to focus on the emotions of *calm* and *joy* as our near-term goals as a way to reach our long-term goals of *thriving* and *flourishing* while engaged in a law enforcement career.

Thrive and Flourish

There's excellent research and a lot of material to help get a handle on strategies for thriving and flourishing.

To start off, let's take a look at two books written by Dan Buettner called *The Blue Zones: Lessons for Living Longer From the People Who've Lived the Longest*, and his follow-up book entitled *Thrive: Finding Happiness the Blue Zones Way*. These books grew out of research he did for the National Geographic Society about areas of the world where people live the longest.

The first thing Buettner learned about the people on our planet who live the longest is that they are *happy*! His research identified nine traits he calls the Power 9®: Blue Zones Lessons. The most significant are: Movement, Purpose, Stress Release, Nutrition, Social Connection, and Social Support.

In the nutrition category is the Okinawan concept of *Hara hachi bu*, or only eating until you are about 80% full. You may also be happy to know that moderate (wine) drinking was involved, and Buettner's research found that "moderate drinkers outlive non-drinkers, especially if they share those drinks with friends." What's significant here is the link between family/social connections and drinking, because these social connections are very important, especially in that they make your family a priority in your life. (I'll add another clue: It's important to choose positive and supportive people to hang out with.)

Another book I recommend is world-renowned psychologist Martin Seligman's *Flourish*. In it Seligman gives concrete examples of what you need to do to flourish in your life. He'll help you identify what you want in your life and how to get there, as well as help you to define and understand the difference between happiness and well-being — critical perspectives for a law enforcement professional to understand. Finally he talks about measuring well-being.

Seligman suggests that your target should be to increase your satisfaction with life, and that since well-being is composed of positive emotion, engagement, meaning, relationships, and accomplishments, the best way to increase your life's satisfaction and to flourish in life is by increasing positive emotion, engagement, meaning, relationships, and accomplishment.

The important point here is to take this information (and anything else you learn during your own research) and apply it *directly* to your life. There are no short cuts to Tactical Resilience™, so you have to be prepared to do the work, daily, for the rest of your life.

Do Your Homework

Before you read on, put this book down for a few moments and ask yourself a couple of questions. Write out your answers and keep them in your notebook.

- What components of a thriving life do you want to build for yourself, and how are you going to do that?
- How do you create joy?
- How do you create and maintain happiness and positive well-being?
  Here, write your thoughts about what you are doing right now in your life.
- What does the concept of "flourish" mean to you?

- How will you add more positive emotion and engagement to give your life more meaning?

  Here, write some thoughts about how you can increase positive emotion, engagement and meaning, as well as positive relationships and accomplishments in your life.

- Write some simple goals for your emotional growth.

The Relaxation Response and Other Strategies for Emotional Management

Now that you've focused on long-term goals for thriving and flourishing, let's talk about the day-to-day goal of maintaining *your calm, collected Self*. Let's find a way for you to calm your mind and body.

Maintaining *your calm, collected Self* is probably the core emotional expectation and positive goal for a modern law enforcement professional. You're expected and needed to be the cool head at the scene of any crisis or tragedy you're sent to. This is an emotional state that will also help you when dealing with a combative suspect or, worse, in a fight for your life. For these and similar situations, I suggest your primary objective should be to master the Relaxation Response.

Earlier, I mentioned Dr. Herbert Benson's Relaxation Response. It's a good goal and offers good measures of how well we manage our emotional responses to negative stresses. I think it also serves as a good benchmark for the emotional subset of stress management in your overall Blue Trauma Management program.

According to Dr. Benson, who is associate professor of medicine at Harvard Medical School, and the author of the book, *The Relaxation Response*, "The relaxation response is a physical state of deep rest that changes the physical and emotional responses to stress… and [is] the opposite of the fight or flight response."

Described simply, the Relaxation Response triggers a dramatic decrease in heart rate, breathing rate, blood pressure, and metabolic rate, and, with dedicated practice, counteracts the harmful effects of negative stress. His original research indicated that you can accomplish this with four things:

- A quiet environment

- A mental device (such as repeating a word or phrase)
- A passive attitude (putting aside distracting thoughts and always focusing on your breathing), and
- A comfortable position.

Further research found that only the passive attitude and mental device were really needed, and these can be achieved and performed as you exercise — as long as the exercise activity is repetitious, and your intent is always to clear your mind of distractions and return your focus to your repeated word so it's in sync with your breathing rate. (You can call this meditation or "quiet time" if you prefer, but there are many ways to accomplish it.)

When I talk about conditioning the Relaxation Response, I believe that this is just like conditioning your body physically, only this is *emotional* conditioning. With regular practice you should be able to intentionally lower your emotional excitation state and bring your body back to a more relaxed state *even if you are not sitting quietly and meditating*. This is helpful in a high-stress situation or after leaving a very negative call or crime scene.

A daily emotional conditioning regime can include any of these types of stress management practices:

- Deep tactical breathing
- Meditation or "quiet time"
- Progressive muscle relaxation
- Creative visualization
- Guided meditation
- Targeting the Relaxation Response — combining a relaxing activity and breathing

Tactical Breath Control

Tactical Breath Control — being able to control your body's physiology by controlling your breathing — is an essential skill for any modern law enforcement professional. Breathing controls many of the body's physiological responses, and by monitoring and training your breathing you can intentionally steer changes in your body (as, for example, through the Relaxation Response).

The main issue in breath control/tactical breathing is simply *becoming conscious* of your breath. The next step is to gain control of your breathing rate. That's easy when you aren't under any stress; but when you're agitated, it's harder to do. That's why practicing breath control every day is so important: You program good breathing habits for the stressful times when you need them. By programming your mind and body *now* with good breathing exercises that slow your body's physiology, you'll be better able to intentionally slow and control your physiology (breathing rate, heart rate and metabolism) when you're under stress.

Many experts, who promote tactical breathing to help you gain control of your emotions, or steady your hands in a shooting situation, propose a straight inhale-then-exhale cycle with no breath holds in-between. This is usually done to a simple 4/4 count, with a count of four on the inhale, and then an immediate count of four on the exhale. The process is repeated over and over again until you achieve the desired physiological state. The only variation on this technique is how long each count is — a very long and slow four count, or a more rapid four count.

Another breath control training technique is to learn to hold your breath for longer and longer periods of time. As I write, there is worldwide competition in progress to see which contestants can hold their breath the longest. Famed American magician, illusionist and endurance artist David Blaine has held and lost the record over the last several years. (You can learn more about his and others' records with the links at the end of this chapter.)

To return to Tactical Breathing: This process uses a specific breathing technique involving deep diaphragmatic breathing to a 4×4 count. I've heard this referred to as "combat" or "box" breathing. You start by taking in a deep breath using your diaphragm, filling 25% of your lungs on each count for 4 seconds, and then exhaling 25% of the air from your lungs on each count for 4 seconds. Repeat this for 4-6 minutes.

In his writings, Lt. Col. [ret.] Dave Grossman, U.S. Army, describes what he calls "Combat Breathing" using a 4x4x4x4 count. This means *breathing in* for four counts, *holding* for four counts, *breathing out* for four counts, and *holding there* for four counts before beginning again.

Any breathing exercise can be used to relax or to energize yourself and can follow any number of counting systems: 12-6-12-6 or 8-4-8-4 (describing the inhale count, hold count, exhale count and hold on the bottom).

You can also try the *purging breath*: simply exhale rapidly to completely empty your lungs. Do it loudly and rapidly, then inhale quickly and push out another breath to completely empty your lungs. Do this three or four times in rapid succession to purge the negative energy you feel, center your mind, and oxygenate your body and brain. There are several examples of all of these in the next chapter.

Breath control can become one of your most effective emotional management techniques and can be employed in a variety of situations. It is very efficient and effective for counteracting the negative stress reactions that occur in the human body and can be used to condition your body to relax.

Heart Rate Variability (HRV)

A fairly new and simple method for measuring your physiological reaction to stress and relaxation is *Heart Rate Variability* (HRV). An article from *The Canadian Journal of Cardiology*, republished by the U.S. National Institutes of Health, suggests: "A heart rate that is variable and responsive to demands is believed to bestow a survival advantage, whereas reduced HRV may be associated with poorer cardiovascular health and outcomes."
Source: http://www.ncbi.nlm.nih.gov/pmc/articles/PMC2903986/

For that reason, and given the fact that there are now lots of easily accessible and inexpensive ways to measure HRV including products, programs and smart phone apps, getting to know how your body reacts to various stimuli and then working to condition your responses to stimuli you choose can be very beneficial in law enforcement.

Quiet Mind Exercises

Quiet mind exercises are designed to help you build strength of mind and condition you to intentionally control your emotional state when you need to.

Many of these exercises are about conditioning a certain response based upon your intention. You set an intention *before* you begin the exercise and then use your time to achieve that state of mind.

Not all emotional activities should be thought of as "exercises" and some should be sessions where you condition yourself to be still, calm or quiet. I believe that learning to quiet your mind by whatever practice you choose is a skill well suited to a policing professional. I will give you some instructions for Quieting Your Mind in the next chapter; but for now, consider the importance of daily conditioning that includes finding the time to quiet your mind.

Find Your Happy Place

When I teach Armor Your Self™ on-site at an agency, I do an exercise with my classes. I didn't invent it; rather it's something I learned sometime around 1986, when I attended the Drug Enforcement Agency's Basic Narcotics Investigators School. What I found most profound was that with only about an hour's worth of instruction I was able to remember and use this technique over the next 30 years.

This technique is a combination of a number of meditation and relaxation exercises. You could call it a guided meditation, but it's really a combination of deep breathing exercises, progressive muscle relaxation and guided imagery. Part of the process is to associate a key word with your experience. I call it the *Happy Place* exercise, and there's an example of how to do it in the next chapter.

Meditation and Mindfulness for Law Enforcement

The Cambridge Dictionary defines meditation as "the act of giving your attention to only one thing, either as a religious activity or as a way of becoming calm and relaxed." The Mayo Clinic weighs in, saying: "Meditation can give you a sense of calm, peace and balance that benefits both your emotional well-being and your overall health. And these benefits don't end when your meditation session ends. Meditation can help carry you more calmly through your day and can even improve certain medical conditions."

Most law enforcement officers dismiss meditation as being too "Woo-Woo!" or without a basis in science. But modern science *is* finding more and more validations for the importance of meditative practices. *Transcendental Meditation* (or TM) is being used to help veterans reduce the impact of PTSD, and some law enforcement agencies are teaching Mindfulness Meditation practices to their troops.

Mindfulness-Based Stress Reduction (MBSR) — or just Mindfulness — is getting more and more attention in law enforcement and also having value in helping with sleep disorders, stress reduction and relaxation.

Mindfulness is a practice of directing and maintaining nonjudgmental attention to the experience of our bodies and minds in the present moment. Mindfulness can be described as *paying attention to what is occurring within one's Self as it is happening*. This can be a very valuable skill in our efforts to manage stress.

Jon Kabat-Zinn, PhD, is the founding executive director of the Center for Mindfulness in Medicine, Health Care, and Society at the University of Massachusetts Medical School. He is also the founding director of its Stress Reduction Clinic, and a professor of medicine emeritus at U-Mass Medical School. He is well-known for teaching mindfulness and Mindfulness-Based Stress Reduction (MBSR) in various venues around the world, and defines mindfulness in this way: "Mindfulness is awareness that arises through paying attention, on purpose, in the present moment, non-judgmentally."

Mindfulness-Based Stress Reduction (MBSR) is a very well-organized and well-researched practice of meditation, group discussions and yoga. The program, generally starting with an eight-week instructor-led course, may prove helpful for your own emotional management process.

For more study of this subject, look at Kabat-Zinn's book, *Full Catastrophe Living: Using the Wisdom of Your Body and Mind to Face Stress, Pain and Illness*, listed at the end of this chapter.

Watch What You Say to Your Self

Self-talk — what we say to ourselves inside our heads — can be very powerful, and yet most of us pay little attention to what we're saying.

I never gave this much consideration until a friend told me it would be good to reframe the very self-critical voice in my head. I thought to myself, "You're crazy! I don't have any voices in my head!" Then I realized that *that* was a voice *in* my head! I started paying attention and, sure enough, there was a lot of chatter going on in there and much of it wasn't helpful to me. The problem is that most of us don't pay attention to this, and yet *subconsciously* our mind is listening and therefore affecting our Self-image, our attitude, our opinions, even our actions

Another friend calls this kind of internal chatter "monkey mind," an Asian expression to describe a mind that's out of control or not in good working order. I think of that expression when I'm trying to calm and quiet my mind.

I'll provide some Self-talk activities in the next chapter, but for starters I encourage you to do two things: *First*, pay attention to what you are saying to your Self in your mind. That conversation is actually very much like a computer's operating system, and it can program you into some very negative and self-doubting beliefs. *Second*, try to change the chatter to positive encouragement, and use positive Self-talk to establish a positive mind-set.

Rx3x: An Emotional Management Prescription for Law Enforcement

In my writing on the CopsAlive Web site, I have offered what I call *Rx3x* as a prescription for emotional and negative stress management for people in law enforcement. The prescription (*Rx*) calls for you to perform emotional management activities three times (*3x*) a day. The Rx3x process uses a combination of mind and body exercises to reduce and manage excessive amounts of negative emotional trauma and stress on days when you're on duty. The process calls for:

1. A 30-45 minute *physical fitness workout* each day, focused upon building strength and aerobic fitness;

2. A 20-30 minute *buffer workout* for negative stress reduction for the transition from work to home, and

3. A 20-30 minute *emotional management session* later in the day, focused on reducing mental stress and fatigue.

I don't have to remind you that a career in law enforcement is surrounded with many dangers, both overt and hidden, and can become very toxic. In the course of an average day a police officer might have to deal with violent offenders, sexual predators, toxic chemicals, auto accidents, drunks, tragedy, trauma, death and destruction — and that's just before lunch break.

Symptoms of excessive and unmanaged negative stress in law enforcement include: police officer suicide, depression, alcohol and drug abuse, domestic violence, heart disease, cancer, disability and Post-traumatic Stress Disorder (PTSD). These "hidden dangers" of a law enforcement career can be the result of chronic or cumulative, unmanaged negative stress, or other unidentifiable things that I include under the heading of Blue Trauma Syndrome.

Everything mentioned above can cause wear and tear on your body, mind and spirit. Some of this negative stress is short-lived and may dissipate quickly. Other emotional traumas are more insidious, may be spread over an entire career, and can lead to chronic problems like disease within your body, mental health issues of your mind, and a depletion of your inner spirit. When coupled with the added risk factors of shift work, fatigue, poor nutrition and inadequate self-care, the situation is rife with major and long-term problems.

Rx3x involves both officers and agencies in becoming committed to changing individual and group responses to these disturbing developments.

Avoid Negative Management of Your Emotions

Now that we've talked about how to create calm, let's focus on three other diametrically opposite pairs of emotions that are of concern to all law enforcement professionals: Calm *vs.* Anger, Courage *vs.* Fear, and Hope *vs.* Despair.

But first, here are some thoughts about what *not* to do.

Sights, sounds, smell, tastes and touch are all connected to our emotional responses, and sometimes they trigger the *wrong* kinds of coping mechanisms. Sometimes when our emotions are particularly raw, or we have bad memories associated with a particular sight, place, sound, smell or taste, we try to cope using negative strategies. Many people and some law enforcement professionals turn to alcohol, prescription drugs, sex, overeating, gambling or overspending to try to soothe their negative feelings. The obvious problem is that, when we are in a weakened emotional state, turning to negative solutions can make the existing problems worse or even create new problems.

Use Positive Ways to Manage Your Emotions

Just as sights, sounds, smell, tastes and touch are all connected to our negative emotional responses, they're also connected to many of our positive memories and emotional responses.

Because of that we can use music, photos, aromas, positive tastes and positive touch to change our moods for the better. Sometimes simple cues like the photos or music on your smartphone can almost instantly change your mood for the better. In the next chapter I'll give you some suggestions, tactics and techniques to leverage this to your benefit.

Managing Anger

Anger is a normal human emotion, but it's one that society doesn't expect in its peace officers. In law enforcement, excessive anger can be a warning sign of unwanted buildup of negative emotions or Blue Trauma Syndrome. Our goal is to maintain the anger/calm balance of an emotionally strong, mature, well-conditioned professional police officer.

The essential point is to determine whether or not you have a deep-rooted natural tendency toward extreme anger, or whether your anger is coming to the surface over an extended law enforcement career. Nonetheless, self-awareness about your anger reactions is important to your personal growth and development. These are things we try to spot in the initial screening process for recruits in law enforcement.

If you think your angry responses to situations around you are not normal, you should seek professional support — just as a professional athlete would seek support from a doctor or sports trainer for a physical injury. Remember, this book is not intended to provide professional mental health advice or treatment recommendations. If you feel that your anger response is excessive, unwarranted or unsettling, you should seek professional mental health support before those negative responses get you into real trouble.

A number of very effective treatments are available these days to assist in managing excessive anger issues. One of these is *Cognitive Behavioral Therapy* (CBT), which is also very helpful in working with cases of Post-traumatic Stress Disorder (PTSD). There are also other talk and problem-solving therapies. The key is to work to manage anger and then to seek professional assistance — and do it early rather than waiting until the problem is out of control. As in the physical realm, most problems are better dealt with when they are small and newly forming. Your job may also be protected if you proactively seek treatment rather than waiting until you are being disciplined for your inappropriate behavior. These are issues to discuss with your personal physician or attorney.

This book is intended to assist you in preventing major problems, whether they are physical, mental, emotional or spiritual. The question of how you stay calm and manage your anger is our primary focus. The next chapter describes tactics and techniques, including tactical breathing, the "Force Field," and the "Count to 10" exercise, all of which can be helpful. Most importantly, getting a handle on anger management needs to be an exploration within your Self to discover what makes you react. Then you can learn how to positively manage your emotional responses so that they *assist*, not hurt, your life and your career.

Controlling Fear

Learning to confront and control your fears is a primary challenge for true law enforcement professionals. The fear/courage balance is one that should not be left to chance, even though we really don't talk about this much in our training. Have you ever had any training specifically to build courage or minimize fear? Maybe, but I'm betting that you haven't.

As a professional, you need to add it to your personal training regimes. We all hope that in the defining moment we will have the courage to be a hero and do the right thing. I think that natural instincts kick in and many of us have been selected for the traits that will make us naturally brave when called upon. But, why leave this to chance when we can devise our own personal exploration into the realms of fear and courage? A lot of training programs, particularly in the military, put you in situations that challenge you to overcome fears and thereby to feel the exhilaration of success and the bravery of overcoming fear. Natural fears — like the fear of heights, of drowning, and of the unknown — are frequently overcome with ropes courses, free diving, Parkour and other activities that meet those fears head-on. Many people who are drawn into law enforcement and the military have natural thrill-seeking personalities and we engage in high-risk sports that allow us to challenge normal limits, like sky diving, bungee jumping, rock climbing, racing, and all sorts of extreme sports that have a high-level of inherent danger.

You can harness these and other activities in your personal training regimen as long as you do things that have a safety and support factor that allows you to take reasonable risks while still having a safety-net or back-up support system. The goal is simply to embrace fear and find exercises that allow you to confront it safely until you learn that you can overcome it successfully or at least manage it well. Overcoming obstacles, challenges and fears give us confidence and help build our positive *Can-Do* mind-set.

You can practice simple exercises in your daily life to build self-assurance by overcoming small fears to develop your courage and confidence. For example, if you're single, try asking someone whom you're afraid to talk to out on a date, and see what happens. We can also go to the extreme by simulating fearful life-and-death situations in our officer survival and shoot/don't shoot training.

The goal is mastery of your fears, and you can develop mastery by starting with small challenges and working your way up to more difficult and daunting fears to overcome. Every law enforcement officer's greatest fear is failing in a life-and-death struggle with a suspect who's trying to kill you or someone else. Training that gives you a chance to practice your responses, whether that be in a hand-to-hand combat or a shooting simulation, can help you build confidence in your abilities and develop the skills you need to control fear and survive the situation.

Creating simulations that give you a sense of fear can be very helpful, such as computer generated shoot/don't shoot simulations or paintball, laser tag or other live-fire training situations. With practice you can learn to manage your emotional responses and develop a feeling of success and mastery. Ultimately, you build courage by successfully overcoming your fears and developing confidence that you can handle the unexpected.

Dealing with Despair and Finding Hope

After my law enforcement friend took his own life and I began talking to others and writing about law enforcement officer suicide on the CopsAlive Web site (www.CopsAlive.com), I learned that many officers who take their own lives mention a "loss of hope" in their suicide notes. That started my own exploration of where hope comes from.

I don't have an easy answer for you, but I've found that hope comes in all sizes from large and worldwide to small and individual. For example, I'm the kind of person who needs a vacation or other future fun activity to look forward to in order to give me a small emotional relaxation goal to shoot for. I don't know too much about global hope, but I know it's my natural tendency always to see the best in people, and when I started to lose that outlook and realized I was becoming very jaded, I knew it was time for me to retire. I didn't want to lose all hope like so many other officers who have taken their own lives.

I believe every cop has seen, and probably experienced, despair. We are surrounded with it in our jobs, and it can become a cloud that follows us around and changes our view of reality. Part of our personal journey in this profession needs to be an objective, unbiased examination of what there is in our lives that gives us hope and what causes despair, and for our own sakes we need to identify and cultivate the roots of *hope* in our personal lives to sustain our professional careers.

Elsewhere in this book I suggest active strategies and tactics for emotional strengthening and conditioning. Connecting with what brings you hope and joy to overcome despair when it strikes is, I believe, best exercised through group discussion and internal introspection.

Finding Joy

Joy is an aspect of life we all need to learn to identify and replicate. As an emotion, joy can support and sustain us throughout our law enforcement careers. Finding joy in our work can bolster our drive to be the best we can be, and finding joy in our personal lives can nourish and preserve us in tough times.

As part of your personal strengthening and conditioning regime, I encourage you to examine what gives you joy in life and then to find ways to develop it and experience it. For the wiseacres out there, I'll simply say that there are a lot of negative influences in our lives that can bring momentary joy without leaving lasting or substantial benefits, and those are not the ones I'm talking about. You can probably start to see that this is the threshold where issues of the emotional begin to overlap with issues of the spiritual.

Try keeping a log of your daily experiences to track how much fun you're having, and annotate the activities that bring you true joy. Making sure we earmark time for adequate amounts of rest, relaxation, and recreation in our lives is very important in maintaining our emotional balance against the toxic effects of our work. I know that the idea of writing personal things in an activity log or daily journal may make you feel vulnerable; but think of it as an exercise in self-discovery and mastery of fear and paranoia. The bottom line (as business management guru Peter Drucker once said) is: "What gets measured gets managed."

Daily Emotional Management Conditioning

None of the things I describe will work for you without regular daily practice. If you want to be able to calm yourself, manage fear or muster courage instantly, your body and mind have to practice these techniques over and over again — the same way you repetitively rehearse an arrest-control or martial-arts maneuver.

In the next chapter I'll give you some ideas, tactics and techniques to experiment with until you find what works for you and to give yourself some variety as you use them. You can also visit our Web site to download some simple forms and worksheets to assist you. Visit the CopsAlive Web site and be sure to check the resources page for other materials to help you. Use these forms to help track your progress and to keep a record of your successes and challenges. As I mentioned earlier, put them into a three-ring notebook so that you'll have them handy and organized when you measure your progress in your personal development. www.CopsAlive.com/aysforms

Strengthen Your Support Systems

I'll talk about this again in the last chapter, but I'll mention it here briefly for emphasis. Three principles are important to building and maintaining your emotional support system:

1. Build emotional support before you need it.
2. Learn to ask for help, and make it safe for others to ask for help.
3. Offer help to others.

"Talking It Out" is an idea that seems to have been lost on the law enforcement profession. But this centuries-old concept has tremendous value in maintaining your emotional perspective. It's not about talking to your buddies over a beer. While social drinking may help in some respects, Talking It Out is about learning to talk to the right people and to many people.

We must learn to talk out our stuff. Talk to a peer support team member, a chaplain or a mental health professional. Talk to a picture. Talk to the mirror. Talk to a grave in the cemetery. Talk to your dog. Talk to your buddy. Talk to your spouse. Talk to someone. But please talk out the *negative* emotions you feel while those emotions are still manageable rather than letting them fester over time and accumulate along with all the other feelings you collect.

The key to this kind of talking is to really let out all of the negative thoughts and fears you might be suppressing so that you can get support and assistance from another person. You might also need their perspective about whether or not you need to talk to a mental health professional. Please don't be afraid of this, as the negative consequences of what will happen to you are far more dire when you keep things bottled inside rather than finding an effective outlet or therapy to manage them.

Remember: It's important (a) to build an emotional support system *before* you need it; (b) to lay groundwork for a network of people who care enough to man up and ask for help; and (c) to ask someone else to listen to your concerns — which may help them as well. This might seem trivial to you right now, but there will come a time when you really need to ask for help with your stuff, and it's better to have that network in place. We all need to lay a foundation for everyone to feel comfortable to talk or to ask for help when they're afraid to bother other people. Start out talking about the recent small stuff and work your way up to those large things that have been bothering you for awhile.

If you want to take a leadership role in this, I recommend the "Make It Safe" program created by police psychologist Jack Digliani, Ph.D., Ed.D., on his or the CopsAlive Web site.
www.CopsAlive.com
www.JackDigliani.com

Grief and Post-traumatic Growth

Grief is an emotion law enforcement professionals have to learn to be in touch with. Because of the very nature of life, you will eventually lose everything you hold dear. This is true for you and for every other human being on the planet. Learning to understand grief will help you on your path through life and may allow you to help others with whom you come into contact both on the job and in your personal life.

I encourage you to learn more about the process of grief and its impact on the people you serve. Emotions hold tremendous power in how we humans react to events, and the more you know about the process the more you will be able to regulate your own responses and the better you will be able to assist the people you serve.

Researchers Timothy Wilson and Daniel Gilbert have done studies on how we humans tend to overestimate the power of both negative and positive events in our lives. We tend always to project our feelings into the future and often have misguided beliefs about how long bad events make us feel bad or how long positive events make us feel good. Their research shows we are frequently wrong about how and how long our emotional reactions will be and will last.

Sonja Lyubomirsky's book, *The Myths of Happiness*, describes many real-life examples of how we "psych" ourselves out about either how long a good event will buoy us up or how long a terrible event will make us feel low.

This can have a profound effect on your emotional state, which is another reason why positive self-talk can be so important in actually working against our brain's natural tendency to err toward negative emotions, or how long the positive emotional high will last. You have to be in the driver's seat when it comes to your emotional state, and positive self-talk and doing regular emotional conditioning can help keep you positive and healthy.

Remember that your goal is to reduce and maybe even remove Blue Trauma Syndrome, and one measure of this in law enforcement is the concept of *Post-traumatic Growth*, which is defined as "positive change experienced as a result of the struggle with a major life crisis or a traumatic event." In their article, "Posttraumatic Growth: Conceptual Foundation and Empirical Evidence," University of North Carolina-Charlotte researchers Richard G. Tedeschi and Lawrence G. Calhoun suggest: "Posttraumatic growth is not about returning to the same life as it was previously experienced before a period of traumatic suffering; but rather it is about undergoing significant 'life-changing' psychological shifts in thinking and relating to the world, that contribute to a personal process of change, that is deeply meaningful."

Homework and Resources for Follow-up

As with everything discussed in this chapter, education, daily practice and measured progress are the best ways to build your emotional management and conditioning plan. Here are a number of articles and other resources to assist you, as well as a list of reading to continue your education.

- Discover a list of over 250 possible emotions from the Sonoma State University Philosophy Department.
http://www.sonoma.edu/users/s/swijtink/teaching/philosophy_101/paper1/listemotions.htm

- Read more about emotional and negative stress management on the CopsAlive Web site.
  http://www.CopsAlive.com/a-stress-management-prescription-for-law-enforcement

- Download some of our documents on stress management.
  - CopsAlive Rx3x Prescription For Emotional and Stress Management 10-minute roll-call discussion guide:
    http://www.CopsAlive.com/suggests?rx3x/aysbook
  - CopsAlive Stress Management Roll Call Discussion Training Key (Rc10m):
    http://www.CopsAlive.com/suggests?rx3xrc10m/aysbook
  - CopsAlive Instructions for Quieting Your Mind:
    http://www.CopsAlive.com/suggests?quietmindinstructions/aysbook

- Additional resources for your Rx3x Prescription can be found in the University of San Francisco Counseling and Psychological Services Relaxation Podcasts.
  - Preparing to Relax:
    http://usf.usfca.edu/fac-staff/citprojects/podcasts/preparing_to_relax.mp3
  - Eight-minute exercise:
    http://usf.usfca.edu/fac-staff/citprojects/podcasts/short_relaxation_activity_9min.mp3
  - Seventeen-minute exercise:
    http://usf.usfca.edu/fac-staff/citprojects/podcasts/long_relax_17min.mp3

- Take a look at this *Psychology Today* article entitled "The Science of Meditation."
  http://www.psychologytoday.com/articles/200105/the-science-meditation

- You can watch David Blaine's TED Talk about how he held his breath for 17 minutes.
  http://www.ted.com/talks/david_blaine_how_i_held_my_breath_for_17_min?language=en

- As of this writing the current breath-holding record is over 22 minutes, held by Stig Avall Severinsen, who is a three-time world free-diving champion and has written a book on the art of conscious breathing called *Breatheology*. You can watch him at:
  https://youtu.be/AqERqQj-ozc

Note: All of these record holders make these attempts under strict supervision and in controlled environments. Don't try this without guidance from your personal physician.

- Stig's Breatheology for optimized health and performance: https://www.breatheology.com/

- Britain's *Daily Mail* article about Stig Severinsen's record: http://www.dailymail.co.uk/news/article-2712984/The-Man-Who-Doesn-t-Breathe-World-record-diver-hold-breath-underwater-22-MINUTES.html

- Here are a couple of papers from Timothy Wilson, Daniel Gilbert and their colleagues who do research on social psychology and affective forecasting and which analyze how we humans tend to overestimate the power of both negative and positive events in our lives.
    - Timothy D. Wilson and Daniel T. Gilbert (2003), "Affective Forecasting," *Advances in Experimental Social Psychology*. 35: 345-411. doi:10.1016/S0065-2601(03)01006-2.
    - D.T. Gilbert, E.C. Pinel, T.D. Wilson, S.J. Blumberg and T.P. Wheatley (1998), "Immune neglect: A source of durability bias in affective forecasting," *Journal of Personality and Social Psychology*. 75 (3): 617-638. doi:10.1037/0022-3514.75.3.617. PMID 9781405.

- Visit the Web site for the National Center for PTSD run by the U.S. Veterans Administration to find the Center's PTSD Coach app (the Psychological First Aid (PFA) App) for your smartphone, along with lots of other useful information. http://www.ptsd.va.gov/

- Here's a good article about the value of managing your emotions: "Happiness Is Best Kept Stable: Positive Emotion Variability Is Associated With Poorer Psychological Health." http://www.apa.org/pubs/journals/features/emo-a0030262.pdf

- A great article from Health-Line on "The Effects of Stress on the Body" can be read at: http://www.healthline.com/health/stress/effects-on-body

- The Mayo Clinic advises, "Meditation can give you a sense of calm, peace and balance that benefits both your emotional well-being and your overall health. And

these benefits don't end when your meditation session ends. Meditation can help carry you more calmly through your day and can even improve certain medical conditions."
http://www.mayoclinic.com/health/meditation/HQ01070

- R.G. Tedeshi and L.G. Calhoun sketch their ideas about Post-traumatic growth in *Posttraumatic Growth: Conceptual Foundation and Empirical Evidence*. Philadelphia, PA: Lawrence Erlbaum Associates (2004), which can be found at: http://data.psych.udel.edu/abelcher/Shared%20Documents/3%20 Psychopathology%20%2827%29/Tedeschi,%20Calhoun,%202004.pdf

Further Suggested Readings

Asken, Michael J., Dave Grossman and Loren W. Christensen. *Warrior Mindset*. Millstadt, IL: Warrior Science Group, 2010. Dr. Asken is the psychologist for the Pennsylvania State Police, and author of *MindSighting: Mental Toughness Skills for Police Officers in High Stress Situations*.
www.mindsighting.com

Benson, Herbert and Miriam Z. Klipper. *The Relaxation Response*. New York: HarperCollins, 2000.

Benson, Herbert and Marg Stark. *Timeless Healing — The Power and Biology of Belief (Integration of Body, Mind and Soul)*. New York: Fireside, 1996.

Buettner, Dan. *The Blue Zones: Lessons for Living Longer from the People Who've Lived the Longest*. Washington, D.C.: National Geographic Society, 2008.

Buettner, Dan. *Thrive: Finding Happiness the Blue Zones Way*. Washington D.C.: National Geographic Society, 2010.

Christensen, Loren W. *Meditation for Warriors: Practical Meditation for Cops, Soldiers and Martial Artists*. Portland, Oregon: LWC Books, 2013.

Cleary, Thomas. *Training the Samurai Mind*. Boston: Shambhala Publications, 2008.

Covey, Stephen R. *The 7 Habits of Highly Effective People*. London: Simon & Schuster, 2005.

Draeger, Lars. *Navy SEAL Training Guide: Mental Toughness*. N.p.: n.p., n.d. (print).

Kabat-Zinn, Jon. *Full Catastrophe Living: Using the Wisdom of Your Body and Mind to Face Stress, Pain, and Illness*. New York: Bantam, 2013.

Lyubomirsky, Sonja. *The Myths of Happiness: What Should Make You Happy but Doesn't, What Shouldn't Make You Happy but Does*. New York: Penguin, 2013.

McGonigal, Kelly. *The Upside of Stress: Why Stress Is Good for You, and How to Get Good at It*. N.p.: n.p., n.d. (print).

Miller, Laurence. *M.E.T.T.L.E.: Mental Toughness Training for Law Enforcement*. Flushing, NY: Looseleaf Law Publications, 2008.

Seligman, Martin E. P. *Flourish*. New York: Atria Paperback, 2013.

Wimberger, Lisa. *New Beliefs, New Brain: Free Yourself from Stress and Fear*. Studio City, California: Devine Arts Media, 2012.

Wimberger, Lisa *Neurosculpting: A Whole-Brain Approach to Heal Trauma, Rewrite Limiting Beliefs, and Find Wholeness*. Boulder, CO: Sounds True, 2015.

CHAPTER 12

Armor Your Self™: Emotionally Training Exercises, Tactics & Techniques

Here are 13 categories of tactics and techniques to help you Armor Your Self™ emotionally. By building your training regimen around three sets of diametric emotions — (a) anger and calm, (b) fear and courage and (c) despair and hope — you can build intentional resilience, or the Tactical Resilience™, you need to endure the emotional rigors of our career. In this chapter I'll also cover grief and happiness, and — most importantly for your emotional conditioning exercises — breath control.

1. Breath Control Exercises
2. Managing Anger/Maintaining Calm
3. Quiet Mind Exercises
4. Promoting Happiness
5. Managing Fear
6. Mustering Courage

7. Mastering Despair
8. Finding Hope
9. Dealing With Grief
10. Positive Self-talk
11. Emotional Mind-sets
12. Other Ways To Manage Your Emotions
13. Habit Seeding, Feeding and Weeding

1. Breath Control Exercises

These breathing exercises focus on the length and time used in each of the following areas of your breathing pattern: your inhale, your hold, your exhale and your hold before inhaling again. The numbers in the following examples show the length of time spent on each of stage of this pattern. In most of these exercises, the actual length of time spent in each stage isn't very important so long as the percentage of time in each stage is consistent with the example.

4x4 Breathing Exercise

The Tactical Breathing process employs a specific breathing technique that uses your diaphragm for deep breathing to a 4×4 count. Start by taking in a deep breath with your diaphragm, and fill 25% of your lungs on each count for 4 seconds, and then exhale 25% of the air from your lungs on each count for 4 seconds. Repeat for 4-6 minutes.

This can become one of your most effective emotional management techniques and can be employed in a variety of situations. It is very effective in counteracting all of your body's stress reactions and can be used to condition your body to relax.

4x4x4x4 Breathing Exercise

In his writings Lt. Col. [ret.] Dave Grossman, U.S. Army, describes what he calls "Combat Breathing," which uses a 4x4x4x4 count. (This exercise is also called "box breathing.") To begin, breathe slowly in for four counts, hold for four counts, breathe out for four counts, and then, hold there for four counts. Repeat the cycle four or five more times.

12-6-12-6 Breathing Exercise

This exercise is the same as other count-oriented breathing exercises, except the lengths of the *inhale* and *exhale* counts (12 counts each) are longer than the *hold* counts (6 each) at the top and bottom of the cycle.

This varies the process for you slightly and may help break any rote patterns you develop. It may assist you to stay focused upon your breathing rather than letting your mind wander (which it may do after repeating one of these other exercises over weeks or months). Here, your focus should be on setting your mind to follow your breathing in and out as you let go of other thoughts while you try to slow you heart rate and relax your body.

8-4-8-4 Breathing Exercise

This is a variation on the 4-count breathing exercises above, except the length of the *inhale* and *exhale* cycles are longer (8 counts) than the 4-count *hold* at the top and bottom of the cycle. Again, varying the process slightly may help you break any routine you develop that isn't effective, and may assist you to stay focused on your breathing. Focus on setting your mind to flow with your breathing, in and out, while letting go of other thoughts. Your goal is to consciously slow you heart rate and relax your body.

Practice Breath Control

We all breathe without thinking about it, but learning to control your breathing rate can help you to consciously control your body's state of agitation. As you improve your skills at consciously achieving the Relaxation Response, try experimenting with holding your breath. In the previous chapter I listed some resources, so that you can learn more about what some world record holders have done with breath control. Of course, these are extreme athletes and you should not attempt some of their feats without appropriate precautions and safety measures. Note also that in order to achieve these really long breath holds, these athletes significantly slow their heart rate and metabolism. *That* is the skill you should be striving for, without concern for how long you can actually hold your breath.

Heavy Sigh

Learn to harness the power of the heavy sigh. A heavy sigh is one of your body's natural coping mechanisms, and one you probably do already without thinking. This tactic encourages you to become aware of sighing. Then, *consciously* use a heavy sigh to your advantage when you need to lower your body's state of agitation. Under stress you often take — unconsciously — a deep breath and then let it out with an audible sigh. What your body is doing is taking in more oxygen and signaling your internal physiology to slow down and purge the various toxins and stress response hormones that the stress response dumps into your bloodstream. By consciously initiating your own heavy sigh, you can *consciously* trigger the same physiological response.

So when you need to collect yourself, and de-stress, try a heavy sigh to get things started: Take a deep breath and then let it out with an audible sigh. See if it works for you.

Purging Breath Cycle

Another breathing exercise is the "purging breath:" a rapid in-and-out breath cycle to purge your stress and oxygenate your brain. Don't do it for too many repetitions or you'll hyperventilate and give yourself a massive head rush. Here's how to do it: Quickly take a deep breath and then quickly expel it through your mouth with a loud whooshing sound. Do this for only four or five breath cycles. Then return to your normal rate of breathing. A cycle of deep purging breaths helps to oxygenate your body and reset your internal biology to its normal processes.

Out-of-Breath Recovery

Finally, another breathing exercise challenge is to work on how quickly you can recover from being out of breath. Most experts suggest the best way to train for this is to do "burst" exercises, such as running wind sprints. You can also couple this with a heart-rate monitor to assist you in focusing your attention on both slowing your rapid breathing and your heart rate to improve your recovery time in both areas.

Heart-rate recovery is an exercise you can also add to your training regimen to see if you can lower the amount of time it takes to return to your resting heart rate. Tracking your resting heart rate over time will also help you focus your training on conditioning your body and mind for higher performance.

2. Managing Anger/Maintaining Calm

The Force Field

When you're faced with a stressful day or situation, there are a couple of things to consider. Most stress management involves regulating you breathing. The 4-count breathing exercises mentioned above are good exercises to use to relax your mind and body. You can do them anywhere (even while you're driving — so long as you keep your eyes open and your mind sharp). You can strengthen these breathing techniques by imagining you're putting an invisible force field between you and a stressful situation or a person causing you stress. As a visualization technique, imagine that the force field is strong enough to deflect all the anger, rage, guilt or whatever is coming your way. Try adding a color to your force field to help keep you calm. Most people choose blue (cops like blue!) because it usually has a calming effect (Imagine blue water or a blue sky.) But you can use any color as long as it gives strength to your force field and adds a calming effect. Someone taught me the "Blue Force Field" technique at the police academy. It worked for me then and it still works now, many years later! In fact I've used that technique many times in my life and career when someone was yelling at or trying to degrade me. This technique works in many situations when you need to repel someone's anger, outbursts, or insults.

Anger Management

Anger management is a term thrown around quite loosely; but for those of us in law enforcement, it is mostly about mastering the art of remaining calm and maintaining composure during stressful situations. It's also about minimizing harmful and negative physiological effects that anger has on your body and emotional state. As you read through these techniques, find ones that work for you and practice them regularly — because these will work effectively only with some prior practice and conditioning.

Count to Ten

You may have heard the old adage of "Count to ten when you are angry" so that you won't say something you'll later regret. This is an excellent law enforcement tactic to incorporate into your professional toolbox to make you better at your job. This gives your rational mind a chance to catch up with your impulsive "dinosaur-brain" response to stress or fear

— an instinctual "fight, flight, or freeze" response which comes from the amygdala, one of the most primitive parts of your brain. Evolution perfected this response so that it kicks into gear much more rapidly than our "higher" rational and intellectual centers. Counting to ten allows your emotional response to calm while your rational Self steps in to help. This simple trick may save your life or your career.

A variation on this tactic — for bigger, more major conflicts with specific people — is to do what American President Abraham Lincoln used to do when he was very angry with someone. He sat down and wrote a letter to whomever he was angry with, and then destroyed the letter. Simply expressing your feelings in writing seems to release emotional pressure and helps you avoid doing or saying something that might ultimately hurt you.

3. Quiet Mind Exercises

Quiet mind exercises are designed to help you build strength of mind and to condition yourself to control your emotional state when you need to. Many of these exercises are about preparing a certain response based upon your intention. You prepare by setting an intention before you begin the exercise, and then conditioning your response to achieve your desired state of mind. Not all emotional conditioning should be thought of as "exercise" activities; in fact, some should create sessions in which you condition yourself to be still, calm or quiet.

Quiet Time

Try this:

- Sit comfortably in a chair (or lie down, if you prefer).
- Let your arms rest comfortably in your lap or on the arms of the chair.
- Set you feet flat on the floor.
- Close your eyes and breathe deeply for a minute or so.
- Get into a slow and gentle 4-count breathing cycle like this:
- Slowly breathe in for a count of 4 and then slowly breathe out for a count of 4. Repeat this cycle to promote relaxation.
- Stay like this for 10, 15, 20 or 30 minutes — however long you prefer.

- Try to let your mind relax and don't think about anything.

- Focus on your breathing as the breath comes into and out of your body.

- Try not to think of anything — simply become a quiet "observer" of your thoughts as they pass through your mind.

- If your mind stays busy, don't worry — just let the thoughts pass and remain an observer.

- Set a timer or alarm for a desired amount of time to signal when to finish.

- When your timer goes off, slowly open your eyes and stretch your muscles.

- Try to repeat this often, perhaps once or twice daily, especially when you're feeling stressed.

Quieting Your Mind

When is your mind quiet? Is it ever?

For this exercise, your goal is to quiet all the thoughts, sounds, images and other noise in your mind. Try to allow your mind to be still while you sit quietly and appreciate the quiet. Find a tranquil, comfortable place and sit with your eyes closed for at least 10-15 minutes. Relax all of your muscles, starting from the top of your head and then progressively relaxing the muscles all the way down to your toes. Try to let your thoughts clear from your mind. As new ones begin, pay no attention and let them slip away. If you find yourself thinking of something, stop and let your mind go blank. See how well you can be still.

This takes practice, and you shouldn't become frustrated if it doesn't work the first few times you try, or even the first many times you try. This takes a lot of practice.

Remember that Herbert Benson, M.D., associate professor of medicine at Harvard Medical School and author of The Relaxation Response, defines it as "a physical state of deep rest that changes the physical and emotional responses to stress... and the opposite of the fight or flight response." At it's most basic, with dedicated practice the "relaxation response" triggers a dramatic decrease in heart, breathing and metabolic rates and blood pressure, all to counteract the harmful effects of stress.

Dr. Benson's original research indicates that you can accomplish the Relaxation Response with four things: a quiet environment; a mental device (like repeating a word or phrase); a passive attitude (putting aside distracting thoughts and always focusing on your breathing), and a comfortable position. Further research found that only the passive attitude and mental device were really needed, and that you can achieve the Relaxation Response with exercise so long as the activity is repetitious and your intention is always to clear your mind of distractions and return your focus to repeating your chosen word in sync with your breathing rate.

Keep after it and work until you can quiet your mind on command. Your goal should be to achieve the Relaxation Response. (See the Quiet Mind Blog article and the Quiet Mind exercise worksheet on the CopsAlive Web site.)

Advanced Quiet Mind Exercise

Once you've become good at shutting out your mind's "noise," you can try an advanced exercise to see if you can shut out external clatter.

Sit in front of a stereo or TV set and pick a station that is mostly talking, like a talk show or a debate. (If people are angry or arguing, it's even better.) Try to shut out the noise you hear in your mind. First, do all the things you did in the Quiet Mind exercise to slow your breathing and calm your heart rate. Then see if you can exclude the noise from the TV or stereo, and see if you can achieve the Relaxation Response.

Calm

The Calm Session is one where you set a goal to calm your entire being — your mind, your body and your spirit.

Sit quietly or lie down, and repeat the phrase "calm" in your mind. Pretend you're a traffic cop telling your mind to slow its thoughts and your body to slow its metabolism and physiology. When you accomplish that, tell your spirit to be at peace. You can set an alarm for 15 or 20 minutes to keep track of time so that you can focus all your attention to calming your Self. You can also add a heart rate monitor or other biofeedback device to assist you in tracking your progress during the session, and track your progress from session to session.

Quieting Your Inner Voice

Sit quietly and try to quiet your mind. Many people hear their thoughts as an inner voice. (Some describe it as "monkey mind" because it is so out of control.) Try to quiet your inner voice. Try not to be judgmental about your thoughts. If you become fixated on one thought, rededicate yourself and focus on quieting *all* of your thoughts and inner voices. Set an alarm for 15 or 20 minutes to keep track of time as you dedicate all of your attention to calming and quieting your mind.

Be an Empty Cup

Be a cup or other vessel, and accept all the thoughts that come to you.

This is sometimes referred to as an "empty your cup" exercise. Set as your goal receiving the message you need to hear. Ask a question and see what answer comes back to you. Quiet your mind and wait for any message or thought that comes to fill your cup. Don't be critical about those thoughts or messages; instead, accept them. Allow your mind to be open to these thoughts; later you can decide what they mean to your life.

Be Water

The opposite of the Empty Cup exercise is allowing your mind to become like water. Let your thoughts ebb and flow like water. Don't try to control them; rather, float with them and allow the river of your mind to guide you on a journey. (You don't need to have a destination.)

There are ancient sayings (often attributed to Bruce Lee) about "being water or being the cup." Lee's quote is specifically about the martial arts, but there are other uses and interpretations of these thoughts as well. Use them to your best advantage.

Lee said, "Don't get set into one form, adapt it and build your own, and let it grow, be like water. Empty your mind; be formless, shapeless — like water. Now you put water in a cup, it becomes the cup; you put water into a bottle, it becomes the bottle; you put it in a teapot, it becomes the teapot. Now water can flow or it can crash. Be water, my friend." (From Bruce Lee: *A Warrior's Journey* (2000); here, Lee was reciting lines he wrote for his short-lived role on the TV series, *Longstreet*.)

What can you learn from this saying?

Still

The Still Mind Exercise is similar to the Calm exercise, but in this case you set your intention to "be still" and simply observe what your mind does. Your goal is to sit still, be still, and allow your mind to be still. This may be difficult because your mind may want to be active or busy or noisy. But just repeat the word "still" to your mind and lead it to slow down and be still.

Be at Peace

Before you begin this session, make it your goal to be completely at peace. Then, sit or lie down quietly and be still.

Allow the idea of peacefulness to wash over you like a warm bath or a flowing river (or in any way that brings you joy and serenity.) Use these sessions to discover what the concept of "peace" means to you and what it feels like to experience it. For more advanced work, ask yourself what it means to be a peace officer and how you can best present yourself as a guardian of a peaceful society.

The Imaginary Emotional Vacation

Close your eyes and imagine your favorite vacation spot, or use your imagination to create your perfect vacation spot.

Can you visualize all the details? Can you feel it, smell it, hear it in your mind? Sit quietly for fifteen minutes (set a timer if you must) and just enjoy your imaginary vacation. Try to create as much detail as you can. Put yourself into the picture or just hover above it. Feel the stress flowing out of your body as you feel relaxation take over. Repeat this trip as often as you need.

What's Your Happy Place's Address?

Take your emotional vacation one step farther.

Set a timer for 15, 20 or 30 minutes. Sit or lie down in a quiet, safe, comfortable place. Relax your body from head to toe by tensing and then relaxing every muscle group from the top of your scalp all the way down to the soles of your feet. Couple this with the 4x4x4x4 breathing, relaxation exercise. Slowly draw in a breath to a count of four, hold it for four counts and then exhale on a count of four. Allow a four-count pause after your exhale, then repeat the process. As your whole body starts to relax, focus only on your breath as it flows in and out.

When you feel calm, start imagining your "happy place." Use all your senses to *really* experience that place by imagining all of its sights, sounds, smells and feelings. Finally, give your place a name. The name should be something simple, and preferably one or two syllables. Repeat that name as you inhale and as you exhale. This name will become your *relaxation word* that you'll always associate with this "happy place."

When you need to escape the day's stresses, you can repeat your relaxation word in your mind as an "address" for your "happy place." As you repeat it, you'll summon up all the memories, including your muscle memories, so that your sense of relaxation will come back to you and help to calm your mind and body.

If you practice this often enough, you'll be able to use your "address" word to call up a physiological relaxation response to help slow your heart, breathing and metabolic rates and your blood pressure. Practice helps to reinforce this process and gives you a regular opportunity to take a mind-body relaxation break from the stresses of life.

The Reverse "What If…?" Game (or How to Turn Off the "What If…?" Game)

Many of us in law enforcement train to play the mental "What if…?" game in order to prepare ourselves for worst-case situations. For example: As you approach the house from which you received a domestic disturbance call, you park your car a few houses away so that no one sees you approach; then, as you walk to the front door you imagine *what* you'd do *if* the door burst open and someone with a gun came running out. And you continue by asking your mind, "What if someone runs out the back door?" or "What if no one answers the door?" It's a mental game designed to tune your senses and keep you prepared for any situation.

Unfortunately, many law enforcement professionals don't know how to turn off this game. They play it 24/7, and it interferes with their personal lives. One danger of maintaining hypervigilance all the time is that you never give your mind or your body's physiology a rest. So use the following exercise to quiet your mind and stop playing "What if…?" 24 hours a day: Decide "I'm off duty now," and consciously try to not be suspicious of everyone and everything. Sometimes this means turning off your mental "radar" and not allowing your senses (including that sixth one of suspicion) to work overtime. Combine conscious breathing exercises with what you've learned from some of the mind-quieting exercises, and allow your mind to go to a place of comfort and rest.

As with many of these exercises, this takes enormous patience and lots of practice. This is an investment in your future health, and putting time into these exercises as early as possible in your professional life can be very rewarding later on.

The "Where Am I" Self-evaluation Exercise

Sit quietly and slow your breathing and heart rate. Allow your mind to quiet and open it up to self-discovery. Ask your mind: "Where am I?" (meaning: "How am I feeling?"), or "How am I doing in the big scheme of life?"

Allow your mind to inventory your physical state, including negative stress level, heart rate, breathing rate, fatigue, etc. Inventory how you feel, what you are thinking, and how your state of joy and well-being is right now. Inventory how well your cognitive functions have been doing lately: How's your memory? How are your communication and problem-solving skills? Finally, inventory your inner spirit: How strong is your sense of honor and integrity? How is your sense of right and wrong? How are your feelings of hope and joy? How is your faith in humankind and, perhaps, your faith in a higher power than your own?

Spend as much time as you need for each session — and you might want to do this exercise regularly. As questions arise, write them down or record them in a journal for later follow-up.

4. Promoting Happiness

Joy Without Guilt

Do you have what people would call a "guilty pleasure?" I know what you are thinking, but it's probably not that!

What I'm talking about is something small and probably inconsequential and won't hurt you when you do it. Perhaps it's the one bad thing you like to eat that your professional police athlete diet won't let you eat it. Or maybe it's something as simple as taking time for yourself to read, hike, cycle or whatever.

If you have one of these simple "guilty pleasures," try indulging, and then examine your feelings about your experience. This will probably evoke some kind of emotion, perhaps guilt. If that's the case, I encourage you to write about the experience in your journal. What were your feelings? Where did they come from? Do you believe the messages your conscience is giving you? How can you grow and learn from this experience?

Jump for Joy

What do you do that brings happiness and joy into your life?

Perhaps an assessment is in order. If you don't have in your life enough activities that bring you a true sense of joy and happiness, then perhaps you need to add some. Look around you, talk to your friends and find out what others do to achieve a state of joy in their lives.

Experiment and try new things. Do things with other people, and do things alone. Compare your feelings and write some notes to yourself. Keep a journal of experiences. Focus on the kinds of things that are positive and nourishing to your mind, body and spirit. Jump at opportunities that will bring you joy several times a week so that you don't get caught in a rut. Jump out of those ruts and get active. One of the reasons the phrase is "jump for joy" is that physical activity often brings our bodies and minds to a happier place.

The law enforcement profession can be very toxic and can drag you down before you know what's happening to you. So, don't become complacent about your happiness and well-being. Set up a calendar that schedules the kinds of activities that nourish and fulfill your personal life. Work can be great — but it's not the only thing in life.

5. Managing Fear

Confront Your Fears

Confronting your fears requires repetition and ongoing conditioning to overcome them. Find small (yes, I said *small!*) things in your life that cause you to pause because they evoke fear or indecision. Work your way through the fear and try to overcome the obstacle. Do as many reps as you can every day. What do you learn when you first recognize fear and then overcome it?

Disclaimer: Again, I don't suggest that you adopt risky behavior to accomplish this exercise. I accept no liability for any stupid thing you do in the name of over coming your fears. *Use your head and be safe!*

Here are some Web site resources for you to do additional reading about overcoming fear:

- http://www.wakeupcloud.com/overcoming-fear/
- http://www.psychologytoday.com/collections/201106/overcoming-fear
- http://www.mindtools.com/pages/article/fear-of-failure.htm

> Always do what you are afraid to do.
> — *Ralph Waldo Emerson*

What's Your Fear Factor?

Do some true introspection and ask your Self what you are *really* afraid of? Think about starting a log or a "Journal of Fear."

Seriously, we only act upon and deal with things that we notice. Only when you really start noticing fear and paying attention to its impacts on your life can you deal with it. And I'm not talking only about those big, ugly fears like dealing with "a man with a gun" call. I'm also talking about those little fears, like saying something to a loved one about a behavior you don't like.

Start to make note, on a daily basis, of times you hesitate or abdicate because of fear. I've already quoted Peter Drucker, who said, "What gets measured, gets managed." Only when we know ourselves well can we truly begin to make positive changes.

How are you going to overcome your fears?

6. Mustering Courage

Finding Courage

Where does courage come from, and how do you enhance it? Before you embark on a quest to explore your courage, you should to do some internal self-exploration to discover your beliefs about fear and courage.

Spend a couple of days observing your daily activities, and watch to see what kind of a risk taker you are. Keep a log of risky activities and courageous events. Write some thoughts in your journal about your beliefs, and then test them in reality. Identify the best possible beliefs about courage and managing your fears, and then create some mind-set statements to use when you're challenged beyond your normal responses. Compare your personal values with your willingness to take risks. In what circumstances would you risk your life? Are you a hero?

Most heroes say that anyone else would have done the same thing in their place. I think that those who have prepared themselves emotionally are really the ones who step up when called upon. Is that you?

The Courage Quest

You have to find inside yourself the place where courage comes from. Courage, like any other muscle, gets strength when you exercise it. Try this exercise, which works well in conjunction with the "Confront Your Fears" exercise to build courage: Find small challenges each day to undertake and overcome. This works better if you are afraid or intimidated to try the challenge. Maybe your challenge is asking for something you want, or asking someone out on a date, or risking embarrassment, or taking an action you think is dangerous. Just as you would do to build muscle, start with small challenges and increase both the number of reps per day as well as the intensity of the risk.

Disclaimer: Once more, I don't suggest you adopt risky behavior to accomplish this exercise, and I accept no liability for any stupid thing you do in the name of building your courage. *Use your head!*

7. Mastering Despair

How Low Is Your Low?

Have you ever been depressed? It sucks.

Depression is very common in law enforcement. Why wouldn't it be? You see some of the worst events and meet some of the worst people on the planet. Depression is a serious and common problem, has clinical definitions, and could require professional assistance to successfully navigate. If you find yourself in this situation, please ask for help and work through it with a professional before it becomes harder to manage.

Even if you're doing okay now, this may still be an excellent time to do some observation and exploration about issues surrounding despair. When I worked the streets, I remember going from call to call, seeing unhappy and desperate people — and I never gave it a second thought. Perhaps I could have been a more enlightened professional.

You have that chance if you choose to open your eyes and observe what the world is like around you. How can you better serve these people? To what resources — beyond the police — could you refer them? What phone numbers do you need to put into your contact list, and what brochures do you need to add to your briefcase or desk? What do you need to learn about depression and mental health that might help you personally and professionally?

Here's your chance to dig a little deeper into an area of human emotion that can return your investment manyfold.

Finding a Life Ring

Swimming in despair can feel like drowning, and for most people it's very hard to pull themselves to safety. That's why it's important to find a life ring before you need it.

Your life ring can be your salvation when your emotional equilibrium starts slipping away. Your life ring can be another person, a chaplain, a peer support team member, an activity or even charity work. Investing in support of others can help assure that others will be there when you need them. Identify your life's support systems and bolster them now before you need to rely upon them. It's also good to get into the habit of asking for a little help for small things now just in case there is a big thing later. Start a list of your personal support team and expand that list to include people you help and serve. Make sure you have support phone numbers and other info in your contact list. Invest time in building relationships and never miss a chance to assist someone else — because you never know when that person might be able to help you.

Put into your personal contact list the phone number for Safe Call Now — (206) 459-3020 — the *confidential*, comprehensive, 24-hour crisis referral service for all public safety employees, all emergency services personnel and family members across the United States.

8. Finding Hope

Plan for Hope

I'm one of those people who always likes to have a vacation planned well in advance, if only just to give me something to look forward to. I've also lived through some dark times, and if I hadn't been able to always find the light at the end of the tunnel, I might not be here today writing this for you.

I believe that hope (beyond just a fun vacation) is something that lives inside all human beings and needs to be nurtured so that it will grow. Hope can be snuffed out, and I've met many people who had lost all their hope. Many of them were cops, and I don't want you to be one of them.

The fertile ground where hope lives is deep inside you — in your values, your beliefs and your faith in something greater than yourself. I believe that hope is fed and nourished by our behaviors, our words and our service to others.

You can plan for and plant hope by creating something to live for in your life. Maybe it's about starting a family, or maybe its about doing charity work. What do you live for? Is it your work? Is it your family?

Ask yourself: What gives you hope? Write down what is important in your life, and make some plans. If you don't have enough on your list, get busy and add to it. This may also include your dreams for the future and your goals in life.

Sometimes we get too busy in life to really pay attention to the things that are most important to us. Figure out what's important to you and add more of it to your life.

Giving Hope

The old saying, "What goes around, comes around," means that what you invest in now will repay you later. That is certainly true when it comes to hope and compassion.

Ask yourself: When can you offer hope? For this exercise, spend some time noticing what gives people hope, pride and joy. Ask colleagues, friends and neighbors. Make some notes in your journal about where hope comes from. See how many times a day you can offer hope to someone else. It's free, and sometimes giving someone hope takes only a few words.

By keeping records in your journal of what examples of hope and compassion you've witnessed, and what lessons you've learned, you'll be better able to share these "real life" stories with people you're trying to help, and you'll be able to give them examples of what has helped others. Who knows? Your exploration may also help you find something that helps *you*.

9. Dealing With Grief

The Grief Examination

What do you know about grief?

I was taught that people pass through a series of stages as they recover from a traumatic event. But the newest research says that's not always true, and that not everyone passes through stages of grief in the same sequence.

So I suggest you do some personal examination and research about grief. What have you seen around you in your work? What kinds of tragic events have you endured personally?

Do some work in your journal about your thoughts and experiences with grief. Do some of your own research and decide how you will cope with grief, and how you can best help others work through their grief. Is it about just listening, or is it about changing one's mind-set? I don't suggest that you try to take the place of victim services — but this may be helpful in supporting friends and family and, particularly your peers in law enforcement.

You can find some helpful information on the Web site of the American Psychological Association.

http://www.apa.org/helpcenter/grief.aspx

Grief Guide

If you choose to do the work and research needed to learn more about the function and process of human grief, you might consider being a Grief Guide for others. Again, I don't suggest you try to replace the chaplains or victim and psych services; rather just become a better-informed law enforcement professional who works to serve a community. That community may well be our own law enforcement community.

Most of us have learned to suppress our emotions — especially grief — and someone needs to take a leadership role to break that log jam and get others to express their negative emotions before those emotions become crippling. Consider joining or starting a proactive peer support team or becoming involved in Concerns Of Police Survivors (C.O.P.S.) and work with co-worker survivors who have lost a partner or peer in the line of duty. Another underserved population are the family members and co-workers of law enforcement officers who take their own lives. These people really need your help (but, sadly, they probably won't ask for it).

10. Positive Self-talk

Give Yourself Some Positive Self-talk

What kind of a pep talk do you need in your life?

Face it: You're the one who's going to be giving that talk to yourself inside your head every day for the rest of your life — so you might want to script some of the more important things you need to say to yourself in order to get them right and so that they last for as long as you need them.

What do you need to hear? What should become your mind's natural response when things get tough? You might say things like: "I've got this," "I can handle this," or "No problem!" You might also say: "Just Do It," "I Can Do This," or "I'll Never Quit."

Program Your Self-talk

What goes on in your head? Do you talk to yourself?

Most of us do, and I believe that if you want to control some of that negative Self-talk, you have to program your Self with positive talk long before you really need it. Programming your Self-talk can help you to automatically come up with emotional strength when you really need it.

Consider situations in which you might need a boost of strength or courage — situations in which you become angry, frustrated, agitated, depressed, as well as in high-stress situations such as vehicle pursuits or life-and-death confrontations.

What is your mind saying in those situations? Consider statements like:

> *I've got this!*
> *Calm down!*
> *Today's the day!*
> *I can handle this!*

Relax!
This is fun!
I love this!
This is the life!

Dealing with Negative Self-talk

Once you begin to work on improving your Self-talk, you'll become more and more aware of negative Self-talk in yourself and in others. Your goal is then to replace your negative Self-talk with more positive statements and to use those positive statements to establish a positive mind-set.

It may be easiest to spot negative Self-talk in other people; then you can see if you can help them by coaching them to be more positive as they program their mind-set with positive Self-talk. I usually say something like "Hey, don't talk to my friend like that" when someone says something degrading about themselves. As you become more experienced, you will start catching yourself more frequently and you can begin to replace negative statements with more positive ones.

It's helpful to keep a log or make a journal record of what you catch yourself saying in your mind to yourself. Some deep-rooted programming from your schooling or childhood might be harder to replace, and keeping a log or record of what you are hearing in your mind might be helpful in working systematically to replace those old beliefs with newer, more positive and more functional ones.

Take time today to listen to your mind as it talks to you and write down the messages you hear yourself saying. Don't be judgmental. Just write in a notebook what you hear; then tomorrow you can analyze your list, and reevaluate your internal programming. Repeat this exercise as often as it takes to rewrite the code of your mind into something more positive and useful. Treat your mind like a computer, and program the code for the life you want to live.

11. Emotional Mind-sets

Set Your Positive Mind-set

Today, try setting a positive mind-set that you want to live by so that you can secure for your life's health and wellness. What words would you say to your Self? What actions would you take today?

In her book *The Upside of Stress: Why Stress Is Good for You, and How to Get Good at It*, Kelly McGonigal, Ph.D., a health psychologist and lecturer at Stanford University, suggests we have the wrong mind-set about stress, and that our negative beliefs and negative mind-set about stress is what's hurting us more than the negative stress itself. What's at the forethought of your mind-set when you're faced with a challenge? Do you believe you're "Unstoppable" or have a "Can-Do" mentality? Do you believe you can handle any challenge, or do you succumb to your fears and doubts?

Sometimes negative thoughts were programmed into us by parents, teachers and life's experiences. You have a chance now to consciously reprogram your mind-set with a positive, optimistic mentality. Choose a mind-set phrase that best describes you, such as "Never Quit," "Who Dares, Wins," or "Just Do It." Pick one or write one for yourself.

Prevention First

Law enforcement is very reactive. Agencies allocate most of their resources to responding to crime, and very few, if any, to crime prevention. This creates a reactive mentality that seeps into our personal mind-sets. We need to think *Prevention First*, especially when it comes to our own health and wellness.

It's much easier to address most emotional issues when they first arise, but most of us wait to deal with our personal challenges until it may be too late. Most of us try to bottle up or bury our emotional problems because we were told to do so, or because we fear our peers will ridicule us if we don't. We need to stop that. We need to prioritize our mental and emotional health, just as we need to adopt a Prevention First mind-set when it comes to looking after our friends. Prevention needs to be our credo, and it needs to be everyone's daily mind-set.

What words would you say to your Self daily to promote a Prevention First mind-set?

Today's the Day

I love positive people, and when their stories of patience lead to great success, that's even better.

My favorite person like that was Mel Fisher, the treasure hunter. Mel was famous for saying "Today's the day" every day. People like Mel, who risked his own time and money in pursuit of a fortune in sunken gold, have to have patience and a positive attitude. Most treasure hunters, I assume, never find their treasures, but Mel did. After searching Spain's national archives in Seville, Mel's team discovered a new clue to the possible site of a sunken wreck off the coast of Florida. Mel, his family and his crew spent over 16 years hunting for the treasure carried by the *Nuestra Señora de Atocha* when it sank in 1622 during a hurricane off the Florida Keys. Despite massive monetary expense, loss of human life, including Mel's son, his daughter-in-law and two divers, he and his team persisted. After a long search, they found the treasure, and after a lengthy court battle victory was theirs. The *Atocha* treasure, worth an estimated $450 million in gold, silver, emeralds and other artifacts, is one of the largest ever salvaged. *National Geographic* covered it in several of its issues and a television special. I encourage you to learn more about this story yourself. But more than that, I encourage you to adopt Mel's mind-set, and say every day to yourself (or everyone around you), "*Today's the day!*"

I think that perseverance has paid. That's one of the main things, just hang in there and do your thing and when people try to tear you down or get jealous, just let it go in one ear and out the other and keep on going."
— Mel Fisher

It Is What It Is

We hear other people (and we sometimes catch ourselves) saying things like, "It is what it is." Some folks interpret such words as a sign of defeat, as in, "I can't do anything about it, and there's no use fighting, so I might as well give in and get used to it."

Maybe. But "It is what it is" is also an exceptionally *affirming, positive* statement which people use everyday to take control of their mind-set. Try saying, *"It Is What It Is — for today."*

Saying "It is what it is" or *"It Is What It Is — for today"* reminds us that it's OK if things didn't go the way we wanted them to, because the earth is still spinning and life goes on. People often say these things to soothe themselves after a painful event and to remind themselves that they shouldn't take life too seriously. These sayings suggest that we shouldn't always expect things to be perfect in our lives.

What do you say when things don't go your way? What do you say to help others cope with their problems? Is there a part of your mind-set able to salvage some good feelings from a bad event so that the negative emotions don't erode your spirit?

Things Change

Another saying people use to dismiss negative events or bad circumstances in their lives is "Things change!" — meaning, "It's no big deal, and life goes on."

Change is difficult for many people, including cops, who want to be in control all the time. Can you form a mind-set so that change in your life doesn't create overwhelming problems for your outlook on life? Can you say to yourself "Things change," "No big deal," "Life goes on" — or something else to dismiss the negative emotions involved with unexpected changes of circumstances?

Just Do It!

Nike's got it right: "Just do it!" isn't simply a corporate slogan; it's a positive mind-set that can give you all the strength you need if only you believe it. In this case it's a positive mental attitude that gets you started: Don't over-think! Go for it!

Never Quit!

Thousands of world-class athletes, elite performers and special operations military units around the world use this mind-set. U.S. Navy SEALs list the phrase "I will never quit" in their Ethos/Creed.

What's your mind-set about quitting? What's your creed, credo, motto or ethos about perseverance? What will you repeat inside your mind over and over when the going gets really tough? "Never quit!" works well for so many folks that I heartily recommend it to you.

Remember that your mind-set is your mind's operating system. But if you don't program your mind-set yourself, you're probably relying on some old indoctrination programmed into you by parents, teachers and many of your old, outdated life experiences.

Be *proactive* and start programming your mind right now: Never Quit!

Psych-Up: "I Can Do This"

Try approaching challenges positively instead of negatively. Try programming your mind-set with "I can do this!" or "I've got this!"

How do you handle a difficult challenge? What do you say in your mind to get through a difficult workout, run, call or crime scene? How do you psych-up your Self for a long, arduous, horrible event?

Programming your mind-set every day during simple activities is the best way to prepare your Self for those rare, overwhelming situations that happen in law enforcement. We start programming our Selves to deal with fear and overwhelm in the police academy, or in military basic training, when we're put through daunting physical challenges such as obstacle courses and other fitness challenges. We continue this process during annual in-service training, and hopefully all that programming pays off.

Don't leave anything to chance. Challenge yourself regularly with physical, mental, emotional and spiritual experiences that test your mettle and evaluate your determination. During these times of Self-improvement, program the mind-set you want to master so that it will be there to support you when you need it most.

Failure Is Not an Option

Oh, but it is — and then what are you going to do? What we're going to do is to learn from our mistakes so that we keep the consequences of any new failures as small as possible.

"Failure is not an option" is attributed to NASA Flight Director Eugene Francis "Gene" Kranz, and it's also the title of his autobiography. Kranz is best known for his leadership in Mission Control's efforts to save the crew of Apollo 13 after a near-fatal equipment failure during the 1970 moon mission, — though, apparently he never used the phrase at the time. Rather, the writers of Ron Howard's film, *Apollo 13*, extrapolated it from Kranz' leadership style, his sense of determination and his personal ethos.

The attitude attributed to Gene Kranz is a great mind-set to help all of us work through tough challenges and (hopefully) bring them to a successful conclusion.

But success isn't always possible. What's your attitude about failure? Can you handle unexpected challenges successfully? What will your mind-set be during difficult times? In the event of an actual failure, how will you handle disappointment, disgrace or dishonor? What will be your mind-set in failure?

Make It Safe

Former police officer-turned-police psychologist Jack Digliani, Ph.D., Ed.D. has an initiative called "Make It Safe" on his Web site.

www.JackDigliani.com

Jack asserts that our job is tough enough without our adding to it by treating one another negatively. We're merciless when we tease each other, and if we're not teasing, we're posing macho, "suck it up" attitudes that usually have no basis in reality.

When we say "We take care of our own," then we should practice what we preach. Jack's "Make It Safe" initiative strives to create a working environment in which it's safe to ask for help. The key is to create a culture whose members don't shrink from asking for help when they need it and who know that help will be available from their agencies and superior officers. Pay attention to your own behavior and language. See if you can catch yourself when you start to be overly harsh to a rookie or begin to excessively tease a peer. Try to find a better way to support them. Teach them, guide them — or simply shut up and *listen* to them.

What are you doing to make it safe to ask for help in your agency? How do you behave towards your peers and juniors? What do you do when you find a peer in need of help? What do you do when your find another employee is harsh or insulting to a peer?

Remember: The supportive culture you create is the one that will be there when *you* need help and have to ask for it yourself. Is the culture you are creating the one you really want for yourself?

Change starts with a few brave people willing to blaze a path for everyone else. "Make it safe" is a mind-set.

12. Other Ways To Manage Your Emotions

Dump the Bucket

How can you remove or manage some of the negative things we all accumulate in our imaginary emotional "buckets" as we work through our careers? One way is to acknowledge what gets added to your bucket every day and to deal with it before your bucket overflows and you require professional assistance or therapy.

The first step is to practice raising your awareness so that you notice those small additions to your emotional bucket right away. The "sound" of something plopping into your bucket might be "Hey, that was painful," or "That hurt my feelings." Acknowledging what just hit your bucket is the first step. The next step is acknowledging, "I need to analyze why that got to me." Noticing these feelings when they're small makes them so much easier to process, and processing them quickly helps to condition your Self to be more resilient to those painful thoughts and feelings in the future. This exercise requires strong emotional maturity on your part. You have to recognize that something hurt you emotionally, and you have to have the maturity to address it.

One way to address emotional pain is by communicating it to the person who caused it by saying, straight out, "That hurt/insulted/offended me." This technique is usually easier when the person causing the pain is someone you love or respect. But it's usually not a good technique to use it with suspects or members of the general public. In those situations, it's best to process what went into your emotional bucket by talking with a peer or by journaling your feelings privately.

Sometimes these emotional pains are caused by events that leave us sad, depressed or even shocked. Those kinds of emotional traumas are very common in law enforcement because we see the worst that society has to offer, or we're involved in crime or accident investigations that leave people or animals hurt, maimed or dead. We are also likely to pick up second-hand trauma by listening to our peers describe their experiences, or by looking at crime scene photos. Be alert to these types of contributions to your emotional bucket, and either avoid them or recognize and deal with them just as you would were they your own experiences.

Laughter: The Best Medicine

What makes you laugh? Is it a person, a TV show, a comedian, a place? What can you call to mind that can make you laugh on command? Is there a picture, a sound, a recording?

Whatever you can put at your fingertips is helpful. Save pictures, movies, TV shows, audio recordings to your smartphone, tablet or computer so that they can be available anytime you need them. Maybe you can find your favorite comedian or comedy routine on DVD or CD to load on your smartphone. What would it take to play these instantly any time you needed to laugh? Laughter can be a very effective stress reliever.

Picture This

Find pictures that make you happy and fill you with joy. Put them where you can find them instantly when you need a boost. Create a photo album; put them in your pocket or on your smartphone; create a slide show or a screen saver on your computer. Use pictures of family, friends, loved ones, pets, children, places, events, things or even just pictures from Google Images that make you smile.

And if you combine these pictures with your other stress-reduction and relaxation exercises, they'll have more power to improve your mood when you need them most. Consider conditioning your mind to react positively to positive images; then, when you need to relax, calm down or cheer up, they'll be there to help you because of the conditioning you've already done to create those relaxing physiological associations.

Music Is Good for the Soul

Most people are profoundly affected by music. Some music lifts you up, while some calms you down. Some music can energize you, while other music can make you feel depressed. Sometimes a certain piece of music will remind you of a person, place or experience from your past. Many of these memories are very pleasant.

Identify music that fits into these positive categories and that works to uplift you. Load your music onto your smartphone or iPod or MP3 player so that you have it at your fingertips when you need it. Find music that excites you and charges you up, as well as music that helps you calm down. Use these recordings when you need to energize yourself, or to bring back happy memories when you are feeling down.

Pet Your Pet

Many people love and cherish their pets. If you are a pet lover, recognize that your pet is an important contributor to your emotional wellness.

Consider time with your pet as a necessary part of maintaining your mental health, and plan accordingly. If it's a dog, map out daily walks, which are good for you and your dog. If it's a cat, work out time to sit quietly and just pet your cat.

This may sound silly, but time with a pet can be very therapeutic. Recognize two things about time with your pet: Regular relaxation time can be good for you and your pet; and during periods of high stress, these interludes can be critical in allowing you to relax and detox from your day's traumas.

Free Flow

The *Free Flow Exercise* is an opportunity to open your Self to what your mind wants, what it's doing and what it's thinking about. Make it your aim to open up your thoughts to everything that's "on your mind," and allow all of those thoughts to pass through your mind like a slide show. Use this time to review what your mind is focused on, and sit quietly and allow the slide show to just present itself to you. Don't dwell on any one thought; rather, allow the flow to pass by as you observe it. Journal about what you learn if you need to work more thoroughly on it later.

You've Got Mail

With the *Mail Exercise*, allow your mind (or a higher power) to send you the messages you need to hear. Don't make it a mind-directed exercise with which you try to force a message you want to come to you. This is a *quiet* exercise to allow yourself to be open to any message of importance so that it can automatically be delivered to your mind's mailbox.

Be Mindful

The process of *mindfulness* is a specific technique used to calm mind, body and spirit. The idea is to be completely present in the moment and allow your thoughts to present themselves without judgment. If you want to learn specific techniques please look at the links at the end of this chapter.

Learning to be aware of and observe your body, your mind as well as important issues about your own behavior is also called mindfulness. Mindfulness is directing and maintaining nonjudgmental attention to the experience of our bodies and minds in the present moment. Mindfulness is paying attention to what is occurring within one's Self as it is happening. This is a very valuable skill for emotional and negative stress management.

Sit quietly and be an observer of your own thoughts. Don't judge them — simply observe and let them pass. Don't become attached to any of them; just passively notice what you are thinking and let your mind wander. Spend 15 or 20 minutes doing this, and then make notes about the experience in your journal. Try it again in a day or so and see what happens then.

Driving Your Observation Skills

The goal of this exercise is to utilize all your senses and skills of observation while driving. Engage your senses fully to the sights and sounds or what's going on around you, to the aromas of the areas you're driving through, and to the feel of the road. What are the cars around you doing? Can you anticipate their movements? Try to observe things objectively, rather than focusing on your thoughts or feelings. This is an exercise in Mindfulness. Observe without judging. You're the dispassionate observer, merely watching without analyzing.

Obviously you *must* still be engaged in the cognitive and decision-making process of driving; in fact you should be *more* engaged than you normally are. The difference here, though, is that you're tuning all your senses to be fully aware and focused completely on the experiences of driving.

This exercise works very well if you're driving with a passenger with whom you can compare notes on what you sensed and what you observed. And it can be very helpful in letting go of the days' work stresses.

Enhanced Awareness Exercise

Enhanced Awareness is discussed in the Armor Your Self ™ Mentally Exercises chapter, but here I'd like to focus on a slightly different objective. In our Trained Observer Training program, we use this exercise to develop and strengthen your senses of observation and cognition. With this version of the awareness exercise, I want you to use any activity to fully engage all of your skills so that your senses and perceptions are fully awake and emotionally aware.

In this exercise, your aim is to be quiet and sedentary as you allow experiences around to pass while you quietly observe them. Activate all of your senses and allow them to flood you with the information that each of your senses perceive. Focus on each of your senses, one at a time, and try to fully absorb each sense's collection of information. For example, as you focus on your sense of smell, sit quietly, close your eyes and try to completely appreciate all the odors that surround you.

This works very well if you are out doors and can experience a wide variety of sensory inputs:

Find a safe, comfortable place to sit outdoors for about 30 minutes. Spend the first couple of minutes getting acclimated to the environment as you take in all the sights, sounds and smells. Try touching and tasting anything that would be appropriate in order to experience the environment totally. Next, spend about five minutes on one sense as you try to exclude perceptions flooding in from your other senses.

Smell

Close your eyes and focus only on your sense of smell. Can you shut out the sounds and sights around you? What can you smell? How many odors are there? What emotions do they evoke?

Taste

Find something in the environment near you — a leaf, stone, stick, etc. (Please avoid things that could be toxic or poisonous!) Close your eyes and focus only on your sense of taste. Describe the taste to yourself. How many different tastes are there in one object? What emotions do these tastes evoke?

Touch

Now, find an object near you that you can hold — a leaf, stone, stick, etc. (Again, nothing toxic or poisonous.) Close your eyes and focus only on your sense of touch. How does the object feel? Describe it mentally to yourself. What emotions do its textures evoke? Is it hot or cold? Can you feel sunlight on your face?

Sight

This time, keep your eyes wide open. Sit quietly while turning your head to observe all the sights, colors, motions, etc. What do you see? Are you really *seeing* it? Describe the colors, textures, brightness, opacity, intensity, etc. How many ways can you describe one item? For this exercise, you might want to take a pen and a piece of paper, and spend just a moment to write a description of one item, listing as many descriptors and adjectives as you can.

Sound

Close your eyes and focus only on your sense of sound. What do you hear? Where is the sound coming from? How many sounds do you hear? Turn your head to enable you to hear all the sounds coming from each direction. Describe the quality of each sound and what it is that makes each particular noise. What emotions do these sounds evoke?

After you have completed these exercises, determine how each and all of your senses made you feel. Ask yourself which (if any) of these activities allowed you to relax or let go of your days' negative stresses. If your answer to any part of this exercise is yes, then these activities might be worth doing regularly.

13. Emotional Habit Seeding, Feeding and Weeding

Emotional Habit Seeding

Habit Seeding is doing simple things to start new positive habits. An example: After years of being nagged to floss my teeth, I just started doing it — and I still do it every day. And success in developing this new, healthy habit has served as a "seed" to remind me that I can create new, *positive* habits any time I want to. In other words, flossing became a master seed that worked for other habits.

I also seeded the habit of writing every day by putting a yellow sticky note on my bathroom mirror where I see it every morning. That's a "habit seed."

What can you do today to seed a new and positive emotional resilience habit that you know you need to do right now?

Emotional Habit Feeding

Habit Feeding is supporting your positive habits either by working with its trigger or its reward to encourage that habit's ongoing success. Sometimes a trigger doesn't work anymore, or the reward doesn't mean as much as it once did. What do you need to do to feed your current positive emotional habits to make sure they continue working?

Emotional Habit Weeding

Habit Weeding is getting rid of negative, unhealthy habits. In order to weed a bad emotional habit successfully, you need either to change or remove the trigger for the bad habit, or you need to change or remove the reward for the bad habit.

There are lots of self-help books and programs on which people spend billions of dollars each year to address this issue. But if you want to try "weeding" on your own, I recommend picking a simple and small "bad emotional habit" to experiment with.

One of my bad habits was eating snacks after dinner while I watched TV. I was raised on the concept of "comfort food"; as a result, I was just "stuffing my face" at night to unwind from an emotional day. To weed this habit, I first tried substituting fruit for sweets. When that didn't work, I tried telling myself not to eat anything after 8 p.m. Finally, I tried not watching TV. It turned out that the TV was the trigger. Once I was able to identify and remove the trigger, nighttime snacking went away. When I was confident I had conquered the habit, I was able to add TV-watching to my life as a reward for the behavior of *not* snacking.

What emotional habits are you going to try to weed? How will you address the trigger or the reward for your bad habit?

Your Emotional Homework

I covered a lot of topics with a lot of exercises in this chapter. I know that everything is not going to work for everyone. How will you personalize your own emotional training regime? Start now. Go back through this chapter and mark or fold back the pages for the exercises you want to try. Plan what you want to do for a week at a time and create a way to record your progress. Remember: I've uploaded worksheets on the CopsAlive Web site to help you with your training plan. www.CopsAlive.com/aysbookworksheets

Resources to Help with Your Training and Conditioning

VIDEO:

- Sig Sauer Academy: Tactical Tip: Tactical Breathing and Threat Scanning After a Violent Encounter:
http://www.youtube.com/watch?v=1bvHq0omtQY

APP:

- Tactical Breather, from the National Center for Telehealth and Technology:
http://apps.usa.gov/tactical-breather.shtml
Tactical Breathing Trainer can be used to gain control of physiological and psychological responses to stress. Through repetitive practice and training, anyone can learn to gain control of heart rate, emotions, concentration, and other physiological and psychological responses during stressful situations. Many of the techniques taught in this application were provided by Lt. Col. [ret.] Dave Grossman in his book *On Combat: The Psychology and Physiology of Deadly Conflict in War and in Peace*. Features:
    - Introduction Narrative to the Benefits of Tactical Breathing
    - Tutorial on how to use Tactical Breathing
    - Practice Mode to help you learn
    - Settings Page to change voice gender and graphics preferences
    - Excerpt Page provided by Lt. Col. [ret.] Dave Grossman that displays several chapters from his book

ARTICLES:

- "How to ease work pressure and fight stress by adding adrenaline to your workout," *Men's Health Magazine,* July 1, 2005.
"The value of adrenaline-charged sports like downhill, mountain biking isn't in stress reduction, by the way. It's in stress production. Researchers at Texas A&M University found that adventure sports such as rock climbing and white-water canoeing call up more cortisol and epinephrine—more commonly known as

adrenaline—than public speaking, the acknowledged champion of redline stress reactions. And in this case, that's a good thing. That's because activities that are physically and mentally stressful help your body react better to stress in everyday life."

http://www.menshealth.com/health/adrenaline-rush

- "Adrenal Stress Response To Crisis (Before, During and After):"
  http://www.nononsenseselfdefense.com/adrenal.htm

- "The Adrenaline Dump: It's More Than Just Breathing:"
  http://www.policeone.com/training/articles/1271860-The-adrenaline-dump-Its-more-than-just-breathing/

- "These are the secrets for 'Tactical Breathing' in combat:"
  http://www.theblaze.com/stories/2012/06/07/these-are-the-secrets-for-tactical-breathing-in-combat/

- Three breathing exercises, Dr. Andrew Weil:
  http://www.drweil.com/drw/u/ART00521/three-breathing-exercises.html

- Five Steps to Mindfulness:
  http://www.mindful.org/five-steps-to-mindfulness/

- Mindfulness Exercises, The Mayo Clinic:
  http://www.mayoclinic.org/healthy-lifestyle/consumer-health/in-depth/mindfulness-exercises/art-20046356

- 16 Simple Mindfulness Exercises, Practicing Mindfulness:
  http://www.practicingmindfulness.com/16-simple-mindfulness-exercises/

- Mindfulness Exercises, The Guided Meditation Site:
  http://www.the-guided-meditation-site.com/mindfulness-exercises.html

- The Fifth Habit of Highly Effective Shooters:
  http://centermassgroup.com/2011/09/the-fifth-habit-of-highly-effective-shooters/

- Breathing Techniques for Snipers:
  http://www.ghilliesuitsonline.com/brteforsn.html

- The Navy SEALs Breathing Technique:
  http://www.ehow.com/how_7740721_navy-seals-breathing-technique.html

- Breathing During Exercise:
  http://www.military.com/military-fitness/workouts/breathing-during-exercise

- Add Reps with Russian Breathing Techniques:
  http://www.armytimes.com/offduty/health/ONLINE.MUSCLE.BREATHING/

- Using Combat Breathing to Conquer Anxiety, Stress, and Fear:
  http://www.selfgrowth.com/articles/
  using-combat-breathing-to-conquer-anxiety-stress-and-fear

- The Importance of Breathing:
  http://military-fitness.military.com/2010/09/the-importance-of-breathing.html

- How Combat Breathing Saved My Life:
  http://www.policemag.com/blog/women-in-law-enforcement/story/2011/03/
  combat-breathing-saved-my-life.aspx

- Tactical Breathing Can Stop Stress on the Spot:
  http://onresilience.com/2011/06/02/
  tactical-breathing-can-stop-stress-on-the-spot/

- The Power of Combat Breathing:
  http://paladinplanet.blogspot.com/2012/05/power-of-combat-breathing.html

CHAPTER 13

Armor Your Self™: Spiritually

I don't pretend to be an expert on spirituality and, of all the chapters in this book, this one has been the most difficult to write because people have such strong emotional responses about this topic, given its ties to religion. But spirituality isn't just about religion; it's also about the *human spirit*, the source of our inner strength, which drives our moral, ethical and honorable behaviors and decisions. Many (though not all) of us find that source in religion, and it seems to me that even those of us without connection to an organized religion still have a spiritual component, a place of inner strength, that is critically important to our self-identity and our very existence. This place of inner strength is also critically important to our ability to successfully navigate and survive a career in law enforcement. So while spirituality is something many of us shy away from discussing with other people, I invite you to explore it for your own growth and well-being.

Why Spirituality Is Important to Law Enforcement

Our spirituality is part of the core, of who we are, and is the home of our honor and integrity. It is where our values and views about right and wrong reside. It's a piece of our humanity which, if corrupted, can erase our ability to make the right decisions for the right reasons, thereby eroding our Self to the point that even we can't any longer recognize ourselves.

If you acknowledge that law enforcement deals with the balance between good and evil, and if you acknowledge that we are constantly confronted with unanswered questions about why bad things happen to good people, then you need to embrace the spiritual dimension of your Self for personal growth, personal strength and, most importantly, for personal protection.

When I say "spirituality" I don't necessarily mean religion or faith, but those things are part of what some people think is important in their spiritual beliefs.

When I say "spirituality" I do mean that place which gives us strength. It is the place from which we all draw our values and integrity and through which we exhibit our honor, courage and fortitude. Spirituality is the internal reservoir that replenishes our inner strength when we are challenged by trauma and tragedy and grief. Some people are certain that this reservoir is filled by God or another deity (or deities); other people believe that this reservoir of strength is built into our DNA or biological coding.

Whatever your beliefs, it may very well be critical to your survival in law enforcement to examine what you believe and, if necessary, explore where such strength comes from. What's important for our purpose here is how you will *build* and *replenish* this strength before it is completely dissolved by the toxicity of your career.

Again — just to be crystal clear: When I use the term "spiritual" or "spirituality" I'm not talking about any specific religion or religious organization. I'm not going to preach to you or suggest that you ought to adopt any specific religious viewpoint. In fact, I won't do any of that because I believe the issue is *larger* than that, and because I believe that a basic understanding of these concepts about spirituality's role in law enforcement can be invaluable to your survival. So I urge you to read on — even if you are resistant to this discussion.

**Revenge
Tragedy Wickedness
Depravity
Venality Debauchery
Dishonesty Rage Indifference
Cruelty Exploitation
Poverty Greed
Avarice Evil
Wrath**

Consider the concepts of Evil, Wrath, Dishonesty, Wickedness, Venality, Poverty, Greed, Debauchery, Revenge, Avarice, Exploitation, Tragedy, Indifference, Cruelty, Depravity, Rage, Child Exploitation, or any of the other disgusting things we encounter in this job. Indeed, consider any question a victim of some tragedy asks you that starts with "why" and then perhaps you can see how it is that any and all of us have a need for the strength and protection of our inner spirit.

None of these "whys" can be addressed in our training and preparation for a career in law enforcement unless we explore this area called "spirituality." And to conduct this exploration, you only have to be open-minded enough to examine the issues and to determine how they affect this career, how they affect you and what you need to do about it.

Balance those negatives above with the concepts below: Honor, Integrity, Honesty, Truth, Justice, Hope, Courage, Love, Faith, Patience, Compassion, Kindness, Charity, Generosity, Altruism, Dedication and Gratitude.

Where do these ideals come from? And how do you build these positive "protective factors" into your life in order to shield your Self from the negative effects of negative influences and risk factors?

These positive qualities can't be defined, or strengthened, with physical, mental or even emotional training.

By my definition I believe that the spiritual side of our Selves is the part of us which deals with issues that are the deepest and most personal to us, and helps us to deal with forces and powers which we sense are beyond our particular Selves. I believe that this side of our Selves refers to various dimensions of larger and more intangible issues such as integrity, values, fulfillment and overall moral character. This is the part of us that is most difficult to describe, feel or reach, and I firmly believe that it is the part of us that is the most vulnerable to the toxic effects of this career.

In his book *Spiritual Survival for Law Enforcement*, Chaplain Cary Friedman writes:
Whether they can express it or not, whether they are fully aware of it or not, the fact remains: People who are attracted to the field of law enforcement and who actually become cops are intrinsically very spiritual people. Don't be fooled by that gruff, no-nonsense exterior, or by the characteristic cop's impatience for all that "touchy-feely stuff." In the ways that really count, in the ways that really define what it means to be spiritual, law enforcement officers are as spiritual as they come.

— Cary A. Friedman, *Spiritual Survival for Law Enforcement*, p. 41
(Compass Books. Kindle Edition.)

Spiritual strength is critical to the survival of our core Selves and is indistinguishable from the values we maintain both personally and professionally. If our spiritual Self is out of balance, then our whole being is vulnerable to corruption from a host of threats, many of which we encounter daily in police work.

Spiritual health then, is a critical necessity for anyone who works in law enforcement. Spiritual well-being is displayed in the compassion, professionalism, integrity and courage of law enforcement professionals. When those who are spiritually unwell show signs of weakness of character, moral powerlessness, and a lack of honor, they are neither compassionate nor professional, and they do not belong in this profession.

So how then do we build spiritual strength? More importantly: How do we maintain and replenish spiritual strength?

I believe that the answers lie in first understanding the importance and make up of your own spiritual Self, and then developing your own routines, tactics and techniques to strengthen and condition a sounder and healthier spiritual core of your being.

This kind of fitness training requires a lot of introspection, examination, discussion and learning. In order to be spiritually fit you must look *inward* and examine your beliefs, values, morals, ideals, principles and ethical standards. You must also *challenge* your beliefs or values, morals, ideals, principles and ethical standards by comparing yours with those of others you respect, and then evaluate your beliefs and standards in relation to those of our society.

To be an ethically sound law enforcement officer you must do this type of exercise often, even daily. It's neither easy work, nor is it comfortable — *but it's necessary*. You can start by asking yourself some of the difficult questions about life and your work.

Ask your Self:

- What do you have to live for?
- What is worth dying for?
- What motivates you to get out of bed in the morning?
- What keeps you awake at night?
- Who teaches you about death?
- What are your beliefs about death and about life itself?

Major Concepts

As you explore your spiritual Self, here are some of the major concepts you will need to examine: Values, Ethics, Honesty, Trust, Integrity, Honor, Compassion, Grief, and Hope. There are also spiritual components to the all the emotions we discussed earlier, especially Joy, Happiness, Love, Fear, Courage, Pride, Loyalty and Gratitude.

Exploring your spiritual Self will probably raise more questions than it will answer. That's OK — as long as you continue your examination and embrace the uncertainty. You may discover that this exploration brings up questions, like:

How will it help me in a fight?
How will it help me at home?
How do I summon this strength?
How do I turn it off?

Spirituality by its nature is about mystery, conundrum and paradox.

The Police Perfection Paradox

There's a spiritual component to the Police Perfection Paradox mentioned in Chapter 5. It's the conundrum created as you try to reconcile your personal expectations with those of both your agency and the public. One or all of these expectations may assume that you'll always be perfect in your decision-making, and yet reality frequently proves decisions you make can't always be perfect. And when you do make a mistake, your agency, the media, the public and your peers will judge you. Their expectations of your behavior frequently won't match those of your actual behavior under stress, and that can create a massive spiritual and ethical conflict.

Sadly, we sometimes make fatal decisions, with the best of intentions, under stressful circumstances with split-second timing pressures. Even when everyone around you says that they understand what you did, you may never be able to emotionally or spiritually reconcile your split-second decision with your own beliefs and standards.

The Police Perfection Paradox is this: You're always under pressure to always be right and perfect because people's lives depend upon you; but when you make a simple mistake, in a split-second, life-and-death decision, you'll be second-guessed by Monday-morning quarterbacks who weren't there and have the privilege of 20/20 hindsight. This can happen in a court of law, in the media and, sometimes, even worse, in your own mind.

Coming face-to-face with the Police Perfection Paradox can be very challenging if you lack professional competence or spiritual strength. It's a damned-if-you-do, damned-if-you-don't snare that heightens reluctance to even ask for help or treatment for problems out of fear that your bosses and peers will think you are weak and won't support you, or ever consider promoting you. This creates a macho style of "strong and silent" policing: Just internalize all of the traumas, tragedies, fears, stresses, anger and other emotions, on the assumption that these feelings can just be bottled up so that they'll eventually just go away.

This simply does not work for anyone. In this kind of a pressure-cooker environment — where feelings, emotions and natural responses to negative stress are bottled up inside our Selves, and when our Selves are weakened with a flawed or flimsy spiritual foundation — it's no wonder that we crack under pressure when we're asked to do the really tough things that we knew we would eventually be asked to do in this job.

If we haven't strengthened our Selves spiritually to assume a sense of honor and a code of ethics and integrity, then we haven't built a foundation of strong values and principles — and we've created a breeding ground for this Police Perfection Paradox to thrive.

Creating a Moral Compass

We all need an internal moral compass with which to navigate through life, one with its directional points based on the core values and beliefs with which we were raised. No doubt these core beliefs and values have been and will be molded by external forces; but we also have a good degree of control over the growth and development of this tool, and thus we can strengthen it and serve and protect our Selves as we navigate life.

If you haven't already gotten all the spiritual foundation you need from your parents, teachers, mentors and religious leaders, then you'll have to do the work yourself. That means forging your own set of principles, values and codes of honor and ethics, and then comparing these with the values and beliefs of your mentors or people you really trust. As you do this, you'll have to ask questions, start discussions and be willing to examine your belief systems. And you'll need to be sure about the sources of your core beliefs and principles and about why they're important to you or to the world.

You'll only really be able to make these examinations comprehensively by writing out your beliefs so that you can read them and reexamine them under the microscope of everyday reality. When you've honed what you've written into statements of principles you can adhere to, you can then begin to discuss them with others and further hone and perfect your personal credo. When you're comfortable with what you've created, you can use these written documents to reinforce your beliefs and principles every day.

As you go through this process, it's important to understand that just because you established your core values by the time you're 20 years old doesn't mean they'll still apply when you're 30 or 50, so be ready to review and reevaluate them regularly.

Once you establish your own statement of values the next step is to examine and scrutinize the values and standards you're held to by your agency and our country. Review carefully your agency's oath of office and its code of conduct or code of ethics, and thoroughly read and memorize our United States Constitution. (If you live and work outside of the U.S., examine the governing documents of your country and region.)

Law Enforcement Oaths and Ethics

Where statements of our personal core beliefs and those of our profession come together are in our oaths of office and the codes of ethics we follow as law enforcement officers. If your agency has these documents, get copies and put them with the material you're creating as you use this book. You'll find them very helpful for stimulating your thinking as you go about writing your own personal oath and code of ethics.

The International Association of Chiefs of Police (IACP) offers a model Oath of Honor as a symbolic statement of commitment to ethical behavior. It reads:

> On my honor,
> I will never betray my badge,
> my integrity, my character,
> or the public trust.
> I will always have
> the courage to hold myself
> and others accountable for our actions.
> I will always uphold the constitution
> my community and the agency I serve.

Source: http://www.iacp.org/What-is-the-Law-Enforcement-Oath-of-Honor

A Sample Law Enforcement Oath:

As a Law Enforcement Officer, my fundamental duty is to serve mankind; to safeguard lives and property; to protect the innocent against deception, the weak against oppression or intimidation, and the peaceful against violence or disorder; and to respect the Constitutional rights of all men to liberty, equality and justice.

I will keep my private life unsullied as an example to all; maintain courageous calm in the face of danger, scorn, or ridicule; develop self-restraint; and be constantly mindful of the welfare of others. Honest in thought and deed in both my personal and official life, I will be exemplary in obeying the laws of the land and the regulations of my department. Whatever I see or hear of a confidential nature or that is confided to me in my official capacity will be kept ever secret unless revelation is necessary in the performance of my duty. I will never act officiously or permit personal feelings, prejudices, animosities or friendships to influence my decisions. With no compromise for crime and with relentless prosecution of criminals, I will enforce the law courteously and appropriately without fear or favor, malice or ill will, never employing unnecessary force or violence and never accepting gratuities.

I recognize the badge of my office as a symbol of public faith, and I accept it as a public trust to be held as long as I am true to the ethics of the police service. I will constantly strive to achieve these objectives and ideals, dedicating myself before God to my chosen profession…law enforcement.

You can find more examples at: www.policecodes.org/police-code-of-ethics

Spiritually in Law Enforcement

I don't believe we can separate our professional law enforcement Selves from our personal spiritual Selves. Both Selves have to be connected and in alignment, otherwise this career will tear you up.

In his book *Spiritual Survival for Law Enforcement*, Cary Friedman suggests that reinforcing our spiritual strength or "replenishing our spiritual bank account" is more about nurturing mature, wisdom-filled idealism than about trying to regain the youthful naive idealism we have when we begin our careers.

He also suggests that spiritual survival in law enforcement requires constantly replenishing our spiritual reserves by drawing on our faith at three levels:

    Faith in God

    Faith in humanity

    Faith in Self

And, Friedman adds:

    The intensity of the career of law enforcement is what distinguishes it from all other careers. In less intense careers, you might be able to get by, or even thrive, without consideration of the job's spiritual dimensions; you might not need strong motivation and spiritual introspection to survive. But, in this intensely demanding career of law enforcement, you just don't have that "luxury." To succeed, you have to be motivated and you have to be "in touch with" — aware of — that motivation, the "why," as Victor Frankl calls it. An officer cannot long survive, and certainly never thrive, without that powerful, robust, healthy, meaningful, personal, compelling motivation.

Law enforcement and police work is specifically about understanding the most basic of human vulnerabilities and weaknesses, and then being able to rise above those influences to enforce the laws of our land fairly and equitably. We are "peace officers" because our core mission is to maintain peace and order in an otherwise chaotic and tumultuous society. We can't do that effectively if we don't have the inner peace and strength necessary to stand apart from society's chaos and tumult *and* still be part of that society.

Your Inner Strength

Part of exploring your spiritual Self is discovering where your inner strength comes from and then learning how to harness and enhance it. Perhaps you call that inner strength willpower or self-discipline, drive or force-of-will; but we all have that reservoir of strength within us.

Your challenge is to discover the sources of your inner strength and learn to leverage its use for good. Perhaps you believe that your inner strength comes from a higher power, from God, or other external sources, or perhaps you believe that this strength is part of you and within you. Whatever your beliefs, you have to undertake this exploration in order to truly be in harmony with your inner spirit. This is the adventure you must begin, because this might be the strength that will save your life or guide you through times of darkness. Most importantly this inner strength will guide you through your life and your career.

Spend some time asking your Self where that strength lies, where it comes from and how best to harness it. Explore the concept of inner peace and how to cultivate it. Be open to the answers you receive, especially if they are not answers you expect. Just being able to conduct this internal examination will make you stronger. Perhaps what you will discover is faith. As Chaplain Friedman suggests, that might be faith in God, faith in humanity, or even faith in your Self.

The Power of Faith

Faith is a very interesting concept. The word *faith* often has a lot of stigma attached to it because most people instantly associate it with religion. By some estimation there are over 4,000 religions on this planet. Because even the concept of religion can mean something very different to different people, let's first consider the broader implications of the word *faith* and analyze what we might have faith in. We might have faith in ourselves, in humankind, in our system of justice, or in the righteousness of our society. By it's very nature, faith requires you to let go of control and invest your trust, sometimes blindly. How do you feel about the generic concept of faith? What do you believe in by trust alone?

If we are to discuss faith in the religious sense, then we need to examine our own beliefs in a higher power or something greater than our Selves. By definition, religious faith has a public aspect or community component, but even privately, religious faith is a belief system that should sustain and nurture us. What are your religious or other belief systems? Do you believe in a higher power? Do you believe in God? How do you explain all that is great and inspiring in our world? Why do bad things happen? Your answers should matter to no one else but to you.

The Merriam-Webster dictionary defines religion as "an organized system of beliefs, ceremonies, and rules used to worship a god or a group of gods."
 http://www.merriam-webster.com/dictionary/religion

Wikipedia defines it as "a cultural system of behaviors and practices, world views, ethics, and social organization that relate humanity to an order of existence."
https://en.wikipedia.org/wiki/Religion

Worldwide, more than 8 in 10 people identify with a religious group, according to a comprehensive demographic study of more than 230 countries and territories conducted by the Pew Research Center's Forum on Religion & Public Life. The study noted: "The vast majority of them are affiliated with one of the five largest religions, namely Christianity, Islam, Hinduism, Buddhism and folk or traditional religions. The folk or traditional religions include African traditional religions, Chinese folk religions, Native American religions and Australian aboriginal religions."

You will have to discover your own beliefs and your own priorities. No one else can tell you what you believe in. You must embark upon this quest alone. This does not mean that you can't learn from others or be inspired from outside your Self; but you need to find a balance between your Self and other's beliefs and belief systems, and if you don't embrace what is solely yours, then you are getting some of your influence from other people and not from within or from that higher power.

Finding Balance

One of the key concepts permeating all of the concepts of Armor Your Self ™ and Tactical Resilience™ is the concept of *balance*. Balance is something we can create in our physical bodies, our lives and our inner Selves. Balance is a core value of the universe and should be one for you, too.

There are lots of examples of balance and there are lots of ways to find it. I suggest that one of the best ways to conduct such an exploration of your beliefs and strategies for balance in your physical life, your cognitive functions, your emotional life and your spiritual life is to practice actual physical balance exercises *while at the same time you examine your state of balance in other parts of your Self or lifestyle.* Try standing on one leg or on top of a narrow balance beam and examine your beliefs about the balance between good and evil, or between right and wrong. You might also explore your beliefs in the balance of life and in the balance of the seasons. You should document the results of your explorations in your personal journal and discuss them with people you trust in your life.

Tactical Trauma Control

The word *tactical* refers to any actions that have been carefully planned to gain a specific result. So if our ultimate goal is to manage our emotional and spiritual well-being, then we need to think tactically. We have to start with the assumption that many, many people in law enforcement will suffer doses of emotional and spiritual trauma throughout their careers. Some of these traumas and injuries to the psyche may be small and insignificant, while others might be overwhelming. The concept of *Tactical Trauma Control* is about doing things *proactively* to prevent trauma — specifically, emotional and spiritual trauma — from having powerful effects on you when it strikes. I don't pretend that you can prevent all traumas that might occur, but I do believe that you can strengthen and condition your Self daily with practices that will help to alleviate or minimize the effects of negative stresses and trauma.

Preparation for Tactical Trauma Control starts (as do all the exercises in this book) by doing a risk or threat assessment and then planning a training and conditioning regime to combat those threats.

First, you should examine what spiritual and emotional threats lie in wait for you. What do you think is your spiritual vulnerability? Where are you weakest emotionally? From these examinations you can develop a strengthening and conditioning regime to produce emotional and spiritual fitness. What do you need to do on a daily basis to strengthen your Self spiritually? Write your thoughts in your journal and use a separate sheet of paper to write your action plan for building Tactical Trauma Control practices into your life.

In the next chapter I'll provide some suggested exercises and tactics you can use to build strength and condition your Self to better manage traumas in your life.

Tactical Decision-Making

Decision-making in law enforcement is complex and often takes place in a fraction of a second. I could have written more about this in the chapter covering mental preparation, but I think it belongs here because any of the split-second decisions we make are based on our inner core values and sense of integrity. How important is your decision-making ability? Former Chief Justice of the U.S. Supreme Court Warren Burger summed it up quite well when he said:

> The policeman on the beat or in the patrol car makes more decisions and exercises broader discretion affecting the daily lives of people every day and to a greater extent, in many respects, than a judge will ordinarily exercise in a week.
>
> — *Address to local and state police administrators upon graduation from the FBI, reported in Frank J. Remington, "Standards Relating to the Urban Police Function," American Bar Association: Advisory Committee on the Police Function, (1972), p. 2.*

The problem with this notion is that I don't remember anyone ever teaching me how to make decisions. It's just like the Trained Observer Training that we never got. So it's up to *you* to create your own decision-making training regime.

First, do an assessment of your person values and ethics. Ask your Self: What are my core beliefs and what would I do to protect them? And: What is my Personal Code of Ethics?

I mentioned earlier that Benjamin Franklin is said to have done some self-examination, and afterward a he wrote down his 13 virtues (or core values). He then used them as a basis for daily study and is said to have reread and written about them every week. Interestingly, the number 13 goes into the 52 weeks of the year 4 times. This allowed Ben to examine each one of his 13 core beliefs for a week at a time, and to do this four times during the course of a year. I have done this exercise and found it extremely valuable, and I encourage you to do the same. Ben's virtues were Temperance, Silence, Order, Resolution, Frugality, Industry, Sincerity, Justice, Moderation, Cleanliness, Tranquility, Chastity and Humility. (You can find Benjamin Franklin's 13 Virtues many places on the Internet if you want to learn more.)

Once you've established your own code of conduct / set of virtues / core beliefs, you need to test them as part of your own internal decision-making process. When I was in training as a young police officer, someone told me about a decision-making mantra to use when I had to make a quick decision. It went like this: "Is it Legal? Is it Moral? Is it Ethical? Is it the Right Thing to Do? If you can answer *yes* to all of these questions, then Do What You Have to Do with a Clear Conscience!"

You can answer these questions only if you are really, really clear about what is legal, moral, ethical and the right thing to do! The next chapter has an exercise so that you can practice this.

Commitment

The final concept for this chapter is the concept of *commitment*. In the spiritual context, commitment is about your pledge, your obligation and your honor.

Most people don't have to be overly concerned about commitment because they have not taken an oath as you have, nor have they accepted your responsibilities as a law enforcement professional or peace officer. It's no big deal to most people if they're late to work or don't meet their obligations, and in many cases there's no one to hold them to their commitments.

In our profession we've made a solemn pledge and sworn an oath to even sacrifice our lives to meet our commitment to society. We need to have a strong moral and ethical foundation of honor and integrity to maintain that commitment. We need to hold ourselves to a higher standard because our responsibilities are of a higher caliber than those most other people face. Therefore it's critical that we fully understand what we stand for and what we are willing to give our lives for.

Mottoes and credos are ways for elite performers like us to establish our beliefs in short, easy to remember slogans. These statements are also strong enough for the general public to know exactly what we mean.

Consider the mottoes of the British Special Air Service: "Who Dares, Wins" and the motto of the U.S. Marine Corps: "Semper Fidelis" (Always Faithful). Now consider some of law enforcement's most prominent mottoes: the Los Angeles Police Department's "To Serve and To Protect"; the Fulton, New York, Police Department's "Proud to Serve"; and the Colorado State Patrol's "An Honor to Serve…A Duty to Protect."

What's your personal motto? Have you ever written a credo? In the next chapter I'll give you some ideas and resources for doing just that. In the meantime, while you're considering the concept of commitment, I'd like you to check out the movement and Web site called "Because I Said I Would," created by Alex Sheen, an impressive young man from whom we can all learn.

www.BecauseiSaidiWould.com

Daily Conditioning/Daily Practice

In order to Armor Your Self™ Spiritually you must consider the concept of *balanced conditioning*. As noted earlier, some kinds of conditioning are active and some are inactive or passive.

Physical and mental conditioning are *active* conditioning processes conducted through physical and intellectual endeavors such as physical strength training, running, aerobics or brain games, solving puzzles and mental gymnastics.

Spiritual and emotional conditioning require you to "go inside" your Self, and so they involve *inactive* or more *passive* forms of conditioning, such as quiet time, reading, study, contemplation and meditation.

These types of fitness conditioning techniques provide balance for the body and the mind, the brain and the spirit. Most people, however, haven't learned how to do passive conditioning, and if you're used to physical fitness training, this form of spiritual fitness conditioning may seem too simple — or, conversely, very challenging. We all need to learn these balanced conditioning techniques and incorporate them into our daily routines. We use balanced training to form our Selves into balanced beings. Creating this balance will also make you more resilient.

How to Train Your Self Spiritually

Spiritual conditioning requires you to do a lot of "soul searching" in order to discover your true beliefs, values, morals and ethics. This requires you to spend time alone thinking, writing and exploring your most personal thoughts. When you feel that you have a handle on your belief systems, you should try discussing them with people you trust. Ask for their opinions and examine their motivations. You might also do more reading and study of philosophical, religious or spiritual material in the library or online. Libraries of written material have been handed down over the course of human history, and most of it is available to you on the Internet using a computer or smartphone.

Through the ages, human beings have created much in the spiritual realm. You might also consider art, sculpture, poetry, music and architecture.

Look at other cultures and explore human history to find beliefs different from your own. Be open enough to consider why those beliefs are different, and examine what value they have. There's a wealth of material for you to examine; and your own beliefs might even change over time. The important thing is to begin the exploration.

Ways To Condition Your Spiritually:

Reading

Self-analysis

Reflection

Meditation

Contemplation

Prayer

Devotionals

Writing

Examining your values and beliefs

Defining your personal mission

Establishing a personal credo

Stating your personal values

Expressing your personal beliefs

Outlining your personal weaknesses

Examining your beliefs about "faith"

Learning about the world's religions

Walking a labyrinth

Reading Scripture

Considering important moral issues

Examining your beliefs about life and death

Examining your beliefs about God

Examining your beliefs about right and wrong

Examining your beliefs about why "bad things happen to good people"

Evaluating your reactions to trauma and tragedy

Homework

The reason this section is in this book is because I believe (and I hope that by now you believe) that *spiritual strength* is critical to your personal resilience and to your ability to survive in the field of law enforcement. It is also critical to building a professional image and credible persona. You will have to decide how much time you need to dedicate to this area.

The next chapter will give you ideas to get you started on your spiritual exploration. But there is so much more you can do, and there is enough in this realm to keep you occupied every day for the rest of your life if you choose to examine it. You will learn that many of these things will come more easily to you as you get older. There is no rush: The world and all of human history will be waiting for you whenever you choose to make the journey of exploration. Good luck!

Questions to Ask Your Self:

What do I have to live for?

What am I willing to die for?

What motivates me to get out of bed in the morning?

What keeps me awake at night?

What are my beliefs about life and death?

How will spirituality help me in a fight?

How will spirituality help me at work?

How will spirituality help me at home?

How do I summon this spiritual strength?

How do I turn this spirituality off?

How do I feel about the generic concept of faith?

What is my religion or my belief system?

Do I believe in a higher power?

Do I believe in God?

What are my beliefs about God?

How do I explain all that is great and inspiring in our world?

Why do bad things happen?

What do I think is my spiritual vulnerability?

Where am I weakest emotionally?

How important is my decision-making ability?

How do I strengthen my decision-making ability?

What are my core beliefs and what would I do to protect them?

What is my Personal Code of Ethics?

What's my personal motto?

How are other cultures and beliefs different from my own?

What value do cultures and beliefs different from my own have for me?

What do I consider important moral issues?

What are my beliefs about right and wrong?

What are my beliefs about why bad things happen to good people?

What are my reactions to trauma and tragedy?

What do I need to do on a daily basis to strengthen my Self spiritually?

How do I build spiritual strength?

How do I build positive "protective factors" into my life to shield my Self from the effects of negative influences and risk factors?

Suggested Reading

Douglas, Robert. *Death With No Valor*. Pasadena, MD: Keener Marketing, Inc., 1997.

Douglas, Robert. *Hope Beyond the Badge*. Pasadena, MD: Keener Marketing, Inc., 1999.

Ferruccio, Piero. *The Power of Kindness: The Unexpected Benefits of Leading a Compassionate Life*. New York: Jeremy P. Tarcher, 2006.

Forni, P. M. *Choosing Civility: The Twenty-Five Rules of Considerate Conduct*. New York: St Martin's Press, 2002.

Friedman, Cary A. *Spiritual Survival for Law Enforcement: Practical Insights, Practical Tools*. Linden, NJ: Compass, 2005. Print.

Hoban, Jack E. *The Ethical Warrior: Values, Morals and Ethics for Life, Work and Service*. Spring Lake, NJ: RGI Media and Publications, 2012.

Jackson, Phil. *Sacred Hoops: Spiritual Lessons of a Hardwood Warrior*. New York: Hyperion, 2006.

Kushner, Harold S. *When Bad Things Happen to Good People*. New York: Schocken, 1981. Print.

Pressfield, Steven. *The Warrior Ethos*. New York: Black Irish Entertainment, 2011.

Sanders, Bohdi. *Modern Bushido: Living a Life of Excellence*. Fort Collins: Kaizen Quest Publishing, 2012.

Sanders, Bohdi. *Warrior: The Way of Warriorhood*. Fort Collins: Kaizen Quest Publishing, 2012.

Singer, Michael A. *The Untethered Soul: The Journey Beyond Yourself*. Oakland: New Harbinger Publications, 2007.

Ueshiba, Morihei. *The Art of Peace.* Translated and Edited by John Stevens. Boston: Shambhala Publications, 2002.

Weinstein, Bruce. *Ethical Intelligence: Five Simple Rules for Leading a Better Life.* New York: MJF Books, 2011.

Articles from the FBI Law Enforcement Bulletin

- Friedman, Cary A., "Embracing the Spiritual Dimension of Law Enforcement" March 2017 LEB   https://leb.fbi.gov/articles/perspective/perspective-embracing-the-spiritual-dimension-of-law-enforcement

- Friedman, Cary A., "Value of Spiritual Survival Tools for Law Enforcement Officers" July 2016 FBI LEB   https://leb.fbi.gov/2016/july/value-of-spiritual-survival-tools-for-law-enforcement-officers

- Harpold, Joseph A., M.S., and Samuel L. Feemster, J.D., "Negative Influences of Police Stress:"
  http://www.fbi.gov/publications/leb/2002/sept02leb.pdf

- Feemster, Samuel L., M.Div., J.D. "Spirituality: The DNA of Law Enforcement Practice:"
  http://www.fbi.gov/publications/leb/2007/nov07leb.pdf

Articles from the January 2009 FBI Law Enforcement Bulletin

- http://www.fbi.gov/publications/leb/2009/january09leb.pdf
    - Feemster, Samuel L., M.Div., J.D. "Spirituality: An Invisible Weapon for Wounded Warriors."
    - McDearis, Thomas R. Ph.D. "Wounded Warriors and the Virginia Tech Tragedy: A Police Chaplain's View."
    - Krause, Meredith, Ph.D. "In Harm's Way: Duty of Care for Child Exploitation and Pornography Investigators."

Articles from the May 2009 FBI Law Enforcement Bulletin

- http://www.fbi.gov/publications/leb/2009/may2009.pdf
    - Feemster, Samuel L. "Wellness and Spirituality: Beyond Survival Practices for Wounded Warriors."
    - Willetts, Jeffrey G., Ph.D. "A Brief Introduction to the Language of Spirit and Law Enforcement."
    - Tuck, Inez, Ph.D., M.B.A., M.Div. "On the Edge: Integrating Spirituality into Law Enforcement."
    - Charles, Ginger, Ph.D. "How Spirituality Is Incorporated in Police Work: A Qualitative Study."
    - Travis, Fred. "Brain Functioning as the Ground for Spiritual Experiences and Ethical Behavior."

An Excellent PDF comparing the world's major religions

- http://sharepoint.chiles.leon.k12.fl.us/mcneilt/Textbook%20for%20World%20History/World%20Religions/World%20Religion.pdf

CHAPTER 14

Armor Your Self™: Spiritually Training Exercises, Tactics & Techniques

Note: I'm neither a chaplain, priest, rabbi, imam, deacon, or shaman; nor do I hold certification in any form of spiritual guidance. I'm not an expert at any of this. What I am is another cop on the same path as you are, perhaps just a few years ahead of you. I've tried all the things I recommend here. Some I continue to do regularly, and some my friends think work great. So try them out, and choose the ones that work for you.

The Challenge Challenge

The *Challenge Challenge* is about investigating your beliefs regarding the nature of this life and the role *challenge* plays in it.

Examine your beliefs about the purpose of your life. Is life supposed to be easy? Is this life really about overcoming challenges for which, at the end of your life, you reap a reward that allows you to relax in peace?

The *Challenge Challenge* is not about determining or even examining what happens at the end of life; but rather it's what happens *during* life. This exercise is a chance for your to explore what you believe about the kind of attitude or mind-set you should adopt to carry you successfully through *this* life.

Our beliefs about challenges, obstacles, tragedies and trauma greatly impact our mental and emotional outlooks on a day-to-day basis. In law enforcement we tend to see the worst things life has to offer, and this frequently leads us to overlook the best that life has to offer. If we never take time to look beyond some of the ugliness of what we see on the job, we may never notice those good things — and that would be a horrible shame.

Making this examination may enable you to discover a way to put challenges and tragedies into a mental perspective that will better allow you to cope with all that you see and experience in your life and career.

Trust Exercise #1

One of the hardest things for cops to *relearn* is to trust others. Spend any time in this career and you run the risk of obliterating your ability to trust anyone or anything. Your challenge in this exercise is to examine your thoughts about trust, and to determine what you can trust and believe.

One key aspect of being able to trust is belief in any higher power or any higher plan in this world. Most people call this *faith*, rather than trust. This kind of faith is not necessarily about religion; rather it's about letting go and just trusting that there is a higher power that we don't and can't fully understand, or letting go and just trusting that there's some higher plan that is well beyond our comprehension.

Spend some time examining this thought. Contemplate it quietly by yourself in your thoughts, or write out your thoughts, or take a walk and contemplate this matter as you walk. Depending upon your thoughts and beliefs about religion, you might want to examine your belief and faith in a higher power; or you might first want to try doing this exercise using the term "trust" instead of "faith" to see what you learn.

Trust Exercise #2

Once you've done Trust Exercise #1, turn to the more challenging Trust Exercise #2, which focuses on your trust in other people. In law enforcement we can so completely lose our faith in other people that we can believe everyone is bad and can't be trusted. This often leads to an "us against them" mentality — or something much worse: "compassion fatigue." It can also vastly interfere with our ability to build and nurture loving personal relationships. Even with support of a loving family and strong friendships, this career is hard enough to get through. It's almost impossible to navigate successfully if we're alone.

Use this exercise to examine your thoughts about *whom* to trust, *how* to trust, and *when* to trust. Ask yourself if you're able to let go of your suspicious nature, and in what circumstances. Analyze the relationships you have with friends, family and other loved ones. What helps you to trust someone? What makes you distrustful?

This is such a serious exercise that if you have a hard time with it, you might consider seeking professional support from a chaplain, peer supporter or mental health provider in order to find answers to strengthen and support your personal and career well-being.

Trust Exercise #3

After you've completed these two Trust Exercises, you should turn to Trust Exercise #3, which asks you to examine your trust in *yourself*. This is truly the most challenging of all the trust exercises — and should not be considered lightly.

Your very life in law enforcement depends on your ability to trust your peers and your own abilities. Most of us never examine our trust in our peers or ourselves because we think it's unnecessary. Taking time and expending energy, to really examine your beliefs about you strengths and weaknesses (which from now on we'll call "opportunities," in keeping with our belief in the value of positive Self-talk) can be a powerful exploration. When you identify opportunities in your own growth and development, you're not allowing weakness; rather you're identifying areas on which to focus your attention for future improvements.

As with other of these very serious exercises, you might want to conduct this examination with the assistance of someone you trust — a friend, a colleague or a peer supporter. If you find that a truly serious examination is needed, please involve a police chaplain or mental health professional. Remember: Taking care of your own spiritual and emotional well-being is an ongoing process, and asking for help or involving a professional is no different that involving a fitness trainer or medical doctor in your other strengthening and conditioning efforts. Remember: You are a professional police athlete and your strength needs to be comprehensive and sustainable.

Good vs. Bad/Evil Exercise

This is an opportunity to examine your thoughts about *good and bad/evil in the world.*

Are there two opposing forces in the world that can be labeled Good and Evil? Where does evil come from? Where does good come from? Do you have the power to influence them in yourself or in others? Even if you acknowledge they exist, what does that knowledge do for you? Are you empowered to know that you are one of the "good guys?" What does that label mean to you? How do you deal with the bad in the world? What's your role in this balancing act?

This is one of the most complex spiritual exercises confronting humankind. Don't expect easy answers, and don't expect that this is a one-time exercise. This examination will probably generate more questions than answers. That's OK.

As with other exercises, spend some time examining these thoughts. You can contemplate this quietly by yourself in your inner thoughts, or you can write your thoughts on paper or a computer, or try taking a walk and contemplating this exercise as you walk. Whatever method or methods you choose, I encourage you to do this exercise many times and examine the differences in your thoughts each time.

How Good Are You?

This exercise is an opportunity for you to examine your beliefs about good and bad *when it comes to your own behavior.* It's one thing to label others "good" or "bad" — but it's more difficult to truly examine our *own* abilities, beliefs, values and actions under the microscope of good vs. bad.

What constitutes good behavior, beliefs, thoughts or values? How do yours rate? What does it take to be *truly* good? What happens if you make a mistake and do something bad?

By examining your beliefs about goodness you will be better able to understand what motivates you, what drives you and where your values come from. None of these things are set in stone, and if you don't like what you discover you merely have to set a course of exploration and discovery to find and develop the values, thoughts and behaviors you believe are necessary. As you make this examination you might want to benchmark your standards in comparison with the values, thoughts and actions of others. Who are your role models? Who are your heroes? It's always good to have examples and goals to help guide you in your journey to who and what you believe you should be.

The Thoughts You Don't Want Anyone Else to Know

I suspect that we all have thoughts we don't want anyone else to know about. Many times these are bad thoughts regarding ourselves or someone else. I'm not suggesting that you talk about these or even write them down, although if you could do that it would probably be helpful. But what I do suggest is that these thoughts can provide an excellent opportunity to explore your spiritual beliefs.

Have a talk with your inner Self, in your head, about these negative thoughts and feelings. Discuss the reasons why they need to stay private and unrealized. Explore why you know or feel they are bad. Do this in your head as an examination of your beliefs and values.

If you feel strong enough, write out your thoughts. I know this might scare you, but if you do write these things down they are very valuable for your own personal review later in life. It will be good to see how far you've come in your personal growth and development, and your personal journal is a great way to document that. I know you are concerned about security and the threat of the wrong person reading your stuff; but if you can solve the security issue, perhaps with encryption on your computer, the benefits of writing out your thoughts can far outweigh the drawbacks.

The Taking of a Life

If you have or are contemplating a career in law enforcement, then you must examine your beliefs about life and death, and you must come to grips with the fact that someday you may need to take a human life. Many people enter this profession with only a cursory examination of this issue and consequently some are ill-prepared to recover from the situation when it is thrust upon them.

To examine this subject fully you need to do some long-term and deep self-analysis about your beliefs and about what you think will happen if you are ever required to take another person's life. Even in very clear-cut circumstances some officers never fully recover from the aftermath, in part because they have not emotionally and spiritually prepared themselves thoroughly in the first place.

Spend the next week examining your beliefs about the sanctity of human life, and examine under what circumstances you would be willing to take a life. Also examine what would prevent you from taking a life. Next, find someone in law enforcement who has been forced to take a life and ask these three questions:

1. What were your beliefs about your ability to take a human life before you did?

2. What have you learned since your experience?

3. What advice would you give others in law enforcement about preparing themselves to take a life?

Sacrificing Your Life

As with the above exercise, do some true soul-searching about whether or not you are willing to sacrifice your own life to save that of another, and under what circumstances.

Spend the next week asking yourself: When you would risk your life? When wouldn't you? What is the difference between the two?

Perhaps you are not willing to risk your life when the odds of success are too small for your survival or of the person or people you are trying to rescue. Perhaps you would risk your life to save a human being but not a horse or pet dog. Maybe you would run into a burning building but not jump into a rushing river.

Create scenarios in your mind and examine your beliefs. Next, find other law enforcement officers or civilians who have risked their lives to save someone or something, and ask why they did it and what they experienced when it was all over. Make some notes in your personal journal about what you've learned.

List Your Core Values

As noted before, included in Ben Franklin's list of 13 Virtues were Temperance, Silence, Order, Resolution, Frugality, Industry, Sincerity, Justice, Moderation, Cleanliness, Tranquility, Chastity and Humility.

My personal list of core or governing values includes: Courage, Humor, Growth, Excellence, Courtesy and Kindness, Leadership, Positive Focus, Love, Justice, Creativity, Family, Artistic Expression, Financial Wisdom.

Now *you* need to spend some time thinking and writing about what you believe in most. The number 13 provides a good goal to help you pare down your list if it becomes too long. But don't worry about numbers. Just brainstorm, and jot down on a piece of paper a lot of words that are important to you. Don't edit — just dump. Then, when you run out of ideas, start paring them down, one by one until you get to your 13 basic, core concepts.

Once you have your primary values listed, write a short description of what each one really means to you. Put this list in your pocket or smartphone, then test and evaluate them for the next week or two to make sure you have picked the right ones for you. If one or two don't fit, go back to your list and pick new ones to test. Do this until you have identified your core ideals and then keep them with you and review them every day as a reminder of what you believe in and value most. Do as Ben Franklin did and explore each value deeply for a week at a time, for 52 weeks so that you will examine all 13, four times over the course of a year. Every year or two you might reevaluate the list to see if it needs updating.

Have Clear Vision

Your life's vision is a projection of what you want to be, to have, to do and to achieve in your life.

Writing a *vision statement* can be an excellent way to become very clear about what you want to happen in your future. Consider spending some time listing all these things. What do you want to accomplish? What do you want to own, have, achieve? Be creative and list everything you can think of. Most of these things will probably be material and tangible, but you should also consider the spiritual. What matters most to you and what would you be willing to sacrifice your life for or in service of?

You might consider going on a solo journey or *vision quest* to truly explore your spiritual destiny. "Vision quest" is a term used by some Native American tribes to describe a ceremony or a coming-of-age, rite of passage for young boys. It involves ceremony and celebration, but the focal point is of an individual journey to a scared place, and usually involves many days of fasting that results in a spiritual awakening. The vision sought is a symbolic message of enlightenment and personal growth. Call your journey a "walk in the woods," a "retreat," or a "camping trip." You might want to try something as powerful as a vision quest once you have listed all the other material things you want.

Define Your Personal Mission

Have you ever thought about what you want to accomplish in this life? Many businesses write and post a *mission statement* so that they don't lose track of their purpose. Perhaps your agency has its own mission statement.

I think you should have your own mission statement, separate from the one where you work, though there might certainly be some similarities among the two. Begin by taking a piece of paper and then write all the words that come to mind about what you want to accomplish in life. Again, don't edit while you write; just put down as many words as you can think of about what's important to you. When you're ready, start looking for patterns and similarities in your list and refine and focus it to address just a couple of major ideas.

The best mission statements are short, clear, concise. A good mission statement is easy to remember and makes a very powerful statement of intention. Our Law Enforcement Survival Institute and CopsAlive mission statement is: "Saving the lives of the people who save lives." That's our mission and it's easy to remember.

Now it's *your* turn. Write some thoughts in your journal and keep wordsmithing until you have found just the right combination. Don't rush this — there's no hurry, because here the journey is just as important as the destination. If done right, this will last the rest of your life — so don't push too hard. Rather, take your time and savor the experience of writing.

Write Your Personal Honor Code

The United States Military Academy at West Point has a Cadet Honor Code that reads: "A Cadet will not lie, cheat, steal or tolerate those who do." The Honor Code of the *United States*

Air Force Academy is similar: "We will not lie, steal, or cheat, nor tolerate among us anyone who does." These institutions also believe that the basis of true strength is Character, which they define as "the sum of those qualities of moral excellence which compel a person to do the right thing despite pressure or temptations to the contrary." The *United States Air Force Academy* affirms, "We'll teach you to evince character in everything you do." The *U.S. Naval Academy* holds itself to high standards of honor, expressed in an "honor concept" which reads:

> Midshipmen are persons of integrity:
>
> They stand for that which is right.
>
> They tell the truth and ensure that the full truth is known.
>
> They do not lie.
>
> They embrace fairness in all actions.
>
> They ensure that work submitted as their own is their own, and that assistance received from any source is authorized and properly documented.
>
> They do not cheat.
>
> They respect the property of others and ensure that others are able to benefit from the use of their own property.
>
> They do not steal.

The *U.S. Coast Guard Academy* defines its Honor Concept this way:

> Honor, as a concept, embodies a way of life, an approach in dealing with ourselves and others. People who revere and practice the concept of honor do not lie to themselves or others; do not cheat themselves or others; do not deceive themselves or others; and do not steal.

Specific to those of us in law enforcement, the *International Association of Chiefs of Police* (IACP) has created a model Code of Honor that reads:

> On my honor,
>
> I will never betray my badge,
>
> my integrity, my character,
>
> or the public trust.
>
> I will always have
>
> the courage to hold myself
>
> and others accountable for our actions.

I will always uphold the Constitution,
my community and the agency I serve.

All of these codes convey admirable ideas and goals. What words best define *your* sense of honor? *Write those words now!* Again, don't rush. Take your time and experiment. If what you have written doesn't translate into your daily routine, then rewrite it until it fits perfectly.

Write Your Personal Code of Ethics

The Merriam-Webster dictionary describes ethics as an "area of study that deals with ideas about what is good and bad behavior." It further describes ethics as "a branch of philosophy dealing with what is morally right or wrong." The main difference between a code of ethics and a code of conduct (i.e., an honor code), is that a code of ethics governs decisions you make while a code of conduct governs the actions you take.

In order to write your own *personal code of ethics*, decide, first, what your core beliefs are about right and wrong, and then make a list of those ethical issues which are most important to you. Don't worry about making your list perfect as you start out. Just put something on paper, and then spend a couple of weeks thinking about and refining your concepts. Write a code of ethics to govern your decision-making.

Once you have refined your personal code of ethics, put it some place where you'll see it every day. Then take the time to read it every day until you know it by heart. It will become a part of your nature and will express your innermost and highest beliefs that will guide your decisions in tough situations. This code will guide you and give you strength when you need it. This will come in handy and help you in making the really tough decisions that come up unexpectedly in life.

The National Council of Nonprofits has a good list of examples for nonprofit organizations. https://www.councilofnonprofits.org/tools-resources/code-of-ethics-nonprofits

The United States Air Force Air University's Web site also has a good sampling of various codes from all the branches of the U.S. military.
http://www.au.af.mil/au/awc/awcgate/awc-ethx.htm

True Your Moral Compass

A compass always finds True North, and frequently in everyday language the phrase "True North" designates "the right path," or the right way of doing things. A *moral compass* finds the true path of honor and integrity.

If you have done the preceding exercises, you will have identified your core values, written your vision statement, mission statement, honor code and code of personal ethics. Now bring all of those writings together to true your Moral Compass.

Use what you've written to identify your strongest and deepest beliefs. How do your ethics align with your values and your code of honor? What are the similarities and differences? How do your vision and mission align with your daily activities at your job? What do you need to do to ensure that all of your most scared beliefs align with your daily activities and decisions? What statement, mantra or document can you use to make sure your moral compass is always pointing to True North as you make decisions every day?

Perhaps you need a credo!

Write Your Credo

A *credo* is like a motto or slogan but with substance behind it. The Merriam-Webster dictionary describes a creed as "an idea or set of beliefs that guides the actions of a person or group." Having a credo that is simple and easy to remember can be particularly helpful to us in decision-making and creating the proper mind-set.

To get you started in writing your own credo, let me tell you a little about *The Credo Project*, a special educational initiative of the Police Chaplain Project that's dedicated to unlocking the power of credo in daily life. "Over the past several years, Rabbi Cary Friedman, author of *Spiritual Survival for Law Enforcement*, and Phillip LeConte, co-founder of the Police Chaplain Project, have sought out members of the law enforcement community who have developed successful, sometimes offbeat strategies for staying spiritually connected to their profession. The journey has revealed the enduring influence of childhood heroes, from The Batman to John Wayne, and the power of young people to invigorate and inspire.

The Credo Project "offers police officers indeed, anyone looking to tap into their highest aspirations — a potentially powerful portal through which to enter the realm of the spiritual."

Spirituality is not just about religion. It's about honor, integrity, ethics and the codes and mottoes we live by. Officers and civilian employees, and law enforcement agencies, need to establish what they believe in and put it in writing.

One way to strengthen and condition your Self to endure the rigors of a career in law enforcement is to discover your core beliefs by writing a *personal credo statement*. To assist you in your endeavors please check out these articles I have written on the CopsAlive Web site.

- What's Your Credo?
  http://www.CopsAlive.com/whats-your-credo/

- A New Credo For Law Enforcement
  http://www.CopsAlive.com/a-new-credo-for-law-enforcement/

Write Your Own Decision-Making Mantra

I was taught this *decision-making mantra* or *decision tree* during my law enforcement FTO program:

Is it Legal?

Is it Moral?

Is it Ethical?

Is it the Right Thing to Do?

Then Do What You Have to Do with a Clear Conscience!

I have heard other mantras as simple as "If you could do it in front of your grandmother, then it's OK." You need to decide what simple, memorable statement you can create that will help you make quick and correct decisions in difficult circumstances. What can you say to yourself? What can you ask yourself to ensure you make an honorable decision? What do you need to create to assist in maintaining your integrity during difficult, ethically challenging situations? This is something much simpler and more refined than a long and complex code of ethics.

Take a piece of paper and write down your most important values when it comes to honor, integrity, truth and honesty. Identify the key words and concepts, and then hone a statement made of a series of questions to exact the best decision from your Self when needed.

Finding Hope

Hope is the one spiritual domain that seems to nourish and replenish all our strength, willpower and resilience. With hope we have unlimited strength to endure hardships and the willpower to resist temptation. Without hope we are vulnerable and listless. Without hope we tend to drift through life as if we were a sailboat with no sails or compass.

The question for you here is: Where does hope come from and how do you get more of it? Each of us has a different answer and approach to this problem. In order not to force my answers on you, do some of your own research and make your own discoveries.

First, define the term "hope" in your own mind. What is it? Where does it come from? Can it be created? *Second*, talk to several other people and ask them about their beliefs concerning hope. Make some notes and compile your findings in your journal. Identify the common issues, and focus on what similarities you think are most important. *Finally*, seek opportunities that will build and replenish hope in your life and use those discoveries to sustain a mind-set of hopefulness and optimism. I truly believe that having the ability to maintain hope is like creating your own spiritual armor for your soul or inner spirit.

Discover Your Inner Strength

This is a five-part exercise:

Part 1. On a day when you are feeling great, powerful and content, take a few minutes to make some notes in your journal or notebook about why you feel so great. Label these notes "Inner Strength Exercise, Part 1." List things like the weather, your activities, your health, your love life, your job situation, your thoughts, etc. Write down everything you can identify on that piece of paper to remember that day and those feelings; then put it aside.

Part 2. On a day when you are feeling low, depressed, sick, miserable or generally sad, do the same exercise. In your journal or notebook, write all the things in your day and environment that are making you feel rotten. List your emotions, the weather, your love life, your thoughts, the situation at work, your interactions with other people, etc. List everything on your piece of paper that relate to your miserable day. Label these notes "Inner Strength Exercise, Part 2." Put it aside and wait at least 48 hours.

Part 3. On a day when you have some free time, take out both pieces of paper — and then a third piece or paper, which you'll label "Inner Strength Exercise, Part 3." Think of yourself as a scientist who's conducting an experiment, and analyze the data you have from Documents 1 and 2. Make notes on Document 3 about the contrasts you see between the day you were feeling miserable and the day you were feeling great. What was the same? What was different? What can you determine about the external forces that affected you, and what you remember about the internal forces that supported you? At the bottom of the document labeled "Inner Strength Exercise, Part 3," create a hypothesis about what gives you inner strength and where it comes from. Using that prediction, write a small note to remind your Self of that inner strength and where it comes from.

Part 4. The next time you find yourself in a challenging situation or having a challenging day, read or remember your note and what it says. Test your hypothesis and make a mental note about whether or not it helped you in that situation. If it didn't, revisit your hypothesis, change it and test your new hypothesis. Keep testing until you find your hypothesis to be correct several times in a row. If your hypothesis proved correct the first time, continue to test it as long as you need to in order to validate your beliefs about inner strength.

Part 5. Use this note or thought as a mechanism to give you strength when you need it. Keep using this process to discover what is unique and special about your ability to be strong, courageous and successful.

This may seem like an exercise that's either too simplistic or too complicated — but I encourage you to explore this matter of where your inner strength lies and how you can best summon it. This exercise is designed to help you notice your core power and abilities and to help you be able to summon them whenever you need to.

Good luck!

Practice Patience and More Patience

I am certain my primary lesson to be learned in this life is *patience*. I have never been terribly patient and sometimes I'm downright impulsive. If you are at all like me, then you need more practice in being patient.

This exercise forces you to look for opportunities to exercise your patience muscle and to test how much you are progressing. The best testing ground for me is while I'm driving.

I'm always amazed how stupid other drivers can be, and that's an excellent time to practice patience.

The first step is to create the appropriate *patience mind-set* and reinforce it with some positive Self-talk. When I'm driving, my patience mind-set involves quickly noticing my irritation and then immediately repeating to myself (silently) the word "patience" and the phrase "calm down." I then reinforce my need to be patient with Self-talk that those nitwits on the road are doing the best they can under the circumstances and that I need to be more forgiving. I also remind myself that they might be under some terrible duress and may be speeding to a hospital right now.

I've never confirmed any of these kinds of forgiving assumptions, but the process helps in the moment. Over the years I've conditioned myself to be more patient, and these days I rarely notice the kinds of things that used to upset me.

Try this exercise for yourself. Right now write down in your journal your thoughts about the importance of patience and list some mind-sets that might work for you. Also list some positive Self-talk phrases to test out the next time a situation tries your patience.

What Lesson Do You Need to Learn in This Life?

Do you believe you have a *prime lesson* to be learned in your life? If so, what is it? This should be something lofty and perhaps somewhat daunting.

I've just shared that my prime lesson has been patience. My need to develop patience was so apparent to the folks around me that when I was working in plainclothes as an investigator my secretary had a placard made for the back of the nameplate on my desk. It read "Patience," with the word gradually changing from red at the beginning to a deep blue at the end. That was enough to set me on a journey of mastering patience. And now that I'm getting older, I'm *starting* to feel like I have a handle on it. To be sure, I still have my days, but now I see the "opportunities" to be patient much earlier in the experience than I used to, and it's easier for me to set the proper mind-set for overcoming my impatience. A couple more years and I might be able to say to my Self, "Yes! I have it mastered!"

The prime lesson you need to learn may not be something obvious to you, but one clue might be something that others tease you about. Spend some time thinking about what your prime lesson might be and make some notes in your journal. If you can identify it, see if you can master that lesson and perhaps move on to a new one. If you are like me and your lesson is more daunting than a simple exercise that only takes a couple of months to master, then you'll have a focal point for your work at growth and Self-improvement. I hope you discover something rather challenging, because this exercise has been very enlightening for me during my life.

Forgiveness Is a Gift

I don't pretend to be an expert at *forgiveness*. I have a very strong sense of right and wrong, and I don't suffer fools gladly. I have heard and read many, many recommendations about forgiveness; I find value in some and none in others.

What I've come to realize is that forgiveness is a *gift*. For many people, it's a gift they give to someone else; but for me it's a gift I give myself. I agree with many people who suggest that you don't need to verbally forgive those who have trespassed against you, but you do need to let it go in your own heart. To me *that's* the gift: letting go of the anger, animosity, frustration and thoughts of revenge, and then moving on with my life.

The gift is to *rid yourself of emotional turmoil and internal negative stresses*. Law enforcement is stressful enough without harboring resentment against one or more people. Life is too short, and your emotional well-being is worth more than that.

I suggest you make some notes in your journal about forgiveness and what your thoughts are about it. Think also about making a list of people you might want to forgive. Experiment with the mind-set that you have to let go of your animosity so that you don't give those people another thought. Does it work for you? Only time will tell, but this is an experiment you can conduct annually for the rest of your life.

On New Year's Day consider what you are grateful for and whom you need to forgive. You don't need to tell anyone else, but try to change your mind-set and let your negative feelings go away. Send me an email sometime and let me know what works for you.

Kindness and Charity

Kindness and charity are fine thoughts, but without action they're just thoughts. What can you do today to demonstrate kindness and charity?

Boy Scouts carry a coin in their pockets called the "Good Turn Coin." It's a lot like one of our challenge coins, but it's a reminder to do a good deed every day. A Boy Scout receives the coin when he's done his first "good turn," and then every time he does something good, he reaches into his pocket and simply turns the coin over or places it in his other pocket. Scouts don't say anything to anyone or draw attention to their acts of kindness. They just do a good deed for its own sake.

I encourage you to consider adding one act of kindness to your day every day. If you can find an opportunity to do more, that's great. In our profession we get so focused on bad things and bad people that we can loose sight of good things and good people we have sworn to serve and to protect. How about if we focus on them for a change?

Maybe this exercise will help you initiate a mind-set of kindness and service. Maybe you already have a challenge coin that you carry in your pocket — use it just like a scout does to remind you to do a good deed every day.

To me charity goes a step higher than simple kindness and involves more work, time or money. Are you involved in any organized charities? Do you volunteer you time to a cause? I encourage you to do something for even an hour a month. For example, many of us in law enforcement find opportunities to "go the extra mile" by bringing food to a needy family or helping a child in distress. What extra mile can you go above and beyond the expectations of your normal call load? This doesn't have to happen on every call — "occasionally" will do just fine. And with the proper mind-set of looking for an occasion to do something kind, you may even find an appropriate off duty charity or volunteer opportunity as well.

Practice Gratitude

Gratitude is such a simple, yet powerful force in life. We take so many things for granted every day; but in order to be truly connected to our spiritual Selves we need to explore the *process* of gratitude.

President John F. Kennedy expressed it eloquently when he said, "As we express our gratitude, we must never forget that the highest appreciation is not to utter words, but to live by them." Gratitude is something to practice and enhance and savor. It is a spiritual process focused not on the Self but on someone or something else. Gratitude requires maturity and grace and it is an art form when practiced well.

Spend time today looking for people and things in the world for which you are grateful. Make some notes or keep a diary for a month. Focus your attention upon people and situations for which you are grateful rather than things and people that piss you off. You'll find that this is a very powerful exercise. See what happens to your attitude after doing this for a month. Really — try it for a month and see if it doesn't change you for the better. (If it doesn't, send me an email and I'll refund the price of this book!)

If you want some extra help, visit the Resources page on the CopsAlive Web site to download a PDF worksheet on the Power of Gratitude. I also wrote an article on gratitude, which you can find at this link:
http://www.CopsAlive.com/gratitude-is-a-cops-most-powerful-tool/

Tactical Trauma Control

Tactical Trauma Control is doing things proactively to prevent trauma — specifically, emotional and spiritual trauma — as well as minimizing any trauma that does occur. This goes back to my core belief about the Armor Your Self™ concept, which suggests that if you strengthen and condition your Self mentally, emotionally and spiritually the way you do physically, then you'll be more fit and more able to endure this job no matter how its toxic nature attacks you. Does this mean you'll be spiritually bulletproof? No. It means you'll have a greater capacity for whole-person resilience — what I call Tactical Resilience™ — by intentionally building strength in all the areas of your being. Remember, too, that Tactical Resilience™ also includes adapting your mind-set, willpower and social connectedness to positively serve and support you.

Now, what can you do *specifically* to control spiritual trauma? I believe spiritual trauma can occur when some threat attacks and your spiritual core has already been weakened or eroded. The first step to preventing spiritual trauma is to be spiritually well conditioned and self-aware. All of the exercises in this chapter are designed to give you spiritual situational awareness to recognize the threats as they appear before you.

Consider how vulnerable you'll be if you didn't know your own spiritual capacity and aren't able to recognize a threat to your spiritual core when it appears. Two such possible threats are the offer or availability of lots of money and the offer or presentation of an appealing sexual opportunity. If you aren't strong enough to resist, or if you didn't see what acceptance of such "opportunities" can do to your life or career, you might be tempted to accept "just this one time."

Therefore, the core of spiritual trauma prevention is to train early and often. If a spiritual trauma does occur — for example, if you see a minor work-rule violation and you let it go unaddressed — then you'll need to return to what you learned in your training or what you've read about honor and integrity, and reexamine your beliefs and priorities. A small spiritual trauma, just like a minor physical burn, often reminds us of our past lessons and reinforces why we shouldn't touch a hot stove — or allow a minor honor code issue to go unaddressed.

A reminder is important here: When confronted and discussed early, simple mistakes don't have to lead to Internal Affairs investigations; instead, they become powerful lessons that avoid such investigations in the future. And if the need to treat the mistake is immense, you need to address it right away, just like a physical or emotional wound and "stop the bleeding." In that situation, seek professional assistance as soon as possible. If you are a religious person, you can seek immediate counsel from an appropriate religious leader. If you don't have a formal religious affiliation, you might consult with a chaplain, a wise elder or a close friend. Whenever you are in doubt about who can best help you, always consider a consultation with your family physician. Just like a minor physical or emotional wound, a spiritual wound left untreated will get worse before it gets better. Early detection and treatment are equally important in all four realms — physical, mental, emotional and spiritual — of your Self.

Since I believe in the power of the "What If…?" game, your exercise here is to anticipate spiritual threats to your core values, and then to write out in your journal your prescribed responses. This kind of mental exercise will always make you better prepared to deal with a real threat when you have anticipated and analyzed it beforehand.

Good luck and stay safe!

Explore Faith

In the previous chapter I wrote about faith, and noted that it can be in God or in humankind or in you. Now it's time for you to make an examination of your life and beliefs in order to determine what you have faith in.

As I've suggested, I believe faith is about investing trust in something you may never see or touch. Start your examination with the question: "What do I believe in by trust alone?"

Examine your doubts, and try this question: "What do I have faith in?" If you believe in God and this exercise seems simplistic to you, try this question: "Where does my faith in God come from and what am I willing to do in service to God?" Write your thoughts in your journal.

Even if you don't believe in God as others might, ask yourself what lies at your spiritual core. Spend some time writing notes about your beliefs in a higher power, a universal force, or what happens after you die. Try to focus on the kinds of questions with which most people struggle during their entire lives — questions like: What is my purpose on this earth? What am I supposed to learn from this life? Where will I go when I die? Will I ever come back here? Will I be reincarnated? Is there life beyond our planet? Is there a greater intelligence in the universe? Is there something that binds all human beings together?

Consider those kinds of questions and perhaps create some of your own. I believe that whether or not you believe in God these are interesting and important questions to ponder.

Contemplate Meditation

Meditation is a four-letter word among law enforcement folks, but I want you to embrace it for just a second. Whether it's called "quiet time" or "emotional calming" or something else, centuries of practice validate the power of meditation. If you want to learn to control your power of will, if you want to learn to master your thoughts and emotions, you have to dedicate yourself to a strengthening and conditioning regime like meditation. From a spiritual perspective, this is the single best technique for getting in touch with your Self and your inner strength. If you want to connect to God or anything larger than your Self, then this is the pathway to that connection.

Many people dabble in meditation, but it requires dedication and mastery in order to truly fulfill your most powerful needs. I encourage you to try it by dedicating yourself to practice it daily for at least a year. Are you up for that? I won't tell you how to do this because, if you are serious, you'll discover a method that works for you.

Consider the fact that meditation has proven to be an effective technique that has strengthened some of the greatest warriors of all time, some of the best professional athletes, and many of the world's best martial artists. Isn't that good enough for you?

Why Do Bad Things Happen to Good People?

One of the most challenging problems facing anyone in the law enforcement profession is the puzzle of why bad things happen. You've probably heard victims of tragedy cry on your shoulder and ask, "Why?" You've probably asked yourself the same question after seeing so many bad and senseless things happen to people who didn't deserve them.

This question can shake the faith of the strongest among us — not just faith in God, but also faith in the human race, and even faith in our ability to protect and to serve others. Nonetheless it is a question worth asking and a question worth pondering.

It's also a question worth discussing. I suggest you start by sitting in a quiet place and just reflect upon your beliefs about the universe, about God and about mankind. What do you believe about life and death, about why things happen the way they do? What do you believe about destiny, karma and fate? What do you believe about chance and chaos and how things work on this planet? What do you believe is the grand plan for mankind — or is there one?

Spend some time quietly with your thoughts while considering the many options that arise from these questions. Write some of those thoughts in your journal. Talk to a close friend about these issues. Let your thoughts sit for a day, a week or a year, and then revisit them.

An Examination of Integrity

All of us in law enforcement talk a lot about *integrity*. But where does integrity come from? How do you get it, and how do you get more of it? Seriously: What are *your* thoughts about integrity? Where does *yours* come from and how to *you* strengthen it?

Take some time when you are alone to review all the journal entries you've created from this chapter and analyze your belief systems about the concept of integrity. What are the components of integrity? How can you lose it?

Then, consider a test: For the next week, look for examples of high integrity and low integrity. If you have time, make some notes about the characteristics of each.

You get extra points if the examples you find of high integrity are about *you*. When did you exhibit high integrity this week, and when didn't you? This activity might give you fodder for discussions with your peers or close friends. Ask yourself how you can build and strengthen your level of integrity and what might threaten it? Do some writing in your journal about any activities to which you might dedicate yourself to build, strengthen or protect your integrity.

Spiritual Joy

In the chapter about emotions I talked about *joy*. In this chapter I want you to examine the *spiritual* dimensions of joy:

- What is joy, and where does it come from?
- How do you get more of it, and how is it different from happiness and satisfaction?
- Where do you find joy in your life?

Now consider the concept of joy from a higher plane or a more spiritual realm:

- How can you use spiritual activities in your life to bring joy?
- Who would be receiving that joy?
- Would it be you or someone else?

When we speak of the spiritual, we think of a dimension above or apart from the physical; thus spiritual joy is *not* about sex, physical fitness or any activity that is of the physical world. How then can you add joy to your life on the spiritual plane?

I suggest that you to sit quietly in a place in which you are comfortable — preferably one that is a place of honor, of importance to you or of a spiritual nature. Do some deep breathing exercises to relax your body and allow your mind to contemplate this exercise. Now let go of your mind and just *be*. Allow answers to come to you naturally, without creating them. When enough time has passed, make some notes about your experience in your journal. Wait at least a week before doing this exercise again and, when you are ready, try it at least six more times, allowing at least a week between each session.

See what happens! Let me know what you discover.

Spiritual Love

Again, let's revisit an emotion in the spiritual exercises chapter. For this exercise we shall examine the higher concept of *spiritual love*. As in the exercise on spiritual joy, I am speaking here about love in a higher plane, dimension or realm of the spirit.

Start by examining your thoughts about love. Write some of them down for future reference. Do you have love in your life? Where does it come from? Are there different kinds of love?

For example: Can you love your job as much as your dog or your mother? If your love for either is different, why is the love you have for your dog different from the love you have for your job or your mother?

You may never have considered these things before, so it's good for your own growth to ask and discover answers that may help your Self to grow spiritually.

Next, you may want to consider romantic love and what it entails. How are love and sex different? How do men and women view love and sex differently? What's the difference between being in love and having love for someone? Can one person be in love with more than one person, and what's the difference? What are your rules, standards or expectations for a loving relationship? What are you willing to do to express your love to others, and what's off limits? Finally, what do you want in the way of love in your life? Do you want to be or stay married, or do you want to love lots of people?

Now that you have a fuller understanding of your beliefs about love, move to a higher plane and explore the concept of spiritual love: Is there such a thing, and what is its purpose in your life?

If you can answer those questions, then ask yourself: How you can bring spiritual love into the forefront of your life?

How's Your Compassion?

I believe one of the most important ingredients in a police officer's repertoire of emotions is *compassion*. Compassion is important — in fact, essential — to effective law enforcement, and all officers should have a good dose of it in their "tool boxes."

But I'm afraid that compassion is also the first thing we lose in this job. There's even a term for that loss — "compassion fatigue" — and it's a real and ugly side effect of our very toxic career. If you believe this as I do, then combating this loss and strengthening and conditioning our compassion is one of the important things each of us can do. Do some writing in your journal about your beliefs about compassion, about what it is and how you get it. Write about where it comes from and how you can lose it. Do some reading on the Internet about compassion fatigue. Then do an exercise to discover your own level of compassion.

Look for opportunities this week to go the extra mile. Be compassionate to someone for whom you may find it a stretch. Maybe you can spend a little more time comforting a crime victim or listening to a witness. Maybe you can be a little less tough with an arrestee by taking more time with them or being more sympathetic. I don't want you to neglect your duties or pander to a hardened criminal — but you know what I mean about opening up to someone who might be a first offender or who is still worth saving.

You don't have to do these things — but at one time you probably did. Some of you are reading this and thinking, "That's just good police work," while others of you are thinking, "He's nuts." The point is to find opportunities to give a little more of your Self to someone on the street or in one of your cases — someone to whom you may not normally show compassion.

Maybe it's getting back to the ways of a rookie, or perhaps it's stepping up to the more mature ways of the samurai or Jedi (pick your favorite metaphor). It's about showing more respect, giving more time, allowing more dignity. And that's all any of us want.

What Do You Believe About Dedication?

What does *dedication* mean to you?

The Merriam-Webster dictionary defines dedication as "a feeling of very strong support for or loyalty to someone or something," as well as "self-sacrificing devotion."

That's a powerful concept. Do you feel that strongly about anything in your life? Perhaps you feel dedicated to your job, your spouse, your children or your faith. It's easy to say you "feel" that way, but if you've never actually explored why you "feel" that way, then it doesn't have as powerful a meaning as it will when you've done the real work of exploration. Now's your chance.

Open your journal and take time to write your thoughts about to whom and to what you are truly dedicated. Pick a topic and ask yourself: How deeply do I feel a sense of dedication to that thing or person? Would I sacrifice my life for this person or that thing? Would I quit my job? Is there a ranking of the things to which I am most dedicated? How do these people and things rank in importance to me?

If you say you're dedicated to your job in law enforcement and that you're dedicated to protecting life, preserving property and defending the country within which you serve, what does that really mean to you? To what lengths would you go to honor that dedication? Would you fall short of such dedication, and under what circumstances? Jot down these questions and list your answers, if you can. Set this exercise aside for six months or a year, and then revisit it. Are your answers still the same? Is there anything you want to change?

Walk a Labyrinth

While the words "maze" and "labyrinth" may seem at first glance to be pretty much the same thing, let's take a closer look. The modern definition of a "labyrinth" is a unicursal walking path with only a single route to the center and back out again. A "maze" by comparison, is a much more complex multicursal puzzle with many branches and dead ends.

One modern use for a labyrinth is to facilitate meditation or contemplation as you walk through it. There's a classic stone-path labyrinth inside the cathedral in Chartres, France, and many others are 7- or 11-circuit replicas of this labyrinth. Today, labyrinths are everywhere and many are open to the public.

A church near where I used to live had one, and I walked it hundreds of times. It was a circular, 72-foot diameter, outdoor pathway of crushed gravel delineated by round 8-inch river rocks. I could always see my goal of reaching the center as I followed the convoluted pathway round and round through 11 circuits that folded back onto themselves. I was unable to keep track of how far I had traveled or how far I had to go. But, because of its convoluted nature I stopped trying to see the end of the path while I walked and thus I became lost in my thoughts until I reached the center.

I walked that labyrinth in the day and night, in rain and snow, and it was always a powerful, contemplative experience. I encourage you to seek out and try a labyrinth near you. You can find many public labyrinths by using the Labyrinth Locator on the Labyrinth Society's Web site.

http://www.labyrinthsociety.org/

http://labyrinthlocator.com/

CHAPTER 15

Now and the Future

What Needs To Be Done

First, let's talk about what you can do, now and for the future. Then I'll talk about what I'm going to do; and, finally, I'll discuss what we both can do, now and for the future.

With the Armor Your Self™ three-tiered approach you have started something.

First, you have learned how to Armor Your Self™ by strengthening and conditioning your Self physically, mentally, emotionally and spiritually. And you're doing these things to build Tactical Resilience™ so that you will survive your career and create a happy, healthy and positive quality of life for yourself and your family.

Second, you've also learned about building systems of support both for yourself and through the concept of Armor Your Agency™ so that you can build that same supportive and protective resilience into your organization.

And third, you've learned how to make changes in our law enforcement culture through the concept of True Blue Valor™. By truly walking our talk we can care for and support each other to resist and overcome the toxic nature and hidden dangers of this profession.

This is still just the beginning. Your challenge now is to continue this effort. Work tirelessly to strengthen yourself. Work just as hard to build systems within your organization that will support and encourage you and your peers toward personal and professional success.

Finally, please work toward positive changes within our profession. We know that mental health is an important *job requirement*, so let's build the systems to support and maintain it for all of us. Let's remove the stigma from asking for help. Let's not challenge those who admit a need for support — rather, give them the tools and systems that will allow them to recover fully from any physical, mental, emotional or spiritual wounds. Let's dedicate ourselves toward building a professional culture that will sustain us and our successors for many decades to come!

Start your journey today by adopting a mind-set of *tactical wellness*. Remember: I consciously and intentionally add the word tactical to everything that I want you to do.

Tactical Wellness

Tactical Wellness is *a comprehensive law enforcement plan that includes anticipation, recognition and prevention strategies to avoid burnout and to achieve personal and professional strength and resilience.* To create a level of wellness that will allow you to survive your career, you *must* take on a training and development regime for wellness and resiliency that equals or exceeds the training regime you adopt for your firearms, arrest control, legal and driving skills.

The key to success here is: *Do the work*! You have to do your homework if you want this to take hold. Nothing happens in life by osmosis. You have to be active and engaged in your own wellness. Begin by practicing the Core-4 PMES principles of the Armor Your Self™ concept to strengthen and condition your Self physically, mentally, emotionally and spiritually. I recommend that you do this for at least 15 minutes a day, every day, for each of the PMES categories.

Remember: You're doing this to build Tactical Resilience™ so that you'll be able to endure and survive the rigors and hidden dangers in your law enforcement career. This is a lifetime training regimen that must be maintained well beyond your career in law enforcement if you wish to build and maintain the resilience you'll need to sustain your health and overall wellness throughout your entire lifetime.

Thrive and Flourish

I don't want you simply to survive — I want you to *thrive* and *flourish* in your career and your life. You can do that if you *practice every day* and *build a System of Systems* based upon good wellness habits. Build these habits on positive tactics and techniques that you've found to work for you. You can then build those tactics into positive habits so that these positive habits turn into routines that become Systems to contribute to a positive, healthy character for you personally, and a positive culture within your agency.

Your *first goal* should be to commit to all that you have learned in this book. In order to become master of these concepts and build personal strength, you must first absorb them cognitively, then emotionally, then physically and, finally, spiritually. You must practice and condition your Self daily.

I've listed three resources at the end of this chapter: *Blue Zones* and *Thrive*, both by Dan Buettner, and *Flourish*, by Martin Seligman. Dan Buettner is a journalist who did very interesting research for the National Geographic Society to discover where on this planet people live the longest. That work was described in *Blue Zones*, and he then refined it with more work for his book, *Thrive*. Dr. Seligman pioneered the concept of positive psychology, and his book, *Flourish*, is excellent. You can find information at the end of the chapter to assist you in doing your own research in these areas.

Daily Practice for the Rest of Your Life

The time to start is now! Begin by building this process into a wellness habit that you practice daily for the rest of your life. I know you may not be able to practice these techniques every day, but you must make this a fundamental part of your mind-set and *never* relinquish your resolve to be a Professional Police Athlete. Sure, you may slip every now and then, and for that you should forgive yourself. But the *resolve* must be there for your lifetime. Your habits will either help you or hurt you, and the choice is yours. I've listed Darren Hardy's excellent book, *The Compound Effect*, at the end of the chapter for your consideration. If you choose to read it, I promise that it will show you how you can use the compound effect to build healthy habits for success; by the same token, that same compound effect can allow your negative habits to to maximize your frustrations and challenges.

The Professional Police Athlete

As a policing professional you *must* think like a *professional athlete*. When you do so, you will organize the tools, equipment, mind-set and support staff you need to encourage your success.

First, *establish your mind-set*. A Professional Police Athlete trains and conditions for strength and endurance every day. You do this because it's necessary for your health and wellness. It's necessary to win the long race of the career you have in front of you. You do this because it's the right thing to do: It's your job, and you are a *professional*. You do this because many people, including your peers, depend upon you. Program your mind-set every day with positive Self-talk and weed out those negative internal messages.

Next, *build your support systems and support team.*

Your support systems may include:

- maintenance of your firearm, body armor, vehicle and other equipment
- the way you prepare your uniform and personal appearance
- the way you have documented your personal values, code of ethics and credo
- the way you create buffer time between work and home and your daily plan for stress management
- the way you schedule your learning, training and personal development time

Your support team might include:

- a personal coach
- a fitness trainer
- a mentor, chaplain, psychologist or counselor
- a supervisor
- your family and friends
- a group of professional advisors, like an attorney, an accountant and a financial planner
- a personal physician, dentist and anyone else necessary to your overall well-being.

Building Willpower

Not only must we all maintain our willpower, but we must also work to build and enhance it. The very act of doing daily strengthening and conditioning practice will build willpower and self-discipline to do the things you need to do, when you need to do them. You'll also learn that as you get stronger physically, mentally, emotionally and spiritually, you will begin to master your life and career. Think of your will as a *muscle* that you need to strengthen and condition regularly.

Every time you meet a commitment or avoid a bad habit, you strengthen your will. You can consciously and intentionally test your Self regularly by making promises and commitments that you *must* meet. When you do, your will becomes stronger. Also, when you intentionally *don't* do things that you know are wrong or are bad for your health, you're also building strength of will. And the opposite is just as true: Willpower can become flabby and weak if you neglect it.

I encourage you to do more research on your own to learn as much as you can about strengthening and maintaining your self-discipline. You'll find that your willpower can be weakened if you are fatigued or not properly fueled. For *The Book of Five Rings*, Miyamoto Musashi spent 20 years of his life as time for reflection, perfection of technique, and seeking other disciplines to broaden his own knowledge as he created a philosophy of willpower.

The Importance of Social Support

The final key factor of the seven that make up the Tactical Resilience™ System is the *Social Factor*. The Social Factor includes many things that we need to nurture and support our well-being and our inner Self. These include love, family, friendships, our peers and our community. At the Law Enforcement Survival Institute, we recognize that in order to build strong and resilient law enforcement officers, we need to build strong and resilient communities. The two go hand in hand. A sick and collapsing community will create sick and more vulnerable police officers, while a healthy and productive community will cultivate professional and effective law enforcement professionals.

I believe that individual, agency and community resilience are a strong triad, and we should all be working to strengthen and build all three. Just as I want you to go beyond mere survival so that you thrive, we should all want the same thing for our agencies and our communities. If we help them thrive, they can help us thrive. The more social connections we have, the more social support we can receive. These things are critical to our personal and professional well-being.

What's Your Plan?

Now is the time to put together your plan to include all seven key factors of Tactical Resilience™:

1. The Physical Factor
2. The Mental Factor
3. The Emotional Factor
4. The Spiritual Factor
5. The Mind-set Factor
6. The Willpower Factor
7. The Social Factor

My specific recommendations are these about how much and how often to train: There are seven days in the week, and you should train for at least one hour each day. During three days of the week, spend an hour doing 15 minutes each of physical, mental, emotional and spiritual strength training. Then on the other four days, spend a full hour one day for physical training and conditioning, one hour on another day for mental training, one hour on another day for emotional strength and conditioning training, and, finally, on the fourth day, spend one hour for spiritual strength training.

Here's a simple list that illustrates this plan:

Day One:	15 minutes each for physical, mental, emotional and spiritual training
Day Two:	1 hour physical training
Day Three:	15 minutes each for physical, mental, emotional and spiritual training
Day Four:	1 hour mental training
Day Five:	15 minutes each for physical, mental, emotional and spiritual training
Day Six:	1 hour emotional training
Day Seven:	1 hour spiritual training

You can find our AYS planning worksheets on the CopsAlive Web site. www.CopsAlive.com/AYSworksheets

Also, look in the resources section at the end of this chapter for links to order *The Armor Your Self™ Toolkit*, a companion workbook for this book.

Areas for Focus

Many people ask me about where to start their routine of discipline and where to place the most focus or emphasis. I always answer: You must start at the beginning, and work through the process to include all seven key factors of Tactical Resilience™. Your emphasis should be on the quality and regularity of your exercises. However, to help anyone who still has a question about focusing, here is my list of the Top Three Wellness Problems in law enforcement:

Problem #1: Obesity

Problem #2: Frequent Fatigue

Problem #3: Anger and Frustration

Therefore, I believe that our Top three Areas of Focus should be:

Focus #1: Proper Nutrition and Getting Enough Activity

Focus #2: Getting Proper Sleep and Learning Fatigue Management

Focus #3: Building Emotional Strength and Developing Our Emotional Calming Abilities

And the Top Three Solutions for these Top Three Problems are:

Solution #1: Willpower

Solution #2: Proper Mind-set

Solution #3: Strong Social Support

These solutions work as a "One-Three" punch: Your Willpower gives you strength to avoid the negative influences, like food, staying up late, not doing your exercises, while your Proper Mind-set forms your intentions about eating, getting enough rest, staying fit, using the Armor Your Self™ Core-4 PMES principles. Finally, having a Strong Social Support network ensures that we don't have to do it all alone — we are stronger as a team, and we all need a little help sometimes. Don't be afraid to ask for help when you need it and don't let small injuries, whether they are physical, mental, emotional or spiritual, fester and compound. Train for success, put in place strong support systems, and then use those support systems.

Be a Leader

Everyone who works in law enforcement is a leader — otherwise we wouldn't be in this career. And the concept of Tactical Resilience™ requires that you go further to step up to be a leader — every day and in many ways.

Be a leader by working to *build a resilient community*. Be a leader by improving yourself and working to *improve your agency and its support systems*. Finally, be a leader by working every day to *build a positive wellness-oriented law enforcement culture*.

And because these are trying times, I challenge you to be a leader to *work tirelessly to improve police/community relations* in whatever way you can. You'll find a link in the resources section of this chapter to download our white paper entitled, "Building Community Support & Public Trust — An Action Plan for Law Enforcement."

I would also like to call on you to be a leader who works to *improve law enforcement wellness research and data collection*. We are an industry based upon data collection and statistics, and yet we do a poor job of keeping data about how we are doing and what impact wellness programs have on our profession. It's simply appalling that *no one* knows exactly how many law enforcement officers commit suicide.

Beyond Armor Your Self™

Armor Your Self™ is about building a primary plan for your life and career. It is also about having a back-up plan that goes beyond mere officer survival to the concept of officers thriving. To do this you need to consider other things as well — things like planning for your life, career, retirement, relationships, recreation, finances, health, growth, and building your legacy. When you are ready and when you want to take the concepts of this book further, I suggest a workbook that I created called the *Armor Your Self™ Toolkit*. This toolkit is a 64-page workbook of planning documents to lead you through the planning process for areas of your life not covered in this book.

The concepts of planning included in The Armor Your Self™ Toolkit include:

Plan Your Life
Plan Your Career
Plan Your Retirement

Plan Your Relationships

Plan to Have Fun

Plan Your Finances

Plan for a Business

Plan Your Health

Plan for Your Growth

Plan Your Legacy

Have a Backup Plan

You can order a copy of this 64-page workbook on the CopsAlive Web site. http://www.CopsAlive.com/toolkit/

What Is Your Backup Plan?

Before you just skip over that last part, ask yourself what do you have as a backup plan to this career? There are probably hundreds of thousands of disabled law enforcement officers in the United States alone, and the number of disabled officers is probably equal or greater than the number of working law enforcement professionals. That is a staggering figure and one that few want to talk about. Moreover, such numbers don't reflect people who were fired or lost their job unexpectedly.

If something bad happened to you, what else could you do for work? What training, education, skills or expertise can you leverage if your career abruptly ends? What financial resources do you have to support yourself and your family in bad times?

More importantly, what are you doing to get ahead in this world? Many cops work second jobs and extra duty, but few have anything left over to show for it. Many of us spend as much or more than we earn, digging ourselves into a huge hole. Have you investigated other opportunities to build a business of your own or to boost your financial investments? Now would be a good time to start asking these questions and building the systems to protect and support you for the rest of your life. Think like an entrepreneur in your career as well as your life.

What I'm Going to Be Doing

Just because I've written this book doesn't mean that I don't need to be doing the same things you are doing to take care of yourselves. I started this project because a friend of mine completed suicide, and in response I've used myself as the guinea pig for most of the tactics and techniques you see here. My personal aim is to live a life in which I continue to strive to thrive and flourish. I'm retired now, and I want to enjoy myself. I have started a number of my own businesses and tried a variety of business models both while I was working and in my retirement. I also want to leave a legacy of my contributions to an improved profession of law enforcement. I will continue to teach seminars, speak to groups, and work to improve agency support systems and build a positive wellness-oriented law enforcement culture. I will continue to work on the triad of improving techniques to improve individual, agency and community resilience. I will continue to find ways to build resilient communities that support resilient cops. Finally, I also will continue the Law Enforcement Survival Institute's research mandate as I work to improve the way our profession collects and manages health and wellness data.

Armor Your Self™ Online Training

I am dedicated to bring this information to as many law enforcement professionals as I can, and to that end we have begun developing an Armor Your Self™ online course. Please visit www.ArmorYourSelf.com to see how that project is going.

True Blue Valor™

I will continue to expand and develop the concept of True Blue Valor™, which will be the focus of another book. You can keep track of my progress on this book at the True Blue Valor™ Web site.
www.TrueBlueValor.com

Armor Your Agency™ Research Project

I have a lot of plans brewing to expand our research to identify best practices in law enforcement agency wellness-support programs, and my Armor Your Agency™ Research Project will be growing. You can follow these projects on the following Web sires.

www.LawEnforcementSurvivalInstitute.org
www.ArmorYourAgency.com

Armor Your Self™ Leadership

There needs to be a leadership and supervision component to Armor Your Self™, and therefore some of the Law Enforcement Survival Institute faculty and I are working on a training program entitled: "Armor Your Self™ Leadership." You can find more information on the following Web sites.

www.LawEnforcementSurvivalInstitute.org
www.ArmorYourSelf.com

The Tactical Resilience™ & Ethical Policing Project (TREPP)

We have also begun to seek funding for The Tactical Resilience™ & Ethical Policing Project (TREPP). Our plan is to bring this kind of training to law enforcement agencies around the United States and to create a "train the trainer" process so that more of our ideas and materials can be made available in the years to come.

This project will also promote resilience research and distribution of a police suicide-prevention training program. To do this we are partners with The Police Foundation to do research on the effectiveness of our Tactical Resilience™ techniques. We are also partners with the Carson J. Spencer Foundation to support its efforts to reduce law enforcement officer suicides, and to distribute its training materials. We are also creating The Centers For Tactical Resilience™ & Ethical Policing to promote the concepts of individual resilience, agency resilience and community resilience, as well as promoting positive and ethical community policing.

www.TacticalResilience.org

The Law Enforcement Officer Community Action Leadership (LoCAL) Project

The Law Enforcement Officer Community Action Leadership (LoCAL) Project is the offspring of our belief that resilient communities support resilient officers and that unhealthy communities promote unhealthy officers. With that in mind, we have created a project that helps beat cops to develop personal leadership skills by promoting old-fashioned community policing strategies in cooperation with neighborhood leaders, with the aim of building social capital and promoting healthy police/community relationships.

We also believe that the Four Pillars of Procedural Justice are the mainstays of Community Policing. These Pillars promote good practice for internal agency interactions, as well as build and maintain community trust. The concepts of Fairness, Voice, Transparency and Impartiality work hand in hand with individual, agency and community resilience, and we will be developing programs and projects that build upon these concepts.

Looking Toward the Future

My hope is that this book will start discussion about law enforcement officer wellness and agency support, and their combined role in building healthy communities. This triad is a synergistic process. None can exist without the others. I hope that I have begun some discussions within our profession about what we need and how we are going to get there. I hope that you've discovered at least one thing that you can do and one thing that your agency can do to make life easier for those who come on to the job after us.

I would like us to change our profession for the better, and for future generations of cops and their families who will be following behind us. I hope that we can make a difference for everyone who works within every law enforcement agency and organization around the world.

I believe that the three concepts of Armor Your Self™, Armory Your Agency™ and True Blue Valor™ are vital to the proper and healthy growth and development of our noble profession as we make our way through this millennium. With the concept of Tactical Resilience™ we can identify and eliminate Blue Trauma Syndrome.

I believe, too, that we can break the Police Perfection Paradox so that we don't foolishly expect our personnel to be super-humans who are impervious to the excessive negative stress and emotional trauma that are part of law enforcement work.

That we need much more research about law enforcement officer wellness is obvious. That's why the Law Enforcement Survival Institute has partnered with the Carson J. Spencer

Foundation in Denver, Colorado and the Police Foundation in Washington, D.C. to promote research in the areas of individual, agency and community resilience.

This book is not the end. It's just the beginning. Understanding the concepts within this book is about saving and prolonging your life. This is just the beginning for you. Your real goals ought to be establishing the quality of life you deserve in this lifetime and then flourishing or thriving during your lifetime.

As I said in the beginning of this book, this process is about *building systems for your Self, for your agency, for our communities and for our profession.*

Epilogue

To assist you with the ongoing process of armoring your Self, you'll find useful worksheets on our Web site.

http://www.ArmorYourSelf.com

None of these things happen in a vacuum, and we are always looking for new partners and new collaborations. If you want to get involved, please contact me through one of the many Web sites I've listed in the resources section, below. Good luck — and Stay Safe and Stay Well.

Our Resources to Support You

- Resources from the CopsAlive Web site: http://www.CopsAlive.com/resources-2/
- AYS Planning Worksheets: www.CopsAlive.com/AYSworksheets
- Armor Your Self™ Systems Building Checklist: http://www.CopsAlive.com/buildsystems/
- Core-4 PMES Quadrants Worksheet: http://www.CopsAlive.com/pmes/
- Armor Your Self™ book information: http://www.CopsAlive.com/ArmorYourSelfbook/
- Building Community Support & Public Trust — An Action Plan for Law Enforcement Whitepaper: http://www.CopsAlive.com/publicsupport/
- Buy our Armor Your Self™ Toolkit: http://www.CopsAlive.com/toolkit/

- Resources for starting your own suicide-prevention program:
  http://www.CopsAlive.com/suicideprevention/

- Total Policing Wellness Project (TPWP), sponsored by LESI and CopsAlive, as "Cops Helping Cops Survive!" Give us your tips, ideas, strategies and suggestions.
  http://www.PoliceWellness.com

- Here are links to all the Web sites within our family of projects:
  - www.CopsAlive.com
  - www.LawEnforcementSurvivalInstitute.org
  - www.TacticalResilience.org
  - www.TrueBlueValor.com
  - www.ArmorYourSelf.com
  - www.ArmorYourAgency.com
  - www.PoliceWellness.com
  - www.PoliceMeditations.com

- You can find and follow us on various social media platforms listed here:
  - Facebook:
    http://www.facebook.com/pages/-Total-Wellness-for-PoliceOfficers/166025807625
  - LinkedIn — CopsAlive: www.linkedin.com/in/CopsAlive/
  - LinkedIn — Total Law Enforcement Wellness Group:
    https://www.linkedin.com/groups/2436139/profile
  - Google+:
    https://plus.google.com/u/0/112889649835010183948/posts
  - Twitter: http://twitter.com/CopsAlive
  - YouTube:
    http://www.youtube.com/CopsAlive http://www.youtube.com/SurvivalTipsForCops

Resources From Other Organizations

- The Blue Zones
  - Web site: http://www.bluezones.com
  - Dan Buettner's TED Talks:
    http://www.bluezones.com/about/dan-buettner/
    http://www.ted.com/talks/dan_buettner_how_to_live_to_be_100.html
    https://www.youtube.com/watch?v=waGHi6aMzh8
  - The Blue Zones True Happiness® Test: http://apps.bluezones.com/happiness

Suggested Reading for Your Further Growth and Development

Buettner, Dan. *The Blue Zones: Lessons for Living Longer From the People Who've Lived the Longest.* Washington D.C.: National Geographic Society, 2008.

Buettner, Dan. *Thrive: Finding Happiness the Blue Zones Way.* Washington D.C.: National Geographic Society, 2010.

Hardy, Darren. *The Compound Effect.* New York: Vanguard Press, 2010.

Miyamoto, Musashi and Victor Harris. *A Book of Five Rings.* New York, NY: Overlook, 1974.

Seligman, Martin E. P. *Flourish.* New York, NY: Atria Paperback, 2013.

Wimberger, Lisa. *Neurosculpting: A Whole-brain Approach to Heal Trauma, Rewrite Limiting Beliefs, and Find Wholeness.* Boulder, CO: Sounds True, 2014.

Wimberger, Lisa. *New Beliefs, New Brain: Free Yourself from Stress and Fear.* Studio City, CA: Divine Arts, 2012.

Wise, Jeff. *Extreme Fear: The Science of Your Mind in Danger.* New York: Palgrave MacMillian, 2009.

Zielinski, Julie. *MGatt's Last Call: Surviving Our Protectors.* Mustang, OK: Tate, 2012.

About the Author

John Marx, CPP is the Executive Director of The Law Enforcement Survival Institute and Editor of the website www.CopsAlive.com. He worked in law enforcement for twenty-three years at both a police department and Sheriff's office. During his career John worked as a patrol officer, detective, media relations officer, hostage negotiator, and community policing administrator. He is an experienced trainer, facilitator and public speaker and holds a lifetime Certified Protection Professional (CPP) credential from The American Society for Industrial Security. John is currently on the board of directors of the Colorado Chapter of Concerns of Police Survivors (C.O.P.S.).

John retired from law enforcement in 2002. When one of his friends, also a former police officer, completed suicide at age 38, John began researching the problems that stress and the other hidden dangers of a career in law enforcement create for police officers. He decided he needed to do something to help change those problems and he wanted to give something back to the profession that gave him so much.

In 2008 John founded The Law Enforcement Survival Institute (LESI) and started a project that evolved into CopsAlive.com. Put simply, the mission of both LESI and CopsAlive is to save the lives of those who save lives! The Law Enforcement Survival Institute gathers information, strategies and tools to help law enforcement professionals plan for happy, healthy and successful careers, relationships and lives and distributes that information through it's training programs and on www.CopsAlive.com and at: www.LawEnforcementSurvivalInstitute.org.

John and the other members of the Law Enforcement Survival Institute provide training on three areas that build personal and agency wellness and resilience. The programs are entitled: Armor Your Self™, Armor Your Agency™ and True Blue Valor™.

For more information, or to book John for a speaking engagement contact:

The Law Enforcement Survival Institute

11757 W. Ken Caryl Ave., Suite F-321, Littleton, CO 80127

303-940-0411

info@CopsAlive.com

info@LawEnforcementSurvivalInstitute.org

INDEX

A

Albers, Psy.D., Susan, 222, 229

Alcohol Abuse/Issues, 3, 19, 22, 27, 36, 110, 119, 140, 146, 150, 216, 223, 243, 254, 314

Anderson, Denny, 260

Anger, 28, 146, 148, 150, 152, 183, 299, 300, 301, 303-305, 313-316, 327, 331, 368, 400, 417

Anger Management, 301, 303-305, 313, 314, 316, 331

Armor Your Agency™, 3, 7, 12, 31, 48, 49, 53, 61, 70, 86, 88-90, 93, 95, 97-103, 106, 108, 124, 132-134, 136, 156, 171, 184, 411, 420-424, 427

Asken, Ph.D., Michael, 198, 324

Atocha Treasure, 348

B

Balance, 9, 67, 193, 196, 201, 207, 212, 229, 232, 233, 235-239, 242, 253, 301, 302, 311, 315, 316, 318, 323, 364-366, 374, 377, 378

Baumeister, Ph.D., Roy, 198

BCOPS, 22, 34, 36, 139, 214, 215

Below 100, 32, 42, 50, 55, 77, 102, 129

Benson, M.D., Herbert, 199, 209-211, 229, 307, 324, 333

Berns, Gregory, 199

Bias, 87, 146, 166, 255, 262, 265, 318, 323

Blue Shame, 14, 148, 149

Blue Trauma Syndrome, 7, 27, 28, 31, 44, 49, 51, 53, 150, 153, 182, 183, 303, 314, 315, 321, 422

Blue Zones, 305, 324, 413, 425

Bradberry, Travis, 222-223

Breaking the Silence, 32, 121

Bucket Management, 303, 304

Buettner, Dan, 305, 306, 324, 413, 425

Buffalo Cardi-Metabolic Occupational Police Stress Study (BCOPS), 22, 34, 36, 139, 214, 215

Bureau of Justice Assistance (BJA), 133-135, 138

Burn Out, 4, 14, 18, 22, 28, 29, 150, 152, 166, 299, 304, 412

C

C.O.P.S. (Concerns of Police Survivors), 115, 127, 128, 345, 427

Carpenter, Sam, 82, 93, 95

Carson J. Spencer Foundation, 32, 121, 122, 421, 422

Center For Creative Leadership, 111

Centers For Disease Control (CDC), 32, 105, 215

Chaplains, 69, 89, 101, 109, 110, 115, 125, 344

Charles, Ph.D., Ginger, 383

Charney, M.D., Dennis S., 199

CISM (Critical Incident Stress Management), 123, 124

Code of Ethics, 78, 83, 161, 186, 369-371, 376, 380, 394-396, 414

Community Policing, 121, 134-138, 164, 184, 188, 195, 421, 422, 427

Community Relations, 134, 136, 138, 184, 195, 197, 418, 422, 427

Community Resilience, 1, 100, 184, 187, 194-198, 415, 420-423

Community Support, 50, 100, 102, 114, 133-138, 194-196, 198, 253, 418, 423

Community Trust, 38, 134-138, 194-198, 253, 370, 418, 422, 423

Compassion Fatigue, 299, 304, 387, 408

Cooper Institute, 126, 127, 203-207, 212

Cop2Cop, 116, 117

Copline, 116, 117

COPS Office, USDOJ, 36, 134, 135, 137

CopsAlive, 5, 12, 14, 25, 33, 54, 77, 88, 94, 101, 103, 106, 107, 115, 120, 121, 122, 125, 140, 159, 168, 177, 178, 208-210, 215, 226, 229, 297, 313, 317, 319, 320, 322, 334, 358, 392, 396, 402, 417, 419, 423, 424, 427

CopShock, 34

Courage, 5, 37, 40, 52, 77, 83, 119, 130, 146, 155, 156, 158, 160, 161, 164, 165, 170, 171, 177, 186, 254, 300, 301, 304, 305, 314, 316, 317, 319, 327, 340, 341, 345, 364-367, 370, 391, 393, 398

Courageous Conversation, 130, 156, 158, 164

Credo, 44, 78, 79, 161, 164, 167, 168, 170, 174, 188, 347, 349, 369, 377, 379, 395, 396, 414

Crisis Hotline, 54, 89, 101, 115-117

Critical Incident Response, 102, 120, 123, 163

Critical Incident Stress Management (CISM), 123, 124

D

Decision Making, 8, 87, 88, 91, 151, 192, 195, 244, 256, 258, 259, 263, 270, 281, 282, 355, 368, 375, 376, 380, 394-396

Depression, 3, 19-21, 28, 35, 150, 154, 204, 254, 299, 314, 341, 342

Dietary Guidelines, 241

Digliani, Ph.D., Ed.D., Jack, 32, 34, 36, 50, 53, 54, 91, 106-109, 119, 120, 124, 131, 133, 159, 176, 196, 320, 351
Disability, 19, 41, 102, 126, 143, 164, 203, 204, 276, 314
Divorce, 4, 19, 110
Domestic Violence, 3, 21, 151, 314
Dooley, Joseph, 110
Dorobeck, Joseph S., 77, 78 168, 188
Douglas, Robert, 34, 381
Drug Abuse, 3, 27, 110, 119, 146, 150, 314
Duhigg, Charles, 73, 75, 85, 93-95, 192
Dweck, Carol S., 83, 94, 96

E

Emotional Survival For Law Enforcement, iii, 34, 177
Employee Assistance Program (EAP), 101, 105, 106, 158, 189
Everly, Jr. Ph.D., C.T.S., George S., 124
Evidence Based Strategies, 40, 137

F

Family Support, 1, 22, 45, 49, 62, 69, 70, 89, 101, 108, 114-116, 124, 127, 128, 163, 176, 180, 194, 196, 253, 304, 306, 342, 387, 414, 415, 419
Fatigue, 3, 16, 21, 23, 24, 27, 34, 36, 50, 81, 87, 88, 125, 148, 150, 192, 201, 216, 229, 232, 242, 244, 251, 254, 266, 299, 304, 313, 314, 338, 387, 408, 415, 417
Fear, 8, 23, 26, 61, 114, 125, 148, 151, 152, 184, 262, 299-301, 304, 305, 314, 316-320, 325, 327, 331, 339-341, 347, 350, 361, 367, 368, 371, 425
Federal Bureau of Investigation (FBI), 32, 112, 120, 167, 375, 382
Feemster, M.Div. J.D., Samuel L., 382, 383
First Responder Business Builders (FRBB), 12, 224
Fisher, Mel, 348
Fitness Trainers/Training, 50, 102, 125, 126, 205-207, 233
Flash Recognition, 257, 274, 286, 287
Flexibility, 204, 206, 237, 257, 258, 262, 270, 276
Friedman, Cary A., 110, 366, 371, 372, 381, 382, 395

G

Gilmartin, Ph.D., Kevin, iii, 34
Grit, 192
Grossman, Lt. Col. Dave, 77, 148, 246, 309, 324, 328, 359
Guardian, 186, 336

H

Habit Feeding, 81, 85, 193, 232, 328, 357, 358
Habit Seeding, 79, 193, 232, 236, 248, 328, 357
Habit Weeding, 85, 193, 232, 276, 328, 357, 358
Hackett, Dell, 34
Harpold, M.S., Joseph A., 382
Harris County Texas Retiree Wellness Program, 142
Healthy Community Network, 118
Hidden Dangers, 2, 7, 11, 13, 14, 18, 19, 22, 30, 31, 38, 42, 43, 45, 48, 49, 51, 54, 58, 74, 98, 133, 171, 179, 181, 182, 202, 299, 303, 313, 314, 411, 412, 427
Holmes, Sherlock, 279-280, 284, 289, 297
Honor, 17, 38, 48, 68, 77, 83, 87, 109, 128, 130, 156, 157, 161, 164, 165, 167, 168, 170-173, 177, 186, 338, 351, 363-367, 369, 370, 376, 377, 392-396, 403, 406, 409
Honor Code, 83, 130, 156, 157, 167, 170-173, 177, 369, 370, 392-396, 403
Hope, 17, 27, 28, 34, 301, 314, 317, 318, 327, 328, 338, 343, 344, 365, 367, 381, 397
Hydration, 7, 50, 87, 201, 224, 232, 244, 251

I

Implicit Bias, 255
Indian Health Services Wellness Program Model, 118
Indianapolis Metropolitan Police Department, 113
Individual Protective Factors, 365, 380
Integrity, 14, 17, 38, 52, 68, 83, 84, 87, 91, 109, 130, 156, 160, 164-166, 170, 171, 186, 254, 304, 338, 363-367, 369, 370, 375, 376, 393, 395, 396, 403, 405, 406
International Association of Chiefs of Police (IACP), 24, 25, 32, 36, 39, 40, 107, 109, 111-113, 119, 121, 122, 124, 126, 129, 133, 136, 138, 170, 175, 204, 370, 393
International Conference of Police Chaplains (ICPC), 110
International Critical Incident Stress Foundation (ICISF), 123, 124
International Police & Fire Chaplains Association (IPFCA), 111
Intervention Plan, 45, 50, 101, 106, 118, 119, 123, 140, 163
Introspection, 27, 318, 340, 366, 372

J

John's Listening Game, 373

K

Kabat-Zinn, Ph.D., Jon, 199, 312, 325
Kates, Allen R., 34
Key Factors, 51, 183, 184, 303, 304, 416, 417
Kim's Game, 272, 273, 290
Kirchmann, Ph.D., Ellen, 34
Krause, Ph,D., Meredith, 282
Kumai, Candice, 222, 229
Kurtz, Don, 22

L

Law Enforcement Officer Community Action Leadership (LoCAL) Project, 195, 196, 421
Law Enforcement Survival Institute, 3, 10, 12, 27, 33, 54, 55, 77, 95, 113, 130, 132, 177, 195, 290, 297, 392, 415, 420-422, 424, 427
Leadership, 52, 61, 69, 90, 91, 100, 102, 111, 112, 118, 123, 131, 143, 147, 153, 156, 158, 159, 162, 163, 168, 174, 184, 186, 195, 206, 253, 320, 344, 350, 391, 421, 422
Los Angeles County Sheriff's Department Performance Mentoring and PPI Initiative, 113

M

Make It Safe Initiative, 26, 32, 36, 44, 50, 52-54, 91, 102, 108, 131, 133, 155, 158-160, 176, 189, 190, 196, 319, 320, 351
Mayo Clinic, 61, 67, 201, 203, 207, 209, 212, 224, 230, 232, 237-239, 311, 323, 324, 360
McDearis, Ph.D., Thomas R., 382
McGonigal, Ph.D., Kelly, 192, 199, 325, 347
Memory, 81, 195, 216, 251, 256-258, 261, 270, 272, 287, 290, 295-297, 300, 338
Mental Toughness, 125, 126, 183, 191, 252, 254, 324, 325
Mentoring, 49, 70, 89, 101, 111-113, 163, 176
Metabolic Syndrome, 19, 23, 126, 203, 213-215, 239
Mind-set, 42, 43, 51, 75-79, 83, 94, 96, 147, 148, 181, 183-191, 196, 198, 211, 212, 227, 248, 252-254, 257, 260, 261, 292, 313, 317, 328, 324
Minnesota Retiree Wellness Program, University of, 77, 142
Mitchell, Ph.D., C.T.S., Jeffrey T., 124
Miyamoto, Musashi, 185, 415, 425
Motto, 54, 73, 77, 78, 91, 161, 164, 167, 168, 170, 188, 349, 377, 380, 395, 396

N

National Association of Women Law Enforcement Executives (NAWLEE), 112, 113
National Criminal Justice Reference Service (NCJRS), 32, 36, 118, 132, 137, 138
National Institutes of Health, 19, 32, 213, 310
National Institutes of Justice (NIJ), 35, 36, 132, 137, 216
National Sheriffs Association, 110
National Suicide Prevention Lifeline, 117
Navy SEALs, 61, 77, 126, 127, 203, 207, 208, 212, 349, 361
New Jersey State Health Benefits Program (SHBP), 142
Nutrition, 7, 33, 87, 104, 15, 127, 163, 201, 202, 206, 209, 217, 218, 222, 224, 226, 230, 232, 239, 241, 251, 305, 306, 314, 417

O

Oath of Honor, 170, 369, 370, 376
Oath of Office, 5, 8, 15, 78, 91, 130, 161, 170, 253, 369, 370, 376
Obesity, 104, 213, 215, 239, 417
Ontario, Canadian Province of, 118
Organizational Protective Factors, 365, 380

P

Peer Support (Proactive), 1, 5, 30, 31, 39, 41, 43, 45, 48, 49, 52, 54, 68-70, 89, 90, 98, 101, 106-109, 115, 116, 119, 123-125, 130, 146, 148, 152, 153, 155-157, 159, 160, 163, 164, 171, 173, 176, 177, 182, 189, 190, 194, 196, 319, 342, 344, 345, 351, 368, 387, 412, 414, 415
Performance, 21, 24, 38, 52, 65, 106, 113, 139, 148, 155, 216, 222, 223, 243, 244, 256, 257, 288, 323, 330, 371
Pew Research Center, 373
Pinker, Steven, 198
PMES, 5, 7, 9, 43, 47, 53, 54, 56, 67, 74, 76, 80, 81, 95, 132, 412, 417, 423
Police Athlete, 42, 43, 46, 74, 80, 86, 125, 132, 147, 201, 202, 211, 212, 220, 239, 315, 338, 388, 413, 414
Police Culture, 5-7, 9, 23, 25, 31, 39, 40, 43, 46, 48, 51-53, 59, 64, 74, 86, 91, 98, 106, 129, 131, 136, 145-178, 184, 194, 196, 198, 211, 351, 413, 418
Police Foundation, 421-423
Police Perfection Paradox, 8, 30, 150-152, 169, 368-369, 422
PoliceWellness.com, 12, 33, 55, 424
Positive Visualization, 77, 185, 191, 196

Post-traumatic Growth, 320-321, 324
Post-traumatic Stress Disorder (PTSD), 16, 19, 21, 27, 34-36, 43, 46, 117-118, 120, 125, 150, 154, 314-315, 323
Potterat, Ph.D., Eric, 77
Pressfield, Steven, 182, 199, 381
Proactive Annual Check-In, 89, 108, 159, 176, 212
Proactive Peer Support, see Peer Support (Proactive)
Problem Solving, 81, 136, 166, 181, 195, 251, 256, 258, 262, 278-280, 296, 300, 302, 315, 338
Procedural Justice, 135, 195, 422
Protective Factors, 365, 380
Psychological Services, 24, 36, 39-40, 49, 69, 89, 101, 106, 107-109, 119, 125, 189, 196, 322, 344
Public Trust, 38, 86, 87, 135-137, 170, 198, 370, 371, 393, 418, 423

Q

QPR Institute, 50, 55, 122
Quiet Your Mind, 9, 196, 207, 210, 243-244, 253, 289, 302, 307-313, 322, 327, 332-338, 354-357, 377, 386, 406
Quinnett, Ph.D., Paul, 50, 55, 122

R

Rc10m, 88, 122, 210, 322
Reaction Time, 195, 216, 251, 254, 257, 258, 264, 270, 277-278, 288-289
Recovery Case Management, 50, 102, 140
Reivich, Ph.D., Karen, 61, 199
Relaxation Response, 67, 199, 209-212, 221, 227, 229, 245-247, 307-310, 324, 329, 332-334
Remsberg, Chuck, 260
Rescue Team Wellness, 122
Resilience, see Tactical Resilience™
Resource Library, 50, 87, 88, 90, 102, 124-125, 138, 164
Riley, Sean, 54
Roll Call Discussion Guide, 88, 120, 121, 122, 322
Rutgers University Retiree Wellness Program, 142
Rx3x - Prescription for Wellness, 209-210, 313-314, 322

S

Safe Call Now, 54, 89, 115-117, 123, 141, 342
Sapolsky, Ph.D., Robert, 34
SEALs (U.S. Navy), 61, 77, 126, 127, 203, 207, 208, 212, 349, 361

Self-care, 6, 45-48, 74-80
Self-discipline, 2, 181, 191, 192, 196, 248, 372, 415, 417
Self-mastery, 181-182, 184, 191-194, 196, 198, 247, 317, 318, 404
Self-talk, 77, 169, 185, 191, 196, 248, 252, 312-313, 321, 328, 345-346, 387, 389, 399, 414
Seligman, Ph.D., Martin, 199, 306, 325, 413, 425
Serve & Protect, 5, 38, 77, 78, 86, 110, 134, 147, 148, 156, 160, 161, 164, 165, 167-168, 170, 171, 172, 173, 184, 188, 194, 196, 301, 369, 370, 377, 401, 405
Shatte, Ph.D., Andrew, 199
Shaykhet, Lee, 234-235
Sherlock Holmes, 279-280, 284, 289, 297
Shooting, 124, 146, 164, 228, 255, 263, 264, 276, 309, 317
Sieg, RN, Diane, 199, 238
Situational Awareness, 195, 257, 258, 261, 264, 270, 271-272, 402
Sleep, 7, 16, 21, 23, 24, 35, 81, 87-90, 164, 193, 195, 201, 216-217, 221-223, 232, 242-244, 254, 281, 312, 417
Smith, Daniel, 297
Social Support, 22, 70, 114, 181, 184, 194-198, 211, 304-306, 319-320, 402, 415-417
Southwick, Ph.D., Steven, 199
Spiritual Survival For Law Enforcement, iii, 110, 366, 371, 381, 395
Stress Reduction, 89, 91, 209, 210, 221, 312-314, 353, 359
Suicide Survivor Support, 127-128
Suicide Tracking, 101, 120
Survivor Support, 50, 102, 115, 127, 128, 157, 163, 345

T

Tactical Breath Control, 8, 227-228, 232, 245-247, 308-309, 316, 327, 328, 359, 360, 361
Tactical Decision, 8, 375-376
Tactical Resilience™, 1, 2, 7, 8, 12, 15, 27, 30, 31, 33, 37, 43, 47, 48, 49, 51, 53, 59, 61, 70, 81, 92, 94, 98, 100, 121, 132, 133, 158, 164, 179-199, 202, 261, 303, 304, 327, 361, 374, 402, 411, 412, 415, 416, 417, 418, 421-424
Tactical Resilience™ & Ethical Policing Project (TREPP), 132, 421
10 PP Challenge, 234, 248
Ten-Minute Trainings (Rc10m), 88, 122, 210, 322
Texas Department of State Health Services, 105, 118
Thrive/Thriving, 41, 48, 54, 133, 179, 182, 183, 194, 202, 302, 304, 305-307, 369, 371, 372, 413, 416, 418, 420, 423
Throw Away Cops, 26, 44, 232
THSC, 43, 44, 51-54, 63-70

Tierney, Ph.D., John, 198
Trained Observer Training, 8, 257, 272, 290, 297, 302, 355, 375
Travis, Fred, 383
True Blue Valor™, 3, 7, 12, 14, 31, 33, 48, 50, 52-54, 61, 70, 90, 100, 102, 129-131, 132, 156-160, 163, 171-178, 184, 196, 411, 420, 422, 424, 427
Tuck, Ph.D., Inez, 383

U

U.S. Department of Justice (USDOJ), 23, 24, 32, 35, 36, 120, 121, 133, 134, 135, 136, 137, 138, 197, 370
U.S. Department of Justice BJA, 134, 135, 138
U.S. Department of Justice COPS, 36, 134, 135, 137
U.S. Department of Justice NCJRS, 32, 36, 118, 132, 137, 138
U.S. Navy SEALs, 61, 77, 126, 127, 203, 207, 208, 212, 349, 361
Ueshiba, Morihei, 382

V

VALOR, 133
Values, 17, 66, 70, 71, 78, 79, 83, 91, 111, 161, 163, 167, 175, 259, 341, 343, 363-369, 375, 376, 378, 379, 381, 388, 389, 391, 395, 396, 403, 414
Vila, Ph.D., Bryan, 21, 32, 34, 216, 229
Violanti, Ph.D., John, 20, 23, 33-36, 39, 214-215

W

Warrior, 33, 37, 77, 83, 147, 185, 186, 198, 257, 324, 325, 381, 382, 404
Weinstein, Ph.D., Bruce, 382
Wellness Program, 47, 50, 55, 57-96, 101, 102, 103, 104, 105-106, 117-118, 133, 136, 138-143, 163, 225-230, 418, 420, 424
Wellness Library, 50, 87-90, 102, 124, 164
Wellness Tracking, 102, 138, 139, 219
Willetts, Ph.D., Jeffrey G., 383
Willpower, 51, 61, 181, 185, 191, 192, 193-194, 198, 199, 305, 372, 397, 402, 415-417

Made in the USA
Monee, IL
05 October 2023

44024525R00254